I AM FIGHTING *for the* UNION

Maritime Currents: History and Archaeology

Series Editor

Gene Allen Smith

I AM FIGHTING *for the* UNION

The Civil War Letters *of* Naval Officer Henry Willis Wells

EDITED AND INTRODUCED BY

ROBERT M. BROWNING JR.

THE UNIVERSITY OF ALABAMA PRESS
Tuscaloosa

The University of Alabama Press
Tuscaloosa, Alabama 35487-0380
uapress.ua.edu

Typeface: Garamond Premier Pro

Cover images: *Foreground*, U.S. Gun Boat *Cambridge*, broadside view, by Alfred Rudolph Waud (1828–1891) (Library of Congress, Prints and Photographs Division); *background*, handwriting of Henry Wells (Henry Wells Papers) and ocean (unsplash.com)
Cover design: Lori Lynch

Cataloging-in-Publication data is available from the Library of Congress.
ISBN: 978-0-8173-2152-9 (cloth)
ISBN: 978-0-8173-6105-1 (paper)
E-ISBN: 978-0-8173-9445-5

Contents

Acknowledgments

Harvey Mackay wrote: "None of us got to where we are alone. Whether the assistance we received was obvious or subtle, acknowledging someone's help is a big part of understanding the importance of saying thank you."

Henry Willis Wells's Civil War correspondence did get the attention of his great-nephew. Henry's brother's grandson, named after his great-uncle Henry, was an educator, museum curator, and author. He was a Columbia University professor who taught poetry and drama for many years. He likewise was a prolific author, writing books on poetry and the plays of China, India, and Japan. He furthermore served as a curator of the Brander Matthew Dramatic Museum. After reading his great-uncle Henry's correspondence, he felt that his namesake had demonstrated the qualities that young boys could learn from. He consequently selected many of his letters and edited them for a book for a younger audience. He never found an interested publisher for this project, though. His transcriptions gave me a head start on the endeavor.

The final product, however, would not be possible without several indispensable people. Tom, Anne, and David Wells made this whole effort possible. They graciously allowed me access to this collection of letters prior to its donation to the Library of Congress. I cannot express in few words just how extremely helpful and accommodating they all were. Anne spent numerous hours helping with many of the trivial things necessary to make the final editing procedure feasible. When I ran afoul of issues during the editing process, and needed information from the collection or required better images of the correspondence than those I took initially, she was always willing to do everything necessary to assist. She likewise helped with some of the most difficult words in the transcriptions. Another significant person involved is Todd Creekman, the former director of the Naval Historical Foundation. He also deserves my thanks for steering the project in my direction and putting me in touch with the family. He likewise had a hand in deciphering the illegible words. Sam Newell also deserves thanks for assisting with my research in the North Carolina records. His knowledge of the mid-nineteenth–century maritime history of the state is exceptional. Thanks also go to Steve Nielsen, who assisted with the research at the Minnesota Historical Society. Mark Mollan, formally an archivist at the National Archives and now with the Coast Guard Historian's Office, helped to steer me to documents now online at the National Archives. As a historian, I am likewise thankful to Henry Willis Wells. Reading his letters has greatly increased my understanding of the United States Navy during the Civil War. Lastly, I must thank my wife, who gave me moral support and, as usual, prepared the initial document and typed a couple of the edited drafts. Without her help it would have taken me many more months to complete the final product.

Introduction

On 18 May 1862, Henry Willis Wells wrote a letter to his mother telling her in clear terms "I am fighting for the Union." From August 1861, when he joined the US Navy as a master's mate, at age twenty, he never wavered on this position. He wrote his family frequently that he considered military service a necessary and patriotic duty.

Henry Wells was like hundreds of other men with merchant marine experience who volunteered to serve in the United States Navy during the Civil War. His years of nautical experience qualified him to join the service as a junior officer. Thus, he was in the part of the ship's hierarchy where he was able to witness some events, consequences, temperaments, and relationships, that senior officers above him and seamen below often could not. With no serious love interest, his family served as his outlet to fully express his wartime perceptions and sentiments. His correspondence fully presents his personality and thoughts, along with his observations and experiences. He had a close and loving family that supported him fully, and his many letters home show this.

Henry Wells was born on 4 July 1841, in Cambridge, Massachusetts, during struggling times for his family. Henry's father, Thomas Goodwin Wells, was the son of a country doctor and married Elizabeth Sewall Willis in 1838. In 1848, after several failed printing and publishing ventures, Thomas left for California to try and make a fortune in the gold fields, not as a gold-seeker but as a banker.

With the help of his brother-in-law, Hamilton Willis, of the banking firm Willis and Company of Boston, Thomas Wells and some associates obtained the capital to begin a banking endeavor. Sailing around Cape Horn on the *Sweden* they reached San Francisco in May 1849. The company was able to prosper because they could charge high interest rates during the gold rush. After six months the venture dissolved, and Thomas partnered with Willis and Company, which put up the capital for a new banking enterprise. Wells quickly became wealthy. On 4 May 1851, just under two years after arriving, a catastrophic fire burned Wells's bank and nearly cost him his life. Frightfully burned, it was four months before he could again hold a pen. He would never fully recover, and with his health shattered, he closed his business and in October returned to the East

Coast. He lived for twenty-two more years continually suffering from his injuries, and no one of the family ever mentioned to him the word *California*.[1]

The misfortune to his father affected Henry and the dynamics of the family. Henry's father's absence in San Francisco and his disability when he returned helped to produce this situation. Henry wrote emotionally detached letters to his father during the war. They were largely financial in nature. Some correspondence did discuss promotion, and occasionally he asked his father for his views on military and local matters. Elizabeth, his mother, was Henry's "tower of strength" as well as that of the family.

The Wells Nuclear Family

Thomas Goodwin Wells, 1804–1873 (Father)
Elizabeth Sewall *Willis* Wells, 1820–1900 (Mother)
Eliza May Wells *Greeley*, 1839–1880 (Sister)
Henry Willis Wells, 1841–1864
Louisa Wells *Wendte*, 1846–1927 (Sister)
Benjamin Willis Wells, 1856–1923 (Brother)
Ruth Lyman Wells, 1862–1943 (Sister)

The Wells family lived in Walpole, Massachusetts, while Thomas worked in San Francisco. By the outbreak of the Civil War, they had moved to the town of Brookline, Massachusetts, now part of greater Boston. The extended family was close, and they all visited one another frequently. During the early family visits Henry penned letters home, but it was his formal education that truly spurred on his penchant for writing.

Henry's schooling was better than that of many during this era due to his family's wealth. By the age of ten he attended a boarding school in Fitzwilliam, New Hampshire, just across the Massachusetts border and about seventy-five miles northwest of Boston. He frequently wrote home to his family with school news and events. His letters showed a bright and inquisitive young man, and as a teenager he developed an interest in politics and social events, a fascination that continued until his death.

At fifteen years of age Henry demonstrated his adventurous nature and signed on for a West Coast voyage on the 1,495-ton clipper ship *Ocean Telegraph* on her first cruise. Built on the Mystic River a few miles from Boston, the vessel belonged to a local firm. Henry's father likely knew the owners and obtained a position for his son on board. During the trip Henry kept a journal. In it he revealed his enquiring character and a desire to learn the duties of the crew and the business of the ship, and even navigation. This journey matured an impressionable young man into a more worldly and cosmopolitan individual.

The *Ocean Telegraph* sailed out of New York and arrived in San Francisco three months and one day later. While in San Francisco Henry remained on board working for his room and board and he returned to the East Coast when the ship sailed from San Francisco. The sea now in his blood, Henry found employment on other merchant ships. He sailed on the ship *Martha Rideout*, the bark *Falcon*, and the ship *Aurora*, the latter cruise lasting until the outbreak of the war. In between voyages he also improved himself with more formal training at the Boston Mercantile and Nautical College, studying dead reckoning and navigation.

His experience on board ships naturally inclined Henry to join the navy shortly after the war began. In May 1861, the Navy Department had the task of blockading 3,500 miles of shallow coastline containing 189 inlets, harbors, and rivers. The navy would also find that one of its main functions would be the protection of army forces and their forward logistical bases and the projection of power.

Henry began the war as an acting master's mate. Master's mates mainly assisted the master in charge of the navigation of the ship, but they also worked and interacted with the other officers to carry out the ship's functions on board. As the most junior officer, master's mates were in a hierarchical position between the more senior officers and the enlisted men. Before and during the war the navy appointed them from the ranks of the most experienced sailors or, as in Henry's case, having years of service in the merchant marine. Master's mates were in a position to perfect their skills for promotion. They messed with the junior officers and wore uniforms, later in the war similar to midshipmen. Henry worked with great energy for a promotion and before the war ended, accomplished his goal, receiving an appointment to acting ensign.

The young man's naval career was quite varied, even though his entire naval service was on vessels that were not warships before the conflict began. He initially served on board the *Cambridge*, attached to the North Atlantic Blockading Squadron, one of the four coastal blockading squadrons. This screw-propelled ex-merchant vessel initially patrolled the waters of the Chesapeake Bay. While on board, Henry witnessed the first day of the Battle of Hampton Roads.

Shortly thereafter, the Navy Department assigned the *Cambridge* to duty off the coast of North Carolina and the blockade of Wilmington. At the war's outbreak most of the Union leadership considered Charleston the most important Confederate port on the East Coast. But by the beginning of 1863, Wilmington, North Carolina, surpassed Charleston, becoming the most important port in the Confederacy. Wilmington's rail connections to Charleston and Richmond linked it to two of the Confederacy's most important cities. There were two navigable entrances into the Cape Fear River with Smith Island lying between them. In addition, Frying Pan Shoals extended over twenty miles into the Atlantic, making the distance between the inlets by sea almost fifty miles while the distance directly between them was only about six. The double inlets required two separate blockading forces. Henry detailed some of the difficulties while stationed off these inlets on his two separate deployments.

On one occasion, the *Cambridge* chased the schooner *J. W. Pindar* ashore during her attempt to run the blockade. A boarding party sent from the *Cambridge* to burn the schooner became stranded. A team that included Henry deployed to rescue the sailors ashore, but a group of Confederates suddenly appeared and captured the boarding party and the rescuers, including Henry.

After a parole from his captors and a short stay in the infamous Libby Prison in Richmond, he travelled back to Brookline, waiting for orders. Only a short time elapsed before the Navy Department assigned him to the diminutive gunboat *Ceres*. This side-wheel ex-merchant vessel operated on the sounds and rivers of North Carolina. Her main duty was that of protecting army positions ashore. Henry was on board during the Confederate attempt to capture Washington, North Carolina. During this April 1863 attack Henry was instrumental in the town's defense, commanding a naval battery ashore during the latter part of the fight.

The young man's exceptional service gained him a transfer to a larger warship. He returned to the blockade of Wilmington on board the USS *Montgomery*. This screw-propelled ex-merchant steamer operated before the war between New York and Savannah. As a warship, she was relatively heavily armed and had an active career pursuing blockade runners.

Henry's next assignment was on the bark *Gem of the Sea*. She was part of the East Gulf Blockading Squadron whose boundaries stretched from St. Andrews Bay, Florida, to Cape Canaveral, Florida. She was also an ex-merchant vessel and Henry's first sailing warship. The bark spent her time in Charlotte Harbor, Florida, on the Gulf side of the state.

The blockade of the Gulf Coast was, in some ways, more difficult than the East Coast blockade. The vastness of the Gulf coast, from Key West to Brownsville, was nearly 2,000 miles and would stymie the federal government's efforts to forge an effective blockade. While the Mississippi River, Mobile, Alabama, and Galveston, Texas, could accommodate oceangoing steam blockade runners, the rest of the coast was perfectly suited for small vessels to run the blockade—particularly schooners.

The blockade of Florida, while not easy, did not have the same strategic significance as the blockade of other areas of the Confederacy. The sparse population of the state and its lack of railroad connections to the rest of the South limited the strategic value of arriving cargoes. Small craft performed most of the blockade running and the shipments mainly benefited the local inhabitants.

Charlotte Harbor was truly in the backwater of the war and little happened here militarily. Henry often showed contentment on this station, while at other times he wanted to transfer to a location where the war was active. Through his hard work and professionalism, he finally earned his first command. In September 1864, as an acting ensign, he became the commanding officer of the *Rosalie*, a small twenty-eight-ton sloop used as a tender to the local warships. A few months later the leadership assigned him to command the twenty-seven-ton schooner *Annie*, also a tender.

The Henry Wells Papers comprise about 600 letters and several journals. Henry wrote just over 200 of the extant letters during the war, mostly addressed to his parents and sisters. Henry also frequently wrote to many other acquaintances, but none of these are known to exist. His correspondence included missives to his first cousin Louisa May Alcott, the famed author. Incorporated in this manuscript are a few of the administrative documents in the collection that relate to promotions, Henry's career, his movements, and his death.

Upon joining the navy, the service placed Henry in a situation that he found to be professionally confining and often degrading; they assigned him a volunteer status. The navy created this group because there was an inadequate number of regular naval officers available at the war's outbreak. Due to the shortage, the navy promoted many of its regular officers, establishing master's mates for acting masters and promoting crew members to master's mates. It also obtained men like Henry directly from the merchant service and gave them status as volunteers. To enter naval service these men had to pass an examination on seamanship, navigation, and gunnery. The department sometimes rushed those promoted from the merchant service to sea without gunnery practice. The service only offered five grades of line officer to volunteers: acting master's mates, acting ensigns, acting masters, acting volunteer lieutenants, and acting volunteer lieutenant commanders.

These men, however, proved to be critical to the navy. The shortage of regular officers was so acute that in some vessels all the officers except the captain were volunteers. By mid-1863, ninety-eight percent of all the naval vessels had volunteer officers on board and nearly half of the ships had all volunteer officers or only one regular officer. The regular officers often viewed the volunteers as less efficient, not as knowledgeable, and unworthy of command. Many expressed the belief that the volunteer officers were not ready for duty on warships.[2] Henry would initially experience this prejudice on each ship he served, yet he overcame these preconceived notions, due to his knowledge and experience as well as his outstanding work ethic, command presence, and good nature.

This does not mean that Henry's service in the navy as a volunteer officer was not emotionally difficult for him. Despite his years of nautical experience and training, the navy assigned Henry a more junior position than many other men with vastly less skill and proficiency. With years of sea duty and training, Henry was highly capable in many areas of his profession. In his correspondence home he discusses the men transferred on board that had little or no time at sea and yet who were senior to him. Nevertheless, Henry and all those like him were important to the war effort. The US Navy would have had a difficult time crewing the warships without these volunteer officers.

Henry's correspondence was always candid. He addressed most of his letters to his mother. He also wrote his two sisters frequently. Eliza, who he often referred to as La La, was about two years older than Henry. Louisa, who he frequently referred to as Lu or Lu Lu, was about five years younger. He wrote less often to his young brother Bennie, who when the war began was only five. His communications were straightforward and to the point regarding those he served with. He frequently discussed the matters raised by his family, giving the reader a window into the news they provided from home that would interest him. Henry frequently shared his opinions, wants, and wishes.

He discussed the weather, his messmates and the officers, his health, homesickness, the challenges of his job, and entertainment. He also expressed his opinions on race as he encountered ex-slaves who came to the Union ships to escape their bondage. His views on race were not different from the view of most of those fighting in the Union army and navy. Henry initially joined to preserve the Union, and he did develop a more accepting position on the issue of emancipation. Other frequent subjects include discipline on board the ships, his attitudes toward the British, and the frequent quarrels in the junior officers' mess. Importantly, the reader will get a great perspective of the war from the view of an intermediary member of the ship's leadership.

Like all sailors he groused when he did not regularly receive mail. He was always eager and grateful to receive news from home. His family supported him by sending local papers, magazines, photos, clothing, food, books, and other personal items. This connected him closely to his family and helped him cope with his responsibilities and the rigors of the service. Henry's letters are also replete with his efforts to improve himself. In his spare time, Henry studied French and read some of the classics of literature and history, but he also tried to improve his professional knowledge by studying navigation and gunnery.

One of the themes that runs through his correspondence is his restlessness. He desired to serve on a warship wherever the conflict was most active. He also was never quite satisfied with his current situation. While stationed on the *Cambridge*, he was anxious for a better command. Yet, his later correspondence regularly relates a desire to be back on the *Cambridge* and under the command of Commander William A. Parker.

Throughout his naval career he continually demonstrated aspirations for advancement. Henry, unlike many of his peers, had family members with political influence, particularly his uncle Hamilton Willis and his father. Willis was a prominent banker who had highly placed acquaintances that included John Albion Andrew, the governor of Massachusetts; Charles B. Sedgwick, the chairman of the Committee of Naval Affairs; and Massachusetts Senator Charles Sumner. The Wells family contacted these prominent men to get Henry an appointment from acting master to master.

Henry did not live long enough to leave a true indication of his potential. Yet, given his talents and drive, his accomplishments would have likely been substantial. His intimate correspondence to his family will allow the reader to sympathize with his challenges, embrace his triumphs and disappointments, and experience his naval career while giving the reader an inside view of the navy from a lower echelon of command. Henry's letters will now be available to speak for him.

The Editing Process

During his naval service, Henry Wells wrote home without ever considering that anyone would see his letters other than his family. He likewise never imagined that his words, thoughts, feelings, and opinions would ever see publication. His writing is overall clear with few exceptions, which is remarkable since he performed most of his writing on shipboard, where the writing surface is usually moving as is the ship. A pitching and yawing vessel at times caused him to leave pen marks and ink spills on some pages.

In order to give the reader a better understanding of Henry's communications, most of his writing remains grammatically unchanged. Thus, it is replete with run-on sentences, incorrect spellings and punctuation, and words without punctuation marks. Notes explaining items in the letters often correct spelling errors, but if the mistake seemed apparent to the reader there is no editorial note. In some instances, Henry received credit for correct spelling when there was no clarity in his true spelling. Brackets do complete some abbreviated words. Henry usually did not supply the complete names of individuals as he introduced them in his letters. The notes provide these when possible.

As did many of his contemporaries, Henry used archaic spellings and abbreviations of some words. For example, he wrote the past principle of *stayed* as "staid." These remain as he wrote them. The abbreviations for second and third he wrote as 2d and 3d; these appear now as 2nd and 3rd. The abbreviation for *etcetera* he wrote as "+e," represented in the text as "etc.," following modern usage. Additionally, to save space Henry used a + instead of the word *and*, now represented within the text as "&." Henry used quotation marks to denote most ship's names. In the manuscript all ship names appear italicized, including the few that he did not put in quotation marks. Words that he underlined also appear italicized.

Henry also separated compound words and these remain as Henry wrote them. Likewise, Henry often left out the second L in several words and rarely used the apostrophe for contractions. For example, he wrote *really* as "realy" and *don't* as "dont." Most of these remain as he wrote them, expecting the reader could understand what he meant. A list at the end of this section contains most of the words he constantly misspelled.

There were a number of common structural and grammatical issues. In order to save paper, which was at a premium on ships, he often used extra space to indicate the end of a paragraph rather than beginning his writing on another line. His intentions were sometimes a guess. He likewise often omitted a period if the sentence ended at the edge of the paper. He frequently used two stacked dashes as a period. These resembled an equal sign. Sometimes his commas appear as periods and periods as commas. For these, he often received the benefit of the doubt, guessing his intent. Henry frequently failed to capitalize the first word in a sentence, and regularly capitalized some words that did not need capitalization. Capitalization errors remain as he wrote them. When his intentions were unclear, the appropriate composition appears.

Henry infrequently struck through words to improve his language or when he changed his mind. The narrative does not contain these stricken words. He also, rarely, repeated words. The omission of these improved the narrative. Infrequently he ran words together, perhaps caused by the movement of the ship. I did separate these. There were a small number of long letters where Henry believed the pages needed numbers to guide the reader. The transcription does not include these numbers. The transcription standardizes the information in the letter headings, but it fundamentally reflects how Henry wrote them.

Fortunately, Henry's writing is clear enough that most of the words were readable. There are some letters where the ink has badly faded and this made the transcription difficult. Henry, like many soldiers and sailors, conserved paper by crisscrossing his writing, usually at the end of the letters when his concluding remarks ran longer than expected. This complicated the transcription. In the more than two hundred letters there were only a few unclear words that were determined by using the sentence as a guide.

Lastly, his great-nephew, who planned to use many of Henry's letters for a book, left his editing marks and a few comments throughout the pages. Since they came at a later date, I did not include any of these. There were also some comments on the letters made by Henry as an afterthought and others made later by contemporary family members. These I have included as marginalia comments.

Most Frequent Misspelled Words

affraid
detatched
differance
differant
dificulty
disapointed, disapointment

dozzen
dredfuly
especialy
eventualy
finaly
generaly
greatful
headach
impossable
leasure
occasionaly
occured, occurance
off (for *of*)
originaly
pleasant, plesent
plesure
possable
preasent
principaly
realy
releaved, releaf
satisfide
sertainly

The Notes

The notes give information that will assist with detail and help flesh out the narrative. The intention was to allow the reader to continue without searching for needed information in order to make sense of the narrative. Most of the notes either provide the full name and rank of individuals that Henry introduces, identify the more important ships mentioned or those that appear more than once, define words and items no longer in use, or provide further knowledge that helps the reader understand the narrative. Since the armament of the warships continually changed, the guns specified in the notes reflect those which the ship carried near the date of the letter.

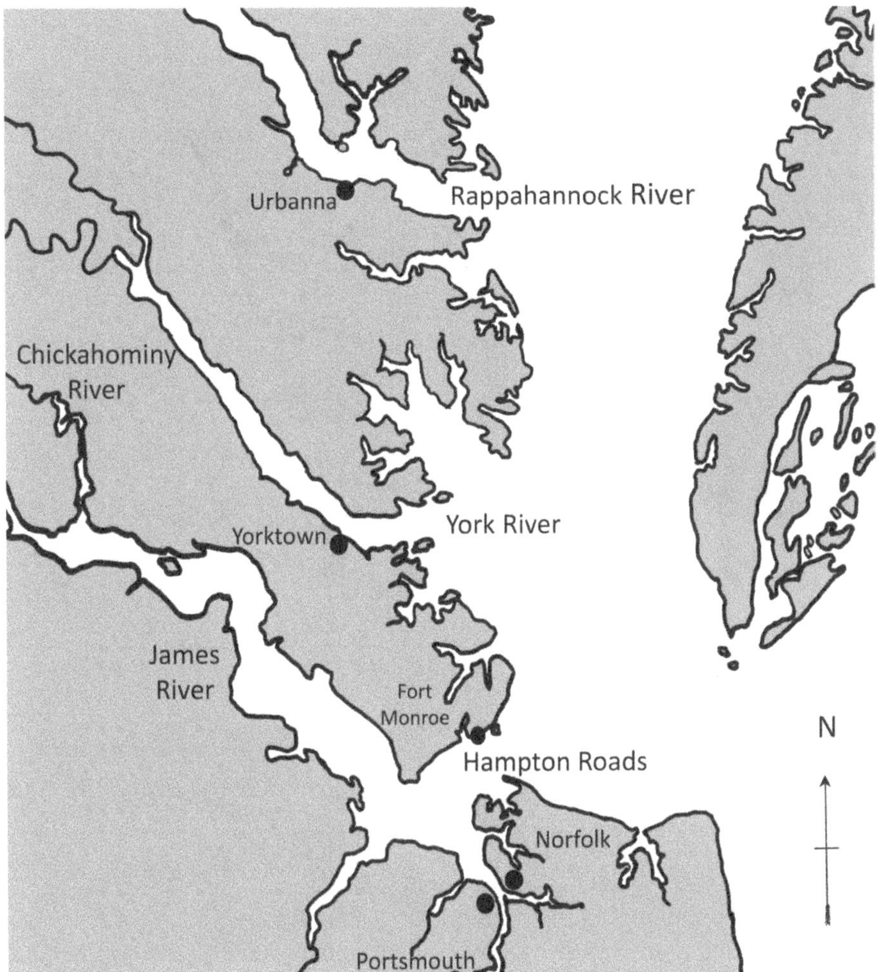

Map 1. The Chesapeake Bay Region

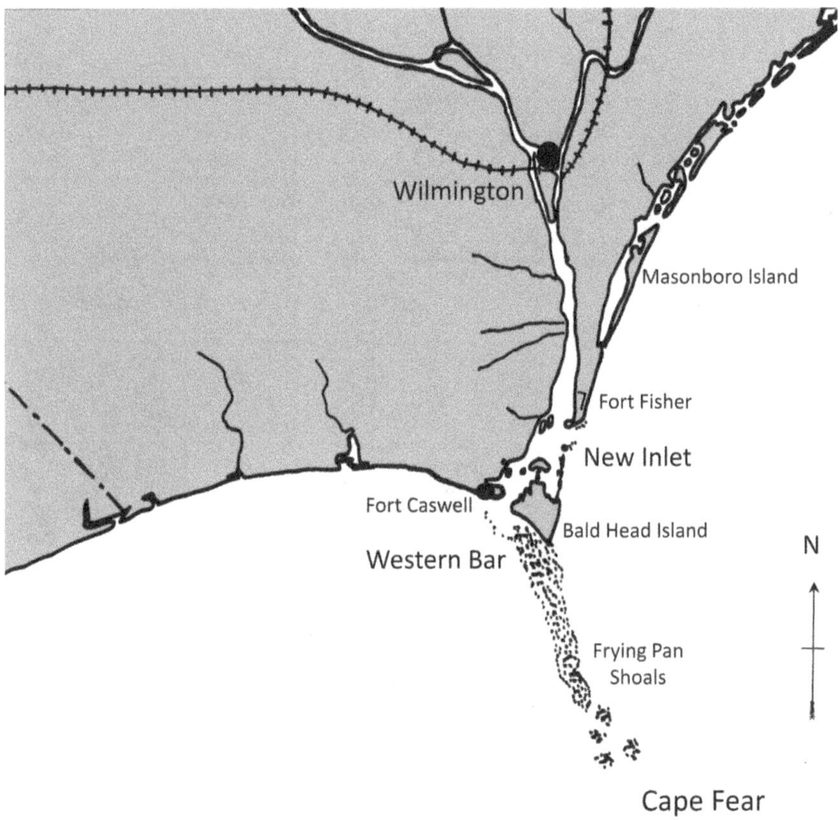

Map 2. The Approaches to Wilmington

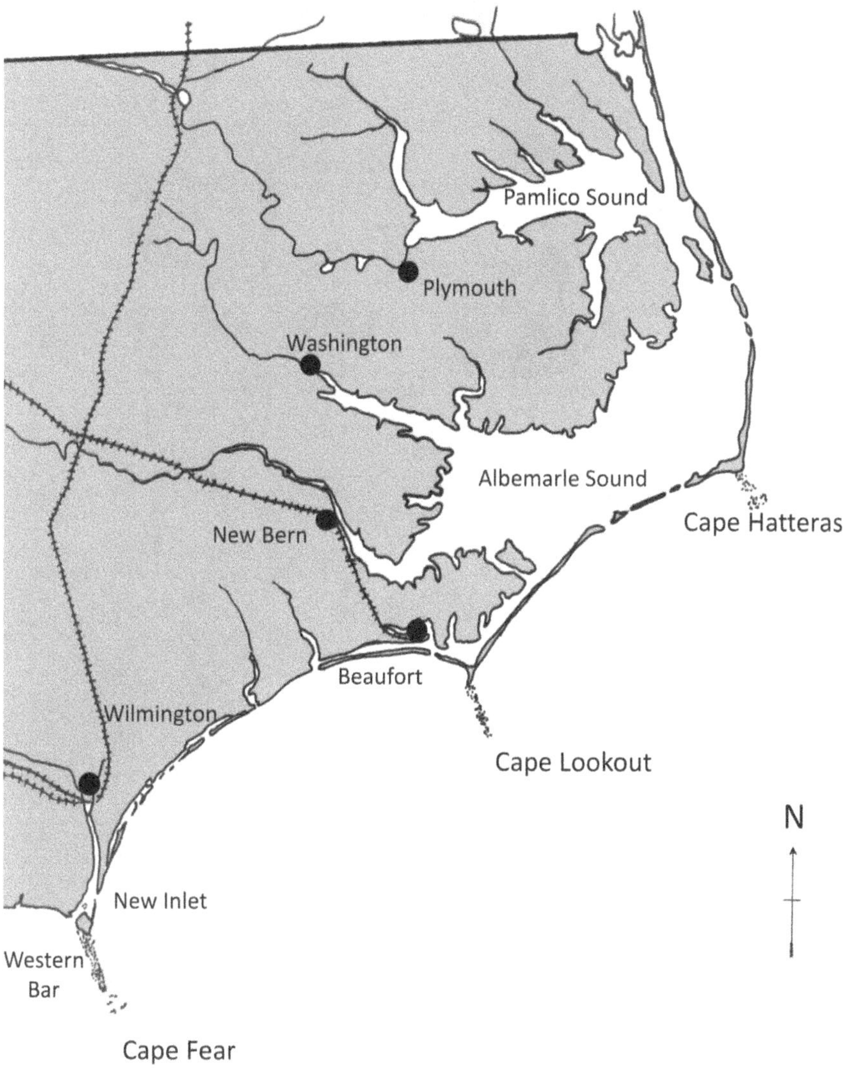

Map 3. Eastern North Carolina

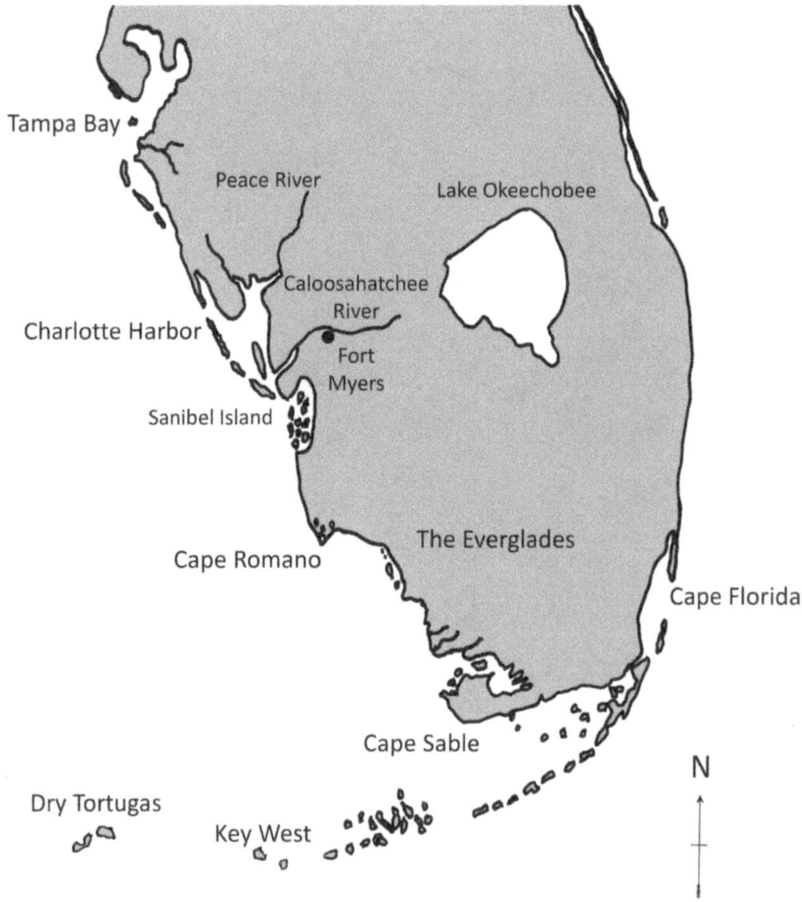

Map 4. Southern Florida

Abbreviations

THE ABBREVIATIONS HENRY USED IN HIS CORRESPONDENCE ARE relatively obvious. The majority remain as he wrote them while bracketed text completes others. Below is a list of those used most frequently in his correspondence.

Act., Actg.	Acting
Adm.	Admiral
Capt, Capt.	Captain
CM, CMD	Commander
Com.	Commodore
Co.	Company
Ens.	Ensign
Ex.	Executive
Gen, Gen.	General
In.	Inch
Inst.	Instant
Lieut, Lieu., Luff	Lieutenant
Mass.	Massachusetts
Obt.	Obedient
Pt.	Point
Pdr.	Pounder
Rec'd	Received
Regt, Reg't.	Regiment
Roads	Hampton Roads
Sch, Sch., Schr.	Schooner
Ult.	Ultimo
Vol.	volunteer

Chronology

4 July 1841—born Cambridge, Massachusetts

6 August 1861—Appointed master's mate for service on board the USS *Cambridge*

7 August 1861—accepts naval commission

10 September 1861—assigned to take schooner *Revere* to prize court

23 September 1861—delivered prize schooner to the US Marshall at Boston

7 October 1861—reported on board *Minnesota*

17 October 1861—returned to *Cambridge*

17 May 1862—arrives in Baltimore while *Cambridge* is under repairs

9 June 1862—*Cambridge* leaves Baltimore for Wilmington, North Carolina

17 November 1862—captured during operation on the North Carolina coast

20 November 1862—sent to Libby Prison

22 November 1862—released on parole

6 December 1862—arrives home in Brookline, Massachusetts

12 February 1863—leaves home for Fort Monroe to await orders

20 February 1863—ordered to the USS *Ceres*

7 April 1863—ordered ashore at Washington, North Carolina, to command naval battery

24 April 1863—appointed Acting Ensign

15 August 1863—detached from the USS *Ceres*

20 August 1863—ordered to the USS *Montgomery*

4 November 1863—medical survey held, ordered to a naval hospital in Norfolk

16 November 1863—returned home (Brookline, MA)

7 February 1864—in transit to West Gulf Blockading Squadron

27 February 1864—reports on board *Gem of the Sea*

15 September 1864—in command of the tender *Rosalie*

16 December 1864—in command of the tender *Annie* (*Anne*)

31 December 1864—died as a result of an on-board explosion

FIGURE 1. The US Gun Boat *Cambridge*. Alfred Waud, an illustrator for *Harper's Weekly* magazine, sketched this drawing of the *Cambridge*. An ex-merchant vessel, the *Cambridge* was just one of hundreds of vessels purchased and converted to serve in the navy. Built in 1860, and purchased by the US Navy in July 1861, this 858-ton screw-propelled vessel initially carried two 8-inch guns and two smaller cannons. (Library of Congress, Prints and Photographs Division)

FIGURE 2. Chase of a Blockade Runner. This image, from the 26 November 1864 issue of *Harper's Weekly*, depicts the chase of a blockade runner at night. Henry would have observed similar scenes during his two deployments on the blockade of Wilmington, NC.

FIGURE 3. The two entrances to the Cape Fear River and the blockading force at each. The top illustration, Old Inlet, was also known as Western Bar and shows the fortifications protecting the entrance. The New Inlet image on the bottom depicts the immense defensive works of Fort Fisher. Both show the various types of vessels used on the blockade. (*Harper's Pictorial History of the Civil War*)

FIGURE 4. Henry Willis Wells shortly after he received his promotion to ensign. Note the more serious countenance compared to that in his sitting portrait. (Henry W. Wells Papers)

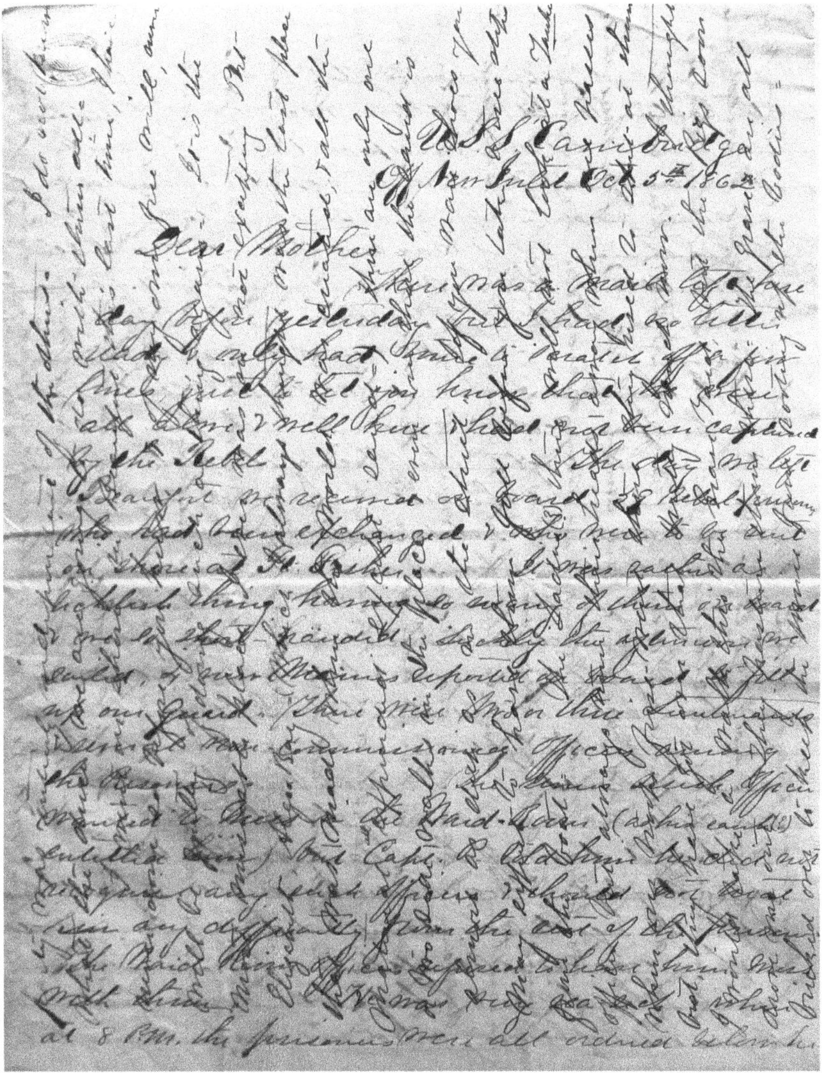

FIGURE 5. A letter from Wells to his mother. This 5 October 1862 letter is a sample of Henry's correspondence home. Note the crisscrossed text. (Henry W. Wells Papers)

FIGURE 6. Henry Willis Wells in his ensign's uniform. This portrait photograph was probably taken shortly after his promotion. (Henry W. Wells Papers)

FIGURE 7. Libby Prison. This was a three-story brick warehouse that held Union officers. It had a reputation for harsh and overcrowded conditions, though mainly after Henry's short stay in late 1862. (Photo by Alex Gardner, 1865; National Archives)

FIGURE 8. Henry Willis Wells memorial marker, Forest Hills Cemetery. This memorial stone is about four miles from Henry's family home in Brookline, Massachusetts. Forest Hills is also the resting place of many other members of the Wells family. The memorial stone also honors another family member, later killed in Africa. (Wells Family)

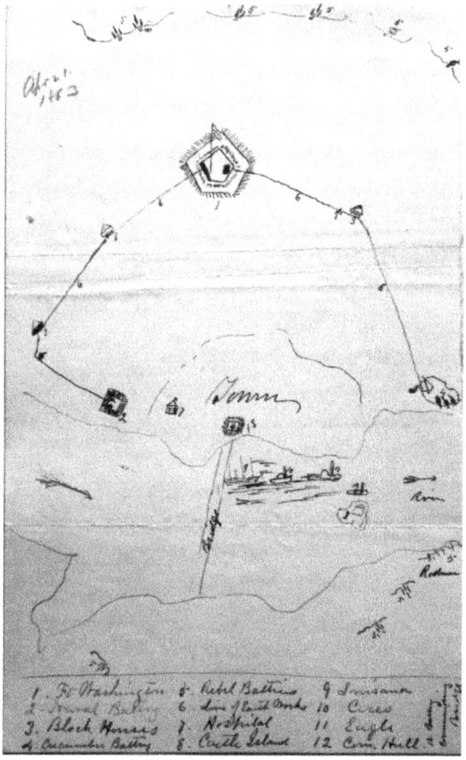

FIGURE 9. Siege of Washington, NC. Henry drew this map to illustrate the Union defenses of Washington, North Carolina, during the April 1863 siege. Henry commanded a battery ashore. It is an enclosure to his 21 April 1863 letter to his mother. (Henry W. Wells Papers)

FIGURE 10. USS *Ceres*. Henry sketched this drawing of the *Ceres* for his sister Eliza and enclosed it in his 31 March 1863 letter home. The warship was a 150-ton side-wheel steamer built in 1856 and purchased by the US Navy in September 1861. She mounted two 30-pounders and two 24-pounders. The navy mainly used her to protect US Army positions ashore in the sounds of North Carolina. (Henry W. Wells Papers)

1

"I Like My Situation First Rate"

Patrolling Virginia Waters

U.S. Steamer *Cambridge*[1]
Navy Yard Boston
August 6th 1861

Sir:

By authority vested in me I hearby appoint you a Masters Mate in the Navy of the United States: to serve on board this vessel and to perform such other duties as may be assigned to you.

You will please to inform me by letter of your acceptance of this appointment.

Respectfully
Your obt servant
Wm. A. Parker
Wm. A. Parker Commander U.S. Navy[2]

Mr Henry W. Wells
Masters Mate
Brooklyne Mass.

Marginalia—Reported to me August 6th

Brookline
August 7, 1861
William A. Parker, Commander
U.S.N. Steamer *Cambridge*

Sir

I accept the position of Master's Mate which you have been pleased to assign me on board the U.S. Steamer *Cambridge*.

With many thanks I remain
Your ob't Servant
Henry W. Wells

USS *Cambridge*
Sep 2nd 1861

Dear Mother

We shall probable go to sea tomorrow as we are under sailing orders. I feel quite nicely.

I am only writing this as a precaution in case we should go off suddenly but I dont intend to send it till I am quite sure that we shall go. I will try to add some more by & by

Henry

USS *Cambridge*
Sep 3rd 1861

Dear Mother

I am getting along first rate, we are not gone yet but I think we shall to day or to night for they have been getting up steam this morning. We are going down to Fort Monroe.[3] Give my love to all Father Mother Sisters brother & grandpa Cousin Lu & Aunti too.[4] I hope Elize is better.

Write to me as soon as possible. In haste from your loving son

Henry W. Wells

U.S.S. *Cambridge*
Sep 7th 1861
At Fort Monroe

Dear Mother

We have just arrived here this morning & as I have a moments leasure I would write you a few lines. We had a pleasant passage down[.] we were a little long about it on account of chasing a couple of vessels. The first one we thought would be a prise [prize] surely for when they first saw us they altered their course & made all sail away from us, of course we followed & gradualy came up with her[.] we soon made her out to be a schooner & when we were with in about six miles we gave them a shot from the Long gun as a hint to come too but they paid no attention to it & kept on so we went on full speed after. When we were within a half a mile he hoisted English colors, but never hove too till we got along side & ordered him to[.] we sent a boat on board in charge of Mr. Eldridge (Acting Master) who examined his papers which were all right so we had to let him go after giving him a blowing up for not heaving to when we fired & so taking us a long way out of our course.[5] We afterwords chased & spoke the packet ship *Victoria*. On Thursday we made a target & put it over board. After getting about two miles from it we hove too &

commenced firing at it. We fired about 7 or 8 rounds apiece & the Captain counted the gunnery pretty good. The best shots were made by the Parrot[t] gun[.][6] we did not hurt the target much but if a ship had been there in stead I think every one of *our* shot would have taken effect. (by *our* of course I mean the forward Pivot gun)

My health is about the same as when I left home if any thing I am a little better[.] yesterday I had a very bad headach & so I went to the Doctor & got something (Pills) for it, which has done me good. As for my cold it has not had a fair chance to get well yet as Thursday night was the first night I had any bed to sleep in other than what I could make upon the floor. We have not got cots after all & this sleeping in hammocks I dont approve of. I like to lay strait.

However dont think I am complaining for I like my situation first rate. When we first started I was told to stand watch with Mr. [Frederick W.] Strong the Sailing Master[.][7] I did not like it at first till I was informed that the arrangement was made so that Mr Strong would not be able to give up his watch to me with out throwing extra duty on the other watch officers he having to attend to the navigation.

I am very glad now that the change was made for not only am I officer of the deck a good deal of the time but being in his watch he calls on me to note the chronometer for him & to work the sights to compare with his. It is splendid practice & he is ready to show me any thing I want to know.

I suppose you would like some description of Fort Monroe but as I have seen only the out side as yet I will defer that till another time. The Steam Frigate *Roranoke* Flag Ship & a number of other men of war are laying here.[8] I expect to receive a letter to day tho' I dont know as I ought to so soon. Write as often as you can. Mr. [Nathaniel] Ottiwell sends his respects.

Give my love to all the family (Cousin Lu and Aunti to) & remember me to all friends especially the Bonds & Joe. Please explain to Jo[e] why I did not write to him as I promised. you know I did not feel able to do any thing the last few days I was at home.

Good by. The Flag is up & we are bound to *keep it there* from your loving son,

Henry W. Wells
Masters Mate

U. S. Steamer *Cambridge*
Off Beaufort N.C.[9]
Sept 10th 1861
Lat obsd 34°. 27′ N Long 76°. 26′W

Sir:

You will take charge of the English Schr *Revere* of Yarmouth and proceed with her to Boston and report to the judge of the District and also to the Commandant of the Navy yard.[10]

You are hereby furnished with duplicate orders to this effect

Respectfully yr obt servant
Wm. A. Parker
Comdr.

To
Henry W. Wells
masters mate
U.S.S. *Cambridge*

Reported on board *Cambridge*[11]

[Endorsement] Reported with schooner *Revere* of Yarmouth Nova Scotia Sept 21st 1861

Wm L Hudson Comdt[12]

United States Marshals Office
Boston Sep 23 1861

Received of Mr Henry W Wells masters mate of the schooner *Revere* & cargo libelled for prize in the District Court Mass Dist.

John S. Keyes
U.S. Marshal

Boston
24 September 1861.

To all whom it may concern

Henry W. Wells, Masters-mate of the U.S.S *Cambridge*, has this day delievered into my custody the bodies of two seamen Wm Pennell, James Pennell, recently of the schooner *Revere* now prize in lying in this port.[13]

C.F. Adams for Prize Commission for the District of Boston in Charleston

Navy Yard Boston
October 4th 1861

Sir,

You will proceed to Hampton Roads with four men belonging to the Gunboat *Cambridge*, and report to Com. Wm. Parker, or in his absence to the Senior

Naval officer present. Transportation for the men will be furnished you by the Navy Agent. Your own expenses for travelling will be reimbursed you upon producing the proper vouchers to the paymaster of the *Cambridge.*

I am Respec
Your obt. Servt
Wm L Hudson
Commandant

To Henry W. Wells M Mate
[Endorsement] Reported on board the *Minnesota* at Hampton Roads October 7th 1861.

G. J. Van Brunt
Senior Naval Officer Present

[2nd Endorsement] Reported on Board the *Cambridge* October 17th 1861.
Wm. A. Parker Comdr

Hampton Roads Oct/4 [1861]
Flag Ship *Minnesota*[14]

Dear Mother

I am going on board the steamer *Rhode Island* this afternoon to go south & join my vessel. I write in great haste to let you know that fact. We heard from the *Cambridge* this morning. They have had a boat expedition in connection with another vessel & got one or two of the boats smashed up in the surf[.] I believe the boats belonged to the other vessel that got wrecked. One of the Masters Mates of the "*C*" (Walter Odine) I think) has died & was buryed at sea. They say he went crazy first & tride to shoot himself—Cousin Louisa Greely knows him I believe. Good by now from your loving son

Henry Wells

I am in a great hurry so you must excuse this awful writing. Give my love to all my friends. I will write every chance I get.

Henry

Baltimore Oct 6th 61
Steamer *Louisiana*

Dear Mother

I am safe on board the steamer that is to take us down to the Fort & I have got all my men.

I had to stay in New York all day yesterday as the steamer did not get in in time for the morning train. One of my men got drunk on the boat & gave me some trouble but I soon bundled him off to bed. we could hardly wake him up in the morning & as soon as we got to the depot he laid down & slept till about three in [the] afternoon. I left the men in charge of Derocher & went over to Brooklyn to see Uncle Lyman & the Dix.

Dr. Morse assistant surgeon of the 17 Reg. M.V. whose acquaintance I made on board the Fall River boat (going to Baltimore to join his Regiment) went with me.[15] & Uncle Parkhurst made quite an impression on him. I did not see Uncle Lyman or Zoueves [Zouaves] at which I was very much disappointed. We left New York at 6 PM on the New Jersey Rail Road. There were a goo[d] many soldiers on board. Recruits going to join different Regiments. There are a party of Zuaves [Zouaves] of the 11th N.Y.V. going down to the Fort with us.[16] We arrived here in Baltimore at about 3 ½ AM & as the boat was not in then we went up to a hotel to stay till she arrived & to get some breakfast. I saw the place where the Massachusetts men were murdered in April & I felt as tho' I would like to pitch into somebody.[17] One of them is going up to the Post Office so I will not write any more now (I left off up there to go to dinner) The *Cambridge* has left Hampton roads. I will write again when we get to the Fort.

Love to all & write soon to your loving son

Henry W Wells

I saw that Colonel of the 11th Ohio who was taken at Rich Mountain & has just escaped, at the Quartermaster's office.

If I dont forget I will tell you about him next time

Henry W Wells

Fort Monroe Monday morning

All safe & sound here. The *Cambridge* is away & I am going with my men on board the Flag Ship *Minnesota*. I could not or rather to tell the truth did not (for got talking with a gentleman and forgot it) mail this yesterday so I thought I would add two or three lines. Love to all. Direct the same as I told you Steamer *Cambridge*. care of Flag Officer [Louis Malisherbes] Goldsborough.

Good by from your loving son
H W Wells

Marginalia penned by the family—About 10 days after the *Cambridge* left Boston she captured a prize & Henry with a crew was put on board of her—brought her into Boston. This letter was written on his way back to join the *Cambridge*. LW [Louisa Wells Wendte] April 1902.

Hampton Roads
Oct 9th/ 61
Frigate *Minnesotta*

Dear Mother

I though[t] I would commence a letter to you before dinner as several of the others are writing.

I am getting along very well on board here & am very well contented to stay here for a while as there is a prospect of the *Merrimac* coming down to attack us before long with two other steamers that they have got there.[18] We expected them last night & got all ready for them but were disapointed.

There was a flag of truce came down from Norfolk monday & brought about sixty released prisoners from Richmond that were taken at Bull Run.[19] They were all badly wounded, most of them being minus & [an] arm or a leg but they seemed in good spirits & would talk & laugh as cheerful as you please[.] There was one of the 1st Mass. Vol. amongst them belonging to Co. I, I believe. I had quite a talk with him. He belonged to Boston & has got a wife & children there, but seems to think if he gets well he should like to go back & have another try at the Rebels. He is wounded in the ankle & was left on the field when the Rebels came up (A Louisiana Reg.) They bayoneted him twice or rather tried to[;] one of the bayonets directed at his breast was stopped by his Testament which he carried there, the weppon went about half through it. He showed it [to] me & said he never should part with it. He says they were treated very cruely. one of his comrades was shot dead for looking out the prison window & another got his arm shattered for the same offense.

It was an awful sight to see the poor fellows & it makes one realise what war is.

There are several officers on board here waiting for a chance to rejoin there vessels. There is the Carpenter of the *Jamestown*, A Midshipman of the *Vandalia*[,] A Masters Mate of the *Gemsbok*[,] an Engineer of the *Flag* & myself.[20]

One of the Lieutenants drills the officers who have just entered the service at the great guns & small arms every day & the masters mate of the *Gemsbok* & I join in with them so I am not losing any thing by staying here.

When the *Cambridge* was here last she had no Mates on board at all, they tell me & they borrowed one from this ship. & I believe there is another away in a prize which makes them rather short[.] So to day the First Lieutenant came to me & said he wanted the mate of the *G[emsbok]* & I should stand watch while on board.

When I arrived this was the only man of war in the roads but yesterday the *Susquehanna* & the *Corwin* came in so we have a little company.

I guess I wont write any more at present & I hope next time I write will be to tell we have captured the Rebel steamers. Good by give my love to all & write soon to your loving son

Henry W. Wells

Hampton Roads
Oct. 13th [1861]
On board Frigate *Minnesotta*

Dear Mother

Tho' there has not much occured since I wrote last I thought I would write again to night if it is ever so little as I know you will be glad to hear from me.

There does not seem to be any immediate chance of my rejoining my ship, which on a great many accounts I am very sorry for. One thing, I am getting *rather* short of clothes, shirts in particular, as I dirtied about half of my stock in that nasty dusty ride in the cars.

I had a talk with Captain Van Brunt about getting back day before yesterday & he promised to send me the first chance that turned up.[21] So all I have got to do now is to wait.

Thursday night we had quite an exciting time. At about 9 o'clock P.M. we saw blue lights burning in the direction of Newport News & pretty soon the steam tug *Lockwood* which was stationed up that way on the look out came down full speed & said that three Rebel steamers were coming down to force there way out & had nearly surrounded her.[22] Of course all was bustle & excitement. The Drummer was call[ed] to beat to quarters. & in a very short time the hammocks were all up, guns man[n]ed & cleared away, & every thing ready for action.

As I had no station I took my position on the quarter deck & made my self generaly useful carrying orders, etc. Everybody was anxious for a fight but we were disapointed, for it was a false alarm so after standing in a drizzling rain for about two hours the retreat was beat & the guns were secured.

Friday we had target shooting[.] we fired one broadside. I did not think they did much better than we did on board the *Cambridge*.

We had services on board here today. The Rev[erend] Mr. Fuller Chaplain of the Mass[achusetts] 16th Reg. Vol. preached the sermon and a very stiring [*sic*] one it was tho' I hardly endorse all his opinions. I have scraped up quite a little acquaintance with him. I have a good deal of boat duty [to] perform now & stand a watch so I dont have any too much leasure time tho' after all I aint doing much compared to what I used to have [to] do when in the merchant service.

Well! it is about the hardest job that I have undertaken for some time trying to write in a Frigates Midshipmans berth here is one Mate drumming a tattoo on the table, two or three more skylarking, a *Shell* fixing a hammock & all talking as fast as their tongues can wag.[23]

Now I think all things considered I will not write any more now as the lights will have to go out pretty soon so good night. Love to all & write soon[.] I guess you need not mind putting care of Flag Officer on my letters as it wont be necessary.

Good by from your loving son

Henry W. Wells

Henry

U.S.S. *Cambridge*
Oct 18th [1861]
Off Beaufort N.C.

Dear Mother

Here I am at last safely back on board the *C[ambridge]* & for all my worrying they did not expect me much sooner. Mr. Maice [William H. Maies] is not here yet tho' he is in the fleet some where trying to find the vessel for he was at Fort Monroe a short time before I got there.

I was missinformed about the sad occurance that took place while I was away. it was poor Ottiwell instead of [Walter C.] Odiorne was taken away. He was only sick about 10 days from the time he first complained of not feeling well till he died, & during the last 5 days & a half he did not have his right senses. As the steerage was rather warm they made him a bed on the gun deck close to one of the ports & had watchers with him all the time[.] When his mind first commenced to wander he was very quiet but early the next morning (his watcher having slept out side of the screen that was round his bed) he sprang up & darted down into the steerage where the rest of the officers that belong there were sleeping before any body could stop him & got hold of his revolver & swore he would shoot the first man that came near him. he seem to have an idea that there was a man after him with a Sharps Rifle & he said that he could fight too. Of course every body cleared out of the steerage in *short time*. but soon after the Gunner went down to try to peacify him. but as soon as O saw him he fired & the shot barely missed Mr. [William J.] Ferguson's head. & he had to retreat. He fired none after that. O had charge of the place for about half an hour when they got the hose along & knocked him down with a stream of water. after they got hold of him he calmed down at once & made no resistance. On the table found *three* revolvers and *two* swords with some ammunition spread out on the table.

It seems strange, but he never spoke of home or of any of his friends all the while he was sick. his mind seemed to run on his duties about the ship & he talked some about prizes etc. He always felt sore about not having had charge of one & I am affraid he allowed his mind to dwell upon it too much.

I will copy you an extract from the Log Book on the day of his death.

"Friday 27th Sept. 1861 From 4 to 6 PM. Gale increasing & ship very laborsome. At 4:40, Nath D. Ottiwell Actg. Masters Mate departed this life after a sickness of 7 days with typhoid fever Aged 25 years.["]

> "For him there tolled no funeral bell,
> O'er him there bent no weeping form
> Wild Nature pealed his parting knell
> Amidst the Anthem of the storm."[24]

And so his light went out in the midst of a tremenjous gale (which very nearly made the ship his tomb together with many others) & as if it had then fullfilled its mission in ushering a spirit to another world, it died away also.

He was buried on the 28th in Lat 34° 04' N, Lon 76° 18' W. The funeral service was read by the Captain. All his effects were sent home & by mistake my great Coat and Sack coat were sent with them but Mr. [Robert D.] Eldridge says he will write for them.

You said something in your letter about my writing to his friends but on the whole I do not think I had better. both Mr. Eldridge & the Dr. wrote after his death & I am affraid anything I could say would hardly releace their minds any, especialy under the peculelar cercumstances of the case. Now I think I had better drop this sad subject & turn to something else.

While I was away the *Albatross* (U.S.S.), who is on this station (& whose commander is "senior" officer to ours I am sorry to say) & the *Cambridge* started a boat expedition for Bgus [Bogue] Inlet to cut out a vessel that was laying there.[25] Three boats went from this vessel & two from the *A*, Lieut [William] Gwin (of *ours*) commanding the whole.[26] They could not find the vessel & in attempting to make a landing thro' the surf the night being very dark the boats got seperated. Our men behaved splindidly[.] Mr. Eldridge who commanded one of the boats went thro' the surf three times trying to find the others but they all got scattered & saw no more of each other that night. The first boat that came back was the Lieutenants & he reported all the rest lost but after two or three hours of suspense Mr. Strong made his appearance & then Mr. Eldridge. One of the boats of the *Albatross* came back but no one knew what had become of the other. In the morning Lieutenant Gwin started with th[r]ee boats to find them & met them coming off. They had stove their boat lost part of their arms (among which were five Sharps Rifles belonging to this vessel) & had been all night on the beach. The inhabitants helped them off. They are mostly fishermen & quite friendly. *So ended the great expedition.*

I stand *my own* watch now & my duties are the same as an Acting Master which of course I like very much tho' I think that before the year is out I shall apply for the Commission. When the ship was at Hampton Roads another master was sent on board named [John M.] Merrill & a masters mate to take the place of poor Ottiwell. So we now have *4* masters and two mates on board & 2 away. Mr. [George H.] Rice the new mate has charge of the Gun deck which was Mr. Ottiwells old station, which leaves five watch officers at preasent so I dont think you need be alarmed about the watching wearing upon me at all. When Mr. Maice [Maies] gets back there will be six—*whew*!

Tafts the Pursers Steward is turned out of our mess he carried his insolence too far to be bourn any longer.[27] The *Roranoke* is along side & the Capt. has gone on board of her if there is a chance I will send this letter by her.

Good by love to all. we shall be in Hampton Roads in about a week. from your loving son

Henry W. Wells

U.S.S. *Cambridge*
At Sea
Oct. 24th 1861

Dear Lu,

Ive spoke the Frigate *Roranoke* yesterday off Beaufort & supposing that she was going north, we sent a letter bag on board, but we soon found she had come to relieve *us* & *we* were going instead so back came the bag with another one from the *R*[*oanoke*] in companie. & now we are on our way for Hampton Roads as fast as the gale that is blowing will allow us. Mr. Maice [Maies] came on the *Roronoke* to join us, so now our mess is complete with the exception of Mr. Odiorne who I suppose we shall find at Fort Monroe. We are all glad to have a chance to go even to such a dull place as Fort M. for it is very monotonous business blockading a place like "Beaufort." We are at anchor most of the time & have nothing to do but fish & watch the sand hills. There are two or three English ships in the harbor waiting for a chance to get out, & wait they will have to I guess for some time. One of them is the *Alliance* the one that flew the Cesession Flag at Halifax NS. & So much fuss was made about.[28] I would rather catch her than all the rest put together—out of spite. I hope I shall find some letters at the "Roads" for me from you all it seems as tho' ti [it] was three months in stead of three weeks since I left home.

I wonder if Eliza has got home yet? it was too bad that I should not have seen her.

I have received one letter from home since I left & so find that you knew of poor Ottiwells death before I did.

I heard that one of the mates had died when on board the *Minnesotta* but supposed it to be Odiorne & never knew it was not so till I arrived on board her. Poor fellow it was a hard fate for him to die in such a way, far from all his friends. If it had been in action we should not have felt so badly. For who would not be willing to die for his country. but as it was, it is sad to think of. He did not seem to suffer much, but was out of his mind nearly all the time he was sick.

How are you getting along with your riding lessons? do you enjoy them as well as ever?

Do you see much of Joe now adays. I hope he comes in often. please tell him I should like very much to see a little of his hand writing.

We shall be at Fort Monroe to night or tomorrow morning I think but I cant tell how long we may stay there, or where we shall go when we leave. I only hope they will give us a new station as all hands are pretty well tired of the old one.

Good by now Luie dear, give my love to all. & write soon & often to your loving brother.

Henry W. Welles

I believe I have got all the letters that were not accounted for when I was at home. at all events I have got two or three old ones.

Hampton Roads
Oct 25th 1861

Dear Mother,

Tho' two letters started for home to day, still I guess I will write another to night. I was very much disapointed not to find any letters here for me. Why cant you try to keep some here in reserve all the time so when I come in suddenly I shall find them?

We had quite a smash up last night between Capes Henry & Hatteras. We ran into a schooner & nearly sunk her cutting her down to the waters edge.[29] on our part we carried away our bowsprit, had the side of the Pilot house stove in & our wood ends started which has caused us to leak a good deal. I was officer of the deck at the time but the First Lieutenant Gwyn was on the deck with the trumpet & giving orders to the helmsman so I am not blamed. Capt. Parker was very angry & as soon as we were clear he demanded to know who was officer of Deck. Lieut. Gwyn took it all on his own shoulders at once like a man & said that he had charge & was responsible so I went clear but I am affraid he will be courtmartialed as Flag-officer Goldsbourough is a very hard man to convince.[30]

There is a large fleet here now. They sail tomorrow I believe for Beaufort, SC (not my station) but we shall not be able to go with them confound it! I am not at all sure but we shall have to go north where we can go into a dry dock. Well! if we cant do any fighting that is the next best thing I suppose!

I wish you (Father) would send me down a pair of boots mine are giving out. I want a half dozen handkerchiefs too. Colored silk are the best I guess. Why cant you send me a nice snug box with those things in it nicely chocked of with some home goodies. you might send it by express (that is if you dont think it a foolish ideer.) If you do send it Direct—Henry W. Wells, Masters Mate on board U.S.S. *Cambridge*, Fort Monroe—*to be kept till called for*. Adams & Co. Express is the one.[31] if there not too expensive I should like to have three or four of those fine flannel shirts that you see gentlemen some our officers ware them a good deal & it saves washing as they dont get dirty so quick as calico ones. I think the blue or brown plaid are the prettiest.

I cant write any more now—(that is to say there is a Boston paper laying on the deck & I want to read it.) So good by. If you conclude to send those things send at once & I may get them before leaving this time. Give my love to all & write heaps of letters to your loving son

Henry W. Wells

I forgot I have not written *about myself.* I am pretty well I thank you only I have got a little cold. Nothing serious however so dont be alarmed. good by again. Oh how I wish I could give you a hug & a kiss!

Henry

Hampton Roads
Oct 27th 1861

Dear Mother

I have been wandering round ever since breakfast in a useless kind of a way not knowing hardly what to do with myself. so at last I have come to the conclusion that I had better write home again tho' I did send a letter yesterday. It was not that I did not want to that made me wait so long before I commenced but because it does not seem as tho' I had any thing to write about however I always feel nearer home when I am writing to you so I'm glad I sat down.

The Commodore says we have got to go south again, *sink* or *swim* for at least two or three weeks when he thinks he shall have a vessel to releave us & then we shall be sent to some Northern port, to go into dry dock & refit generaly. We may get away from here the last of the week tho' I am not sure, as there is a good deel to do. Tomorrow morning we are going to run all the guns aft & lighten her forward as much as possable so as to give the Carpenters a chance to work at our Stem, as the leak is supposed to be there.

Our new Masters Mate is in trouble. he went on shore the day we got in & got on a spree & came on board rather the worse for it. He has charge of the Gun Deck, spirit room, etc. during the night the Engineer with the Firemen etc. were at work making some repairs to the engine & at 12 mid. the First Lieut. wanted to have grog served out to them, but knowing the state Mr. Rice was in, gave the keys to the Gunner who attended to it. The next morning Mr. Rice went on shore in the market boat with out leave & did not come off till an officer was sent for him. He received a severe reprimand & I suppose that would have been the end of it if he had kept quiet but instead of that he went below & insulted the Gunner & tried to get up a fight. The first Lieu heard of it & called him up onto the quarter deck & put him under arrest. I am affraid he will lose his appointment[.] I am very sorry it should have occured for he was trying to get a commission as Acting Master & now I suppose his chance is not worth counting on.

The Fleet has not got off yet but they will go soon I suppose[.] Nobody knows sertainly where they are going. The *Unidilla* [*Unadilla*] is here & I am going on board to see Edward May if I can get a change before they sail.

I received your letter (if you call it such) yesterday sent via NY Naval Lyceum & was glad to hear enough to hear from home if it was ever so little.[32]

I dont think it is worth while to send letters to the Lyceum at N.Y. as the one at Charleston is just as good, & I would not send *all* that way either—but most to Fort Monroe direct—with simply my name & that of the vessel. I shall probably get them if sent either way—as I have already received four letters all directed different.

The reason that I did not get letters while I was on board the *Minnesota* was that they were directed to the *Cambridge* & the Flag Officer entirely ignored the preasence of so humble an individual as myself so they were sent on board the *Rhode Island* & I received them after I got on board my safe vessel. What is Uncle George's no. on Mills St.? I told cousin Sophy I would write to her & I dont know how to direct. I hope I shall get some more letters before I sail, write lots and dont be affraid about my not answering them. Why dont Joe write me? I wish you would ask him the *next time* he *comes over* to *our house* as I shant write him again till I [get] one from him. I wish Eliza & Lu would too. I wonder if they are aware that I have not received letters from either since I have been in the service except the one I had from E. while I was at home.

I am getting along very well & am on good terms with all the officers & enjoying my self as well as I ever do away from home. My duties are very light & such as I like. I have charge of a watch & occasionally I have to go in a boat on duty—so I have a great deal of leasure which I manage to get rid of without much trouble[.] I made a resolution when I found how much time I was going to have, not to read novels except in the afternoons & to devote the fore noons to study or useful reading. We have to send in our reckoning every day the same as at first so I shant get rusty in my navigation. I guess I wont write any more now. Give my love to all & write me a good long letter,

From your loving son
Henry W. Wells

Hampton Roads
Oct 29th 1861
USS *Cambridge*

Dear Mother

As we shall probably leave here tomorrow I thought I had better write once more any way, tho' I guess you would not complain of a scarcity of letters since we have been laying here.

The report is, tho' I can't vouch for the truth of it, that we are not going back to Beaufort at preasent, but are going up the Rappahannock 'in' stead, if that is the case—& the First Lieutenant says so;—why we shall have a chance of doing a little fighting for our country which I think every man in the ship would be glad of.

We have been coaling all night & are hurrying everything along as fast as possible so I think there is something up. We are going to leave with out a bowsprit but I dont think it much loss, in fact I dont know but that it is an improvement. The fleet sailed this morning. Where for? it was dreadful aggravating to see them go off & to stay here.

There was a court of enquirey held on board here yesterday about our collision. I had to appear and give my evidence. The court consisted of a Commander, two Lieutenants, with a Secretary. They will continue the investigation to day.

Mr. Rice I am glad to say has been reinstated again. I was affraid he had got himself into a serious scrape, but they concluded to let him off.

We had quite a time here sunday. Nearly all the officers *except* two or three of the *highest* & a good many of the men, were more or less intoxicated. & those of us that were sober had hard work to keep the rest from getting them selves into trouble. —A very pleasant way to spend sunday!

I went on shore for an hour yesterday it is the only time I have asked for liberty since we have been here for I would not give a cent to see all there [that] is there it is all an old story there with me now.

I have not seen Mr. May & as his vessel sailed this morning of course I shan't at preasent.

The mail has not come on board yet, but I hope to hear from you when it does, & then I will add some more to this short letter but for the preasent good by, give my love to all from·your loving son

H.W. Wells

Afternoon
It is all right we are going up the 'Rappahannock' & sail this evening. We shan't stop there long tho' I guess as we have not got much coal. Good by

From your loving son

Henry W. Wells

U.S.S. *Cambridge*
Oct 31st 61
Off Rappahannock River

Dear Mother

The First Lieutenant has just sent down word that there will be a chance to send off some letters at eight o'clock by the steamer *Rescue* so I have just time to scratch off a few lines to let you know that I am well & that we are all safe on our station.[33]

We arrived here yesterday afternoon & releaved the *Valley City* (gunboat) who has gone to Baltimore for repairs.[34]

This morning we saw a boat coming off from the shore with a flag of truce flying. we were under weigh at the time standing in to the mouth of the river. On running down to them we found it was a flat boat with 21 contrabands in it (18 men & 3 women) who had just escaped from their masters.[35] We took them all on board & I guess a happier set of darkies never were seen. one of them wanted we should fire a gun to let their friends know that they were all safe. it was great fun to hear them talk, but I have not time to tell you much about it now. We took four from the *Valley City* before she left so that with what we got at Fort Monroe we have now over 30 on board, which is rather more then we want tho' a few come very handy.

We ran up the river about 30 miles to day with out seeing any thing of any consequences more than a beautiful country, & then came down again, just before we got out of the river we ran ashore and stuck for about an hour but we got off with out any damage. There are a couple of Rebel steamers up the river some where but we did not meet them. They exchanged shots with the *Valley City* the other day & drove her back but I suppose they will not like to try it with us as we are much more heaver [heavily] armed. I can not write any more now as there are some of the rest [who] want to use the desk. So I must bid you good by. I shall expect to find lots of letters when I get back to the Fort which will be about 10 days from now I guess.

Give my love to all, & do *write* lots to your loving son

Henry W. Wells

I have got a knife from one of the darkies. it is quite a primitive affair & I [plan] to put it into my cabinet. We have got a new messmate, a midshipman named Cushing[.][36] we have got [al]most as many officers as a frigate now. Captain, Lieutenant, 4 masters, 4 masters mates, midshipman, Gunner, Carpenter, Doctor Pu[r]ser.

Rappahannock River
Nov. 7th 1861
U.S. Steamer *Cambridge*

Dear Mother

As I received two letters (dated Oct 29 & 31) day before yesterday by the *Rescue* I will now commence an answer. I don't know when I shall have a chance to send it before long tho' I guess.

Quite an exciting affair came off here yesterday tho' I did not participate in it. I suppose I must begin at the beginning & tell you the whole story. So to commence—In the morning I heard that there was an expedition on foot to cut a schooner out of Corrotoman River.[37] I went to the First Lieutenant & volunteered to go, but he said that no more officers could go than those already promised as they could not be spared from the ship. I urged him as far as I could with out giving offense but it was no go & I only got the promise that I should go next time. There were four officers, Lieut. Gwyn, Mr. Eldridge, Mr. Strong & Midshipman Cushing & 30 men. They went in the little *Rescue* with one of our boats in tow.

The *Rescue* is a small tow boat (or was before the war) & mounts 1 gun on her for[e]castle. They started at 12:20 PM. & were soon out of sight up the river. They expected to be gone about 2 hours, but 3 o'clock came & we heard nothing of them, but a little later & we heard a gun faint in the distance followed by two others in quick succession & shortly after another. Then we heard no more for some time. This made us very anxious for from the reports of escaped slaves (of which more by and by) we had been led to suppose that the Rebels had no force there more than Pickets and Guards & no artil[l]ery. At a little after 4 we saw the *R* coming out from behind the point firing as fast as possible with great guns & small arms. Our boat was in tow but no schooner. Of course we were in a great deal of suspense & I guess there were a hundred different conjectures as to what they had or had not done.

When she came within hail, the men in the *R* gave three cheers which we answered with right good will for we judged by that that it was all right, which was the case. For they had gone up with out any opposition & found the sch. there aground loaded with wood & wheat & after parting two lines trying to get her off they set fire to her. They laid by her till the fire was so far under weigh [way] that it could not be put out & then started down stream. but this time the Rebels were ready for them with two Rifled Howitzers & a body of riflemen & they had quite a smart engagement. The steamer had two shot holes through a canoe lying on her house & one or two ropes cut but no men wounded which was very remarkable as for one spell the rifle balls were falling all around thick. on the whole the whole thing was very satisfactory.[38]

Nov 8th. Well! I wish I always had as much to write about as I have this time tho' I have not much time now for I have just heard that they are going to send the *Rescue* to try to put a mail on board the Baltimore boat to night & I must not loose the chance.

To day we have been Shelling the town or village of Habana [Urbanna] because the contrabands reported that there were three companies of Rebels there & that the women & children had all left the place.[39] We fired 90 rounds & the *Rescue* 40. I fired 21 from the Parrot[t] gun, for the 1st Captain of her was sick & I took his place. during the action the *R* sent in a boat to bring out a canoe that was laying near the beach but the rebels drove them back with rifles.[40] We could not see the extent of damage that was done the place on account of a greater part of the houses being in a hollow but as several of the shell exploded right amongst them I think it must have been considerable. I can hardly hear now, the guns are ringing in my ears yet.

Last night we picked up 9 negroes (but that is getting an old story now as we get more or less almost every night.) One of them came off in a little dugout all by him self. The first thing he said when he came on board was "Tank de Lord I haint got to work no more for dem dam Soderners." He is quite an intelligent darkie & will lie as fast as he can speak. he came from the neighborhood of Habana [Urbanna] & was delighted when he found we were going to attack the place. His name (so he sais) is George Washington Weeks. Day before yesterday a canoe came off with a party in her of darkies who came from the same plantation as some already on board & it would have done you good to have seen them meet each other. (Golly! how is yer) They were all in the land of freedom sure, so they thought. One of them was perfectly white & had red whiskers.

Capt. Parker asked him what he wanted on board but he said he was a "slave man" & come with the rest. They all say that the Southerners are quite wrathy against us & only want we should *land* to give us a good thrashing. "But Lord massa dey'ed run like sheep." I could write you lots more about it, but the *R* will leave in about fifteen minutes so I must close.

I delivered that message to James Begley. he has written twice & wish me to write to that effect.

We had a Court Martial on board a few days ago to try a man named Fitch for leaving his post when on sentrie with out being relieved. by the Articles of War that is death but the Court stopped one months pay & gave him extra police duty for the next two.

Well I must not write any more now so good by, till I have another chance. Give my love to all & write often to your loving son

Henry W. Wells

We cracked our after pivot gun during the bombardment.

Rappahannock River
Nov. 9th / 61
U.S.S. *Cambridge*

Dear Mother

Sunday has come round again & with it a desire to write home so here goes. I sent off a letter night before last which I hope you received as I gave you a short account of some of our doings in it.

We are hopeing that some contrabands will come off from about Habana [Urbanna] so we can hear what damage was done to the place. We have 40 about of them on board now but they dont come off so fast now as at first on account of not being able to get boats. The white[s] having seized them all & taken them to places where they have troops to guard them. We have great sport on board here with the darkies. Night before last we had a crowd of them aft on the Gun Deck singing & dancing, & it was about the richest thing I ever saw[.] we had a regular hoedown. & one of them sang Dixie with "secesh" words (how old Abe Lincoln wished he was back splitting rails again & how Southerners took Washington? etc. etc.)

I like our new messmate thus far very much. he & I are together a good deal. He is rather exclusive in his ideas, but as it dont come in my direction I dont let it trouble me.

We all like our new station very much & I hope we shan't be sent back to Beaufort again. There it is the same thing over & over again but hear there is some life (& more death?) & we are always doing something if it is only oystering or picking up runaway negroes. The white people along the shore here according to all accounts are in a dreadful rage against us & I expect if they get hold of any body belonging to this vessel or the *Rescue* they will show no quarter but the thing is to get hold of us. (Please excuse those finger marks down at the bottom of this page I don't know how they got there for my hands *look* clean.)

What has Cousin Isa gone to Fayal for? seems to me there was no talk of it when I went away. I should think Mrs. Kent would miss her very much.

Where is cousin Clara going to live now she is married & what are Kinnie & Lu going to do with themselves for you say they have sold the house?

By the way my sack coat has turned up. I hope Miss Ottiwell has not put herself to any trouble about it. As to the Box I think under the circumstances it was better to keep it back for a while, tho' as it happend if you had sent it I should have got it. I guess I would not send it now untill I know something different about where I am going. When you do send it if you like I wish you would put in two or three books History or anything interesting & *useful* & my French Book. I wont promise to study it but think I will.

I dont smoke very bad now so you need not be alarmed about me in that respect. & I have been for the last three weeks wading through *Great Expectations* (in the afternoons) it is very good but does not come up to what I expected, having heard so much said about it.

I wish you would send me a *Boston* Paper occasionaly I never can get them at the Fort to the northard of New York. & I like to read the local news. I wish I could go with you this morning to hear Mr. Clarke. The Dr. reads services here every Sunday but oh! so miserable compared to ours & then besides we have no sermon[.][41]

Well I have come to the end of my paper so I will finish & give some of the rest a chance at the desk. The *Rescue* is going down to the mouth of the river to intercept the Baltimore boat to night & we hope to get a mail. at all events we shall have a chance to send one. Good By give my love to all & write soon to your loving son

Henry

U.S.S. *Cambridge*
Nov 11th 1861
Rappahannock River

Dear Mother

I have just come off watch & as there is a mail going off tonight I thought I would write you a few lines for I know you like to hear from me as often as possable & so I never like to let a chance slip with out improving it.

We are about to experience quite a loss, for Lieutenant Gwin is going to leave us & another Lieutenant has arrived to take his place. He is ordered to the Brig *Perry* as commander of her I believe. We are all very sorry to loose him & I think he would rather stay himself for a sailing vessel can not do much in this war. & he thinks a subordinate position here better than a command there. Our new Lieut. is quite a young man named Miller.[42] He may be a very nice sort of a man but I dont think he will come up to our old one by a good deal, in fact I hardly think there are many in the Navy that would. I guess from all I can hear & see that Capt. Parker is rather put out about it too.

Mr. Cushing & I went oystering to day. *Close the letters in the steerage!* That is the order so good by, love to all. From your loving son

Henry

Rappahannock River
on board U.S.S. *Cambridge*
November 13th 1861

Dear Sister

Last night we ran out into the Bay & stopped the Baltimore boat & sent on board for our mail which we obtained[.] Amongst the rest I found three letters for me which you may be sure I was glad enough to get. One was from Mother dated Nov. 8, one a family letter (Nov. 2) in which Lu & you shone forth with Mother, & the other was from Joe. I have sent several letters lately so I have not much news to impart still such as I have you are hastily welcome to.

Lieutenant Gwyn left us yesterday to the regret I think of every soul on board. He came down into the steerage & bid us all good by before he left & he was very much affected & the tears stood in his eyes all the while. He went away in the *Rescue* to Hampton Roads. When they started the crew all man[n]ed the rigging & gave him three rousing cheers. After they laid down from aloft they seemed to have lost all spirit & looked as tho' they had lost their best friend. I am affraid we never shall get another Lieut. equal to him. I don't like to express my opinion of Lieut. Miller yet as I have not yet seen enough of him to warrent it.

The *Rescue* took with her between 30 & 40 Contrabands which we picked up. We have kept a few on board of the most intelligent, but *not* the one that we had here in the steerage. He was so *dirty* & *lazy* that we all got so disgusted with him, that when we found the rest were going one of us went to the Captain & asked him to send "George" along too, which he accordingly did.

I hope you won't be shocked but realy I dont think much of these *niggers*. They are but very little better than brutes, so Stupid, Lazy & ignorent! of course there are exceptions & we have got four or five on board here now that are realy quite intelegent men considering the way they were brought up. but as for the rest I am glad we have got rid of them. We have not had any new arrivals for some time on account I believe of their not being able to get boats, what there are being all guarded.

The last letter I wrote home closed rather abruptly on account of the mail leaving sooner than I expected. I was just telling about Mr. Cushings & my oyster party. We started at about 12:30 – (confound my pen it just dropped out of the holder & made that great ugly blot) – (leaving the *Rescue* along side of the *C[ambridge]* taking coal from her,) armed with sharps rifles, in one of our boats with a canoe in company. We towed the Canoe down to one of the Oyster Beds & left her there to rake oysters (There were three darkies in her & a boatswain's mate) while we took a cruise along the shore.

We saw a whole lot of Canoes hauled up on the beach all together & were sorely tempted to make an attack thereon (notwithstanding we were ordered not to go with in *Rifle* shot of the beach,) but were prevented by the shoalness of the water which would not let us go within 50 yards of the beach. So after a while we commenced shooting *at* ducks. We had not fired more than half a dozen shots when we saw the *Rescue* cast of[f] from the *Cambridge* & beare down on us full speed. When she got down near us we saw the men all at quarters & every thing ready for action for it seems they thought we had been fired on from the shore they having heard the reports from our rifles & seeing us so close in shore, & so came to have a hand in the game. They were all disapointed at loosing a brush Lieutenants Gwin and Miller being both on board of her, but as our oyster boat was doing splendidly they did not blow us up for alarming them as we expected they would.

Well I guess I wont write any more now so I will bid you good by. Tell Joe he will find a letter for him in the Brookline office for I have forgot his town number. I shall get the box all right I have no doubt & I am glad it is sent.

Give my love to all & write often to your loving brother

Henry

U.S.S. *Cambridge*
Nov 15th / 61
Chesapeake Bay

Dear Mother

The steamer *Valley City* arrived at the Rappahannock River this morning & releaved us. So we are now on our way to Fortress Monroe & shall be there probably at 5 P.M. We hope now to be sent North but we cannot be sure of it till we are on the way everything in the navy is so unsertain. The *Valley City* brought down another Act. Master for us, named Nelson I believe. We have got now almost as many officers as the Frigate *Minnesota*. I dont know what to make of it.

I suppose I shall find my box at the Fort all right. I will let you know as soon as I get it. I hope to find some letters there too. I do not know that I may be unreasonable in my saying that you do not write often, but when a mail bag comes on board of a ship it is quite an event & it is a great disapointment to see others getting letters & find none for me, still that does not happen very often.

I think Miss Ottiwell must be mistaken about her brothers clothes for he had no cloth suit. he ordered one but was not satisfide, or from some reason or other did not take them. so he only had one uniform coat & a sack [coat] both of which I believe were sent. I believe I told you in one of my letters that I had found that sack of mine.

I hope you will not be shocked at the opinion I expressed in my letter to Eliza a day or two ago, but you must remember that you have never seen *slaves*. I don't consider slavery right any more than I ever did. but if what I have seen is a fair sample of slaves it seems to me that nine tenths of them would starve to death in a very short time if left to their own resources for they are a dreadful lazy set. of course there are exceptions & we have got 6 or 8 on board, smart active men[.] one of them is a carpenter & *our* Carpenter, Mr. [Theodore D.] Wilson, says he understands his business, & he has got him in his gang. Three of the others were first rate oystermen & we used to go after oysters almost every day while we lay in the river & had as many as we could eat of as fine ones as ever you saw.

We are all on the *qui vive* [on alert] to know what has become of the Naval Expedition[.] we have heard that they were at Hampton Roads.[43] I hope not unless they have accomplished their object. But we shall know in a few hours.

I dont fancy our new Lieutenant much, not that I think there is any thing realy bad about him, but he is what we call an "Old Betty" & *so* different from Lieut. Gwin! however I guess I shall get along with him well enough[.] I wont write any more now but if I get a chance I will add a few lines later after we get to the Fort.

Good by. Give my love to all & write as often as you can to your loving son

Henry

U.S.S. *Cambridge*
Nov 17th 1861
Newport News

Dear Mother,

Here we are hard & fast I expect for some time at least, off Newport News, taking care of the *Congress* Frigate & the *Cumberland* so that the Rebels shan't hurt them.[44] It is expected (from information received) that they will make an attempt to destroy the vessels here in a day or two with fire ships so Com[modore] Goldsboro[ugh] thought it best to send a smart vessel like the *Cambridge* to look out for them & as I said before—here we are—about 2 miles farther up the James River then [than] the other vessels "Right in the fore front on't."[45] It is quite an aggravation to a good Union man to lay at anchor where we are now, for on one side we have the Federal camp & batteries in sight & on the other we can see that dirty red & white flag flying over the heads of Tratiors. Well I suppose we shall thrash them all in good time.

By the way was not that splendid, the taking of Slidell & Mason by the *San Jacinto*[.] Hurrah for the Navy![46] I wonder how *John Bull* will like it? Our cause seems to be looking up again. What with Port Royal[,] Kentucky & the *Bombardment of Habana* [Urbanna]—I think we are doing finely.

I have received my box & think the contents quite jolly. The shirts are splendid[.] the boots are a little tight but I think I can ware them. I am much obliged to you for remembering my weakness for Olives. Tell Lu that I shall have to devote a special letter of thanks to her for the contents of that envelope I put in[it] in my breast (pocket) at once to have it as near my heart as possable. I ate Claras wedding cake about ten minutes ago, (that is, part of it), & am much obliged to you for sending it to me. I have got the neck tie on now. (dont think I am going to spoil it right off but it is Sunday you know.) & also one of the shirts which came just in the nick of time for we are having quite a cold spell now. I gave out a lot of tracks [tracts] today. I am almost affraid there is too much soldier in them tho,' for the sailors for you know they are very particular. I think the monthly journals are first rate. You have no idea how pleasant it is to receive a package from home after being away for some time.

I received a nice long letter from Eliza day before yesterday which I answer soon. (if not to night) tho' our letters crossed which I always think sort of agravating.

Captain Parker is as pleasant as ever & I very seldom have a watch but what he walks the deck a while & has a talk. He told me to day about his visit to the Flag ship. He sais the first thing Com[modore] Goldsboro said to him was, "How many officers have you got? does the Navy Department allow you five Masters?" "No sir." "Well I'll see about it." & the next thing we knew Mr. [John M. Merrill] Merril and Mr. [Henry L. Sturges] Sturgess (the one that joined us at the Rappahannock [)] (I thought his name Nelson when I wrote before) were ordered away so now we have only the three Masters that we had when we left Boston. There are three of my messmates standing round the table on which I am writing talking as tho' their tongues were hung by the middle so as I have arrived at the end of my paper I will bid you all good by with lots of love.

from your loving son
Henry

U.S.S. *Cambridge* Nov. 17th 1861

Sir

Having received orders to make out a written statement of the treatment of the two prisoners on board prize Schooner *Revere*, placed in my charge on the 10th of September, I have the honor to make the following report.

On taking charge of the vessel I proceeded according to orders from the executive officer to place the two men in irons.[47] The object as stated being to prevent their rising & retaking the vessel.

For the first two or three days the men were confined in single irons in the day time, & double at night. After that as they were quiet & orderly I allowed them their liberty during the greater part of the day but confined them at night.

They were treated as well under my orders as the circumstances would admit.

I remain sir, very Respectfully

Your Obt. Servant
Henry W. Wells
Masters Mate

Commander Wm A. Parker
USS *Cambridge*

U.S. Steamer *Cambridge*
Off Newport News
Nov. 20th 1861

Dear Lu

I have been waiting for some time for you to finish that letter of which I received the first edition but as it does not seem to be forthcoming I have made up my mind that I had better write myself.

I am very much obliged to you for that picture that you sent in the box. I shall take great care of it[.] I assure you & only wish I had a better one (or the original?) but it would not do to try to cut Joe out you know.

By the way how does he behave? does he come over occasionally? If he dont I will give him a overhaul when I get home. We are still laying here at Newport News waiting quietly for the rebels to send down fire ships & burn us up—if they are smart enough—which I have no doubt they think they are. I only hope they will try to do it before we leave the station: for we have got every thing ready for them & it would be a pity to have had the work for nothing.

The Pilot has just come back from a oyster excursion & brought 10 bushels of oysters with him. & we have got two darkies here now *shucking* out our share for us.

Here is a nice growl here in the steerage so I will just knock off writing for the prasent.

Nov. 21st Well I have just been to quarters & now I will try & finish my letter. I left off rather abrubtly yesterday on account of a growl that two of my mess mates had. it did not amount to much yet they made a good deal of noise at the time which made it next to impossable to write. Some how since the changes that have been made in our mess we do not get along so smoothly as before. It is hard to say exactly where the fault lies.

Today is "Thanksgiving" & we are going to try to have a regular Thanksgiving dinner[.] I don't know how well we shall proceed tho' for it is pretty dificult to do much where there is no market. How I wish I could come home & surpprise you as I did two years ago, however perhaps I may be able to be at home Christmas & that will be better.

We have quite a little fleet here now. There is the Frigate *Congress* 50 guns, Corvette *Cumberland* 24 guns, Steamer *Cambridge* 6 guns, Steamer *Hetsel* [*Hetzel*] 2 guns, Steamer *I* 2 guns, Steamer *Lockwood* 1 gun.[48] There is a rumor that there is going to be an attack on Pig point soon & that the vessels here will run in & cover the landing & like wise shell the batteries. I hope it is true!

I have just been on deck to witness the sale or poor OHares effects. It is the custom at sea when a man dies to sell his clothes & whatever else he has at auction to the highest bidder & then send the money to his friends. Sailors always bid higher than the actual value of articles put up particularly when they know that the friends of the man are poor.

I cant say much tho' for the decorum with which such sales are carried on if they are all the same as the one I have just seen. The Master at Arms is the man that carries on the sale & there is more fun than a little made out of it.[49] However the men paid a great deal more than the things were worth for OHare was very poor & his mother & two or three young brothers & sisters depended on him entirely for support. We are making up a subscription for them.

I will not write any more now as I have nothing to say[.] Give my love to Mother Father & Eliza G[r]andpa & Ben—in fact to all that it will do to send *love* to. & remember me kindly to the rest.

from your loving brother
Henry

US Steamer *Cambridge*
Newport New[s]
Nov. 24th 1861

Dear Mother

I received a nice long letter from you night before last (dated Nov 19th) & will now try to answer it tho' the steerage is so noisy just at preasent that I don't know how well I shall succeed, one singing "The Bold Privateer"[50] & another spinning yarns to make the rest laugh. & the rest all differently employed in an equaly edifying manner for Sunday.

All the harmony of our mess has been destroyed during the last week & quarreling is the order of the day now. I am heartily sick of the way things have been going on. [William H.] Maies & I thus far have kept as it were neutral, while the war of words has been carried on by the Carpenter & Gunner on one side & the remaining members of the mess on the other. It has been brewing for some time but the open outbreak came on Thanksgiving Day.

Part of us wanted to have an extra good dinner but the Warrent Officers would not have any thing to do with it.[51] So we took a collection from those that wanted it & sent on shore & got some chickens, eggs etc. Of course all the preperations made the dinner come a good deal later than usual. So the desenters ordered the Steward to get another dinner at the usual time for them. Which he did so they had their dinner & we had ours. but I must say tho' it was a first rate dinner, it was spoilt for me, for I can not enjoy any thing of that sort when it causes a quarrel to get it & it did not seem much like Thanksgiving. Well ever since some of them are growling all the time. There I will not spoil the next page with that subject.

I received that newspaper (or papers section) that you sent & am much obliged to you. I wish you would send them oftener as I like to see a Boston paper occasionaly.

I wish you would offer my congratulations to Miss Annie Sullivan. I think who ever this Mr. Urann is, he is a fortunate man & hope he is worthy of her.

I wish Father would write me a *war letter*. I want his opinion on the capture of Slidell & Mason & how it will effect our relations with England. I would rather see a war with her than have them given up, confound them they have been trying to get a pretext for a war all along I believe. but if they try it I rather think they will get more than they bargained for. I for one had much rather fight against them than my own Countrymen if we must fight. Is there realy any chance of Mr.

Clarkes going into the army[?] Somehow it does not strike me very pleasently. I think he is altogether to[o] good a man to go into the army it seems as though he would be out of place there. I do not mean by that that there are not plenty of good men there, but do not think there are any like Mr. C. He is altogether to[o] good to be shot & we can't spare him.

Such ones as the Chaplain of the *Cumberland* aint good enough for it would be a shame to send him before his Maker. A man that when he is asked to perform the burial service for a fellow creature sends word that "it would be more convenient to wait till after dinner," as *he* did in the case of our poor shipmate O'Hare, keeping the funeral waiting half a day that he might not have a cold dinner. It was seriously thought of by some on board of here to have the funeral go on with out a Chaplain as he seemed to care so little about coming. He was buried on Newport News Point. I was not able to go as I was officer of the deck at the time, but those that did said that the service was as short as it well could be.

I have just come off watch & it is now after four but I will try & finish before dark. We are anchored to day two or three miles farther up the river than the rest of the men of war here, & close in to the northern bank. We are right abreast of the extream outer Pickets of the Federal forces here, & can see them quite plainly with out a glass. This afternoon Capt Parker left his Spyglass (which is a very fine one) on deck & I have been taking a survey with it, & moralising on the sad effects of war. Out of more than 50 houses I should think that were in range of my glass, not one was inhabited. They were all burnt or sacked some had their sides stove in as if by shot & of others nothing is left but blackened chimneys. & those that still stand had their windows all broken & doors stove in & were more or less dilapidated[.] The only life to be seen was the sentinels posted at intervals & occassonaly mounted officers going there rounds.

They had quite a jubille in camp last Thursday[.] The Massachusetts Boy[s] seemed to be enjoying them selves hugely, if music and bon fires are any sign. Well I can't write any more now so good by give my love to all from your loving son

Henry

I enclose $10.00 as part payment for the money that I borrowed from Father when I was at home[.] I would send the rest but cant get bills. I know Father that you don't care whether it is returned or not but I feel better to do it.

2

"I Hope They Are Going to Give Us a Chance to Do Something at Last"

Blockade Duty

U.S. Steamer *Cambridge*
Off Mouth of Chesapeake Bay
November 29th 1861

Dear Mother

I hope you will not think I have forgotten home because I have not written for some time, but I have been pretty busy for the last few days trying to get my Log written up as I was a long ways behind hand in it & it will have to be sent into the Capt. on the 1st of next month I suppose.[1]

I suppose you saw in the papers the account of that brilient engagement that the *Cambridge* had with the Rebel batteries on James river? We were all very much interested on *reading* it, as it was the first we *knew of it,* & are much obliged to the Editors of the various newspapers for giving us such a good name. It was absurd tho' wasnt it? for our vessel to engage the enemy with out any one on board knowing any thing about it. we all had a good hearty laugh about it I can tell you. The whole story grew out of two long boats going a little way up the river & firing a few shots at one of the batteries. we hardly heard of it at Newport News so you can judge how much of an affair it was.

Commodore Goldsboro has *Blacklisted us sure* enough I believe. Day before yesterday we were ordered to proceed to Fort Monroe & we made sure then that we were going North, but when we got there we were ordered down here to guard the Light-boat & overhaul all vessels bound in or out that pass the Capes of the Blockade & endorse their papers so that if they are overhauled again trying to go in to any southern port, they can be made prizes of instead of only being warned off. It is not a very agre[e]able station the only redeaming point being that we can get a mail once or twice a week. We are completely exposed here & a gale would make us very uncomfortable. Capt. Parker has allowed us to put a stove down here in the steerage (a thing that is not allowed in another steerage in the service I think) which makes us very cozy & warm down here, but Alas we are in a state of Civil War (in the mess) & therefore cannot enjoy anything much. it has been brewing for some time & at last the opposing parties elected a Caterer to suit them selves & so the Carpenter & Gunner have *seceded from the Union* & have appealed to foreign powers for assistance. (in other words to the engineers mess to take them in & the Captain to allow it.) The successful party I am sorry to say however is sadly demoralized. but as the neutral party (Maies & Wells) is inclined to side in with them we shall soon be able to ["]conquer a peace" (It is nearly a parallel case with *the great* struggle aint it? I never thought of it in that light before.

Well I hope we shall have a quiet time after a while for I am sick & tired of living the way I have over the last month.

We saw the Steamer *Constitution* at Fort Monroe. & she passed out close to us since we came here[.] She is a magnificent vessel.

I received two letters while there one from you (dated the 23rd) & one from Joe.

I am glad you think I improve in my letters. Now that I have got my Log written up I will try to make them longer, only I hope in doing so I shall not make them stale & dry.

I do not see how I can do any thing for Uncle Lyman for of course I have no influence & I should not like to ask Captain Parker to recommend a man that he never saw or I either, for of course he would want to know all about him & I should be in a very awk[w]ard position to have to say that all I knew of him was what I had heard. I am very sorry for him & if I thought I could help him any I am sure I would.

I like Lieut. Miller a great deal better now that I am getting used to him.

I am afraid there is no chance of getting home again this year now we have been shoved down here tho' I may be mistaken[.] I am sorry that I shall not be able to be at home on Christmas as I had hoped to be but there it is.

We expect to get a mail tomorrow & I hope to receive a letter or two from home. Oh you dont know what a satisfaction it is to hear from home when away amongst strangers.

Well I guess I will not write any more now so good night. Give my love to all the family & remember me to friends.

Write as often as you can to your loving son.

Henry

U.S. Steamer *Cambridge*
Off Capes of Virginia
December 5th 1861

Dear Mother,

I wrote you a very hurried note yesterday asking you to send me some clothes. I hardly know what to do whether to tell you not to send them or to let them come & miss my chance of getting them. I need them badly tho' & I guess you had better send them.

We are not going to stay here but a day or two longer, at least that is the report, but are going to Hampton Roads to coal & then wait orders which means I think & hope that we are to join the expedition that is fitting out there.

I hope they are going to give us a chance to do something at last.

I wish you would send me some medicine. I am not very well tho' I dont know exactly what the matter is, but I am spitting flem [phlegm] all the time & blood with it a good deal of the time[.][2] I have a dull headache too a great deal. & I feel a somewhat as tho' I should like to get into an action & get shot, that is, I am rather low spirited I suppose. If you can make anything out of those symptoms & will send me some thing for it I should be glad tho I dont think it is any thing very serious & might pass off of it self.

We ran in yesterday to the river Light ship & sent a boat to the fort which brought out the mail. & I received a letter from Eliza & Louisa which I will answer soon.

Our life out here is very monotonous & it is my own private opinion that we are not half doing our duty, for we do not board or even speak half of the vessels that pass in or out here. however that is none of my business. we have been laying at anchor all the time but yesterday we got orders to keep under way all day & only anchor in the night, so now we [are] puffing around generaly.

I am affraid I have not written lately as often as I used but you must excuse it for it is not that I think less of home by any means, but some how I have not felt any energy even to write home which is the greatest pleasure that I have.

The Carpenter & Gunner have left our mess & by the majority vote of the rest we are now drawing our rations. Maies & I were against it but all the rest were for it so we gave in for the sake of peace. We shall live cheaper I suppose but I for one have lived as long as I want to on Salt Beef & hard bread. "M" & I however are going to lay in a few little things on our own account or as Maies says "For our private tooth." I hope we shall be able to get along with out any more trouble tho' I must say I have my doubts however sufficient rule the day etc.

The papers seem determined to give us credit for what we do not do. I hear one of the Baltimore papers has published an account of an action between the *Cambridge* & *Yorktown* in which the '*Y*' was compelled to retire. I suppose when we do have the good luck to do something they will take no notice of it what ever & so square accounts.

I am very glad to hear that Uncle Lyman has at last got his commission. I hope I shall be able to get one before long tho' I dont see much light yet.

I dont know when I shall get home. I was in hopes to be there Christmas but must give up that idea. you know the fates are against my being at home on that day.

Well I must bid you good by as one of my messmates is waiting for the desk.

Give my love to all & write often to your loving son

Henry

Dec. 6. Please send those things at once. I wish Father would keep an account of what the clothes that are got for me cost for you know I am on high wages now & ought to pay my own bills. Our mess is in a state of smash again, but from a different cause. I will tell you about it next time. in haste

Henry

U.S. Steamer *Cambridge*
Hampton Roads
Dec 10th, 1861

Dear Mother

We have just come into the Roads & I have received your letter of the 7th.

We are only going to stop here 24 hours & then we are off for Cape Henry again, where I suppose we shall have to spend the best part of the winter. Well, it is one comfort, that we shall get our mails often, & perhaps it will not be so bad as that after all.

I heard the most agravating piece of news a day or two ago that ever was thought of. Only think when we were releaved from our station at Newport News our orders were actually on board, to proceed to New York for repairs, & were afterwards countermanded by the Flag Officer because the *Daylight* needed them worse than we & he had no other vessel to send.[3] The *D* has gone to Baltimore & when she comes back we are in hopes to have a chance.

I shall be very glad to get that box for I am in need of *thicker* clothes, tho' to day does not seem much like it for it is as warm as summer.

I am better than I was tho' not quite as I could wish yet, but you need not feel at all anxious.

I sent a box of oranges to you by Adams & C[ompany] Express. I got them from a Fruiter that we boarded yesterday for a mere song & could not resist the temptation of sending home some to you, I hope they will arrive safe. We have had a perfect feast of oranges & Bananas & for once I can say I have eaten as many oranges as I could.

I wish I could have sent you some of the Bananas but they were so ripe that they would have spoiled before you could have got them. Those little ones that are in the box they call Sweet Limes & are very nice. we could only get a few of them. Please excuse the looks of the box it was the only one I could find in the ship.

Mr. Cushing has been released from arrest[.] They only did it to frighten him for frightening us. *Tit-for-Tat* you know.

Mr. Maies has been rather unfortunate lately first he was sick, he had just got over that when yesterday he fell & hurt his knee so badly that he can not walk & has to lie in his cot. I am very sorry for him for he is a nice man.

I am glad Uncle Lyman has been ordered to so good a vessel as the *Brooklyn*[.][4] I wish I was on board one just like her. for in spite of every thing I can not but think we are going to have a war with England before we get through our difficulties, & then those are just the vessels that will have to do the fighting.

Well I can not write any more now for the mail will close directly give my love to all. Tell Lu I will write to her next time.

Write as often as convenient to your loving son

Henry

US Steamer *Cambridge*
Off Cape Henry
Dec. 13th 1861

Dear Mother,

We are just running up towards Hampton Roads to get our mail & I have just time to scratch you a few lines.

Yesterday I had a chance to get my *name up* as sailors say, which I improved I believe to the satisfaction of all concerned. & I will now tell you all about it. Yesterday morning at day light we saw a ship in Lynhaven Bay apparently amongst the breakers[.][5] We hove up our anchor at once & stood in to see if we could get her out & if not, to destroy her for the Rebels have a battery on the shores of the bay & we expected every minute they would open on us. (I suppose they could not bring their guns to bear on us tho' for they did not fire at all).

We ran in as near as we dared on account of the shoalness of the water & then lowered a boat. The First Lieut. would not trust the usual boarding officer to go in her but ordered Mr. Wells to take his place & go & see if we could render him any assistance.

When I got to him I found that he was within a half a ships length of the breakers, in fact you could almost jump from her stern onto the white water. He had anchored a good distance from the shore but during the night had parted one of his chains & drifted in. They did not seem to have the least idea what was to be done & had made no preparations what ever. They seemed to be on the Happy go Lucky principal. The Capt. was "dreadful anxious didn't know what he should do, hoped we [would] help him off etc. etc." The mates seemed to be the least intelligent of the whole crowd & take them all together they were the shabiest set I ever saw on board of a ship.

As soon as I found how the case stood I went back to the Steamer & ran a line down to the ship & then bent both the ships hawsers together & bent the small line on for them to haul it on board the 'C.' It took his & all the hawsers on board the *Cambridge* to reach from one vessel to the other.

I took entire charge of the ship during the time I was on board, & did not take yes or no from any of them. While we were waiting for the 'C' to get her anchor, I made them get their kedge up out of the hold & bend in [it] on to the chain that had parted so as to have something more than 1 anchor to let go in case the hawser parted for it was blowing quite fresh. but fortunately nothing of the sort happened much to the disapointment of the rebels I guess, quite a number of whom had collected on the beach. Nothing but the preasince [presence] of the Gunboat prevented them from boarding her. Tho' they would not have had much of a prize if they had for she was in ballast. The name of the ship was the *A.M. Lawrance*[.][6] I took dinner with the captain who was very greatful for the service done him.

We towed him about three miles of[f] shore & then left him. I took it as quite a compliment from the First Luff [Lieutenant] sending me on such service. But he seems to like me very well & places a good deal of confidence in me I think. I notice he always pays as much attention to any sugestion that I offer about things concerning the ship as he does to any of the Act. Masters. & what is more he very often follows them. In fact he seems to like me & as a natural consequence I like him better every day.

Well I have arrived at the end of my paper & pretty well filled up this side into the bargin so I guess I will not write any more. By the way you never acknowledged the receipt of the $10. Treasury note I sent home some time ago. did not you receive it? I hope I shall find the Box at the Roads. I am very anxious to get it. Good by now. My conscience smites me for not having answered Lu['s] letter before this but Mr. Mai[e]s is laid up & I dont have so much time now as usual. Give my love to all & *remember me to the rest.*

Write often to your loving son

Henry

US Steamer *Cambridge*
Off Cape Henry
Dec. 15th 1861

Dear Lu

I am ashamed of myself for not having answered your nice letter before but . . . . . . Thu[s] now I wont try to make excuses for I know it is all my lazyness.

I am in a flourishing state just at preasent & a great deal better than I was both in mind & body so I shant have much occasion for that medicine that Mother sent me & which I received yesterday. not exactly all right for one bottle (the Aconite) was smashed but that is no matter for I have that vial that Dr. Wild gave me for my sore throat just before we left Boston which will answer all purposes.[7] I have not much confidence in my box it is so long since the pellets were medicated.

Mr. [Charles C.] Pennington one of our Engineers is going to leave us. He used to live in Longwood but now lives in Roxbury. He is a real nice man & understands his business but he has been fairly never [let] out of the ship by that *miserable object* our Chief Engineer, Mr. Brennan a man who I most thoroughly dispise. Mr. B. was jellous of him because he knew more than he did & so took every oppurtunity to annoy him. So Mr. P has sent in his resignation.

Our Mess has politely speaking gone to the Devil. At the first on the month all except Mr. Maies & myself wanted to live on their rations so we had to give in[.] Now every body is disgusted (as we knew they would be [(]M. & I) for we have been thro' the mill you know.) but they cant get out of it till the end of the month at least. & it is nothing but gruel the whole time. Maies & I have got about sick of it & have all most made up our minds to board ourselves & let the rest take care of themselves as that seems about the only way to have any peace.

When you see Mary Lovett I wish you could ask her (not from me you know) if she ever received the letter I wrote her while I was at home & if she did, if she ever answered it. She told me if I would write to her she would answer my letters so I suppose either he[r] letter or mine must have misscarried & I want to know which.

Everything is going on quietly here now & it is difficult to find materials for a letter[.] nothing has occurred worth mentioning since we hauled that ship out of Lynhaven Bay. We are living in constant hope of being releaved tho' there does not seem to be an amediate prospect.

I suppose now it would not be at all strange if we should hear at any moment that England had declared war against the Northern States. Well if they do I have faith for one in the ability of the States to thrash them again as we have twice before.

What does Father think? I wish he would write me a little war sentiment for I have the greatest confidence in his judgement.

Realy I have nothing more to say & as I think a forced letter must be rather stupid I wont write any more to day. Give my love to all the family & remember me to all friends[.] Dont forget to ask M.L. Good by & write often to your loving brother

Henry

Dec. 16th How I wish you could give me one of your bear hugs this morning!

H.

Tell Joe I have received his letter & will answer at once.

US Steamer *Cambridge*
Off Cape Henry
Dec 17th 1861

Dear Father

This letter will introduce to you Mr. Pennington one of our Engineers who has been detached from this vessel.

As he is going north he has kindly offered to go out to Brookline as I thought you would like to see any body who has just come from here & can give you a better idea of our doings than fifty letters. & I think it will give you a great deal of satisfaction to see him. I know it would me if the case was reversed.

What do you think of the English news? it looks rather black I think, but if it comes to war I for one am ready & willin to fight as long as I can hold a sword & that too with a better heart than against my own countrymen, Rebels tho' they are. I have got a great deal of the old prejudice against the English which has been increased since this war commenced by the way they have carried on. & I would rather come to blows than see Mason, Slidel etc. given up, why! I should be ashamed to fight under the flag of a country that would do such a thing.[8] All I want now is to get transferred to some First Class Sloop of War or Frigate where I can see some service.

If the slaves rise which I suppose they will, (or rather have since Charleston is burnt), that the Southerners will have their hands full at home & will leave us comparatively free to make an attack on Canada. I think a war from such a cause would be a popular one & that there would be no lack of soldiers.

Please write me your opinion on war matters generaly. I know you do not write much but I am very anxious to hear from you.

I will not write any more now as I have got to go on watch directly.

Mr. P will tell you all about me.

Love to all from your
Loving son
Henry W. Wells

U.S. Steamer *Cambridge*
Hampton Roads
Dec 18th 1861

Dear Mother

We have just come up to the Roads to coal & I take the opp[o]rtunity to write you a few lines. Mr. Pennington our 2nd Assistant Engineer leaves us today he is going out to Brookline to see you. I asked him to because I know you will be glad to see him as my friend & having just left me. I send a short letter by him to you by way of introduction.

I have succeeded at last in getting a cot instead of my hammock to sleep in which is quite an improvement as I can lay straight now & sleep so sound that they find it hard to get me *up* in the morning which you know is a very unusual thing for me.

Our Boat has just gone on shore & I hope it will bring back my box which by your letter ought to have been here some time ago. Have you received the Oranges yet?

I got my mileage a day or two ago $88.30 which was pretty well I think when my ticket cost me less than $10. good for Uncle Sam!

I think it will be splendid to have a Billiard table at the house it is good exercise & pleasent amusement at the same time. I dont see how you can keep the large Attic room warm in winter tho.' but where there is a will there is a way I suppose. I think it is well not to send the coat at preasent as I can get along out here with what I have & I would rather have it all nice & new when I get home or North. Tell Grandpa that I am ever so much obliged to him, he could not have sent my any thing more acceptable for I was counting myself $25 out, what I got north for that very purpose.

I enclose you a postage stamp (1c) it may be common enough for ought I know but I have not ever seen one like it, so I thought I would send it.

Our mess is pretty well cleared out now there is only 4 of us left & the Pilot has gone into the Engineers mess he could not stand the rations & I should not think he would when the government pays $30. a month for him. At the end of the month I think we shall split again for Mr. Maies & I will not live one hour longer than is necessary in the way we have been doing. That confounded fool of a midshipman has done it all[.] it was the way he carried on more than any thing else that made the Carpenter & Gunner leave our mess, both of them *men* & that is a great sight more than he is for he is neither sailor Gentleman or any[thing] else but a conceited puppy. You may laugh for it is rather a different opinion from what I expressed in the first place about him, but I have had a better chance to know him now.

My box has just come & I have been opening it. O Mother that Photograph Book is *splindid*. Is not that one of Cousin Isa capital! They are all first rate tho.' Tell Lu I am ever so much obliged for the contribution but think under the preasent aspect of affairs I shall have to take out the two at the end of the book.

The stockings & mitts are fine & I shall value them the more knowing the pleasure that Eliza takes in that sort of work. The Boots fit nicely[.] Father had them made for himself did he not?

Please give my respects to Mrs Tollman & tell her that I am ever so much obliged for those checkerboards & shall have no trouble in disposing of the extra ones. & I think they will give a great deal of satisfaction. I have not time to write any more now. I am ever so much obliged to you all & hope to see you before

Boston is blockaded. I received your letter of the 16th. I am pretty well now. Good by from your loving son

Henry

US Steamer *Cambridge*
Hampton Roads
Dec 22nd [1861]

Dear Mother

We are just st[e]aming up towards the Roads to send our mail on shore & I have just time to scratch of[f] a few lines to you

I feel ashamed of my self for not having a letter ready & have very little excuse to offer except that I ment to do it yesterday but was prevented by being employed all the morning giving assistance to one of Burnsides Expedition, the Sch[oone]r *Skirmisher.*[9]

Oh! Dear I have just had to go to quarters & so lost my time to write.

I am very sorry but will try to give you a longer one next time. I am better now than I have been for some time which I know you will be glad to hear

I enclose a $10. dollar Treasury Note toward paying Father for the money he lent me for traveling. There the boat is called away! Good by love to all from your affectionate son

Henry

U.S. Steamer *Cambridge*
Off Cape Henry
Dec 24th 1861

Dear Mother

I was very much disapointed in not hearing from home last Sunday but I suppose I deserved it for not having a better letter to send home it is the first mail we have had for some time that I *have not* heard from home & I am determined that I will not deserve such luck again[.] We go up to the Fort about the first of the week and then along about the middle.

Tomorrow is Christmas, how I wish I could be at home with you all, but it seems to be my fortune never to be home on that day. Last year I was on board the *Ocean Telegraph.* Where shall I be next? Every thing is going on quietly as usual here. We are making preparations for a grand dinner in our mess tomorrow & are going to invite two or three of the ex members.

The last occurance of interest here was our sending assistance to the sch. *Skermisher* [*Skirmisher*] of Burnsides Expedition. She came in during the night & anchored about a mile from us. In the morning at daylight we made her out with her colors in the rigging Union down. Of course we hove up our anchor at once & stood down for her & the First Lieutenant ordered me to board him & see what assistance could be rendered. I found he had lost one of his anchors & as it was blowing very fresh he was affraid he might part his other chain & go on shore. So he wanted us to tow him down to the Roads. I therefore went back to the *Cambridge* & ran aline to the sch. & as usual put on "*Uncle Sam*" & took charge while the steamer was towing her. They had a miserable crew all boys[.] The officers had to steer themselves & they were 7 day[s] from New York here. Our Midshipman was mad enough at my having the job he says they only let him go when it is all smooth & well but when there is any thing out of the way they send some one else which is about so & right enough too, as every body acknowledges, except himself. He has sent to the Department asking to be detached from this vessel & it will be a day of Thanksgiving to every officer on boa[r]d when he is ordered from the vessel for he makes himself generaly disagreeable to all. it is all self with him. Well I wont dwell on the subject any longer as it is not a plesent one.

You remember my man Dan Derocher who was so useful to me in my prize? Well I have been trying to get him a position as Petty Officer ever since I got back & I have only failed in it from the fact that there are no vacancies, for the First Luff has promised to give him a chance as soon as possible & there is not a man in the ship that is thought more of by the officers.

Dec. 25. I wish you all a Merry Christmas.

We have just had a smash up with the U.S. Steamer *Valley City* our luck you know & just *my* luck to be in charge of the deck at the time, but I dont see how I can be blamed for we were at anchor & she ran into us[.][10] The First Lieutenant says that he does not see how we can be held answerable tho' there will be a Court Martial I suppose. It is very unfortunate that I should happen to be on deck at both of the collisions for it has a bad effect even tho' I am not to blame & will hurt my chance of promotion I am affraid. Ah! well after the war is over I dont care much whether I stay in the Navy or not.

Our Damage is not very serious as effecting the safety of the vessel but will cause our carpenter thinks our being sent to a dock yard at once as our stem is all knocked one side in a manner that will injure the steering of the vessel & can not be fixed while we are in the water. We do not know what damage the *Valley City* suffered for as soon as the collision occurred she turned back for the Roads with out stopping to see whether we were sinking or not. The accident occured at 8 P.M & we expect that a steamer will be sent down from the Roads before morning to see how we are getting on. I can not write more to night as it is most 10 o'clock & lights go out at that time. If I have time I will add more tomorrow. Good night love to all from

Henry

Dec 26 We are on our way to H. Roads I have got [to] go up & take charge of the deck & so can not write any more now good by

Henry

I enclose $10.

U.S. Steamer *Cambridge*
Off Cape Henry
Dec. 27th 1861

Dear Father

I received your letter yesterday & was very glad to hear from you. I dont know but it was rather selfish in me tho' to ask so many times that you would write for I know that it troubles you a great deal. Now I have got this letter I shall apreciete it all the more however & will try to make it last some time.

I am very glad to have your opinion on the English question tho' I must say if Concessions mean the release of Messrs Slidel & Mason I would rather see a war, bad as it would be for our country. I think even in our present situation we could give as good as we take. And whether Messrs S & M are released or not I am very willing to have a brush with John Bull after we get through with the Rebels.

Christmas Day passed away pretty quietly tho' some few got drunk. Mr. Odiorne got himself into trouble & lost charge of the Gun Deck & now has to stand his watch with one of the Masters. One of the other officers has taken his place. I came very near getting myself into a scrape in a very foolish manner & I expect I should if it had not been that the First Lieut. likes me & was willing to put the best construction on it. You see I had the middle watch & at 4 o'clock Mr. Maies relieved me. We were talking in the wheel house & the Quartermaster joined in & after a little he remarked that it was a cold morning & something to drink would not go bad & I said well come down below & I will give you something. (I had a bottle of whiskey in my locker which I had had sometime) So he came down & I gave him a drink. I thought no more of it & turned in but in the morning at breakfast the Pilot came down into the steerage & said that Thompson was drunk & that they had accused him of giving him the licker & had put him off duty. Of course I could not allow that so I went right on deck & told Mr. Miller, the First Luff that it was I that did it & would take the consequences for I did not wish the Pilot to take the blame for what I did.

I expected he would suspend me at once & report to the Captain but he only said he was sorry that, it was a bad practice giving men licker & hoped I would not do it any more. Some one stole the bottle out of my locker after I gave the man his drink & the Pilot was tight so I drew my own conclusions as to he took it. But I am glad it is gone & have made up my mind not to drink & bring on board another drop of spirits while I am in the ship. The Quartermaster however had more licker than what I gave him & I have found out since that the Pilot gave it to him.

As it has turned out I do not think the affair has hurt me any.

The Steamer *Valley City* was not much injured by her collision with us. she only lost one of her boats[,] had her main rigging carried away etc. She went to sea again last night bound to Hatteras. There is a report that we shall be relieved tomorrow or next day by the *Daylight* & go to Baltimore for repairs. I dont believe it, but still it may be so. We are going up to the Roads tomorrow at any rate for we have only 4 or 6 tons of coal on board. What do you think of the news from Ireland?

Good by give my love to all. & write me again when you feel like it. In my two last letters I enclosed $20. I am very well now.

From your loving son
Henry

Please tell Eliza & Lu that I have got envelopes already directed to both of them but dont intend to send them till I know what has become of them as they have not written for some time & they both owe me letters.

Nothing *short* of six pages will turn aside my wrath from them, possably 4 might do from Lu as it troubles her more to write than E.

US Steamer *Cambridge*
Off Cape Henry
Dec. 31st 1861

Dear Mother

I received you[r] letter Saturday & as we shall probably go up & send a boat in to the Fort tomorrow I will now answer it, tho' I hardly know how I shall make up a letter for there has not been any thing going on here worth mentioning except that a schooner went on shore here a day or two ago. We could not send her any assistance for the wind was blowing right on shore & the surf was too high for our boats. There was quite a large force of Cavalry on the beach & I suppose they had possesion of the vessel. She had coal in but I dont think they will be able to get any of it.

Eve. I must finish tonight as we are going to send our boat up in the morning & I shall have the watch so I shant have time then. I should have written more this morning but we have only one desk & the Gunner wanted to use it to make out his quarterly report.

The Sloop of War *Brooklyn* passed in Sunday. I suppose Uncle Lyman was in her. I hoped I should be able to go on board when we went up but she went out this morning so I have lost the chance of seeing him which I am very sorry for but I suppose I shall have a chance by and by.

A boat with four contrabands came off from the shore to us a day or two ago which was rather a surpprise as we thought when we left the Rappahannock we had left the darkies too. We did not get much information from them.

I am sorry to write you so short a letter but realy I have not much to write about. We are having a very mild winter here & have had no very severe gales yet. We are expecting every day to hear that Burnside has started on his expedition.

I wish you all a happy New Year. Good by Love to all & write often to your loving son

Henry

Jan 1st 1862. We have just got the news from the Pilot Boat of the giving up of Messrs Slidel & Mason. I would rather have seen a war & shall now live in hope of seeing one. Darn the English!!! I hope I shall have the satisfaction of fighting against them before long. Good by, I will not wish you a happy new year for we are not going to have one. War & happiness dont agree.

Love to all from your loving son
Henry

US Steamer *Cambridge*
Off Cape Henry
Jan 4th 61 [1862]

Dear Mother

We went up to Hampton Roads on New Years day & I was very much disapointed in not receiving any letters from home. It seems to me that my sisters are forgetting their brother[.] I hear from them so seldom but I find no fault with your letters for I know you write as often as you can. I dont think however that Eliza or Lu realise what a pleasure it is to receive letters when a person is away from home & friends. if they did I am sure that they would find time to write oftener.

Every thing is going on quietly here & there has nothing occured worth noticing since I last wrote. We are expecting the Frigate *Niagara* & the Steamer *Constitution* in here ever[y] hour now. Some anxiety is felt about the latter as she sailed from Boston several days ago.

We had the Pilots on board of here for two days on the lookout for them as both the Pilot-boats got disabled at the same time, but yesterday another one came down from Baltimore & took them off.

Thursday I signed the Pursers accounts for the end of the year & I find that am $100. ahead on his books. I think that is pretty well considering for I have $25. on hand besides.

I am quite well now & have not used any of that medicine so it will do for next time.

It is [al]most time that the *Daylight* came down from Baltimore & I am rather inclined to think she will releave us tho' I would rather stay here than be ordered there which I am affraid we shall be as they are so busy at the Northern yards.

Jan. 6th. We are on our way to the Roads for coal, & I take this oppurtunity to finish this letter.

Yesterday an English Frigate the *Immortilite* passed in bound to Annapolis[.][11] They sent a boat on board of us for news. The *I* is a large steamship but I dont think she would be a match for one of our vessels of the same class. One of her Lieuts. came on board & he was accompanied by the littlest Midshipman ever I laid eyes on. I could hardly keep from laughing when he came on deck he looked so important. I have heard a great deal about English men of war but I dont think that one much of a credit to them for she was awful dirty & the boats crew looked dreadful slovenly for a Sunday morning.

The U.S. Sloop of War *Jamestown* passed in in the afternoon & looked finely tho' she was farther off than the other.[12]

We have had quite a cold spell of weather for the last two or three days[.] The thermometer is 29° this morning & the decks are glazed over.

We are nearly up now & I must close for I shall be wanted soon to take charge of the deck. We have turned our Steward of our mess before the mast for stealing etc.

Good by now give my love to all & write often to your loving son

Henry

U.S. Steamer *Cambridge*
Off Cape Henry
Jan 9th 1862

Dear Mother

Since I wrote last I have been quite sick but I am nearly well now & I shall turn to again to morrow I guess for there is a rumor afloat that some of our officers are to be detached to join Burnsides Expedition & I want to be counted in on that you know if possable. We are going to send a boat to the Roads tomorrow & then we shall know something more about it I suppose.

I can hardly tell you what is the matter with me, but I had a dreadful bad sick headach & was very feverish. I have only been laid up three days but it has pulled me down a good deal & I am quite weak now[.] You may be sure I wished my self home more than once while I laid in my cot tho' my messmates were very kind & did all they could for me. but that is not like home care after all. I sometimes almost wish I could have a real good *sick* at home for the contrast sake[.] I dont know but it would be more satisfaction than being well away.

The last time we were up to the Roads I received your letter of the 1st & Lu's of the same date tho' finished apparently rather later. Please tell her that I will answer it as soon as I feel a little stronger.

The Carpenter is making a desk for Mr. Maies & I, so I shall be able to write a little more at my leisure than I have been able before.

I am glad you liked Mr. Pennington we all found him a very pleasent shipmate on board here.

I can not tell you much news not having been on deck for some time and as I am not quite over my headach yet I know you will [excuse] my sending so short a letter.

so I will bid you good night give my love to all & write often to your loving son

Henry

I enclose another $10. which will make $40. the sum I borrowed from Father. & I wish you would let me know the amount that those clothes cost that I sent for so I can send that too. H.

U.S. Steamer *Cambridge*
Off Cape Henry
Jan 14th 1862

Dear Lu

I received your nice long letter several days ago & now set down to answer it.

It is blowing a heavy gale now & the ship is rolling badly so you must excuse me if I do not write extraordanaly well. We had a sweet night last night, snowing & sleeting the whole time which is bad enough on board here for those who have to be on deck as we have no protection in the way of bulwarks whatever. I had the morning watch & found it pretty severe I can tell you.

Burnsides Expedition has sailed & I hope they arrived at Hatteras before the storm commenced for if they did not I am affraid that a great many lives will be lost for they had the crazyest set of steamers that ever I saw got together. The schooners were by far the best part of the fleet. I think it is disgraceful that the Government would not find better vessels to transport her troops. We are all hoping soon to hear of an onward movement on the Potomac. I think it is full time now.

Yesterday a large Steam Sloop of War came down the bay & went into the Roads & we can not think what vessel it can be unless it may be the *Pensacola* which has been blockaded at Washington for so long by the Rebels. I hope it is her for she will be quite in addition to our fleet, besides the disappointment to the Rebels in not being able to prevent he[r] escape.

There has been a new Engineer ordered to this vessel in place of Mr. Pennington he is a young man named Haden & is junior to the others, he seems to be a very pleasant sort of a fellow but I hardly think we shall find him equal to Mister P.

When I ask you questions why dont you answer them? I want you should answer that which I *asked you* in my *last letter with out delay*. So Dont fail.

I received a long letter from Eliza last time we were up at the Fort which I will answer with *speed*. You must not think at home because you do not get letters so often now as you did a while ago that I am remise in writing, but we dont go up so often now as we did so I can not send them. I never miss an opportunity of letting you all hear from me tho' sometimes my letters from various causes are rather short.

I am getting quite over my little sickness now & feel quite smart again.

Dont you realy think you could find time to write to me a *little* oftener? It dont seem to me as tho' I ever saw your time so occupied that you could not find time to do what you wanted to.

Dont feel above leaving (him! Teaching) the little Irish children to sew etc. it is a good work & I think the Irish deserve it well now, they are doing splendidly this war.

If I knew Tom Pecks address I think I would write to him it is a pity to loose all ones all old associations & I should be glad to open a correspondence with him. Why dont Joe write? I have not had a letter from him for an age.

Well I seem to have arrived at the end of my paper so I will close here. Give my love to all the family & remember me to all friends.

Good by

from your loving brother
Henry

US Steamer *Cambridge*
Off Cape Henry
Jan 18th 1862

Dear Bra Ben

I received your letter last time I was at Fort Monroe & I will now answer it.

I am quite well & was not confined to my cot but a very short time.

I am glad to hear you are getting along so well at school & have been promoted to higher classes. I hope you will continue to improve & be a very good boy at home besides & not give dear Mother any trouble.

The sailors are doing very well only three or four being on the sick-list & I don't doubt they would be very much obliged to you for your kind inquiry if they knew any thing about it.

I am sorry Father would not put any Patriotics in your letter for you, but then you know you had the satisfaction of writing it all your self which of course is the pleasantest way of writing letters.

I am very glad you approved of those oranges I sent home. I thought you would like them.

I dont think there is much danger of my ships being wrecked at present so you need not let it worry you. I think I may come home in about a month tho I am not sure.

I am affraid the Rebels would feel very bad if they knew you wished to have them killed but I will try nevertheless to do as you want me to if I get a chance.

I shall be very glad to receive your picture paper when you get ready to send it. We do not have many on board ship.

I am very glad to hear you make your self useful about home shoveling paths & chopping kindling wood but you must be careful not to cut yourself with the hatchet.

I wish you would give my love to all the family also to the girls.

I shall be very glad to hear from you again when you find time to write.

I can not write any more now as it is almost time for me to go on deck so I will bid you good by with much love from your brother

Henry W. Wells

U.S. Steamer *Cambridge*
Off Cape Henry
Jan 19th 1862

Dear Mother

We are going to the Roads today or rather we are going to send a boat in & I have just time to write you a few lines.

I am quite well now, better than I have been for some time so you need not feel any anxiety about me.

I received your short note & Lu's letter also the one from Bennie which I have answered as I think it well deserved it. & I will write to Lu next time.

I dont think there is any danger of our ships being unable to weather any gales that we may have so dont let that worry you, besides it is a chance if we leave here much before spring any way, they are so busy at all the Yards now. & I dont much think they will send her to Baltimore.

After Com. Porters expedition sails we may have a little chance but not before I am inclined to suppose.

I am sorry Eliza is so poorly I hope she is better now. What is the matter? is it the same old complaint?

I hope I shall find a letter at the Roads but somehow I dont feel as tho' I should get one it is so short a time since we were there.

Every thing is going on as usual. Mid. Cushing we have turned out of our mess & now Mr Maies & I are alone. we shall have a quiet time at all events & that is worth the five dollars a month more that it costs us. I enclose $10. towards paying for those clothes that you sent & I shall keep sending till you tell me what they cost. Good by, give my love to all & write as often as you have time to your loving son Henry.

[Is] There any discount on Treasury notes in Boston? They charge us four percent at Fort Monroe & I think it is a swindle. I have written a letter to Joe & directed to the Care of Mr. Lincoln 13 India St.[13] I wish you would ask him if he has received it.

U.S.S. *Cambridge*
Off Cape Henry
Jan 22nd 1862

Dear Mother

As we shall go up to the Roads tomorrow if the weather will permit I have just set down to write you a few lines.

There has not much of interest occured since I wrote last except that we have had another collision (not in my watch tho,' thank God!) with an English Brig. Very little dammage was done on either side, but it was a very narrow escape & what is worse, this time, the fault was all on our side as the Brig had hove to some time before we came up with him. The Pilot will have to take the blame I suppose tho' they may hush it up so little dammage done.

We seem to be very unlucky in respect to accidents & I am very sorry for it on Captain Parkers account. Our vessel does not answer her helm quick enough for one that has to be round amongst others so much as we do here & we have had several very narrow escapes.

I am affraid I have lost quite a lot of my clothes which I sent to Baltimore to be washed[.] it is about three weeks now since they went & we have not heard any thing from them[.] there are several other officers in the same scrape[.] We have often sent them before & have always received them with in a week. it will be a pretty severe loss to me as nearly all my draw[er]s & undershirts were in the lot besides two of those flannel shirts that you sent me & several others. I dont know whether to ask you to send me more or not, but I dont know but you might as well send me a couple of suits of under clothes[.] I like *flannel* draws not tight ones the under vests I like to set snug please sew loops on the first so that I can keep them up. There were several things that I was going to ask you to send me but now I have got sat down I can't think of them. One thing I want very much which is some sort of Portfolio or cheap writing desk to keep my writing paper in[.] if you send a desk I dont want a very large one.

I dont like to send for too much because we *might* (tho' I dont think there is much chance) be sent north before it arrived[.]

I want a half a dozzen more collars. & ask Father if he wont get me a hundred or so Manville cheroots (is that spell right)[.] Now that I have these headachs I find a pipe most too strong. I must smoke something & they are very mild. I want to pay for these things so do oblige me by sending the bill of these as well as the other things. If you should put a big cake or any other home goodies in I wont offer to pay for that but will dispose of them at short notice[.]

I wish you would remind Eliza that there are two or three Photographs that she promised to get me which I should be very glad to receive especialy one. Why did not you put yours in that book[?] I don't think it complet with out it.

I did not get any letters the last time I was at the Roads but I was not very much disapointed as I hardly expected any. We generaly go up Wednesdays and Sundays so perhaps you can time your letters so I get them every time.

We have great old times here in the steerage now, skylarking the whole time pretty much. We get some awful cracks now & then but alls fair in war you know and I never saw a better set together for not getting mad at those sort of things. A while ago Mr Fergusson & I were carrying on & he got a musket & commenced charging on me so I grabbed a broom & we went at it till at last I hit him an ugly punch right over the eye (an accident of course) which cut a deep gash. The mark is there yet he took it as it was meant tho.' Today my face is all one sided from another reencounter that we have just had. Not very pleasant that but we should all die here if we did not have some excitement. Two of them are at it now. The other night we had a grand set to, every man against every other & the result was in about 10 seconds we were all in a grand pile in one corner of the steerage. I never laughed more in my life. The First Luff sent down to know what the trouble was he thought we were fighting I suppose. & no wonder for we must have made noise enough to have roused the whole ship. One has to look sharp for himself in the morning he is bound to be capsized out of his cot.

Well I cant write any more now as I must get ready to go on watch. If you send the box, do so with out delay. Good by give my love to all & write often to your loving son

Henry

I think it would be as well for you to get a receipt for the box from the express company as then we might recover it in case I should miss it.

Pls [please] put in two towels & some toilet soap also something to read useful & interesting both.

I think you will find my gold pen in my sanctum in one of the drawers of the [left blank] I dont know how to spell it but you know what I mean. I would like to have it very much as my short pens are about gone.

I wish you would send me Bennie's measure for a shirt (it wants to be pretty full) and a pair of pants & I will get one of the sailors to make him a regular man of war suit. send me the size of his head too for a cap. I can get every thing that is necessary here. Mr. Maies has quite fallen in love with his picture & says he will make it himself. don't disapoint me now. for the pants all I want to know is the length & size round the wast send me six skeins of embroidering silk red, white, & blue; two of each.

U.S.S. *Cambridge*
Off Cape Henry
Jan. 23rd 1862

Dear Lu

I received your short note about a week ago & I will now answer it tho I have not much time before going on deck. We were going to send the boat to the Fort to day but it is so rough that we shall not be able to. We shall go up now for our mail tho' as soon as the weather will permit. we generally go about twice a week.

I think I ought to receive at least three this time as I got none last. I am glad you explained to me why Mary did not write for I must confess I felt rather hurt about it.

I have got quite a bad cold now but that you know is nothing strange for me. We have been having damp nasty weather for some time & that is what has brought it on I suppose.

We had another collision a while a go with a brig (English) he carried away his flying jibboom (you ought to know what that is for I remember showing you on that picture of the *Flying Cloud* in my room).[14] The only damage we received was, one of our boat davits was bent up but the Engineers have straightened it so now no one would know where we were struck. it was a wonder that the boat was not smashed to pieces but it fell down out of the way by one of the Davits capsizing & was only scratched.

I hardly know what to write you about. There is nothing doing here of interest[.] We have had stormy weather for some days past and have been laying at anchor most of the time. Whenever it rains the hatches are on & then it is as dark as pitch here an oil lamp only serving to make darkness visible[.] We are allowed 5 candles a week so we have to keep them for evenings & in the day time in such weather our principal employment is skylarking or sitting round the stove keeping it warm & spinning yarns[.] we have got several adapts at that here for tho' our mess only consists of two yet the warrant officers & Engineers are here most of the time the stove acting as a kind of magnet to draw them together. On the whole we have first rate times, but I don't get a chance to study much.

Mid. Cushing has to stand watch now with Mr. [Samuel] Very. they wont trust him to take charge by him self which rather cuts him as he has always pretended to be senior to Maies & I. The First Lieut gave me a compliment & a reprimand at the same time. You see I left the deck in charge of Mr. C a few moments to run below. & when I came up the First Lieut. told me that I had done wrong for said he The Captain has selected five officers who he can *put confidence in* to do that duty & none other could be allowed to take that responsibility.

I have just come off watch & a busy one I have had. A while after I went on deck I saw a schooner well in shore making a signal of distress. it was blowing very heavy but we got under way & ran down to him. It was the Sch *Ocean Ranger* from Portland for *Philadelphia*, 21 days out. he had lost the head of his fore mast & both of his anchors & had also sprung his bowsprit. So we took him in tow & are now on our way for the Roads[.] So you will get this letter sooner than I expected after all.

Before I finish I must tell you of the last joke of the season. One of our quartermasters (as big a fool as ever put his foot on board of a ship) insulted one of his messmates & got reported to the First Lieut. Mr. Miller heard the case & told old Morse that he must make an apology before all his mess. So he went down at dinner time & said "Gentlemen" "If I've done any thing that I am sorry for I want to know it[.] I did not mean Lewis particularly when I said that I meant the whole of you." With that they all made a break at him & made him get down on his knees & take it all back. They frightened him dreadfully & then let him go. Wont that a great apology.

Good by Love to all from
Henry

US Steamer *Cambridge*
Off Cape Henry
Jan. 29th 1862

Dear Mother

As we shall probably go up to the Roads tomorrow, weather permitting I will take Time by the forelock[15] & write you a line today. I received your letter of the 22nd on Saturday as you will have heard by the letter I sent Eliza on monday. We [steamed] up to the Roads on that day but as I did not expect to get any letters so soon after having received such a begget, I was not disapointed at finding none.[16]

In my letter on Saturday I sent for some things which I need very much & I hope they are on the way by this time. I am sorry that I have to send so often but it cant be helped. We have often sent clothes to Baltimore before & never lost any. The last happened to be the biggest one that I have sent & that seems to be gone. There are several of us in the same box, the Capt. included. We have sent to Baltimore about it but I dont expect ever to see them again.

The Gunboat *Daylight* is at the Roads, but I dont think she is going to releave us for she has been there three or four days. besides next time we go up we are to take in 3 months stores for the Carpenters & Gunners departments which I dont think would be given us if there was any intention of our being sent North at present. So I hardly expect we shall be ordered any where before spring. I suppose you will be rather disapointed but the longer we stay the more chance I shall have of getting a Masters commission when I do get home.

I received a long letter from Mary on Saturday. how pleasantly she writes! I should be very glad to get letters from her oftener.

Poor Richard, he has had a hard trial but I think how that he has made a discision he will gradualy think less about it. If Lu had been a little older I should have called it a most cruel thing for her to do, but I doubt if she realisis now what he has felt. I think one of these days she will regret the loss she has made more than a little [Marginalia "*Never* L.W. 1902"]

I received Bennies picture paper give my love to him & tell him I am much obliged to him for his attention & hope he will rite to me again when he has leasure. I hope he is not going to have the Whooping Cough. I thought he had had it once.

There has not been much of interest going on here since the Light-boat went ashore of which I told you in Eliza's letter. We have had the satisfaction of watching the Rebels since, stripping the copper off of her, etc. with out attempting to drive them off. We are all mad enough about it I can tell you[.] it seems such a shame when we might have gone in & knocked her to pieces or burnt he[r] as well as not. It might have been rather dangerous to have sent boats in (tho' I would have liked to have tried it.) but there was no reason why we should not have thrown in a few shells to have shown a proper resentment at least. But Capt. Parker thought it wont worth the trouble so we have done nothing.

I have sent home now $50.00 I believe. you have received that much have you not? & I will send the rest soon. I dont like to put too much in one letter for fear it might get lost. Let me know what the other things cost when you send them.

I have not received any Boston papers for nearly two weeks. I like to get them very much for the local news. & we very seldom can buy them at the Fort.

Do tell Joe that I think he is getting very unreasonable. I have not received a letter from him for some time & have written him two since the last. Either he or I dont direct the letters right & I dont think it is me, so please tell him my direction & get his. As for Old Point Comfort being better than Fort Monroe for a direction I cant say about only I believe that I have received all letters that were directed to the fort & so judge that to be very good. As I have passed the end of my paper I think I will stop now, perhaps I shall find time to add a few lines before the letter goes.

Good by give my love to all & write often to your loving son

Henry

I enclose $10.00 on a/c [account]

U.S.S. *Cambridge*
Hampton Roads
Jan 31st 1862

Dear Lu

We came up here this morning for our stores & will lay here all night so I take this opportunity just before going to bed to write you a few lines. I received your letter to day & was very glad to hear from you. So you are going to go in town to school? I hope it wont make you proud. I think it will be a capital thing for you tho! & I hope you will improve your advantages.

I am quite well now with the exception of the last end of a bad cold which I have been having so you need not worry your head & retard your studies *old* lady about my bad health & *want of exercise*[.] I think that last applies a little to your case, dont it?

I sent a letter to Mother to day with a $10.00 Treasury Note enclosed which I hope will arrive all right. I was in hopes to get an answer to my letter about having some more things sent me, to day but I suppose it is most to[o] soon and so may come tomorrow tho.'

I am very sorry to hear that Bennie has got the Whooping Cough, however I will try & not feel anxious as you say he only has it lightly. it is a great pity that he should have to loose his school for so long tho' aint it?

I am glad you like my new coat so well, I hope it will fit. it was very kind in Grandfather was it not, if it had not been for his help since I joined the service I am affraid I should have been in debt now instead of being well ahead on the Paymasters Books.

Your connundrums were so-so, it took me some time to see the point of the Ramrod "specialy the *licker*[.]"[17]

The reign of peace is over in our mess now & war is to commence to morrow, again. Mr. Maies & I still hang to gether tho,' & will continue to do so as long as we are in the ship I rather guess, he & I get along first rate. When any battle comes off I will send you a list of the killed wounded & missing also a full account by your *Special Correspondent*[.] I expect we shall have some gay times now.

Burnside seems to be doing rather poorly & I am sorry for it, but I hope soon to hear better accounts.[18]

Three or four of Com. Porters fleet were here at the Roads this morning but they all got underway & went to sea, but I dont know where they have gone unless it is to join Burnside. They were schooners mounting two guns, & a very heavy mortar (13 in).[19]

I do wish our armies would make an advance if we are not able to do it now I dont think we ever shall be. & I am affraid that the European nations are beginning to think so to.

Well, Lu darling I have got the middle watch so I must not set up any longer as it is most 9 o'clock, so good by[.] Give my love to all & write soon to your loving brother

Henry.

Feb 1st. The mail will go in a few minutes but I thought I might as well add a few lines so you could have the latest date you know. We have got a beautiful nice rainy day to coal in, but never mind I have not got to be out in it, I had my share last night. I am hoping to receive my box soon perhaps I may get it to day tho I hardly expect it.

We have got the confoundest set of officers on board of this ship that ever were got together I believe, a party of them can never go on shore but what some of them have to come off drunk. I have got so disgusted with it that I have knocked off drinking all together tho' I never carried it to excess. Yesterday two of them were suspended & another stuck on shore all night. He is not on board yet & I dont know what they will do with him when he does come.

Well dear good by love to all the family & remember me to all friends

Henry

Ain't that a pretty envelope? Henry

U.S. Steamer *Cambridge*
Off Cape Henry
Feb. 3rd 1862

Dear Mother

I received your letter of the 29th & also the Box before we left the Roads which was not till Sunday. The contents of the Box was very satisfactory[.] I think that that *Little Harry* that you mentioned was a very foolish boy & I will try & not let your Major follow his example. I will also be careful about the olives which by the way I was rather hoping all this time that you would send. I have not opened the Preserve yet as my Guava Jelly is not quite gone. So you see I am not a very greedy boy.

Those draw[er]s are just what I wanted. I would rather have one pair of them than two of such as you sent before, for to my mind they are more comfortable & less expensive.

The cigars were just what I wanted & I think Father got them very cheap.

I am very glad you did not send the coat I do not require it here & it would only lay in my locker & get defaced. I shall want it when I get home & not till then I think so dont send it unless I write particularly about it.

The soap was the only thing that I was disapointed in what I wanted was some nice soap for the hands. (Brown Windsor or something of that sort.) We have got *bushels* of Castill on board.[20] However it dont matter as I got some at the Fort that will do very well.

And now about books etc. I will try to study tho it will be a pretty hard matter to accomplish much I am affraid. Capt Parker told me the other day I might go in his office & study if I wanted to, in fact he recommended me to post myself on Navigation etc. in case I should be required to pass an examination for Act. Master. But then it is awful cold in there & I am affraid I may catch another bad cold however I guess I shall try it. I make no hesitation about sending for what I want for after all what is the Expressage when you think how much more everything would cost if I bought them here so you must not think I am thoughtless or extravagant in sending so often.

I hardly know what books it would be best to send for. I[t] does not seem to me as tho' I could do much at French as I have no one to teach me the pronunciation. I want Hardee's Tactics tho.'[21] I will think what books I want & tell you next time I write.

Tell Lu I am very much obliged to her for those Atlantic Monthlies. I will take great care of them & bring them all back safe. Also Uncle Hamilton's Books.

There is nothing of interest going on here. We changed our Pilot when we were up to the Roads, Mr Seward having obtained leave of absence.

We have two messes in the steerage now, Mr. Maies & myself in one & Mr. Odiorne & Mr. Cushing in the other. We have got along very well so far. & I hope there will be no trouble, as long as they leave us alone there will be no trouble, but neither M. [or] I will take any more humbug from them that is certain.

We are having a real *old Fashioned* snow storm now & are laying at anchor at our station.

I may not have a chance to send this for two or three days in which case I will try & add a few lines more but for the Preasent good by[.] Give my love to all & write often to your loving son

Henry

I enclose $10.00 on a/c.

US Steamer *Cambridge*
Off Cape Henry
Feb. 7th 1862

Dear Mother

As we are going up this afternoon or tomorrow to the Roads to put a boy on shore who is to be discharged as unfit for duty, I can not resist the temptation to send you a few lines tho' it was only yesterday that I sent you a letter.

Every thing is going on here as usual & I can hardly think of any thing to write you about, but never mind[.] I know it would give you satisfaction if I only wrote that I am well & closed at that.

Your cake is generaly approved of throughout the steerage. at any rate I have not heard a desenting voice or found any body unwilling to accept of a piece.

Mr. Nelson was very much pleased with his book & wished me to thank you very much for him.

I wrote a letter to Mary the other day & sent it by the same mail as my last home. I hope she will receive it. but I did not direct it in care of any body as I was not quite sertain about Mr Lovett's news tho I believe it is John O. is it not?

In my letter to you I enclosed $10.00 which I hope you received all right. I think that that clears off every thing except what came in the last box. does it not? I find those Atlantic's very interesting. last night I was reading Dr. Windships experience & was very much amused at his first attempt at public speaking. There was another very good article in the same number "Love & Skates."[22] Tell E & Lu that I shall expect to find them both U.P.'s or F.S.D's at least on my return home.

It is a rainy day & I feel sort of rainy myself partly I suppose because I did not get much sleep last night, having the middle watch. but I shall have all night in to night & that will make up for it in a measure.

We have heard from Lieutenant Gwyn he has got command of one of the Gunboats on the Mississippi.[23] I am very glad & only wish I was with him, one would see service there at any rate. & he is a man who that if any thing is going on he is bound to have a hand in it.

There, I have us been eating a piece of cake & feel decidedly *refreshed*. I can not pessuade any of my messmates that olives are nice. occasionally one of them eats one, but they seem to think they are doing me a great favor by it & make faces enough over it to drive a horse from his oats. They wont accept a second one on any consideration. They seem to think that would be carrying friendship too far.

Well I think I have done pretty well. when I sat down I did not think I could find enough to say to fill up one page & now I am on the fourth. Pray look at the quantity & not the quality tho.'

Give my love to all. By the way Joe will find a letter for him in the Brookline Post office if he will take the trouble to go there for it. Please tell him for they get all their letters in town & might not think to go to the Post out there.

Write often. (I got no letter yesterday)

From your loving son
Henry

US Steamer *Cambridge*
Off Cape Henry
Feb. 9th [1862]

Dear Mother

Sunday has come round again & with it the desire to write home again tho' I am much in the same fix that I was last time, that is I have got nothing to tell about, so you must excuse me if I do not write a very long or interesting letter.

We went up to the Fort day before yesterday & I received a joint letter from Lu & Eliza which I will answer shortly. By the way this is the third one I have written you since I received one. if it was any one else I should not like it but I know it aint because you dont think of me & I know also how little time you have so do not think that I am complaining Mother Dear.

I have been thinking about the books but I hardly know what to send for. I would rather trust it to Father. I want some thing standard which will be both interesting & instructive, history perhaps. I have long wanted to have M. Thiers *Consulate & Empire* but I believe it is very expensive.[24] I want Blunt's Coast Pilot any way & would like to have it sent to me.[25]

I have been trying to accomplish something in the way of study this week. It is like working a sailing vessel against wind & tide to try to do any thing here in this noisy place, still I believe I have done a little. I have been at work on my navigation in which I need some brightening up.

I found those Atlantic Monthlies very interesting & am much obliged to Lu for sending them to me. I have read "Birdofreedom" and enjoyed it hugely, his matrimonial affairs especially.[26]

Evening.—I was obliged to knock off this morning there was such a noise here in the steerage. & now it aint much better. I dont mind skylarking week days but I *do like* to have quiet sundays, that is an impossibility here tho' it seems. How I wish I could be at home to night & sing with you. I often think of my sunday evenings at home. After all sunday *is* the best day in the week tho' I can well remember when I thought it an awful bore. I remember once when I was little (I wont say young for you might laugh) I made a most serious resolution that if ever I arrived at years of discretion I never would go in side of a church.

I wish I could hear Mr. Clark[e']s voice again in our little church. it would be a real satisfaction. Well, perhaps I may in six or eight weeks & in the mean time I shall be doing my duty at all events & there is a good deal of satisfaction in that to. I wonder if he would write to me? I should like to get a letter from him ever so much. I suppose he does not have much time tho'[.] I wish you would remember me to him, in fact give my love to him & tell him that my Hymn Book has been a great satisfaction to me.

What do you think I had better study besides my Navigation & Gunnery I am in a very docile state of mind just now & will take up most any thing if you will only send me books.

You need not look for me at home before the first of April. & I should not be supprised if I did not get there then. it is dreadful tedious here tho' & if they would only change our station I would not care so much.

Well Mother dear Good night send me the books soon if you think it worth while. Give my love to all & write as often as you can to your loving son

Henry

US Steamer *Cambridge*
Hampton Roads
Feb 11th 1862

Dear Mother

We are up here at the Roads coaling ship & I take this opportunity of answering the two nice letters that I received this morning tho' I sent one this morning that will go in the same mail as this.

Please Ma. P.r.e. pre s.e. n.t. sent present.[27]

Enter Orderly. "Mr. Wells, the First Lieutenant wants you to take charge of a boat:" "I. I. Ill be right up, tell him." & so that ended my afternoons writing[.] it is now about nine o'clock in the evening but as I have all night in I think I can spare you an hour of it. The watch are at work coaling ship & of course are making a beautiful noise over head, but there is nothing like getting used to these things.

I am very glad you have got those Photographs for me & I long to see them in my book.

You say that every body at our church is working either for the Sanitary Commission or the countrabands, now I know my advice is not worth much but at the same time my *tenix* is that I dont know any thing about the first more than that such men as Dr Bellows[,] Mr Knapp etc. are engaged in it & that the object seems to be a very good one, but as for the last I would not worry my self at all about them.[28] They will do well enough, there is plenty of work for those that want it here & I dont see as they suffer any for clothes or any thing else, of course I only speak of those at the Fort but I guess there are as many here as any where else. If I was you I would do what I could for the San[itary] Com[mission] & let the countrabands take care of themselves.

I sertainly hope that Edward Hooper will not go on such a wild goose chase as you spoke of.[29] Why the very idea strikes me as particularly absurd. In the first place the negroes as I understand it, are set to work for the government as fast as they come in. & even allowing that they had time to go to school how could he expect to learn them any thing in the midst of all the excitement of the seat of war where the chances of a battle may be a matter of almost life & death to them. I dont suppose any thing I could say would influence him any only I think he will find him self in a very disagreeable position if he goes south & will bring back a very different opinion of the slaves from what he takes with him. There aint more than one in a hundred that is capable of learning, in my estimation. I must say I have got pretty well disgusted with what I have seen of them.

If you send those books send them at once as there is a rumor (tho' I dont place any confidence in it myself) that we shall go north in a week or so. There has been so many such reports that I dont think it hardly worth while to stop the box on that account only be sure & get a receipt for it from the Express co. when you start it.

Well I have got to the end of my paper & as it is getting late will bid you good night give my love to all & write often to your loving son

Henry

US Steamer *Cambridge*
Off Cape Henry
Feb. 13th 1862

Dear Father

I have been talking with Lieut Miller today about getting an appointment as an Act. Master. he says he will help me all he can & advises me to make an application. both Capt. P[arker] & he will approve of it. He says however as this vessel is only a steamer, that I had better get letters from some one that I have sailed for as he thinks that that would make a great deal of difference in my chance of success. so I write you to ask you to see if you can not get them. Those that I had before are in one of the little draws in my secretary up in the sanctum. I wish you would get them & if they will do send them on & if any of our friends know Mr. Welles why a letter to him might help a great deal, or a letter from any *big bug*. you know what I want & if you can get any thing for me send it as soon as possible dont over look that letter of Capt. James Taylor or the one from Mr. Clough if you can find them, also my Navigation by Mr. Spear[.]

We spoke the U.S. Steamer *Stars & Stripes* this morning & they informed us of the victory at Roanoke Island grand is it not?[30] I think a few more such will finish this Rebellion & then—England next *I hope*.

We came down here yesterday and as we have got in coal & water for four or five weeks I dont suppose we shall go up again for some time but that will make no difference about letters for we shall send our boat up the same as usual I suppose.

15th. We shall go up for the mail tomorrow if the weather will permit (which I very much doubt as it is hailing now) & so I will finish this now & have it ready. Every thing is going on quietly as usual except that a disposition is shown by steerage mess No. 2 to renew the quarrels which have destroyed our harmony here for the last few months[.] it has been quite quiet for the last three weeks & we were in hopes it would continue so, but peace dont seem to be for us any more than for the country.

They dont seem to be inclined to trouble Mr. Maies & I tho,' this time but are at the Carpenter & Gunner again & have decidedly the best of it so far I must confess. I do dislike to have to live with men (or boys some of them) who can not get along with out quarreling all the time. That is one great reason why I am anxious to get ordered to another vessel. but any way I dont see why I should not have the rank & pay of a Master now, after having done the duty of one for the last 5 months to the perfect satisfaction of all concerned when I see a great many others that have not been to sea half so long & some even that dont even pretend to be any thing in the way of seamen, getting it.

Do try & get me letters as soon as possible as I want to send on at once. Good by. Give my love to all,

from your loving son
Henry W. Wells

Off Cape Henry
Feb. 15th 1862
U.S. Steamer *Cambridge*

Dear Eliza

What do you think of that?[31] I was all all out of paper & had to borrow some & this is what I got. My taste does not run in the line of this sort of paper generaly but an occasional indulgence will do no harm I guess.

I received your letter of the 2nd some time ago & feel rather ashamed of my self for not having answered it sooner. I dont know as I have got any particular excuse to offer tho,' so I do not know as it is any use to try to find one.—Supper is ready so hold on a bit.—

There I have eaten supper, smoked a cigar, & had the pleasure of hearing some fine singing since I commenced this letter. Our firemen have splendid voices some of them, & sing very finely. We have a concert almost every night in the fire-room.

Our mess quarrels have commenced again, not exactly our mess either. You know Mr Maies & I form one mess here & Mr. Odiorne and Master Cushing (he has not got to years of discretion yet so I wont call him Mr.) form another. The Gunner & Carpenter live in the steerage but mess with the Engineers[.] Well, steerage mess No. 2 have commenced an attack on the Warrant Officers in a series of petty annoyences with in the last two or three days & the others of course have tried to retaliate. but so far I must say tho my sympathies are all on the other side, that the youngsters have got the best of it.

At the last tug Mr. Maies and I got rather the best of them & they have been rather careful since not to interfere with us & as we are two peaceable men as long as they dont trouble us we leave them alone. A kind of armed neutrality, you know.

I shall be very glad to get the Mary's and Clara's photographs. send them as soon as you can. & also Aunti & Mrs. Wilds those are two that I did not expect to get but none the less glad to have.

As long as you are not going to Montreal, I am sorry that you have been so disapointed, but at the same time (Excuse me dear) I can not help feeling a kind of tacit satisfaction that you are not going to visit that *mean contemptable* province. Confound them I only wish we could have a chance to take away a little of their conceit. "barking dogs dont bite" (not much)

Day before yesterday we saw a steamer coming in all covered with flags[.] we stood for her & found she was the U.S. Steamer ~~*Cambridge*~~ (there is no much talking going on that I can hardly think strait & there is one of the results.) *Stars and Stripes* from Roanoke Island with news of the victory. We are going up tomorrow if the weather will permit to get the newspapers so as to have the particulars.

Realy La La I dont know as I have any thing more to write I guess I will stop here. Tell Lu I will write to her next time & that I am sorry that I should have delayed so long. but I have got the middle watch to night & so can not write another letter as it is most time to turn in.

Good by give my love to all & write me a nice long letter soon.

From your loving brother
Henry

United States Steamer *Cambridge*
Off Cape Henry
Feb. 17th 1862

Dear Lu

Dont think because I have started on a large sheet, that I have got lots to say & am going to fill it up. Oh no! I only took this because I could not get any other. For I have got nothing to say or tell about & the reason why I write at all is because I am ashamed to keep you waiting any longer for an answer to your letter which I received almost two weeks ago.

It was only day before yesterday that I sent home two letters one to Father & another to Eliza which I hope will be duly received especialy the one to F. which was important.

Sunday I went up to the Fort myself in the boat & was happy to find three letters at the Post Office for me which I considered a quantity about equal to my merits & was there fore satisfide & did not growl.

One of my letters was from cousin Sophia telling me all about the farewell given to Mr Hooper by the church, it must have been very gratifying to him to have them show so much interest in his welfare. He is a noble fellow & I wish him every success tho' I have doubts of the utility of any such scheme & I am afraid he will find he has a hard row to hoe but he will have the feeling that he is doing what is right to spur him on & may be able to accomplish more than I think. I hope he will prove that I am mistaken at all events. & may God prosper him in his good work is my prayer.

I am glad they have given him a hymn book he will find comfort in that I know, when he is far away from home & friends, the feeling that it came from *our* church will cheer his heart whenever he opens it I am sure. What a good church we have got! & with Mr Clark at the head it seems to me like a nother home when I think of it. every body seems so united there all loving each other & Mr. Clark. It makes me feel home sick to think about it especialy on sundays. How much I have to loose by having choosen the sea for my profession, still perhaps I am better here than I should be at any thing else so I must not complain, if it had not been right I should not have come.

I must get ready to go on watch now as it is raining & I must put on my rubber clothes. I will finish this when I come below again.

Evening—I have just finished my after supper smoke & will now finish my letter.

Mr. Eldridge Act. Master (the best one on board by the way tho' they are all very good) has got a furlough of three weeks from the Department on account of his child being sick & we are going up tomorrow to put him on shore it is very doubtful whether he comes back to this vessel again as he is ordered at the experation of his leave to report at Washington, he will be a great loss to us, but Capt. Parker is going to write to the Secretary asking to have him ordered here again.

When Lieut Gwyn was ordered to take command of the *Tyler* on the Mississippi he applied to have Mr. Eldridge with him but as there were no vacancies he did not succeed, he may be sent there now tho' & on his own account[.] I hope he will for he will have a chance to see some service there. Oh! dont I [wish I] was there? Wont it splendid? The way those Gunboats attacked Fort Henry. There is a report that Fort Donelson is taken too, you will know whether it is true or not before you receive this.[32] Hurrah for Burnside!!! Matters do begin to look cheering at last, now if we can only have some fine weather to give McClellan a chance & then "*On to Richmond*"![33]

I am glad you passed such a good examination at our new school, & am not at all surpprised that you broke down on the spelling[.] it seems fated that all the younger members of the Wells family should be poor spellers, so of course you are not to blame for submitting to the *Fates*.

I have enjoyed reading those Atlantic's very much & will try & keep them in good order till I get home tho' it is pretty hard to keep a book of that sort in good order on board of a ship—Talking of ships—You asked me to rig you a little vessel to put in your room, in your last letter, now I am not much of a jack knife carpenter so I have got one of the men to make one for me. It is almost done now & I hope you will like it. Its a schooner.

I am very glad that there is a chance of my getting Clara's photograph, but I want Mary's most tho' of course I shall be disapointed if I dont get both.

Well aint I smart, here I am almost to the bottom of the fourth page, whether you are the gainer or not you must judge for your self.

Give my love to all & write soon to your loving brother

Henry

I received two newspapers from home yesterday & two from Joe.

I received Mothers letter containing a photograph of Mrs. Wild. I dont think it is a good one at all it is not half so handsome as she is Cousin Libby sent me a very good one of Auntie Bond.

U.S. Steamer *Cambridge*
Off Cape Henry
Feb. 19th /62

Dear Mother

I received your letter of the 14th on Sunday and now set down to answer it tho' I dont think we shall go up for several days, however I dont like to wait till the last minute & then not write half a letter.

We went up to the Fort yesterday to put Mister Eldridge on shore he having got three weeks furlough from the Department on account of some of his family being sick. I am afraid we shall not get him back here again as he is ordered to report at Washington on the expiration of his leave.

It will not make much difference to me tho' if I succeed in my application which I do not feel a great deal of doubt of. I hope Father will get those letters for me as soon as possable as I am anxious to get the thing under way. I would rather my project should not be mentioned to any one out of the family except of course to those who father may ask for letters.

I shall have a little more to do now as Mr Eldridge's leaving, leaves only 4 watch officers, which is enough tho' in all concurrence[.] Mr. Odiorne expected to get his watch but Lieut. Miller would not trust him, so he is to stand with Mr. Strong.

Our Chief Engineer Mr. Brennon has sent in his resignation, I dont know the reason sertainly but believe it is because his Father is sick & he can not get leave of absence. I dont think any one will be very sorry to have him go for he is not very well liked here. I believe that that is all the news that there is afloat here except what we get from the New York papers.

I am much obliged to you for sending me the account of the proceedings against the *Revere*[.] after I read it I sent it into the Captain.

I believe all the papers that you send come strait[.] I like to get the Boston papers very much for the local news.

I shall begin to look for my box now soon. I forgot to ask you to put in a Nautical Almanac for 1862 in, but it is no great matter as I can get one some where I guess.

I wish I could come home & see you all if it was only for a day. I am beginning to feel quite homesick if we were only doing something I would not care but to be laying down here off Cape Henry four or five months is most too much. I am very sorry but I have not been able to do any thing about Bennies suit as yet. I thought I could get the cloth that I should want from the Paymaster but I find he has only satinet which will not do at all.[34] I tried at the Fort was no better success tho' the man told me he should have some in a few days so I shall live in hope. I am sorry for I know you will be disapointed but perhaps I can fix it all right after all.

I dont like that Photograph of Mrs. Wild a bit that you sent me. I hardly knew who it was at first. did you like it? I am sorry very that I shall not get the one of Mary but I suppose she will have some more taken one of these days. How about Clara's?

You mentioned having heard once from Aunt Ruth, what was the news?

I hope that the report that reached us that Fort Donelson with Generals Johnson etc. have been taken is true[.] it will be splendid if it is—& 15000 prisoners too[.] Mr Very (one of our Masters) says that that last is like "winning an Elephant at a raffle." "What are you going to do with them now we have got em? it will cost more to feed them the [than] the Devils are worth[.]" according to all accounts our gunboats got pretty severly handled in the last scrape.

Matters do begin to look brighter dont they? I hope soon to hear that Burnside is in possession of Norfolk & then we will see what their famous *Merrimac* is made of.

I suppose there is no chance of Mc[C]Lellan making any move till we have a little dry weather & it dont look much like that at present for it is raining like the mischief on deck & what is worse I have got the first watch. We have not had more than two or three fine days this month I believe. I think that the cisterns *up stairs* must be most empty by this time.

Our famous Mid[shipman] is trying dreadful hard to get his head broke & I should not wonder if he succeeded after a while. He knows that man of war rules protect him & he takes a mean advantage of it to cast slurs at some of the others down here. human nature will not stand every thing & the first thing he knows he wont know any thing as the saying is. One of the officers made a complaint against him to the First Lieut. the other day but Mr. Miller said, he would not mind him he was a miserable thing & not worth paying any attention to. So you see what his superior officers think of him. You need not think from what I have said that he is making his attacks on me for he dont & I hope he wont for I dont think I would put up with any more from him with out taking hold of him.

Thursday Morning. I had to leave off last night & go on deck to stand my watch & I will now finish this letter as for some reason or other, we are going up to day tho' it is not our regular time.

The pilot-boat just ran alongside of us & told us that Savannah was taken.[35] what glorious news we are having now from all quarters! it realy begins to look as tho' we were doing something. Now if they would only send the *Cambridge* somewhere so that we could have a hand in the game, such as shelling Sewells Point & Craney Island, I would be satisfide.

Give my love to all & write often to your loving son

Henry

Feb 23rd. Highly Important! Three days later from Henry! Nothing of interest. The thick slate of the Roads having delayed the decent of the *Cambridge* of Fort Monroe. A moment now in contemplation. The Post Office to be carried by storm Express ditto. ditto.

Yours in haste from your especial correspondent

H.

US Steamer *Cambridge*
Off Cape Henry
Feb. 24th 1862

Dear Father

I received your note yesterday about my application for a masters commission, & asked Capt. Parker for a letter when to my utter astonishment after a great deal of circumlocution he told me he was afraid I was not quite old enough, did not doubt my seamanship etc. but thought I had better wait a *year or so* & then I should be older, did not like to take the responsibility of recommending so young a man. if I did not prove fully up to the mark the Department might come down upon him, etc. etc. etc. & finely ended by refusing to recommend my appointment.

I was thunderstruck for it was only two or three weeks ago that when we were talking on the same subject he gave me every encouragement & said he would be willing to recommend me. So I consider that Capt. P. has done a very mean & dishonorable thing.

I hope that I have not put you in a false position as well as myself?

It does seem as tho I was born to be unlucky whenever I set my mind on any thing & work hard to get it, just as I think I have succeeded it slips away & I am as far off as ever.

To be told to wait a year when men with not half the sea experience that I have had & no knowledge of a man of war are receiving appointments over my head every day is most to[o] hard to be born. with most any other man I might have succeeded but Captain P. is so cautious and afraid of committing himself & dont seem to releaise that I have been to sea any length of time because I seem young. he seems to think that a man can not be a man unless he is 40 or 50 years old, in which I respectfully beg leave to differ. I told him that I considered my self a great deal better fitted for the position than Midshipmen that are getting it now[,] some of whom have not seen a years service all together. But as he is a regular officer of course he did not see it in that light & allowed that they received a scientific education to fit them for their positions tho' for my part I dont see how all the book[s] in the world can teach a man how to manage a ship in a gale of wind. & if the Mid. we have on board of here is a sample of them & their education I would not give mine for it wheather it got me the rank of Act. Master or not.

But never mind long before the year is out I will be promoted or shot or resign I dont care much which.

If I was at home I would try for the appointment whether Capt Parker approved of it or not & I think it could be got too, for he can not say but what I have done my duty & more to[o] ever since I have come on board this vessel.

I only wish we could have a good hot action so that a man might have a chance to distinguish himself. if the chance was offered, I would do my best to improve it I assure you. Good by now give my my love to all

from your loving son
Henry W Wells

U.S. Steamer *Cambridge*
At Sea
Feb. 26th 1862

Dear Mother,

This morning we went up to the Roads for wood & water but we had hardly let go our anchor before we were ordered to get under way at once & go down the coast to assist the *R.B. Forbes* which was ashore 30 miles to the southard of Cape Henry together with two or three other vessels, which were wrecked in the gale of day before yesterday.[36]

One of them a Ferryboat, the *Hoboken*, a crazy tub, we saw drift out of the Bay ourselves being unable to make headway against the wind which blew fearfully, but much to the astonishment of most of the officers on board of this vessel, no attempt was made by us either to save the vessel or crew.[37] The crew of the *H[oboken]* which drifted ashore on Cape Henry were rescued by the Steamer *S.R. Spaulding*[38] & taken to the Roads where they denounced the *Cambridge* in no measured terms, & said they drifted with in a mile of us & made signals of distress which we refused to answer. She did not come nearer than three miles of us however & if she made any signals we did not see them. That is no excuse for us tho' as we knew very well what boat it was, & that she was not fit to stand any kind of a sea. But if we had gone to her assistance we should have been obliged to put to sea afterwards as we never could have got to windward again in such a storm & that would have been *very uncomfortable* you know. so the poor fellows were left to their fate, tho' thank God they have been saved from death.

Yesterday was a fine day & we might have gone out then & looked for her. but no, it was a little rough & it was much better to lie at anchor. So today when we went up to the Roads we had the satisfaction of being informed that a vessel had gone ashore on our station with out our knowing it, for she was wrecked on the Cape & if we had not been well up the bay we should have seen her.

I am afraid that Capt Parker will be Court Marshaled for it. I am very sorry, tho' I do think he treated me very meanly about my promotion. But after all I am afraid he deserves it for it sertainly was a very strange thing for him to do.

Of course as soon as we received our orders we got underway & started down the Bay[.] on passing the Cape we saw the *Hoboken* high & dry, broke in two. as the crew had been taken off of her & our object was mainly to save life we left her for another time & kept on towards the False Capes where we met the Tug Boat *Cohasset* with the officers and crew of the *R.B. Forbes*. They reported the vessel thoroughly burned before they left her, so all we had to do was to turn round as they told us that there were no other vessels ashore, & we are now on our way back. We were all in hopes we should have a brush with the Rebels, but this is a sample of our luck ever since we have been in commission. When we were off Beaufort we did not have any work to do but as soon as we left two or three ships ran ashore there & the Blockading vessels had the fun of burning them.

We met with an accident which prevented our going in the Port Royal expedition.[39] We were then sent up the Rappahannock, while we were there the Rebels kept very quiet but as soon as we left they got up Batteries so as to make it pleasent & warm there. Then we went up to Newport News. Nothing was done while [we] were there but as soon as we left the Gunboats had a fight, & now here, others are allowed to do our work. it is shameful & I am disgusted.

Mr. Odiorne a Master's Mate on board of here has made an application for an act. master appointment through his friends & expect[s] to get it. he is younger than I am and has only been two voyages at sea as boy or o.[rdinary] seaman. Now if he can get it why can not I? who can get letters from such men as Capt. Taylor to recommend me backed by Gov. Andrews[,]Senators Sumner, etc.[40] I wish Father would try what he can do. It is no use for me to write for if I sent a personal application other than through the Commodore no notice would be taken of it.

I do not feel myself satisfide with my present rank as I feel myself qualified to take a higher. & besides I do want to get clear of this ship & go where I can see some service.

I wrote a letter to Father two or three days ago but I did not get a chance to mail it today so it will go at the same time as this. It explains how my first plans were defeated.

It is [al]most time for my watch so I can not write more now[.] I hope tomorrow I shall be able to tell you that we have burnt the wreck of the *Hoboken* but I suppose as usual some other vessel will have the pleasure of doing that.

Good by now give my love to all & write often to your loving son

Henry

P.S. I am much obliged for that Photograph tho' I had to look at it three times before I mad[e] out who it was. I hope to receive that box soon.

Who on earth was that Masters Mate that you told me about in your last? Surely he could never have been to sea, to be so imposed on, or else he must have been (excuse me) very *soft*. At all events is it fare that such men (or boys) as he should rank with those who have been to sea 5 or 6 years? I say it is not!

Every thing is very quiet in our mess lately. Mr. Maies has received a letter from Lieut Gwin offering him a chance as 4th Master in his gunboat. I dont think he will go tho' as Capt. Parker will give him letters to the Department, he has age on his side you know & I am sure I am glad that he has so good a chance to get promoted.

U.S. Steamer *Cambridge*
Hampton Roads
Feb. 27th 1862

Dear Mother

I sent you a letter this morning, but as I have just received one from you I will answer it at once.

It makes me so mad I can hardly think to find myself so confoundedly imposed on as I have been about this promotion afair & still more so to think what a false position I have put you & Father in. If it want that it would be little better than mutiny I would give Capt. P[arker] a good large piece of' my mind on the subject & if ever I meet him on equal terms I will too.

I wrote you what I thought best to be done yesterday, but if Father does not approve of it, why I suppose I must wait till I get home & try not to think any more about it at present.

I was very much disapointed about the books which I expected to receive this time, but perhaps it is best to keep them now, if the application is made, if not send them at once. I want something to occupy my mind for I am disgusted with every thing here.

There! in a fit of mine I went just now to Lieut. Miller who is realy very frendly to me, & told him how I was situated, he said at once that he would give me a letter stating that I had performed my duty as a watch officer & Masters Mate to his entire satisfaction & advised me to try the captain on the same tack which I have done & the results I hope to enclose in this letter, but I have not got them yet. I feel a good deal better now than I did an hour ago.

We were all genuinely disappointed in our hopes of a brush yesterday, but as usual we were behind time.

I dont know as I have any thing more to tell you about as I wrote last night. We are up here taking in stores & I hope we shall not leave before tomorrow as if we do this letter will be delayed which may do some harm to my prospects considering what I wrote in my letters to you & Father.

Good by Give my love to all & write often to your loving son

Henry

As we may leave here before tomorrow I will send this wheather I enclose the others or not.

H.

US Steamer *Cambridge*
Off Cape Henry
March 2nd 1862

Dear Mother

As to day is sunday I think I can not employ a part of my time better than in writing home tho' I do feel as tho' I had not received as many letters as I ought for the last ten days or two weeks they having been limited to one for each week. I think my sisters might write a little oftener. I know you write as often as you can so I dont mean to blame you in the least. You must have received a pretty large lot of letters from me last week, four went in one mail. The way of it was that two of them were sent ashore in the morning, & afterwards receiving your letter I sat down & wrote the other & had sealed it up to go in the mail bag when the Capt. sent me his note which I had just time to direct & pass into the boat as it was shoving off. I hope you received it & also the one of Lieut Millers which I sent the next day.

When you write I want you to tell me all that is done, the steps taken etc. about the affair & if convenent send me the copies of the letters used[.] I have copies of those which I sent to you. I think Gov. Andrew's a very good one.

Mr. Maies has made an application to the same effect to the Department through the Capt. & Flag Officer. I hope he will succeed.

I believe I told you some time ago that Mr. Brennon our Chief Engineer had applied for his discharge. He has got it but has not left us yet.

For some time past several of the Fire-men and one or two of the seamen have been getting up a band of minstrels. They had a dress rehearsal last night (preparitory to a performance on deck) which was realy very good, in the Fire Room. Only a *select few* were admitted[.] I was amongst the number. They were all blacked as negroes & had five pieces of music—viz[41]: a Guitar, Accordian, Tambourine, Triangle & Bones.

The effect was very fine & would have made a good picture. The place was not very brilenetly [brilliantly] lighted & the Machinery round them & above gave every thing a kind of infernal look which formed a striking contrast to their music songs & jokes, it looked so sombre and heavy.

I enjoyed it very much for set[t]ing aside the novelty of the thing their music & singing was very good indeed some of them have got very fine voices.

We had quite a spell away from our station last week it was quite a relief. I realy felt like a bird set free when we got out side of the Capes of Virginia on our way to assist the *R.B. Forbes*. it did seem good to be on the blue water again & to be out of sight of land at least on one side. We were at the Roads two days taking in wood, water, coal, & provisions.

We are back here now tho' & are likely to stay for ought I can see for some time to come.

Joe sends me the papers now quite often. I like to get them very much. Please tell him I received No. 8 Saturday.

March 4th I do not feel very well today & hardly know what to do with myself so I think I will write a few more lines to you, for when I am out of sorts I always feel better after writing home.

To day is the anniversary of President Lincoln's inauguration. What an eventful year it has been for the country. I hope this war will all be settled before another year passes away, but I think the South will take a good deal of whipping before they give in. I almost dread the attack on Columbus.[42] The Rebels will make a very determined stand there I expect & with Beauraguard to lead them, it will be no childs play to drive them out. I think we have got an army there tho' that is equal to the task & I hope we shall soon hear that the place is taken.

I hope we shall hear some more news of Burnside soon & of Sherman too, at Savannah.

We had a very blustering night last night & it blows very fresh to day. We should have sent a boat up to the Roads if it had been pleasant but as it is we must wait till tomorrow. I am not sorry either for Wednesday is my letter day you know, so I shall expect quite a lot of letters when we do go.

I hope my box will come in the course of the week tho' I dont know but that is most to[o] soon to expect it. I dreamed last night that it had come.

I shall enclose $10.00 on account. how much that will leave me in debt. I believe $15.00 not including the books is it not?

Well I can not write any more now as I shall have to go on deck pretty soon[.]

Give my love to all. Tell my sisters that I am ashamed of them, & if I dont find any letters from them when we get our next mail I shall be doubly so. Good by from your loving son

Henry

March 5th. Something is the matter with our Engine so we can not move to day & there-fore will not be able to go up to the Roads. It is not a very pleasent day & perhaps we should not have gone up any way so it dont make much difference.

Two of the Sound steamers came in past us this morning, the *C. Vanderbilt* & *Commodore* bound to Annapolis I believe[.][43] I wonder what is up now? I hope something that we can join in.

US Steamer *Cambridge*
Off Cape Henry
March 6th /62

Dear Mother

Our boat went up to the Roads to day & I received your letter of the third. From the way you spoke I judge you had not received the letter of Lieut Millers which I enclosed to you on Saturday. I hope it has not miscarried. I shall not ask Capt. Parker for any thing more in the way of letters if I have to go with out the promotion[.] There are plenty of merchant ships afloat thank God, & I have not got to depend on the Navy to get along or on its *regular officers* either.

I shall not send Capt. P. the note that you made as I dont think it would be exactly the thing, not ship-shape you know.

I have been disapointed about that Box so often now that I am tired of thinking of it. You can send it or not just as you like & think best.

Why—I have just been looking over what I have written. & I guess I wont write any more to night. I dont feel well & am cross & dissatisfied with every thing & I find the feeling will get on to the paper in spite of me. I can not write a pleasant letter feeling so.

Perhaps I will write more in the morning if I have time we shall go up as Mr. Brennon is going to leave. Good by love to all from

Henry

March 8. We did not go up yesterday on account of the weather. We are under way now & I suppose will send our boat in today.

If you have not received Lieut Millers letter let me know at once & I will try to get another.

Yesterday morning two steamers hove in sight coming in, it was blowing very heavy & they were both light river boats not made for rough water. One of them was towing the other. When they were within about two miles of us the leading one let go his tow & started for the Roads at full speed. as he passed us we saw that his bulwarks were all swept away forward, paddle boxes stove in, etc. The other steamer sank shortly after. as usual we laid by & watched them but never made any motion of getting under way to assist them.

Do rub out all the last half of the page I have just written as I should be ashamed to have any one else see it.

I am absolutely disgusted with every thing that is done here. it is just outrageous & *nothing* else.

Why last Saturday we passed close down by the wreck of the *Hoboken* & saw the Rebels landing her machinery etc. & we never offered to fire a shot at them to help them along [last four words circled by Henry] or to destroy the vessel.

If some one did not belong to a state so far North I should strongly suspect that he was rather of a sesesion tendency. Let me know all about what you are doing or have done as soon as you can. I like to have the Box but you can do as you think best. I can write no more at present. Love to all from your loving son

Henry

U.S. Steamer *Cambridge*
Hampton Roads
March 8th 1862

Dear Mother

To day is a black day in the history of this war[.] The Rebel steamer *Merrimac* with several others have come down & beaten our Fleet. It is humiliating to acknowledge it but so it is. we have been decidedly worsted in to days fight. God knows what will happen tomorrow. The Sloop of War *Cumberland* is sunk, the Frigate *Congress* burnt. The Frigate *Minnesota* is ashore but we are in hopes to be able to save her more especialy as the Erricson battery has just come in & will go up imeadietly to protect her.[44]

We took a part in the fight, tho' we were not there till the hottest of it was over on account of towing up the Frigate *St. Lawrence* which was at anchor down in Lynnhaven bay. We were only struck twice & no great damage done.[45]

The Rebels have not exagerated in their accounts of there famous ship—that. . . . [He penned a drawing in the letter] is the way she looked.

Our loss on the first three vessels which I named must be fearful. I *can not* give you a more circumstantial account at present as I have been on the go ever since morning, it is now ten P.M. & I have got the middle watch. we shall have another battle tomorrow I suppose. Thank God! we have an iron clad battery to meet the *Merrimac* a wooden ship can do nothing against her.

All praise to Capt. Van Brunt he fought the *Minnesota* splendidly.

We had a very narrow escape from being taken while laying by the *St. Lawrence* who got ashore. The *Merrimac* tried to cut us both off but we got the *St. L.* in tow & got clear. The *Lawrence* gave the *M.*[*errimac*] two splendid broadsides, it was too dark to see the effect but one thing I know & that is that the *M.* did not fire any more but put back towards Sewalls Point. I cant write any more now. If I live I will give you a full account tomorrow.

Good by, love to all. The Capt. of the *Roanoke* swares (so the report goes) that he will attack Norfolk tomorrow if he sinks every ship in the fleet.

Well, well, I will try & not disgrace my name or country. Dont fear for me, there is many a mother that has lost her son to day. And if God wills that my life should be taken remember that he doeth all things well.

God bless you all. Good night from

Henry

US *Cambridge*
March 9, 1862

Dear Mother

The *Monitor* has attacked the *Merrimac* & seems to be getting the best of her.[46] We are ordered down to Beaufort to blockade the *Nashville*.[47]

In great haste
Henry

[This letter is no longer extant and was transcribed from the original, which, after the war, Louisa found in a scrapbook.]

An account of the memorable engagement of the *Monitor* and *Merrimac*
US Steamer *Cambridge*
At Sea
March 9th 1862

Dear Mother

We are on our way to Beaufort N. C. for the ostensable purpose of helping to blockade the Steamer *Nashville* but it is the general impression that there is going to be hard fighting there, at all events we are informed that a strong force of gunboats are concentrated on that station.

I shall not have a chance to send a letter for two or three weeks I suppose but I write now so as to give you an account of the events of the last two days while they are still fresh in my memory.

I will begin at the beginning, prefacing with the fact that three or four days ago the U.S. Frigate *St. Lawrence* came in past Cape Henry bound into the Roads but having a head wind anchored in Lynnhaven Bay, where she was on the eventful 8th.

Yesterday morning we got under way & steamed up to the Light-boat to send our boat ashore. after that we cruised about till after 1 PM the time appointed for its return when we went back to the Light-boat to pick her up. When we had the boat hoisted up & were turning around to go back to our station some one saw several steamers coming out from behind Sewalls Point, which proved to be the *Merrimac* & two other Rebel steamers[.] one of them carried the French flag at her mast-head, for what reason I do not know unless they thought the French men of war would take the matter up if we fired at their flag. They were very much mistaken however if they put faith in any belief for we sunk her with a broadside from the *St. L* but of that in its place.

They saw them from the Frigates *Roanoke* & *Minnesota* at the same time we did I should judge for immediately after the *R*[*oanoke*] hoisted a recall for all boats & fired a gun. The *Minnesota* got underway at once & started up to meet them, the *Roanoke* soon followed but as her shaft is broke she had to get two towboats alongside first. As she made no signals to us Capt. Parker hardly knew what to do as he was affraid to leave his station with out orders, but his mind was soon put at ease by seeing the *St. Lawrence* signalizing us, so we ran down to her to find what she wanted, which was to "Tow him in the direction of Norfolk till we got orders to stop." You may be sure that suited us first rate for the other vessels were hard at it by this time. We soon got a hawser to him, but no sooner did we set taught [taut] on it than snap! away she went. so we had the work to do over again which took a good deal of precious time, however we finally got fast to him with two hawsers & started for the scene of action. we could not see much of the position of the vessels, tho' at that time the firing was heaviest in the direction of Newport News. The vessels stationed at that point were the Frigate *Congress* 50 guns & Sloop of War *Cumberland*—24 guns, both sailing vessels. Those that went up from the Roads to take part in the engagement were the *Roanoke* 40 [guns], *Minnesota* 40 [guns], *Mystic*-4-[guns]. & several boats mounting one or two guns.

The Rebel force consisted of the *Merrimac*, *Yorktown*, *Patrick Henry* & two others.[48] The first two are iron plated & I believe one of the others. As we came into the Roads we met the *Mystic* coming back in tow of another steamer from which I judge she was disabled tho' I have not been able to assertain her battery was very light however & could not be of much service in such an engagement as we soon found ourselves mixed up in. Just as we got a breast of Sewalls Point we saw a puff of white smoke & then a whirr as a Rifle shell came between our masts & exploded beyond us. a minute after a nother came & cut away the *St. L*[*awrence*'s] fore-brace. We then opened fire, as did the *St. L* giving them a perfect shower of shot & shell. We soon got past out of range of the broadside guns tho' our pivots bore for some time longer. One shell from our Parrott (the last one we fired at the point) was as pretty a shot as ever was made, it landed right alongside of one of the guns they were serving & burst. I did not see that gun fired again. While we were firing on the point the *Roanoke* passed us under sail going back to the Roads. On account of not having steam he could not get near enough to be of much service. We had all been wondering what had become of the *Cumberland* as we did not hear any thing of her & could not see her spars over the point. but now as we advanced to our horror, there was the *Cumberland* sunk with her spars out of water on an angle of 45° (which accounted for our not having seen them) & the *Congress* worse still—surrendered, & two white flags flying. shortly after a tug-boat came to us with the comfortable assurance that the *Minnesota* was hard & fast aground. We had more that half suspected it all along for she lay so quiet with the *Merrimac* across he[r] bows at long range raking her with every shot. Capt Van Brunt fought his ship splendidly. he could not bring any guns to bear on the *M.*[*errimac*] but kept his broadside in a perfect sheet of flame playing on the others, so that at first we thought he was on fire, it was not very effective however as the enemy chose his own distance & had very heavy guns.

The *St. Lawrence* now took the ground, & at about the same time the *Merrimac* commenced playing on us both. one shell exploded right over our poop cutting away our main trysail sheet & wounding Mr. Cushings hand slightly. another I saw coming right in a line for me & thought that I was gone. I stood my ground tho' & the shot struck the guard right under my feet. Those were the only times we got hit tho' the shot was flying round us in a very uncomfortable manner for a nervous person. We did not fire much then as were doing all we could to get the *St. Lawrence* clear of the bottom.

The *Merrimac* now with one or two others[,] I do not exactly know how many as it was quite dark then, started down towards the Roads to head us off & left the *Minnesota* alone as I suppose they thought they had her safe enough & could finish her when they got ready.

By the time they got abeam of us however with the assistance of a Tug we got the *St. L.* clear & in tow & started down. as soon as we got fairly started we went back to our guns. We watched for the flash of their guns & then fired for that as it was so dark that we could not distinguish them they all set so low in the water. The *St. Lawrence* gave them two splendid broadsides which sickened them & they ceased firing. Those last broadsides sunk one of their gunboats for we saw her spars sticking up in the water, this morning.[49] Soon after we came to anchor in the Roads. We now saw a bright light in the direction of Newport News which proved to be the *Congress* which the Rebels had set on fire at 12:30 AM she blew up. it was an awful explosion & shook our vessel from truck to keelson[.] it was a splendid sight but one that I do not want to see again (unless it is an enemy that suffers & then I dont care[)]. – 8 bells!!! I will finish this by & by it is my watch on deck now.

On our arrival at the Roads we were told that the Ericsson Battery *Monitor* had arrived with two other gunboats which cheered us up a good deal as in the crippled condition of the fleet the *Merrimac* & her iron clad consorts might have come down & cleared the Roads with out much dificulty. The *Monitor* went up & laid by the *Minnesota* all night.

In the morning at daylight we saw the *Merrimac* with two other steamers laying off Sewalls Point at anchor. We got under way but had to anchor again as the Act. Flag Officer would not let us go up. I was then sent ashore for the mail & to gather particulars as to that part of the engagement which related to the *Congress* & *Cumberland*[.] The latter it seems was run down by the *Merrimac* with that iron beak of hers. The crew of the *C* tried to board her but could not find any place to get in, & while they were assembled for that purpose the slaughter was awful, the Rebels pouring grape & canister into them all the time.

After finishing her & it did not take long she took up a position under the *Congresses* stern & raked her fearfully the shot sweeping the full length of the deck. Capt. Smith sliped his moorings & run the ship ashore after which he surrendered. The Rebels took all her officers & Marines prisoners but told the crew they might clear out as fast as they liked.

While I was on shore the *Merrimac* started for the *Minnesota* to destroy her I suppose, but found a slight obsticle in the way in the shape of a vessel that carried heaviry [heavier] guns than she[,] was shoot proof & had the extra advantage of being so small as to afford no mark to fire at, in other words the *Monitor*[.] The two went at it with a will & you will know of result of the action long before you receive this & before I know it my-self. for shortly after the engagement commenced an order came from the Department to send the *Cambridge* to Beaufort. We started at once much to the discomfort of the officers messes as none of us had laid in any sea stock of provisions. We are a pretty looking vessel to send any where. With our bow stove from our old accident, our stern all tore to pieces in trying to pull off the *St. Lawrence* last night & a shot hole through our side. Well I guess the old *Cambridge* is good for repairs next time we come back.

I tell you we were all mad enough to be sent off right in the middle of a battle, but the orders of the department have to be obeyed. Capt. Marston (the Senior Officer[)] gave us great credit for the part we took in the affair. The Navy had been taught a lesson that it will not soon forget I am thinking. We were too confident & despised the Navy of the Rebels & we have had to suffer for it as the army did for the same thing at Bull Run.

Well as this is the twelfth page I guess I will close now. Love to all from your loving son

Henry

Please save & send me all the papers relating to this affair as having witnessed it I should like to hear what the Reporters say.

US Steamer *Cambridge*
Off Beaufort N.C.
March 11th /62

Dear Mother

We are now back here on our old station off Beaufort & tho' not much of an improvement on Cape Henry still I am glad of the change. Variety is the spice of life you know.

We arrived here last night & found on the station the Steamer *State of Georgia* & the Barque *Gemsbok*.[50] The first will have to leave in a few days as she is short of coal but I am in hopes that there will be one or two others here be fore that as if there is not I do not see what is to prevent the *Nashville* from running out when she gets ready for one steamer is not enough to blockade her in here & if she once got out we could never catch her as she is a very fast vessel & we are rather slow.

We can see her with our glasses very planely in Beaufort Harbor, & from appearances I think she is taking in coal.

It is rather stormy to day but as soon as the weather settles we are going to run in & have a shot at her with our Rifle-guns. I may be able to tell you with what result before I close this letter as I shall not have a chance to send it till the *State of Georgia* sails.

I have writen you an account of our Battle with the Rebels off Sewalls point which I hope you will receive. please save me all the papers relating to that unfortunate affair.

I hope the *Monitor* succeeded in beating the *Merrimac.* Was it not a shame to send us away at such an exciting time. We are very anxious to hear the news. I hope the papers will give the *Cambridge* the credit which she deserves, for we saved the *St. Lawrence* & Capt. Parker ought to receive great praise for the way he staid by her. He nearly lost his own vessel by it. For one spell we all made up our minds that there was no escape for us, but to fight till we sunk, but thanks to that broadside from the *St. L.* it did not turn out quite so bad as that.

I received your letter before we left the Roads, & am glad that my affairs are going on so nicely. Wheather we succeed or not I want it understood that I foot the bills. I think it is a capital idea Uncle Hamiltons going to Washington. I am sure he will be able to accomplish the object if any one can. I only hope if successful I shall not be ordered to fill the vacancie on board here arising from Mr. Eldridge's absents it would not be very plesent to go from the steerage to the Ward Room as it would be apt to make hard feeling amongst my present messmates. However I am counting my chickens before they are hatched it will be time enough to think about that when I get my appointment.[51] I suppose May is with you now? I hoped I should be at home when she made her visit but it seems I am to be disapointed. I think I shall be home soon now tho.' We can not stay here long as we have very little coal & water. We are also short of ammunition which is difficult to obtain at Fort Monroe. We received a good deal of damage too in the late action, so that if ever a vessel needed overhauling we need it now. If you have not sent the books, do not—as now that we have changed our station I might never receive them. Give my love to all at home. Of course direct the same as before. Good by from your loving son

Henry

U.S. Steamer *Cambridge*
Off Beaufort NC
March 18th 1862

Dear Mother

This is the third time I have commenced a letter since Sunday, the day the *State of Georgia* started for the Roads. One of them I capsized a bottle of ink over, & the other which I wrote yesterday on the eve as I then thought of an engagement, I tore up just now, as under the present circumstances it would not be just the thing to send.

The *Nashville* has run the Blockade again & is now on the ocean raising the old Nick with our commerce I suppose.[52] I only wish it was the government & not the merchants that will have to suffer thereby. It is no more than what I expected when the *S of Georgia* left, for it is all folly to expect one steamer to blockade a vessel like her in a harbor like this especialy where the Blockading vessel can not steam more than one knot to the others two.

I suppose there will be an awful hue & cry made about it & that the *Cambridge* will get greatly abused for letting her get out. I hope those that sent her here will get at least a little of it.

Last night at about 7.30 we were setting in the steerage talking when all of a sudden down bolted the Doctor with his case of instruments under his arm (All ready to *carve* off some poor fellows arm or leg on our *mess table*) & asked us if we had not heard the call to quarters. You never saw a party broken up quicker in your life. every one grabbed his sword & revolver & made a rush for his station. My station is on the forecastle you know, a beautiful place to see what is going on by the way. It was dark as pitch on deck & we could see nothing, but the *Gemsbok* who was farther in, had just fired a rocket which was the signal agreed upon if the steamer was seen coming out. We had hardly got our guns cast loose before the *G* commenced firing us fast as posable. We stood in the direction where her shells were exploding & fired several times tho' we could see nothing[.] Soon after the moon rose but tho' it made it quite light we could see nothing & so after running out a little ways we concluded there was some mistake & stood back & spoke the *Gemsbok*. The Captain came on board here

& told Captain Parker that the *Nashville* had gone out. He said he was sure he had hit her twice. Even then we were all very doubtful as to her escape for we could not bring our selves to think that she could have got out so far but what we could have seen her after the moon rose.

However as if she was out it was no use to chase her in this *tub*, & if not, as she might come out before the night was over the Captain thought it best to anchor where we were & wait for morning to prove who was right.

At daylight there was many an anxious eye directed towards the harbor of Beaufort but no steamer was to be seen, so we were forced to believe that she had evaded us.

I dont think there was any one aboard here that ever expected to *take* her, but we did expect to *see* her & have a chance to send our *complements* & a few specimens of the Parrott projectile to show to their English friends when they report themselves as having run the Blockade.

Well I will not write any more on that subject it is bad enough to have to think about it.

We confidently expected as we were the only steamer on the station that she would show fight but I suppose they will find it pleasanter to prey upon Merchant vessels that to run the chance of getting hard knocks. So we have to bear our disapointment the best way we can. I have a few more little private opinions on this subject but I guess it is just as well not to write them. They will keep.

We had target practice to day with our eight in[ch] Parrott guns, but every body was so downhearted & disapointed in not having a chance to practice on the *Nashville* that it did not amount to much. The shooting was very poor & did not begin to come up with that which we made at Sewalls Point the other day, which was very fine & Capt. Parker was complimented on it by the Senior Officer Capt. Marston of the *Roanoke*.

We hope to be releived in a day or two & then to be sent North tho' that last is very doubtful I am sorry to say.

I am more & more anxious to get out of this vessel. I am very willing to fight for my country but I want to be led by a man that I have confidence in. to be in a vessel that wont take *quite* two miles to turn round in. I hope Uncle Hamilton will succeed in his mission.

Cape Henry has quite spoilt us aboard here in regard to letters[.] it is only little over a week since we left H Roads & yet we are all in a stew to get news from home. I dont think there is a vessel in the fleet where a mail-bag will be more welcome.

March 20th. The U.S. Gunboat *Chippewa* arrived here yesterday to help blockade the *Nashville* (48 hours behind time).[53] She brought us news of the result of the action between the *Monitor* & the *Merrimac* which you may be sure we were glad enough to here. She brought us no mail but I suppose she came off in a hurry the same as we did & did not have time. We expect the *State of Georgia* back tomorrow & she will bring it of course. We shall not be able to stay here much longer as we are short of every thing. but it is no matter as one steamer is enough to blockade this place *now*, with the barque to help her. I see the papers do not say much of the *Cambridge*. The *Monitor* has eclipsed every thing & deservedly too. The *C* did her duty tho' for all that & saved the *St. Lawrence*.

Give my love to all at home & write just as often as you used to when we were off Cape Henry & then I shall get a whole lot of letters when the mail does come.

Good by now from your loving son

Henry

U.S. Steamer *Cambridge*
Off Beaufort N.C.
March 23rd 1862

Dear Mother

The *State of Georgia* arrived here yesterday from the Roads and brought us about a bushel of mail amongst which I found three letters for myself. One of the 10th from Eliza, of the 13th from Louisa & yourself & another of the 17th from you, which I will answer now.

I always like to write home on Sundays, it seems the most appropriate day I feel nearer to you all when I am doing so.

I am getting quite home sick nowadays & shall be glad enough to see home again, tho' I am afraid that our last achievement of letting the *Nashville* escape will not improve our chance at all of being sent north, in fact I should not be at all surprised if we were kept on this station to pay us for it. but realy it does not seem fair to blame us for it was almost an impossability for one steamer to blockade such a vessel as her.

We have quite a fleet here now, (which is in accordance with the old addage of closing the stable door after the horse is stolen) *State of Georgia* 9 guns, (senior Officer com.[manding]) *Cambridge* 6 guns, *Chippewa* 4 guns & *Gemsbok* 6 guns. The first three are steamers you know. But we may need all our force after all for there is a heavy Confederate steamer expected on the coast every day said to mount 16 guns coming from Liverpool. I should not believe the report if it was not that it came from an official source, The Flag Officer having sent Capt. Parker a description of her. She is as likely to come here as any where & (if she is made of wood) I hope she will, but I would a little rather not fight any more iron clad ones unless I can be in something that will give at least a shadow of a chance of success.[54]

We shall not be able to stay here many days longer, in fact I think unless one of the other vessels supply us with water, we shall have to leave Wednesday, for we have got very little on hand. Our coal is getting pretty short too.

I am afraid that I shall not get my promotion, from what you said in your last letter. Well I am sorry but I guess I can survive it. As long as the war lasts of course I shall stay in the service, but after that if they arnt of a mind to promote me why I can go back to the merchant service again & not feel very bad about it either.

Perhaps however Uncle Hamilton may succeed. I have great confidence in him & believe that if the thing can be done he is the man to do it.

Evening. We are on our way to the Roads. What started us off in such a hurry I do not know but what ever it was, I am very glad for I hope (tho' I hardly dare to) that we shall be sent north.

Just before we left the Rebels set fire to a Portland Barque that was taken by one of their Privateers during the first part of the war & has been lying here ever since[.][55] She makes a fine fire. I can take more satisfaction in looking at her than I did at the burning of the *Congress*. I think Burnside must be coming for there have been large fires around this vicinity for two or three night[s] past. I wish we could be here when he attacked the place but I suppose there is not much chance of that.

Our Midshipman expects to leave when we get to the Roads, on account of his health. I am very glad on account of our mess & also (a little selfish you know) I shall probably have the 3rd Division under my command.

I wrote you a letter two or three days ago but I shall put this in an other envelope as that is as much in that as will go for one stamp, & then you know you will have two letters. Two is better than one any day!

I am *very* sorry that I could not have been at home when Mary was at our house[.] I expected to have been at [as] it was quite a disapointment to me.

I suppose you saw Joe often enough did you not? or has he give up his attedement?[56]

I should like to have seen Eliza's acting I should think she would look splendidly on the stage for you know (you need not read this out loud unless you want to) I think her very handsome off of it. I am very glad she was so successful.

I shall not write any more in this letter to night but will add a few lines more in the morning if I have any thing to say.

Give my love to all, at home. From your loving son

Henry

March 25th. We are in Hampton Roads. There is a strong fleet here & I think we can whip the Rebel fleet when they see fit to come down. Mr. Eldridge has rejoined. yours in haste

Henry.

US Steamer *Cambridge*
Hampton Roads
March 25th 1862

Dear Father

I received your letter with the enclosures this morning & as I was prepared by Mothers last letter not to expect much, I was not very badly disapointed at the result of the application on my account.

I have been thinking about it for some time & made up my mind that if not successful in this attempt to let the matter drop till we are sent north, as there the vessel will probably be put out of commission & then I shall stand a better chance at least I think so.

Flag Officer Goldsboro[ugh] is awful mad about the *Nashville* affair and Capt. Parker has had to take it hot and heavy. He told him (at least I heard so) that if there was any worse place than Beaufort on the coast he would send him there.

We are taking in provisions & stores for three months & will be off somewhere no one knows where as yet by Friday or Saturday I think. No North for us at present I feel confident.

I can not blame Com. G[oldsborough] altogether. There has been a great lack of energy in this quarter on several occasions & I cant say but what he has had cause enough to be down on us. Still he has no business to send us to sea in our present state. There is a rumor that there is to be a survey held. I only hope it is so as then we may have some chance.

We picked up two contrabands last night that came from Norfolk. They say the *Merrimac* (*Virginia*) will be down tomorrow. I dont care in fact I am rather glad. We have a strong fleet here now & with the assistance of the "Cheese box" I think we can settle her. They are fitting up the *Vanderbilt* to run her down. (if one sinks the other will too I think). I was on board of the *Monitor* to day. Such an animal! I dont wonder the *M*[*errimac*] could make so little impression on her. There is nothing to shoot at. I will not attempt to describe her as of course you know all about what she is, in fact I dont know but what you saw her when you was in New York.

It is getting late & I can not write any more to night. Give my love to all. Tell Grandpa that I am very greatful for his kindness in endevoring to get me my promotion. I feel just as much obliged as tho' he had succeeded. Please thank Uncle Hamilton for me too.

Well good good night from your loving son

Henry

It would be no kind of use to apply to the Commodore *now* for promotion even if I had the best of letters. he would not give it to me to spite Capt. Parker, his recommendation is I consider of no value at all just now.

26th. There is a survey to be held this afternoon. I will let you know the result as soon as I know it myself. We hear that Beaufort NC is taken.[57] how aggravating. We left the day it happened I believe.

Henry

US Steamer *Cambridge*
Hampton Roads
March 28 [1862]

Dear Mother

I received your letter of the 26th this morning.

We are very busy now & I have only time to write you a few lines just to keep you posted you know.

I think there is no chance of our coming home at present the survey having been indefinitely postponed. We are building up a barricade of sand bags in the wake of our Engine & I am in charge of one of the boats bringing them off & am writing this while they are discharging my last load.

It looks as tho' we were going where there was to be some fighting. Have we any accounts in the paper that you may see of the escape of the *Nashville*, we are all interested in that aboard here you know. Large bodies of troops are arriving here constantly.

The boat is ready

Henry
Love to all

U.S. Steamer *Cambridge*
Hampton Roads
March 29th 1862

Dear Mother,

We are going off to day, where, I dont know but I am inclined to think back to Beaufort N.C. tho' I may be mistaken. Of course I will let you know as soon as posable of my whereabouts, so keep on directing my letters as usual till I know of any change be needed.

We have been very busy since we arrived here & I have not been able to write much. Tell Lu that I have not forgoten her altogether & will answer her letter as soon as I can.

We may be sent up some of the rivers around here & if so we will try to make our mark. I hardly think however that the Flag Officer will favor us as much as that however he has no love for this ship.

I am expecting the mail off every minute as I hope to get a letter from home by it tho' I received one yesterd[a]y.

I see by the papers that Wendell Phillips was mobbed at Cincinnati.[58] It seems to me that he must have been crazy to have represented himself as a disunionist in any Northern city. he has no right to expect any sympathy from a people who are fighting for a Union which he says he wishes to see desolved.

I dont believe in slavery or in Phillips either I think both would be better out of the country.

What *have* the missionarys been doing down at Port Royal[?] I see the most absurd accounts of them in the New York papers. Is Mr. Hooper amongst them yet? Do write me all about it.

Joe sends me all the papers (Boston) he must mail me almost every day I get them so often. It is very thoughtful in him is it not?

Aint it a shame that I have missed Mary's visit? I am real provoked about it. I suppose she will be gone before you receive this.

The reason why we did not get any more credit in the papers for our work in the *Merrimac* affair was not because we did not do much but because we left so soon after & did *not* leave some one behind to blow for us to the reporters.

Give my love to all & keep on writing as usual to your loving son

Henry

US Steamer *Cambridge*
At Sea
April 1st 1862

Dear Mother

We are now on our way to Wilmington N.C. The Flag Officer has kept his word for it is the worst station on the coast[.] those who have been there say that Beaufort is not to be compared with it as there is no lee there at all & we shall get the full force of every gale that blows. I am fairly discouraged, they never will give us a chance to do any thing as long as we stay in commission & I dont suppose they will send us north till our engine breaks down & we have to be towed there. I wish I could get out of her but dont see how I can unless I resign & I dont want to do that while the war lasts if I can help it.

We called in at Beaufort this morning to give the vessels there their mails. The town has been taken but the Fort holds out yet so there will be some fighting there I suppose. it is just our luck to be done out of it.

I only got one or two letters while we were up at the Fort. & as those did not bring me very good news they did not improve my spirits much. I hope we shall get a mail down here soon.

There was a report that the mail was not allowed to leave the Fort while we were there. if that was the case it accounts I suppose for your not answering my letters, as you could not have received them. Midshipman Cushing left the ship while we were there & we were all glad enough to see him go as he has made trouble enough since he has been here.

Oh! Dear I never was so home sick after a years voyage as I am now. I wish we could take another prize so that I could be sent home in her but if we did I might not be the one choosen for that duty.

I shall be glad when the war is over so that I can go back into the Merchant service. Perhaps I can get command of a vessel then. & that is better by far than being under the thumb of about 15000 senior officers every one of which you have got to obey or run your chances of a Court Martial.

I wish we could have one good smashing fight[.] I think it would wake us all up on board of here & do us good. Idleness is becoming oppressive.

Well I dont know what you will think of this letter but it has released my mind considerable to write it.

I am not alone in my feelings most of the officers are as down hearted as I am. We came here in the hope of being able to serve our country but we find we are not allowed to do it. Our Captain is a nice man enough but in my opinion is not fit to command a man of war in these times he has got no energy & will take no responsability which is not forced upon him.

We never should have been in that affair in Hampton Roads if the Captain of the *St. Lawrence* had not ordered us to take his ship in tow.

I will not write any more now but wait till we get in our station. Love to all from

Henry

April 2 We are on our new station now. We burnt a sch. this morning. I have writen an account of that affair to Lu. I enclose you a piece of the 'Sesesh' flag found on board.

from your loving son

Henry

The bunting is some what scorched from the fire.

April 4th The *Fernandina* sails tomorrow I believe. Alls well nothing going on. Be sure & have plenty of letters to come back by the Barque. Love to all. Henry

What do you think of my stitching prowess?

U.S. Steamer *Cambridge*
Off Wilmington N.C.
April 2nd 1862

Dear Lu

You must excuse my delaying so long in answering your letter, but we have been so hurried lately that I hardly had time for any thing. I do not mean that I have been hard at *work* all the time, but there has been a great deal doing on[.] I have been worried in mind never that in body about a good many things.

We are now on our new station we arrived just in time to see a bit of fun which I will now tell you about.

The *Mount Vernon* (Steamer) & the Barque *Fernandina* are the vessels blockading here.[59] This morning early they saw a schooner trying to run the blockade. The *M.V.* [*Mount Vernon*] gave chase, & as we soon after hove in sight the Barque came out to see who we were.

When we got in we found the schr. had run ashore & the crew had left her. The *Mount Vernon* was making preparations to pull her off. as soon as we found out what they wanted we lowered one of our boats to carry our hawser to them to bend on to theirs as the *MV's* was not long enough alone to reach. Mr. *Wells* took charge of the boat. When I got there I found they had already got a small warp to the schr. & I was ordered to underrun it with one of the *F's* [*Fernandina's*] boats to help me & take the hawser to her which I did.

When I got on board I found her in charge of one of the Masters of the *M.V.* She was hard & fast ashore & the tide fast leaving her. her name was the *Kate* of Nassau N.P. [New Providence]. The crew had set her on fire before leaving her, but it had been put out before I arrived. She was loaded with salt & we found a *Sesesh* flag on board (badly burnt) (a piece of which I will enclose to you as a *trophy*.)

We hove overboard part of her cargo but the tide left her high & dry so of course we could not get her off. indeed she was hardly worth it as the fire had dammaged the vessel very much & the cargo would not be valuable if sent North. The Rebels too opened fire on us from the shore with muskets but their shot all fell short.

Under the circumstances it was thought best to destroy her so after turning over most of he[r] cargo to make sure there was nothing under the salt, we set her on fire in three places, & left her, tho' not till she was too hot to hold us.

I enjoyed the whole affair very much & we are all inclined to think our new station not so bad after all.

I have got several trophys from her, one thing a South Carolina button off a soldiers coat found on board.

The *Fernandina* leaves tomorrow or next day for Hampton Roads, besure & have plenty of letters there to come back by her.

I will not write any more now as it is getting late.

Love to all & write when ever you can find time to your loving brother

Henry.

U.S.S. *Cambridge*
Off Wilmington N.C.
April 6th 1862

Dear Mother

Tho' there is no immediate prospect of my being able to send off a letter, still I dont know what may happen & therefore like to have one on hand in case an opportunity should occur.

I wrote both to you & Lu by the Barque *Fernandina* (also to Joe) which I hope you will receive as I have given you an account in them of our burning a schr. down here. The *F*[*ernandina*] sailed on the evening of the 4th. at about 12:30 we heard two or three heavy guns out side & saw signal lights burning. The *Mount Vernon* signalised us to go out & see what the matter was. (we thought most likely the *F*[*ernandina*] had got aground or the shoals)

We ran about 12 or 15 miles & met the *Fernandina* standing back for the anchorage. We hailed him to find out what the matter was & found that they had had a mutiny on board, & wanted our surgeon as two or three were wounded on board. One of her officers came on board here & told us how it happened. It seems that a few of the men had got hold of some spirits & became very noisy. The Officer of the Deck sent one of the Masters Mates down below to have the noise stopped which he did, but they soon commenced worse than ever. The Captain came on deck to see what the matter was & he & the Officer of the Deck went forward together when one of the men kicked the Captain in the face cutting it badly. The C[aptain] ran for his sidearms & told the rest of the officers to arm them selves which they all did but one who refused but afterwards came on deck with them & with very little resistance allowed the men to disarm him.

One of the men wrenched the Captains sword away from him (he regained it however) & stabbed him in the thigh with a sheath knife, upon which the Captain shot him. after that the men gave in & several of them were put in irons.

The man who was shot is not dead but dangerously if not mortally wounded, the ball struck him in the lower part of the Abdomen & went right through him, but Dr. Richardson thinks he may recover. It will be just as well for him if he dont however for if he gets well he is sure to be hanged, I suppose. In war time such men have to be dealt severely with. I would not like to be in that officers shoes that refused to assist in quelling the mutiny. He is sure of being turned out of the service & he may think himself lucky if he get[s] off as easy as that.

We hope to see another vessel down here soon & I suppose we shall as the *Mount Vernon* can not be kept out much longer as he[r] boiler is defective. The *Fernandina* left yesterday.

Off New Inlet. April 11th. Last Monday the *USS Monticello* arrived off Wilmington, but we got no mail by her, at which we were very much disapointed. On Tuesday we came round here to New Inlet (one of the entrances to Wilmington to the Northd of Frying Pan Shoals). We are all alone here tho' the Sloop of War *Jamestown* ought to be here as it is her station but I suppose she is taking a cruise outside.

We have just been out side in chase of a schr. I was in hopes that it would be a prize & that I should have a chance to get home in her, but I was disapointed as she proved to be a vessel loaded with government stores for Port Royal.

Off New Inlet April 14th 1862. We had quite a disapointment this morning. At daylight we saw a steamer standing down towards us so we got under way &

stood out to meet her. She proved to be the *Rhode Island* (Despatch Boat) & hailed us telling us they had our mail & fresh provisions for us. So we sent off our boats in great haste thinking our selves very fortunate but our pleasure did not last long for when the boats returned they had fresh meat to be sure, but no mail it was a mistake. Too bad wasn't it?

I got a bad fall two or three days ago & hurt my back a good deal[.] I was rather nervous about it for a while but it is better now. I tripped on the combings of the hatch & fell down the steerage ladder striking on my hip & small of my back. I have been rubbing it with Arnica.[60]

If I get a chance to send this letter before we go up our selves I wish you would send my box to the Roads at *once*. We shall be there about the last of this month. I want some sort of a bed quilt, some (2 or 3 Pr.) white pant[s], white handkerchief[s] socks etc. also stock ties.

April 20th. – The USS *Victoria* arrived hear to day.[61] When we ran out to speak her they told us that they had our mail, but as before we were disapointed as they only had two or three official letters for the Captain.

The *Jamestown* is laying here at anchor now in company with us[.] The *V*[*ictoria*] has gone around the other side of the shoals.

We shall leave here tomorrow or next day for Hampton Roads I think as we have only about 40 tons of coal left, & we have lost one of our anchors with 40 fath[om]s of chain.

Captain P. expects to be sent up to Yorktown to assist in the attack on that place if the work is not done before we arrive which I hope it will not be.

A week ago yesterday the *Cambridge* Minstrels gave their first grand concert on the Gun Deck. Every thing went off first-rate. The Captain & other officers were among the audiance & all seemed to enjoy it very much. I think I have seen worse on the stage.

Two or three days ago we spoke a schooner from the West Indies. I boarded her to see that all was right & then finding she had some fruit I *confiscated* a considerable amount of Pine Apples, Oranges & Bananas. (Paid for them tho,' a mere song) We have had quite a feast off of them. I only wished I could send some home so that you might enjoy them also.

There was a schooner loaded with horses knocking about here for two or three day[s] becalmed & jamed here on the shoals bound to Port Royal so finely we took him in tow & carried him out side clear of the shoal & gave him a fair start.

April 22nd. – We are on our way to Hampton Roads now. I suppose we shall get in some time to-morrow when I hope we shall get a nice large mail. I am afraid tho' that it has been sent down to us & that we have missed it. it will be too agravating if it should turn out to be so.

I suppose it will not do now to send the box as it would not arrive until after we sail, if we are sent down the coast again so I will tell you what you do.

If you find we have gone south again, send the box at about the 20th of May. (to be kept till called for) to Fortress Monroe. I think that will be the best plan.

April 23rd. We are inside of Cape Henry now & almost up to the Roads. So I have not time to write any more[.] I will let you hear from me again soon. I enclose $20.00 which please hand over to Father on my a/c.

Good by now. love to all from your loving son

Henry

US Steamer *Cambridge*
Hampton Roads
April 24th 1862

Dear Mother

I sent off a letter yesterday so you will know by that that we have arrived at the Roads.

I believe there is now no doubt but that we shall go back to Wilmington again as soon as we get our coal etc. in.

I want you to be sure to send that box so that it will be here on or before the 20th of May as realy I need the things which I have sent for. In regard to the pants remember that I want *white* and no mixture. I have no clothes fit for warm weather now & from the taste we had last time, I know I shall feel the want of them. I have taken to wearring paper collars lately. Suppose you send me a hundred Garcats (Chokus). On a box that I have got here the kind I want are marked "No. 8 English B." I suppose you have made up your mind about the books before now so I will say nothing about them but let you send what you choose. (Send two or three Latin books if you think best).

I received five letters yesterday three from you one from Eliza & one from Cousin Sophy. also a host of papers from Joe (but no letter how was that Joe?) He is very attentive to my wants in that respect & I am very much obliged to him. I am sorry he is not satisfide with my letters but realy I *think* I write as good ones as he does. Sometimes he writes me a real good letter, he knows how when he has a mind to, but at others they aint hardly worth reading so I try in such cases to give as good as I take.

Please tell him I demand as & act of justice (to my much abused self) that he keep all the letters that I write him till I get home. I will do the same & then we will allow & impartial judge to decide between us, which has the most cause to growl at the other. Of course in such judgment I rule newspapers out for if they counted I should be "like the little boat—a long way astern."

I am very glad to hear that Edward Hooper is getting along so well in his good work & am also glad that I was mistaken in what I said about it. He ought it succeed!

You mentioned in one of your letters that Lu had writen to me. I have not received any letter from her for about two months, but I suppose she does not have much time now that she is going to school, so I dont feel at all hurt about it.

It is very strange that Uncle Lyman's letters should all miscarry how do you direct? I think it ought to be Lyman Wells—Act. Master—U.S. Sloop of War *Brooklyn* Gulf Blockading Squadron off (Where? I dont know)

I hope that I shall hear from home again before we leave but I suppose it is doubt full as I am afraid you will not know that I am here in time. Write by return of mail & I may get it. Keep writting all the time just the same as if I were here for our mails are *sometime* sent down to us & you would not like to have us have a mail & I not get a letter I am sure.

Good by now. I will answer E's letter soon. From your loving son

Henry
Love to all.

U.S.S. *Cambridge*
Hampton Roads
April 25th 1862

Dear Mother,

I wrote yesterday but I want you to hear from me as often as possable while we lay here so I will send you a few lines to day.

We are not getting along very fast with our coaling, however it is not much matter as the engine is out of order & it will be two or three days before they can repair it. I only wish I had known before that we should stay so long as you might have sent my trunk if I had been aware of the fact. As it is however, wait till the 20th as I said in my last. I have written home twice since we arrived, twice I sent $20. in each letter which I hope was duly received. I shall send some money in this letter also.

I sent a box to Lu yesterday (no, day before) if any thing is hurt in it, let every thing be & I will fix it when I get home.

The *Galena* (iron clad gunboat) arrived here yesterday towed by the Steamer *Baltic*[.][62] I have not been able to ascertain whether any thing was the matter with her own machinery or not that she required to be towed. she looks very formitable tho' no match for the *Monitor* or the *Merrimac* either in my opinion single handed, but of course she is a great addition to our force here. I have not seen Steven's battery yet.[63] I am very anxious to do so, as I have heard very interesting accounts about her. she is laying up towards Hampton & not in sight from our anchorage.

We do not anchor now where we used to. The Fleet are all anchored below the Fort so that if the *Merrimac* comes down she will have to run the gauntlet of the

Forts before she can get at the vessels. The iron clad boats are up above however.

I have just been on board the Flag Ship on duty. Confound that Commodore Goldsboro[ugh], he abused me like a Pickpocket. He wanted to know if we had got our water in? I told him no. "Why the D—l haven't you? Do you expect me to bring it to you? What are you doing? Have you done anything since you arrived?" "We are coaling, sir." "Can not you coal & water too? Get a waterboat alongside at once, sir, do you understand? I expect you will report the vessel ready for sea at once," etc, etc., etc. till finally I beat a retreat as fast as possible. Confound him, I wish I could tell him a piece of my mind!

Mr. Odiorne is in trouble again. He went ashore in charge of the mail yesterday & while he was up at the Office some of the Officers came down and shoved off in the boat with out waiting for him, so he was left ashore all night. It is strictly contrary to orders from the Flag Officer for any one to absent themselves from their vessel over night, & he is therefore suspended for it. I dont see how he could help himself & I think it very unjust, but the First Lieutenant dont like him & I am afraid he will be broke. It is too bad & I am very sorry for him. There is not much going on here in the Roads just now. I understand a vessel tried to run up to Norfolk this morning & was captured by one of the Tugs but I dont know how true it is. Good by Love to all from your loving son

Henry

U.S.S. *Cambridge*
Hampton Roads
April 26th 1862

Dear Mother

We are all bustle & hurry as the Commodore is determined to get us off to night. I dont think he will succeed tho.' Nobody cares now whether we go, stay, sink, or swim they find it is no use they only get abused for they'r pains when they try to hurry things along[.]

When we left Boston I dont suppose there was any vessel in the service that had a better or more willing set of officers than we, & now nobody cares as I said before to do anything more than just what comes in their way, so they have to. It is all the Flag Officers doings (d-m him) (leave that out if you like).

I am expecting every minute to be called upon for boat duty. I have been in the boats all the morning bringing off wood etc. in a rain storm & am wet through & of course feel very comfortable just now but it is no use to change my clothes when I shall have to go out in it again directly.

I have not received any letters since the first day we arrived at the Roads, the last was dated the 16th[.] why have not you written since?

I can not write any more now so good by. I dont know whether I shall be able to write again love to all. inclosed $10.00 which makes $60.00 which I have sent since our arrival here.

We are for Wilmington I believe. From your loving son, in great haste—

Henry

U.S.S. *Cambridge*
Hampton Roads
April 27th 1862

Dear Mother

We shall sail to day & I dont know wheather I shall be able to send this or not but will take my chance & write you a half a dozen lines.

I caught a bad cold yesterday but as we are going south (at least I am quite sure that we are) I shall soon throw it off I guess. I have written every day since we arrived, but have received no news from home since the first day. My last date is the 16th.

I have sent home $60.00 since we have been here & shall include $10 more in this.

Good by now give my love to all & write often.

One of our Petty Officers was discharged yesterday on account of his health. He is going to Boston & said he would go out to B[rookline] & see you. I gave him a few lines of introduction in great hast[e] while I was on shore yesterday. He is a nice old man, he was Nurse in the Surgeon's department on board here. He may not go out to B[rookline], so dont place too much reliance on it. I gave him the note because I knew you would be glad to see anyone that came from here.

Dont forget the trunk on the 20th of May

From your loving son
Henry

U.S.S. *Cambridge*
At Sea
April 29th 1862

Dear Mother

We are on our way back to the Roads our engine having broke down. The accident occurred night before last when we were off Cape Hatteras in a thick fog. It could not have happened in a worse place, but fortunately it was not so bad but what we could run at slow speed for a few hours. We could not stop to sound, as once stopped the Engine could not be started again. Perhaps you may not understand, but Father will comprehend at once, the pleasant position we were in, on the edge of Hatteras Shoals one of the worst places on the coast, in a thick fog with a disabled vessel.

Providentialy at about noon the fog lifted & we ran for Hatteras Inlet & anchored about 4 miles from the Forts which our Navy took last summer.

We then blew off all steam & the Engineers found a large hole in one of the steam pipes. They fixed it as well as they could & we are now on our way back to the Roads.

I suppose we shall *have* to go North somewhere now as they (the Engineers) say it can not be repaired on board the ship. Possably it may be fixed at the Roads, but they do not think it can. Baltimore will probably be our destination.

I received a letter from you the other day we left Roads, dated the 25th in which you said "you almost wished our Engine would break down," so now you have your wish, & I am glad of it as it has turned out.

Where ever we go I am in hopes I shall be able to get two or three weeks liberty. I shall try hard at all events.

In one of the papers that Joe sent me there was an extract from one of Mr. Clarks sermons on the state of the country which I was very much interested in, how I wish I could have heard the whole of it.

I did not receive any letter from Joe the last time I was up in the Roads. just scold him a little when you see him, from me, if you know how. I wrote him a letter in answer to the one I expected to get & sent it so you see I have *sold* my self.

Is it Mr. or Mrs. Wm Bellows that is so sick? You wrote the handle to the name so indistinctly that I can not make out. Do you know where Ned is now? he ought to be in the service.

I see by the papers that Mr. [Edgar] Van Slyck who was second mate of the *Ocean Telegraph* is an Act. Master on board the Gunboat *Port Royal*. He is a smart man.

I have written you so lately that I have not much more to say now so I will bid you good by[.] I will let you know as soon as I can what is to become of us. I hope soon to be able to kiss you all.

Good by Love to all from

Henry

Tell LaLa if I don't come home forthwith I will answer her nice long letter at the first oppurtunity. Dont have time to write any to speak of except to you when we are lying in the Roads. There is so much to do. Mr. Odiorne is released from suspension.

Baltimore
May 17th /62

Dear Father

We arrived here this morning & I am stopping for today at Barnums Hotel but shall get a boarding house as soon as possable as the *Cambridge* will [not] be ready for sea for four or five weeks, I think from the looks of things.[64]

They have got the propeller unshipped & are having the shaft taken out which envolves taring up a part of the deck. our steerage is in a state of wreck every thing in a heap.

I am sorry to say that I was robbed in New York of my pocket book containing about $10.00 in cash, my ticket & baggage checks. I recovered my baggage by proving it mine & borrowed $20.00 of Uncle Parkhurst. I have to buy another ticket & I am afraid I shall come short now as the Paymaster has not come back yet

Direct my letters to the *Cambridge*, Baltimore.

I can not write any more at present but will send home a good long letter as soon as I get astablished some where.

I wish you would send that money to Uncle P. as there is no prospect of my being able to for some time to come.

Good by now. Love to Mother & all the rest of the family from your loving son

Henry

Baltimore
May 21st 1862

Dear Mother

I have got nicely established here now in a private boarding house. Mr. Odiorne and I room together.

We do not have much to do when we reported[.] Mr. Miller said he wanted one of us Mates on board all the time but that we might arange it to suit our selves how we stood so we take each 24 hours on & 48 off.

I was on duty yesterday & Mr. O has to day. Tomorrow is M. Maies day, & O & I have an engagement with one of his (Odiornes) friends who is going to take us round to see the fortifications etc. etc. There is quite a party of Ladies & gentlemen going I understand. Odiorne has a good many relations & friends here, & I think we shall have a very pleasant time while we stay here, tho' I shall be glad enough to get off to sea again.

We shall probably be detained hear all of a month more tho' I hear that Capt. P. said we should get away in two weeks. He expressed himself very sorry that I had been sick but was very glad that I was able to have home care & attention.

Mr. Odiorne was in a little while ago & tells me that Mr. Miller is detached from the *Cambridge* & that another master has been ordered to her. In that case I suppose Mr. Eldridge will be our Executive Officer unless the new Master is his senior which I hope is not the case. I suppose a good many of the officers will be glad of the change but I dont know as I am particularly. Mr. Miller was always very kind to me & of course I had no fault to find. Mr. E is a nice man & takes a great deal of interest in the service but I am afraid he will not be strict enough with the men.

I dont think we shall ever get a man like Lieut. Gwin again.

We have a very pleasant boarding house. There are about 20 boarders here, half of whom are secession sympathizers, but I suppose that is the case in every respectable place in the city. They keep very quiet & dont trouble us with their opinions, nearly [all] the ladies are on that side.

When we first came here Mr. Odiorne asked Mrs. Peters if she required any references. She said she usualy did but would not of us as our appearance was sufficient, he gave her one or two nevertheless.

We have a fair view from our window the house being situated on a hill near the center of the city. We are only a short distance from Baumans Hotel & handy to every thing. The place was recommended to us by one of Mr. O. friends.

I wrote home day before yesterday. I hope the letter was received. If it was not ask Father if he will send Uncle Parkhurst $20.T as I had that amount from him when I was there as my money was all stolen. I think it was rather my fault as I was careless but it has taught me a lesson which I dont intend to forget.

I was rather amused at Uncles when I arrived at the door upon seeing [large ink blot] D. F. Wells on a door plate above that of [large ink blot] P.P. Wells. I will write again soon. Good by love to all, do write often. From your loving son

Henry

Baltimore
May 25th 1862

Dear Mother

I received your letter of the 21st day before yesterday.

Every thing is going on here about the same as when I last wrote, except that since Mr. Miller has left Mr. Very who is at present act. Ex[ecutive] officer keeps two of us Mates on board all day instead of one so our leisure is rather cut down and I dont think I shall be able to study much.[65]

I have not seen much of the new Master yet[.] He is quite young, belongs to the regular Navy & *has never been to sea a day* a valuable addition to our list of officers! besides as he is in the regular service of course he ranks all the other officers & so I suppose will be executive officer unless Capt. Parker will not allow it.

It is very pleasant any way to have such men stepping in over ones head all the time. It makes me indignant to think of it. I do not see any prospect of our getting away in less than four weeks tho' they may take a start & shove the work ahead in less time.

Last Thursday O[diorne] & I went up on top of the Washington Monument here & had a splendid view of the city surroundings.

We after words went to the water works & saw the reservoir etc.

I cant write any more now as I am going to church.

Afternoon—I went to the Catholic Cathedral this morning[.] I believe it is the first time I have ever heard a service in one of their churches since we lived in Boston. I remember going there once there with one of the girls, (Brebe I think).

The singing was very fine to day but as for the rest it did not seem much like religion to me, Except the address which was on the life & character of Pope Gregory VII. I could not understand a word of the service. & whether it was Latin or English I am sure I dont know.

I was disapointed in the building, it was not so fine as I expected from what I had heard tho' very handsome. I shall not go again there.

When I got back from church I sat down & read a little in my Hymm Book & then looked over my Photographs etc. of friends at home.

What a contrast there was, must have been between the service I heard this morning an[d] the one in Indiana PP. Oh dear I wish I could have been there.

Thursday night I went to a Union Concert, it was splendid, the Hall which holds over 5000 people, was crowded. As I was invited I had a seat on the stage close to the singers & enjoyed it very much. The audience was very enthusiastic & at some of the songs the cheering was tremendous. The Star Spangled Banner had to be repeated as also one or two others. I have marked those which seemed to take best in the programme which I send you.

I can not write more now as I have got to go down on board.

Good by love to all a[nd] write often to your loving son

Henry

I am as well as usual I think, at all events you need not feel anxious about me[.] I have had no return of feverishness.

Baltimore
May 27th 1862

Dear Mother

I dont think it is hardly fair. I have been here over a week & only heard from home once while this makes the fourth letter I have written.

I dont feel much like writing to day as I have a headach but as I was afraid you might feel anxious if I did not on account of the disturbances here, I though[t] I had [better] send you a few lines.

I have just been cutting a few pieces from one of the papers to give you some idea of what is going on hear.

I saw a part of the proceedings myself but tho' I think the men that suffered richly deserved it. Still I don't like to see a mob of two or three hundred men attacking one or two.

I saw them try to hang one man to a lamp post but the Police recovered him.

Several others got severely handled while I was in the crowd, but I did not stay long. I have too much respect for the uniform I wear if nothing else.[66]

Sunday eve I went up to Franklin Sq to see a Gentleman & while we were there (O[diorne] & I) were instrumental in saving two mens lives probably, who were attacked by half a dozen rowdies armed with revolvers. We interfered & as they knew Mr. Larabee (our friend) & saw by our uniforms we were union they let them go.

One of them staggered up to us with a Navy revolver in his hand & said "All he wanted was to see a live Rebel, he'd give his coat to get hold of one." A few minutes after they left us we heard them firing at some one. We started off to see if we could render any assistance but they had gone off in chase of some one & we did not see them again.

I found out afterwords that one of the men that we saved was Mr. L[arabee'] s brother but that on account of his being a secessionist they were not on speaking terms.

The Police were very active & did all they could to keep the peace. The city is quiet now, every other man one meets is a Policeman.

We have bad news from General Banks, & will have to withdraw some of his red pins.[67] I see the three months men have been called out again in Massachusetts do tell me if any one goes that I know.

Has Prescott Wellman gone with the 7th N.Y.S.M.?[68]

If I was Joe I'd volunteer now. its a good time perhaps his company will go.

What does Gov. Andrew mean or is it a mistake about that answer to the call for more troops? Surely the Old Bay State is not going to be backward[.]

I wish you would send me a Boston paper occasionaly they are hard to get here.

Mr. Maies is promoted to Act. Master, but I dont know where he will be ordered to yet. Our repairs are going on slowly.

I will not write any more now. good by give my love to all & write often (if only a line) to your loving son

Henry

Baltimore
May 30th 1862

Dear Mother

What is the matter? Why does not any body write to me? I dont know what to think wheather you are sick at home or what. I have only had one short letter since I arrived here & I dont like it a bit.

I wish you would try to write as often as twice a week, that is amongst you. Here I am hardly five hundred miles from home with mails running twice a day

& unless something is the matter that I dont know about I do think that I have been rather neglected. I might as well say it as feel it.

I wont write anymore now as I dont feel much like it or any thing else this eve. Do please try to let me hear from home a little oftener while we stay here if you only have time to write two or three lines.

Good by Mother love to all from your

Henry

Baltimore
June 1st 1862

Dear Mother

I received your letter yesterday just after I had sent off [a] rather hasty note about your not having written.

I am sorry now that I wrote it but I did feel rather hurt at not hearing from home for so long especialy as Mr. Odiorne was getting letters almost every day & it made me feel as tho' I was a little neglected. So I wrote what I did, but you'll excuse me wont you Mother? I dont very often get taken that way.

I am very glad to hear that Joe has volunteered even tho' he may not be sent to the seat of war. I think he will feel better satisfied with him self to be able to know, when this war becomes a matter of History that he at least offered his services to his country & it was not his fault that he was not allowed to go.

I wish they would send the 4th Battalion on to Baltimore. The 7th New York is here you know. I would try to see Mr. P. Wellman but do not know what company he is in or what rank he holds. I have enquired of several members of the Reg't at a venture but none of them knew any thing about him.

Baltimore is very quiet now after the excitement & riots of the first of last week, but no one can tell how soon they may break out again.

I wonder what news is in store for us tomorrow, of course there will be something Sunday is the famous battle day in this war.

I believe I told you in my last that Mr. Maies has been promoted to the rank of Act. Master, he is ordered to remain on board the *Cambridge*. I am rather sorry for it as I think it would be pleasenter for him & us both if he had been detached & ordered somewhere else. we have five masters now & no Lieutenant. I hope we shall get one tho' for if we dont we shall be badly off for an Executive officer for Mr. Eldridge is sick at home & there is some doubt wheather he will be able to rejoin before the ship sails & if he dont I think that either of the other masters would be worse than none.

I think it doubtful if Mr. Very goes to sea with us again tho' he is on board at present. & I understand the Doctor has resigned but I do not know whether that is true or not.

The *C[ambridge]* is on the Dry dock again & things look now as tho we might be at sea in less that two weeks. but there is no telling what may turn up to detain us. The *Gemsbok* is here repairing. I dont know but I told you of that before.

I am still living on shore but now that Mr. Maies is promoted I have to be on board most of the time. I dont have time to read or study much so I cant make you any report on French.

I attended the 2nd Unitarian Church this morning, it is some what similar to Mr. Clarke's. It is a free church, they have a service very much like ours & every body sings. They seem to have a very nice minister. I talked with him a little while before church. The communion is different from ours. After he had finished his sermon he came down from the Pulpit & stood behind the Table and made a few remarks on the occasion. Said that he thought the Lords table one to which we all ought to be admitted, & invited all to come forward who wished to join in the service. Those who wished to partake of the communion than got up & stood round the table in a semi circle & handed the bread & cup to all they then returned to their seats & he finished the service.

He does not make it so impressive as Mr. Clarke. but apart from our own church I like this one better than any other I have attended & shall go there the rest of the time we stay here. Well I guess I will not write any more at preasent as I believe I have told you every thing of interest. As my letters benefit the whole family I think my sisters might write with out wanting for a special correspondant.

Good by love to all from your

Henry

Baltimore
June 5th 1862

Dear Lou

I received your letter day before yesterday & will now answer it tho' I am afraid I shall not return you so long a one as I received.

We (that is Capt. Parker[)] has received orders to sail tomorrow but we can not do it so there is no use talking for even if the vessel was ready, which she is not, he (Capt. P.) is engaged on a Court Martial (trying the mutineers on board the U.S. Barque *Fernandina* [)]& of course can not leave till it is over which will not be for several days.[69]

Mr. Very one of our Masters is detached from the *Cambridge*. I do not know whether to be sorry or glad a little of the first I think tho' Mr. Odiorne is overjoyed as he & Mr. V did not get along very well to gether.

Our Doctor resigned but the Dep. refuse to accept of his resignation at present. One of the Engineers is also trying to get away. I hope he'll succeed. We have no Lieutenant yet but hope soon to get one tho' I am greatly afraid we shall not.

They have taken away our gun that was cracked & given us instead a Boat Howitzer which is not worth a d__readful sight[.] It is a brass gun. 24 Pr. We (O & I) shall move on board tomorrow as our steerage will be habitable by that time.

I dont care how soon we are at sea now as it is rather expe[n]ssive business staying here tho' I am having a very fair time.

One of the boarders here is Mr Houston Engineer in the Navy.[70] He was on board the *San Jacinto* at the Mason & Slidel affair, & boarded the *Trent* along with Lieut Fairfax. He was up here in our room the other night & gave us the whole account of it. Talking about their reception in Boston. At the meeting at Faneuil Hall the whole audience shook hands with the officers & he says his hand was so lame after it that he could not use it for three days.[71]

He staid at the Parker House while in B[oston] & when he went away the proprietor refused to receive any payment.

He speaks very highly of our old Gr. Mountain City.[72]

I should think it was rather a strange time for Mr Copeland to be at home when the Division to which he belongs is in need of every man. It is rather warm down there just now. What set you out against him so suddenly tho'? I thought you liked him? I am glad it is so however for so far as I am concerned I never want to see him again.

Well as I have arrived at the end of my paper I will close here. Good by. Love to all, & write often to your loving brother

Henry

Baltimore
June 7th 1862

Dear Mother

I received your letter yesterday & now I will answer it. I wrote to Lu day before yesterday.

We are under orders to sail tomorrow & O & I will move on board to night, I shall be glad enough to get away tho' I have had a very good time since we have been here, still I want to be down the coast again where there is something going on. We have no idea at present where we shall be sent tho' I myself, think we shall be sent to Wilmington N.C. I wish they would send us farther south, but there is not much chance.

I joined a Union League here last night & was initiated.[73] There are sertain signs by which members of the League know each other when ever they meet the same as the Masons do you know. I think it a very good thing in a city like this where there are so many secessionists. For if one of the members is attacked in the streets, by means of sertain signals he can raise a crowd of supporters in a very few minutes.

I find the Union sentiment here in B is much stronger than people north are generaly willing to allow.

The Troops are moving through here very fast now, several Regts left yesterday for Fortress Monroe & the 12th NYSM went on to Washington this morning. The 7th NYSM have taken charge of Fort Federal Hill & the 13th of McHenry.[74]

There are 500 wounded men expected here to day from McClellan's Army.

Great news from the West is it not! As to my not finding Prescott Wellman I do not think it strange as there are so many new men in the Regt. now & besides I dont think any of them would be apt to be very well acquainted out of their own company.

From your account I should think the Cadets were enjoying them selves hughly down at the Fort. I can't help being amused at the ideas of their being caught in such a scrape. I expect by this time that they are pretty well sick of playing soldier. How long are they going to stay there? 8 *months*?

What did Mr. Tilden leave Fitchburg for?

I do not know as I have got any thing more to write you about so I think I may as well close here.

I am afraid M. Eldridge will not be able to go to sea with us tho' he is here. He sertainly is not fit. The Doctor has succeeded at last in getting his discharge, & Mr. Very has also left us.

Good by now love to all & write often to your loving son

Henry

3

"If They Would Only Put Me on Board a *Man of War*"

Off Wilmington

Chesapeake Bay
June 10th 1862

Dear Mother

We left Baltimore yesterday bound I believe to Wilmington NC to shell out those Forts. There is quite a large fleet going there I believe. I have not been well at all for the last few day[s] tho I have not been obliged to lay up yet.

Our new Master does not stand watch & Mr. Eldridge left us the day we sailed, so there are only three of us including Mr. Odiorne to stand. I am glad they have made O[diorne] a watch officer. We are very short of officer[s] now & of men too, & twenty of what we have got are new recruits & as green as grass the most of them.

I have got sole charge of the Parrott Gun now & I shall take great interest in drilling my men so that they will not be second to any on board the ship.

I shall not write any more now as it is getting late & it is my middle watch. You need not feel anxious about me. I shall soon be well.

Good by love to all from your loving son

Henry

U.S.S. *Cambridge*
June 14th 1862
Off New Inlet, Wilmington, N.C.

Dear Mother

I have just come off [my watch] & have just a few minutes before the mail closes to write you a line.

There are six steamers off here now & three more round the other side of the shoals. We expect Com. Goldsboro[ugh] down in a few days with more force & then we shall attack the enemies works. We have great hopes of success.

I wish the *Cambridge* had her old crew & officers on board. Our new men are the poorest set take them all together that I ever saw put on board of a ship.

so ignorant, lazy, thickheaded good for nothing that it is enough to drive a man crazy to have any thing to do with them. And we are so short of officers too. Only three to stand watch & two of them masters mates!

I dont like Mr. Strong for Executive either. I dont think him well fitted for the position.

Mr. Maies has changed greatly since he has been promoted & I think a little inclined to give the cold shoulder. I wonder if I should be so to a man that I had been so friendly to, if placed in the same position? I might but it does not seem to me as tho I should.

I have been quite sick ever since we left Baltimore tho' I have not laid up. The Doctor said I ought to but I told him I would not as long as I could stand on account of there being so few of us. So I kept on & did the best I could. I am a little better to day. You thought I looked poor when I was at home but I wish you could see me now (indeed I do)[.] My cheeks stick right in & show where the bones are located very planely.

I hope I shall be all right before the attack is made on the Forts but sick or well, if I can stand I am going to have a finger in the pie. You know I have charge of the Parrott gun now & I want the Rebels to hear her *speak*.

They have the Red Flag flying on shore[.] I wonder if they dare fight under it. (It means no quarter you know.)

We shall coal at Beaufort N.C. now & there is no telling when we shall come north of that.

I hardly know how you ought to direct to me. Either to B-[Beaufort] or care of Flag Officer. I think you had better try both.

Good by now. love to all. I am getting better so you need not be anxious. Scatter your letters so I shall be sure to hear from some quarter.

Good by again from your ever loving son

Henry

(I hope my next letter will not be dated "off" but "at" Wilmington NC)

Henry

USS *Cambridge*
Off Wilmington, N.C.
June 23rd /62

Dear Mother

The *State of Georgia* sails tomorrow for Beaufort NC & for Hampton Roads so I will write you a few lines to go by her.

We left New Inlet Thursday & came round here to be preasent at a Court of Inquiry on the escape of the *Nashville* from Beaufort. They finished to day & we leave to night for New Inlet again. There are eight steamers here to blockade both sides which is quite an effective force.

I am a great deal better than when I wrote last tho' not quite well yet. You must ask Joe to excuse my not having writen to him but I have not felt much energy to do any thing. I dont have a great deal of time now either as there are only three of us to stand watch.

Mr. Maies has changed very much since he has obtained his promotion. I hardly speak to him now.

He should not let his dignity run away with him too much tho' for Act.g [acting] appointments dont last for ever, & when the war is over he may have to come down a peg.

I hope we shall make an attack on this place in the course of the week but we know nothing sertain. I think we can drive them out with out much trouble tho' I may be mistaken.

Mr Odiorne & I dined with the Captain yesterday. If it had not been that I did not want to show the Capt. disrespect I would have refused the invitation, as we have been on board the ship about 10 months & this is the first time he has ever invited us. We went however & had a very nice dinner, five courses & then coffee and cigars. I suppose on account of our being young men, he did not have wine so we contented our selves with ale & claret, which I have no doubt was a great deal better for us.

Captain P[arker] is very pleasant at his table & made us feel perfectly free & easy so that we had a very pleasant time.

I like our new Doctor very much & have more confidence in him than I had in Doctor R. His name is Ezra Pray a New Hampshire man.

I have not studied any as yet but shall commence soon. in fact I intended to have done so today but I had to attend the court this morning & was on watch in the afternoon so I have had no time. Odiorne & I are going to study French together.

Supper is ready so I can not write any more now. Address my letters to Beaufort N.C.

Good by, love to all & write often (because I shall only get about one letter in three I suppose)

To your loving son

Henry

U.S.S. *Cambridge*
Off New Inlet
June [27] 1862

Dear Mother

We have had quite an exciting time here this morning tho' we have not done much yet I am sorry to say.

This morning at daylight we saw a steamer close in shore heading towards New Inlet. We at once started (we were under way at the time) to try & cut her off, followed by the *Stars & Stripes* our consort, & we succeeded in doing it but we could not prevent them from running the vessel ashore which they did right under the guns of the Fort.[1] Both vessels opened fire on her & we saw her crew leaving at quick time. After a while the Fort opened & after throwing one or two shot at us they fired several at the steamer (to make sure of our not getting her afloat I suppose.) We keep up our fire till 7 o'clock & then knocked off to rest the men & let them get breakfast.

At 9 we turned too again & stood closer in. we did not fire many rounds before the Fort opened again & this time threw shell all around us tho' luckily none took effect but it got rather hot quarters and we "Got out of that Wilderness" quicker than we went in. As all our firing then, had to be at very long range the damage done was not very extensive & not at all satisfactory. I dont think she was struck alltogether more than six or eight times tho' a great many in fact nearly all came very near. I fired 42 rounds from my gun.

At a little after 10 AM we hauled off again & what we are going to do now I do not know. *I* think & not alone, that we ought to send round to the other side for some Gunboats, there are four there & two of them have 11 in[ch] guns which are just what we want. We may try to cut her out & burn her to night, there is not an officer or I think a man on board who would not gladly volunteer, if Captain Parker would only give the word, but I am afraid he wont. You know what I have always said every body seems to feel it now more than ever. I wish I was in some other vessel.

I received very unexpectedly four letters & two papers from home three days a-go via Fortress Monroe & the Gov'[ment] Despatch boat *Massachusetts*.[2] You may be sure I was glad enough to get them & will answer Eliza's & Lu's soon.

I think I would not give up the old direction altogether, but send a letter that way now & then, I would *not* direct to the Commodore.

We shall start for Beaufort N.C. in a few days after coal[.] I hope I shall find letters there but hardly expect it yet as I think you have had hardly time enough.

By your letter of the 16th I judge you did not receive the letter I sent on shore by the Pilot when he left us off Cape Henry. I am sorry you did not receive it tho' it did not amount to much.

July 2nd We leave this evening for Beaufort N.C. for coal so I must close this letter.

Yesterday the USS *Chippewa* came down from there. She brought a few letters for us & among them I found one from you dated the 23rd. I was surpprised for I did not expect to hear so soon from that direction.

When we first came down here I thought we should not get letters very often but I do not see but what we are doing very well. Beaufort will be a good direction for any letters tho' I would not give up Fort Monroe altogether.

We have not done any thing to that Rebel steamer since the day we chased her ashore & we have had the mortification of seeing them land her cargo on the beach. I suppose they will save the greater part of it tho' the vessel will be a total loss. I dont know what to say or think about it. We wanted to cut her out but Captain P thought the risk too great & perhaps he was right. The Captain of the *Stars & Stripes* volunteered to go himself but as Capt. P is senior officer he could not allow it. I volunteered to go for we have been so unlucky all along that it seemed a shame to let the vessel slip through our fingers. I would have been willing to have run any risk for the sake of destroying her.

Well as I have got two or three other letters to write I guess I will stop here. I am most well now. Good by love to all from your loving son

Henry

I enclose that article (letter) of Chas. Summner as you requested.[3] I think it very good indeed. Has Lou gone yet I will try & write to her before we leave Beaufort. I shall write to Joe also. Please tell him he will find the letter in the Brookline Post Office as I do not know how else to direct.

We are having very warm weather here & I find white clothes quite an institution.

USS *Cambridge*
Beaufort N.C.
July 4th 1862

Dear Mother

As this is my birth day I feel as tho' I could not let the day pass without writing home. I dont think I should be able to bring my mind to write to any one else except to you, for without being exactly sick I feel decidedly used up & as soon as my watches are up, want to go & lay down & keep quiet till my turn comes round again.

It is too bad I can not be at home with you on my birth day this year, only think I *am* a *man* now! I have not found that it makes much difference in ones feelings tho' as yet.

I hope you are having a plesant day in Boston, it is cloudy & blustering here.

Yesterday after noon the Guns from Ft. Macon announced to us some great news they fired one hundred [shots] (no they did not, it was 93) & soon afterwards we heard that *Richmond was taken*? What glorious news. None the worse because we have been expecting it for so long. We can not get any of the particulars for there is no *regular* Post Office here or any thing else for that matter that I can find out. I would give a good deal for a New York or Boston paper today.

We arrived here yesterday morning. It did look good to see the old Fort which we have watched so many tedious hours, with the glorious Stars & Stripes floating over it. I felt a decided inclination to cheer when we passed it. The harbor presents a very different aspect now from what it did when we were blockading it. Then there were only two or three vessels laying here & now there are 40 or 50.

I have not been on shore yet. I me[a]nt to have gone to day but did not feel hardly able. It is not much of a place, nothing more than a good sized village, but I am very anxious to see the Fort, which was so receintly bombarded & also the field works which our troops constructed before the attack.

We have been coaling ship all day to day much to my own private disgust for I think a Man of War of all things should keep National Holidays. We have not even fired a salute. The U.S.S. *Bibb* & a Revenue Cutter laying here both saluted together with the Fort at noon.[4] Soon after the firing the Captain of the *Bibb* came on board in great haste for our Doctor (he had none, for some reason or other) having blown a man's arms off firing one of his guns. The Doctor has not returned yet so I have not been able to learn the particulars as yet.

I wish the next time you write you would send me a lot of postage stamps. They are not civilised here sufficiently yet to have such things & I dont like to have my letters franked. Send at least a Dollar worth. Do send me plenty of papers too for they have none here. The Weekly Editions would be the best would they not?

Yesterday evening I received a letter from you, dated 23rd & directed to Fort Monroe, how it got here I do not know & now that I have receved it I do not know as it makes much difference[.]

I am glad Louisa is going to the White Mountains. I hope she will have a real good time. She will have plenty of exercise there I should think. I suppose E has gone before this. I realy feel ashamed at not having answered Lu's letter yet but realy I have not felt much like writing. I wish Cousin Lu Greely would write to me. I suppose I ought to write first. I will soon.

I hope Mr. Knapp is not dangerously sick? I did not know before that he had gone to the Peninsula.

Who on earth has been fool enough to marry Dan Wells? Of course no one that we know. I did not think that he had agr[e]eable qualities enough to please any one.

Well I think I will not write any more now.

Good by, love to all (that includes Cousin Lu you know & as she is one of the family I shall not feel bound to name names every time) from your loving son

Henry

U.S.S. *Cambridge*
Off New Inlet
July 12th 1862

Dear Lu

I feel ashamed of myself for having made you wait so long for an answer to your letter. I know you will excuse me tho' for I have not been very well for some time past and have not felt equal to doing any thing more than just what was absolutely necessary. I even gave up smoking for a while & you know I must have been pretty hard pressed when I would do that. I dispose of a double allowance of cigars now to make up for lost time.

I do not have so much leasure as I used to, as there are only three of us to stand watch & what with that, & drilling our Divisions, we do not have much more time than what we require for meals & sleeping.

I have charge of the 2nd Division now. Yesterday Capt. Parker came forward while I was drilling my men & after watching them a while he said, "They are doing *very well Sir very well indeed.*" I feel very much flattered for he does not very often say what he thinks. But my Division sertainly is (tho' I say it) the best drilled in the ship, & all hands acknowledge it too. The men seem to like me & try to do the best they can. So that tho' two of my men have been on the Sick list almost ever since we left Baltimore.[5] My gun is worked quicker & better than any in the ship.

Mr. Maies Commands the 1st Div. but he is very unpopular with the men & they will not try to please him. He very seldom exercises them with out having one or two punished.

Since he received his Masters appointment he has been very overbearing, & is not the same man at all, that he was before.

On Fourth of July (we were at Beaufort N.C.) we heard that McClellan had taken Richmond, but just as we were leaving B[eaufort] a report came contradicting it & stating that he had been defeated with a loss of 10000 men. We have not had any news since so you may judge in what a state of suspense we are in. I would give almost any price for a newspaper now of late date.[6]

There are two vessels here with us now, the *Monticello* & *Stars & Stripes*.[7] Yesterday we were all laying quietly at our usual anchorage, Fishing, when all of a sudden we saw a puff of smoke on the fort & whiz came a shot right over the *M[onticello]* and struck in the water about half a mile beyond. We were astonished I can tell you, for we had no idea that they had guns that would reach any where near us, & if any body ever saw three anchors come up quicker than ours did I would like to see that man.

We fired two shots from our Parrott gun but they both fell short.

We have a cannon duel here almost every day between the *Monticello* & the Fort, for Lieut. Braine who commands that vessel is never satisfied unless he is under fire.[8] He is [Commanding] Officer & I wish I was with him.

In your last letter you asked me who & what a Lieut. of Marines was. His rank is the same as a Lieut. of shore soldiers & he messes in the Ward Room. I am sorry I should have to decide against you. but so it is.

I suppose you are up at the White Mountains before this. I hope you will have a splendid time. You must write & tell me all about what you are doing.

Love to all at home. If you are with Uncle H. remember me to him also, in fact consider yourself supplied with several, loves, regards, etc. to distribute around to any of my friends that you may meet. Good by from your loving brother

Henry

U.S.S. *Cambridge*
Off New Inlet
July 13th 1862

Dear Mother

To day is Sunday so I am going to write you a letter for I always feel nearer home on this day than on any other.

We are having very hot weather down here & it is almost impossable to find a place cool enough to set down[.] I am in a very comfortable place just now however, right under a wind sail, (if you do not know what that is I guess Father can tell you.) so that I get all the air that is moving.

We boarded a schooner yesterday & got a paper of the 7th of July so we have heard a little of the news, & bad enough it is. look at it in any way you please.

We heard a rumor just as we were leaving Beaufort N.C. that 'McC'[lellan] had been defeated & that the news we had received the day before was false, but we knew nothing sertain till yesterday. What effect has it had North? I hope there is no desponding & that there will not be any trouble in raising the fresh troops that are called for. Joe will have a chance to go now I expect if he realy wants to, & I have no doubt he does. Will the Cadets go?

I do not see any mention made of the 1st Mass. in the paper that we got. I hope Dr. Wild has been spared.

We expect to get a mail in a day or two by the *Penobscot* & then I shall get the particulars I suppose.[9]

We have a cannon duel here almost every day now the *Monticello* is stationed round on this side. Her Captain believes in following out to the very letter the Article[s] of War that enjoins every commanding officer to annoy the enemy all that lays in his power. So he goes poking round every now & then throwing shell into the fort or some of the batteries giving them no peace & braving their fire with perfect indifference. I wish with all my heart that our Captain had half of his energy[.] we are not worth our salt so far as troubling the Rebels are concerned except so far as simply preventing vessels from running in & out. We take fine care to keep out of range of the Fort. Ah! Well. I hope before the war is over I shall be able to get into some other boat.

I am a good deal better than I was the last time I wrote & hope soon to be all right you need not feel the least uneasiness about me.

I have not received that letter from Mr. Clarke yet that he was going to write me. I suppose he has forgotten it. I dont know but it seems he might tho' for I remember now that I promised some time ago to write to Cousin Annie G. which I have not done as yet.

Now Cousin Lu nead not get out her pen to scold me in a letter, for I shall at once retire behind my ill health which I am sure ought to protect me from an attack on that score.

Mr. Odiorne wants the desk to write up the ships Log on so I shall have to close now tho' perhaps I will add a postscript by & by. Good by love to all from your loving son

Henry

U.S.S. *Cambridge*
Off New Inlet
July 18th 1862

Dear Mother

I received your letter of the 30th June last Sunday night by the *Penobscot* & will now answer it as I expect another vessel will leave for Beaufort tomorrow or next day. It is aranged now so as to have one gunboat in B. all the time as an additional safeguard. So each of the vessels take turns of going up & stopping a week, during which time they fill up with coal, stores etc. The *Stars & Stripes* is there now. She ought to be back Monday, when we shall get a mail. The *Mystic* I believe is going up to take her place[.][10] I think we shall have to go up next tho' it is not our regular turn as we are getting short of coal, again. We burn more than any other vessel on the station as we keep under way almost the whole time.

I am getting more & more disgusted every day with the way thing[s] go on board here & would give almost any thing if I could get ordered to another vessel.

Mr. Strong our Executive Officer is a miserable affair who thinks he knows a great deal & makes a big fool of himself at times, he is not liked at all & those who were the most glad when Lieut. Miller left the ship, would gladly see him back now.

We are full as much like a merchant ship now as a Man of War. Both are very good things in their place. But as Old Aunt Dinah said in Uncle Toms Cabin "I'd like to be (in) one thing or turrer".

We have a new Masters Mate now, his name is Durgin, he was Yeoman & Capt. Parker has got him promoted.[11] He is a very good man & I am glad that he has got the position but I should have much preferred that he should have been ordered to another ship. I think this promoting a man & keeping him on board the same ship is a very poor practice. unpleasant all round.

I hope in Mercy if I am ever promoted (which I begin to despair of), that I shall be transferred—any where. I would almost as leef go on board of one of the old hulks that they have up a[t] Hampton Roads for store ships.[12]

There has not been any thing doing since the last time that I wrote & we are all as dull as you please. We have had very hot weather till yesterday morning when it commenced raining & has kept on ever since[.] It is about as bad tho' a[s] having it hot for the hatches are all on which makes our steerage like an oven, now that we have got no ventilators. As I write it seems as tho I could hardly breath it is so close.

I am almost well now so you need not give yourself a moments uneasyness about me. If it was not so hot down here I would write to Cousin Lu but give my love to her & tell her I dont think I could get through another letter without fainting which would be very annoying as there is nobody handy to bring me too in good shape besides they would just as likely as not pour a whole bucket of water over one. (I know I would if I caught any body doing such a thing as faint on board ship)

Well I wont write any more now as I have arrived at the end of my paper. I think if Joe has so much leasure he might write to me. I have not heard from him since I left home. I suppose E[liza] & Lu are up at the mountains before this. Give my love to all & write as often as you feel able to your ever loving son

Henry

I hope the Postage Stamps are on their way.

I am very sorry to hear that Dr Wild has been wounded[.] I hope he was not made Prisoner during the Retreat?

I think it is a real shame about that engagement of Miss Wellmans being broking off & poor David off in California away from all his friends. After all he has gone though I am afraid it will discourage him altogether.

U.S.S. *Cambridge*
Off New Inlet
July 23rd 1862

Dear Mother

The word has just been passed through the ship that there will be a chance to send letters tonight. & I have just time to scratch off a few lines to you before going on watch[.] We did not expect any vessel would go before Sunday or I should have had a letter ready.

Last Sunday the *Stars & Stripes* came down from Beaufort & brought us a mail. I received four letters two from you (4th & 10th of July) one from Lu areal nice one, & one from Joe.

I feel ashamed of even having complained of not hearing from home[.]

I shall answer Lu's letter very soon. did you read it? I think it the best letter she ever wrote me.

There has not been any thing going on here since I wrote.

They say on board the *Penobscot* that a schooner ran the blockade last night.

I dont believe it, but if it is so it serves us right for yesterday we chased a schr (which was acting very suspiciously) off shore for 30 miles & just as we were with in two miles of her (near enough to have brought her too with our bow gun) we turned round & gave up the chase.

Oh Dear I wish I could honorably get out of this miserable, inefficient, vessel[.] I would be willing to serve the Government three months for nothing if they would only put me on board a *Man of War*. I have lost all interest here & all respect for most of my superiors. I expect I shall have a row with Mr. Maies before long. I long to hive [give] him a strong piece of my mind.

I am sorry you do not receive my letters regularly. They start from here once a week.

I am sorry you think they will have to draft troops in the North, it is a great pity. Well they will not have to force any of *our* family to serve

I am sorry Joe seems inclined to *back out*. I hoped he would feel differently about it. In such times as these I do not see how any young man of spirit can be satisfied to stay at home & *read the papers* when men are wanted [to] defend his country against traitors especialy when drafting is talked of.

Do keep me posted as regards foreign affairs as we seldom see the papers here. Is there any chance of intervention? What does Father think?

I hope soon to hear from Eliza. but I suppose she will be having such a grand time that she will hardly know when to find a spare moment to write.

I must not write any more now as I am keeping others waiting.

Good by love to all from your loving son

Henry

I hope my stamps are under way. it is very inconvenient to be with out them.

Marginalia on page 3—

What a lot of sorrys.

I have made a mistake. See next page

U.S.S. *Cambridge*
Off New Inlet
July 24th 1862

Dear Sister

I received your nice long letter last Sunday & was very glad to hear from you.

I fully agree with you in being sorry that I could not have been at home on the 4th[.] it is a very forlorn feeling to be away from one's home on a birth-day at any time & I dont know as I felt any worse this time than I did when I was 20 or 18 years old.

It may be a great satisfaction to some to be of age & *free*, but for my part as I have always since I was old enough been my own Master. I have none of that feeling & always want to be the same at home as I have been, Fathers Mothers *Boy*. (*also Brother*).

I felt almost like crying when I read your letter, to think how I used to tease & torment you in *old times*. I wonder now, that you did not learn to hate in stead of loving me & I am sure if you had I should have had no one to blame but myself for it.

Well well there is no use in crying over what is gone & past. But I wont do so any more "not if I know myself, & I think I do."

I hope you are having a splendid time up at the mountains. The base idea of there being snow there is enough to drive me crazy down here in this suffocating atmosphere. I would not mind it so much if it was a clean pure heat, but it is [a] sort of damp & sticky kind of heat which is very unpleasent.

I wish I was with you but as I could not give up my duty to pleasure & as one can not be in two places at the same time, it is foolish for me to do so.

I am sorry you should have all been so anxious at home about me perhaps I exagerated my sickness in my letters, tho' I hardly think I did. I was not obliged to give up my watch tho' for about a week it was as much as ever that I could stand it. I am nicely now, tho' this hot weather makes one feel miserable all the time.

I hope you are mistaken about Joe. I hardly think he would back out after having once volunteered. I should be very sorry to believe him so wanting in spirit.

Since I wrote you last we have got a new mess mate, his name is Durgin & he was formerly Yeoman of this ship. (The Yeoman takes charge of all the ships stores, that are not in the Paymasters Dept. i.e. Gunners Carpenters, Masters etc.). Capt. Parker recommended him to the Dept. he is a very good man & we get along first-rate. Still I would rather he would have been ordered to some other ship, as it is apt to make trouble, taking a man from forward & making a officer over the heads of his former associates.

We have been as quite & stupid here as you please for the last week or so, in fact we (the C) have not seen any fun since the Steamer tried to run the blockade. & that want much as we only made fools of our selves there.

I realy think it would seem good to be shot at again in a sociable kind of way.

Well my dinner is ready so I must leave off now.

Give my love to Uncle H. & Aunt Louisa. Write when ever you have time.

From your loving brother

Henry.

U.S.S. *Cambridge*
Off New Inlet
July 27th 1862

Dear Mother

I can not let Sunday pass with out writing a few lines to you. I should feel as tho' the day was not well spent if you did not have part of it.

We are having very hot weather here, tho occasionally the Clouds gather & we have torrents of rain for a few hours which cools the air for a time. It is too hot to do any thing & I should not like to have you ask me how I am getting on with my French etc. I am about well now & I do *mean* to begin & study. At present my principal employment is standing watch & smoking of which latter I do a large amount.

Every thing is very quiet here now, the *Monticello* is at Beaufort coaling so we have no *big gun* duels to pass away the time[.] Capt. Braine seems to be the only man here on the station that has any ambition to do any thing but he has enough for two. (*bigoted*) I wish we had a man of his stamp here as——First Lieutenant, of course.

I had a bit of a blow up with Mr. Strong yesterday. He was *Tightudly Slight* [slightly tight] & used language in speaking to me that I would not put up with. So I reported him to the Captain who made him apologize & take back all he had said. He has been a[s] good as pie ever since. I hope we shall get another man before long tho' if we can not get a regular Naval officer, I dont care much.

The *Monticello* will be down tomorrow or next day I think & then I hope to hear from home again. I did not get a letter from you by the *Mystic* but I got one from Cousin Louisa so that I was not with out a letter from home[.] I also received one from Eliza. My letters come very regularly now, I guess I get all that are written. I hope you get all mine?

I sent for some letter stamps while I was in Beaufort as we could not get any there or in Newbern. I suppose they are on the way before this, in fact I expect to get them by the *M*[*ount Vernon*].

We spoke the USS *Victoria* this morning, from the other side of the shoals, going to Beaufort for repairs, having broke down.[13] I happened to have a letter ready written to Lu which I put on board of her. I directed it to Father so that you could read it at home, as I had not time to write any more.

We shall go to B[eaufort] some time this week I think. I mean to see something of the place this time. Well I have arrived at the end of my paper, & as I have nothing more to say will now bid you good night[.] Love to all from your loving son,

Henry

I have written to Cousin Lu-

I have written to Joe & directed to Brookline please tell him. This goes by the *Mt. Vernon*. July 31st all well

Henry

U.S.S. *Cambridge*
Off Old Topsail Inlet
Aug 3rd 1862

Dear Mother

It is sunday & I again take up my pen to write you a few lines.

We are on our way to Beaufort N.C. again for coal & are almost there as you see by my heading. We expected to have started about a week ago but the Commanding officer on the station would not let us. he said we had burnt our coal in a very useless manner & we had got to stay a reasonable time coal or no coal. He was about right for we have been underway every day almost, whether there was any thing in sight or not. He gave Capt. P.[arker] (through another officer) a regular blowing up & ordered him to lay at anchor till one of the other vessels that were coaling came down to relieve him. It was rather rough especialy doing it in so public a manner, & sending an officer junior to Captain P. to give the orders instead of giving them in person.

There have been two prizes taken on the station since I wrote last on[e] a brig was taken on the other side of the shoals, so I did not see her, & the other on our side, a little sloop of about 60 tons from Nassau bound to Baltimore? & Captured by the *Penobscot* trying to run in to Masonborough Inlet.[14] Her name was the *Lizzie*.[15] The Captain said she ran out from here about a month ago, & did not attempt to deny that he was trying to get back. She was loaded principaly with salt but had blankets & one or two large cases of Farina on board & some other things. The Captains on the station held a consultation & concluded she was not worth sending north, so made up their minds to destroy her[.] We took out the Blankets & a few other things worth saving however we are taking her crew up to Beaufort.

The *State of Georgia* came down this morning from Fortress Monroe & by her I received a letter from you dated 18th (postmarked 21st) & a paper of 17th. You see I was right about ocassionaly sending a letter to the Fort, it is so pleesent to receive something by every conveyance. I sertainly have no cause to complain about my letters now for I get them very regularly. I am sorry you do not have the same success in getting mine.

Father was mistaken about Lieut McCook of the *Stars & Stripes*. He is a regular officer but rather a young one, he was with Burnside's expedition & promoted for gallentry.

I have been very nearly a year in the service now. It hardly seems so long.

I think I shall apply to Capt P soon for the vacancy as master that exists on board this ship, not that I would not give all my old shoes to get out of her, but I may as well make the best of a bad job & better my self *if I can*[.][16] I would like to be with Uncle Lyman now!

How is it about Major Long. Oh! Dear I wonder if they ever will attack this place. I long to see a little service.

Good by now give my love to all keep lots to your self from your loving son

Henry

USS *Cambridge*
Beaufort NC
Aug 5th 1862

Dear Mother

I received a letter from you yesterday dated July 24th & I now take up my pen to answer it.

I was a little disapointed in not receiving the letter stamps which I sent for the first of last month. I have borrowed some expecting mine would have arrived before this so that I could return them, and it is very annoying not to be able to pay them back, as it is impossable to get them here. I wish you would forward me some as soon as you receive this letter.

I have not been on shore yet & think very likely I shall not go this time. I dont feel much like it, & there are always plenty that do want to go & some must stay by the ship.

Mr. Huntington is going to stand watch now so I shall not have quite so much to do in future which will be quite a relief for tho' I am not sick now, still I never feel over & above smart in this oppressively hot weather.[17]

Aug. 7th I was interrupted the other day & so did not finish this letter. This morning I received the papers from home a Tribune & Journal.

We have got through coaling now but will not leave here before day after tomorrow as our week will not be up before that.

There is nothing going on here of interest enough to write about. & it is too hot to think so I hope you will excuse me for not writing so long a letter as usual this time.

I see by the papers that the C.S.I.C.S. *Arkansas* has played her game & made fools of us on the Mississippi.[18] I should have thought the *Merrimac* affair would have been warning enough to us, not to be caught napping. I hope they will not serve us the same way on the James River.

The *Tyler* that had the running fight with the *Arkansas* is Lieut Gwyns boat.

I am very sorry to hear that Joe shows so little spirit in not being ready & willing to serve his country in such a time as this. Will not the 4th Battalion go to the seat of war?

How is the recruiting in Brookline there will not need to be any draft there I hope?

I am expecting every day to get Lu's letter from the mountains which you spoke of in your last[.] it ought to be here by this time I should think.

Good by now give my love to all from your ever loving son

Henry

I wish that you would send me that Photograph of mine (card) if it has not been disposed of. There was a spare one you know.

USS *Cambridge*
Off New Inlet
Aug 12th 1862

Dear Mother

The mail is just going to leave, & I have got one of the officers to relieve me from [the] deck so as to write you a line or two just to say that I am well. I am sorry that I should not have had a letter written, but we have had such notoriously hot weather for the last week that I have not been able to muster up energy enough to attempt any thing. Our steerage is like an oven. & in the wheel-house the coolist place in the ship the thermometer has ranged from 90° to 100° in the daytime (I am not exagerating) & in the night not lower than 88°. So you can judge what the heat has been in the sun, or down in the hold where we live.

We have just received news that there is another formitable Rebel Privateer afloat mounting 8 guns I hope she will come this way. I can not write any more as it is my watch on deck.

Good by love to all from your affectionate son

Henry

USS *Cambridge*
Off New Inlet N.C.
Aug. 17th 1862

Dear Mother

I have now taken up my pen to commence you my regular sunday letter. I do not intend to write much to day & in fact I do not think I should have made the attempt at all if it was not that I am afraid if I do not that I may be caught napping as I was last time, with nothing ready, for I have got a bad *cold* in *my head* & am so of course quite miserable. When I went to bed last night I was not well, & was a little feverish so I got to sleep with out being properly covered up, the result was as might be expected I woke up in the middle of the night chilled through, & in the morning with one of *my* colds. Odies (Odiorne) is a brick.[19] He insisted in standing my watch for me & was quite indignant because I wanted Durgin to take it as O.[diorne's] watch & mine came together which would give him 8 hours on a stretch but he said he did not care & would stand it. He is a good fellow & it is a real comfort to have at least one gentleman for a companion. I always thought a Man of War was the place to look for gentlemen, but there are very few here. There is not a very large proportion of them any way amongst the Volunteers I am sorry to say.

Since I wrote last our ship has under went a General Inspection by a board of officers, according to orders from *Admiral* Goldsborough.

We passed a very creditable examination (so they said & I saw their report.) There is something going on here now worth writing about. We have had very sultry, hot, weather lately & I believe I told you in my last. It is not very bad to day tho' in fact it is blowing a gale of wind. last night it blew so hard that the *Victoria* could not hold on & so had to slip & go to sea. She has not got back yet.

It seems an age since I have received any letters from home tho' I believe in fact it is not more than 10 or 12 days.

I wish I could see you all if it was only for even so short a time for I assure you I am getting very homesick.

Well I will not write any more now, but will try & add a few lines before the mail goes, if not, good by love to all from your loving son

Henry

Notice!!! Parts in parenthesis must *not* be read out *loud*
U.S.S. *Cambridge*
Off New Inlet
Aug 22nd /62

Dear Mother

I received your letter of the 10th this morning & you may be sure I was delighted to hear the joyful news. Do kiss little Ruthie for me as soon as you receive this.[20] I like the name very much both from association & the name it self which I always did fancy.

It is too bad I can not see her. I suppose she will be quite a sizeable miss before I get home. You must send me her Photograph as soon as she is big enough to have it taken, you will wont you?

It was only yesterday that I was turning it over in my mind whether I would rather have another brother or sister in the family & I concluded I should prefer a sister (Two remarkable boys is enough for one family, & of course we could not put up with anything else)[.] You see Eliza & Lu are getting pretty well along & the first thing we shall know they will be getting married, (Bennie will be at a Scotch University) & then you will want some body to keep the house from seeming lonely & girls are better than boys for that. Then again when the *big brother* comes home from the wars a scared veteran with a wooden Peg? it will be very handy to have a little sister to wait on one, bring slippers (slipper) etc. You see I am looking forward to my own comfort! Bennie's nose will not be out of joint! Of course not!

Well it is my candid opinion (what malicious thing[s] these candid opinions are!) that it will be a capital thing for him, as he will not get petted so much now that there is a baby in the house tho' of course nobody will love him any the less.

I started a short letter home this morning before I received my letters. Since

I wrote it I have been quite sick, laid up in fact, much to my disgust. I am better today, in fact I think my letters have quite set me up having such good news. I received four, one from you of the 10th one from Cousin Lu of the 1st (a real nice letter) (she sent me some stamps I imagin[e] she remembered that I had asked to have some sent, & in the excitement at home they had been forgotten. it would be just like her, whether I'm right or not she is a dear cos Lu, aint she) One from Lu of August 3rd from Walpole telling me all about her doings at the Mountains but not much Walpole news, she will tell me that next time I hope. Really the Post Office stamp on the back of the letter did call up a host of pleasant thoughts of old times, when the "Pecks" & I used to build houses & Rabbit pens under the old maple by the brook. Those were happy times when we had no care on our minds & nothing to do (after we had learned our lessons) but to enjoy ourselves. I wish I could live it all over again, from the time Father took me out on the Tavern Piazza & asked me which house I thought was ours? & how I guessed right because that oval carving over the front Door took my fancy. All the memories are pleasant but *one*. I never shall forget the day when they told me down at the Post Office in Mr. Crosbys store that Father was burnt almost to death & I must go home & tell you. I remember then how, young as I was, I would rather have cut my hand off than have done it & how I staid in the entry & cried till you found me & made me tell what was the matter. But if I dwell on that subject any longer I shall not be able to finish my letter. On Dear I wish Fire Proof buildings had never been invented[.] I hope Lu will give me a full account of all the changes in W[alpole] both of people and things.

I shall answer her letter before the mail goes again that is unless some extra chance of sending letters occurs.

I also received a letter from Mary Lovett this morning she sent me a Tin Type as a p[r]oof she said that she meant to send me a card when she had some more taken.[21] I do not think it is very good & shall not return Eliza's till I get the other, unless E is very anxious to have it, if she is, of course I will send it back, always providing she will write her self & ask me to, for it would be quite refreshing to see her hand writing again it is so long since I have been favored in that way. But I wont be unreasonable for I know she has been very busy lately[.] However as soon as things get settled down I shall expect an extra long letter to make up for the delay.

I believe before I commenced my episodes on my letters I was telling you that I had been sick. Well, you have the first edition in the last letter. Influensa much as usual, I pretended to take the Drs. advice & *took* Aconite & Bellodona[22] (hold on a bit I must go take some now I ought to have an hour ago but I quite forgot it) alternately instead (also home letters)[.] I am much better to day & mean tho a little weak to go off the list tomorrow[.] I suppose *Dr. Prey* would say that diet & salts had done the work but *you* & *I* know better! Now dont be anxious I am doing first rate.

Who has enlisted that I know? I hear that the 4th Bat. is going to fill up & make a Reg.[iment] so I suppose Joe will go. I wish he had shown a little more spirit about it. I gave him a little of my mind the last time I wrote him & as he has not answered my letter I suppose he is a little offended. He ought to go tho' there is no two ways about that. The Cadets are going are they not? Will Millard go?

In your letter you mentioned having written on the 27th I think. I have not received that letter yet. The 28th is babys birth day is it not? Well I think I (Hurrah for Banks!!!) have written a pretty long letter for a sick man so I will leave off now as I am rather tired.

Good by give my love to all (please include the baby in future) & write as often as you feel able, have time etc. to your loving Boy

Henry

U.S.S. *Cambridge*
Off New Inlet
Aug 22nd 1862

Dear Sister

I received your letter of the 3rd from Walpole this morning before I was out of bed, together with two or three others. I am not sure that I should have been up yet if I had not got them for I have been in bed pretty much all the time lately. I am better to day tho' I am happy to say & I lay it principaly to the good news from home. How do you like having a younger sister? Of course, you have seen her before this. I wish I could.

I like the name very much & I am glad Father choose it. Any name that *he* liked I would have been perfectly satisfied with. But Ruth I think is a real pretty name. Wont Aunt Ruthie be pleased? I wish she was North with the rest of us instead of being down in Georgia. I know she would be much happier for her sympathies are all Northern I am sure.

I want—(Oh Dear! Durgin will persist in reading the N.Y. *Herald* out loud to me though he knows I have read the paper as I did not let him have it till I was done with it. I keep on writing but he wont take the hint & keeps on reading so you must excuse any blunders that I may make). —The next time you write to me, that you should give me all the Walpole news, tell me all about the people & the doings *et ceteria* for it seems like old times to hear about that place.

What is Josiah Bellows doing now. Why is he not in the army? has he not any of the old Bellows spirit? Who have gone to the War from old W? Has any body. Ned Bellows No 2. where is he? & Fred Bensons & the Hollands, the Kiteridges & O where is Herbert Bellows now? Elbridge & Waldo? I think that there are quite a respectable number of questions for you to answer. Tell me of all our old friends. The High School the stores. Who has Uncle Edwins store now? In fact I want general information on matters in general & those in particular.

I am glad you had so pleasant time up at the mountains, tho' it was a pity you lost the view from Mt. Washington. it must have been much pleasanter for you to have Quinn with you than if you had been alone.

I wonder Uncle Hamilton does not get some position in the army. I should think it would just suit him.

On to Aunt Louisa now. The air at the Mountains agrees with her does it not?

We had quite an exciting chase after a steamer a few days a go, she was burning soft coal which made us think that she was English especialy as she was trying to get away as fast as possable, we caught her after about 5 hours chase. she proved to be the US transport steamer *Swanee* from New Orleans for New York, they thought we were a Privateer I believe.[23] We got N.O. papers from her which were quite a treat.

The news to day seems quite encouraging. Banks did splendidly did he not? Also on the lower Mississippi I am very glad to hear that the Ram *Arkansas* is destroyed. if Wilkes will do the same for the new Merrimac.

Well as I have arrived at the end of my paper I will not write any more at present. I would have written to you on white paper but I did not have any in my Port Folio & I did not feel like getting up to get more besides I know you will not mind what sort of paper I use. Good by darling love to all from your ever loving brother

Henry

US Steamer *Cambridge*
Off New Inlet
Aug 29th 1862

Dear Mother

I sent off several letters day before yesterday but as I do not know how soon I may have another chance I think I might as well commence a letter now & then I shall be sure & have one ready. I have not heard from home since I wrote last, tho' has been a steamer down from Beaufort, but she brought very little mail matter for any one, so I have no reason to think that you have not written, on the contrary I feel sure that there are letters some where on the route. The mails are very irregular at Beaufort you know & some times letters are over a month coming. we got letters last time (that is one or two of the officers did) that were written in June.

They have passed an act in Congress changing all the uniforms in the navy. Mine is altered very essencialy. It is now a single brested coat with 9 buttons in front, 4 on the Tail as before & none on the sleeves. The same sort of cap as before with the addition of a silver anchor in front.

I think it is a regular outrage to make us change our uniform when we are only here on temporary service, & our pay is barely sufficient to support us Masters Mates with out having such an additional expence tacked on us as buying an entire new set of uniforms. I dont mean to do it, unless I am forced to. I am going to ware out my old clothes first & by that time I hope the war will be over. If I could only get promoted now it would be quite a saving for them with a little alteration my coats would do. The only change in a Masters uniform is a different shoulder strap & a stripe of gold lace on the wrist.

I dont much expect that I shall be able to get promoted tho'. if Lieut Miller had stayed here I should have stood a good chance but Mr. Strong & I dont get along so well together & Capt. P.[arker] is a man that is very easily influenced. I have not had any trouble with Mr. S.[trong] since I reported him but I think he talks to the Captain about both Odie's [Odiorne] & I and tryes to influence him against us. Well! this war like every thing else will have an end & then the service may go to the____well any where so I am out of it.

I do wish you would not forget to send me some letter stamps. I think I have written for them 6 or 8 times at least. Cousin Lu sent me a few (9) the last time she wrote, but they are but a drop in the bucket. I used four of them last mail & I believe I owe the rest tho' I have not paid them yet, & I dont mean to tell I can get some more, but shall use them especialy to write to cousin Lu with & you will have to pay 5 cents for your letters till you send me some.

We picked up some contrabands day before yesterday six in all four men, a woman & a child. They were completely used up having been in their canoe, from 2 o'clock in the morning till four in the afternoon with out any thing to eat & wet through all the time[.] Two or three of them could not stand when they got on deck.

The head man amongst them is a very intelligent darkie, & he gave us quite an interesting account of matters & things on shore[.] He says they are drafting all the men from 12 to 60 for soldiers. & there are very few men left here now except barely enough to guard the Forts, & those who are working on the vessels for he says they have a Navy Yard at Wilmington & are building two Rams & are going to iron them.[24] They have bought up all the old *axes* & *ploughs etc.* which they could find for that purpose.

His Mistress told him that "they" (the Yankees) would kill him if he went on board the Yankee vessels, & that all the negroes were running about the streets in the Northern cities starving to death but he sais he heard that they were going to put him in jail & flog him for somthing he had said so he thought he would run away & take his chances for he would as soon die as be flogged as some had been. They make them take off their shirts & then tie them down & flog them on their backs with what they call a paddle which is a broad flat stick with holes in the end they strike with. They take the paddle & dip it first in water & then in sand. The first blow raises blisters & the next breaks them etc. Very *chivalrous* occupation aint it? When they catch them trying to run away they kill them at sight.

Well I guess I will not write any more to day. So good by, love to all. if I do not send this soon I will add a few lines. I am pretty near over my cold now, so you need not be anxious about your loving boy.

Henry

U.S.S. *Cambridge*
Off New Inlet
Sep. 2nd 1862

Dear Mother

Contrary to my usual custom I did not write a letter Sunday as I had dispatched one only the day before, but I will try to make up for lost time now as I suppose there will be another vessel going to Beaufort in a day or two. The *Mystic* will be down tomorrow or next day I think & then we shall get letters from home again, if the mails have not been stopped which I hope is not the case.

The last steamer that was up there did not get any mail for any of the vessels so my latest date from home is Aug. 11th. I hope to get several letters this next time tho'.

The Despatch boat *Massachusetts* was here this morning, direct from New York & brought us besides *ice* & fresh provisions, papers of the 29th. Oh Dear nothing but bad news in them. What are our Generals thinking of? So far as I can see we are about where we were after the battle of Bull Run & that thousands of lives have been sacrificed for nothing. I see General McClellan is back on the Potomac again. I think they might spare some of the Gunboats now to come down here & attack this place, perhaps they will. One (the *Octarora*) has come down at all events, & a formidable boat she is; one of the side wheel boats with a very heavy armament[.][25] She was Flag ship of Com.[modore] Porters Mortar Fleet on the Mississippi[.] Three of our vessels have had to go north within the last month (*Mt. Vernon, Chippewa, & Victoria*) for repairs so we have only seven vessels (including the *O*[*ctorara*] now) one of which is always at Beaufort coaling. Half are on this side of the shoals under command of Capt Parker & the rest on the other side under Capt Armstrong of the *State of Georgia* who is Senior Officer of the whole.[26]

I cannot help wishing at times that I was in the army. it seems so hard to be laying here quietly while our armies are being driven back, & are fighting all the time. Of course some one has got to blockade but I wish it was not me, besides I do not feel as tho we were doing all that laies in our power & that makes me the more dissatisfied.

We lay here, two or three miles from the shore & see the Rebels throwing up batteries all along the coast with out attempting to molest them, which I can not help thinking is very wrong. Their works are twice as strong now as they were when we first came down here & will require a very strong force to take them.[27]

I wish Father would write me[.] We get the papers so seldom that I feel as tho' I knew very little of the true state of things, & should like very much to have his opinion on the state of Country generaly.

It is getting dark so I will not write any more now. Love to all. My health is better than it has been for some time. Good by from your loving son

Henry

U.S.S. *Cambridge*
Off New Inlet
Sep. 7th 1862

Dear Mother

I sent you a letter by the *Monticello* a day or two [ago] but as there will be a mail go tomorrow or next day I will write a few lines now.

We have not heard any news from the North since I last wrote & we are anxiously waiting the arrival of the *Mystic* from Beaufort for it seem[s] as tho' there must be some very heavy fighting going on now, from the positions of affairs the last time we heard.

I am glad you sent me a Boston paper last time. do mail them often. We never can get them at Beaufort & only occasionaly New York ones. & it is realy refreshing to see the *Journal* now & then.[28] When one comes on board it has to go the rounds, there are so many of our officers, Massachusetts men.

Mr. O[diorne] & I are getting along nicely with our studies, & we do not find time for much of any thing else in our watches below. I am glad we have commenced it as it makes the time pass away pleasanter to feel that we are accomplishing something for our selves, tho' we are not it seems to be allowed to do much for our country. Mr. Durgin is quite studious & studies Navigation when off duty. He is not quite so far along as O & I, & so we help him. He is a very pleasant messmate, (tho' not a gentleman exactly) & we three get along first rate together & have not had a hard word since we left Baltimore. Quite different from what it was last winter when we were quarreling all the time.

I imagine you all round the Piano now singing as we always do Sunday evenings. How I wish I was with you, if it were only for that one pleasant hour. I wish all the men that are now away from their homes, serving their country had as pleasant a one to think about as I have! How objectless life must be to a man who has no *home*, (a new house does not make a home according to my notions). Why if I had no home to look forward to at the end of my voyages it seems as tho' I should want to jump overboard & make an end of myself at once.

I wish you would send me a Photograph of the baby as soon as she is old enough to go out. I will not object to having you on the same card. Now do have some taken. I do want to see how little Ruthie looks.

You said in your letter that you wanted to have that piece of Poetry of Lu Alcott's preserved, so I will send it back in this letter.[29]

I think you had better send me some more stamps as those which you sent before seem to have *stuck* some where between here and B[rookline].

I will not write any more now as Mr. O has got Peter (the Frenchman) down here & is practicing the pronunciation of various hard words, & who can write where such jaw-breaking words are ringing in ones ears as *Mercredi* etc. besides I do not want O to get to windward of me.[30] Good by, love to all & a kiss (especial) for the baby from your loving son

Henry

The mail goes early tomorrow morning I believe so I shall not be able to answer L's letter this mail. Will do so next time with out fail H.

U.S.S. *Cambridge*
Off New Inlet
Sep. 14th 1862

Dear Mother

It seems an age since I have heard from home tho' it is only about two weeks the reason being that the last mail was lost in the Steamer *Arrow* which was sunk some where in the neighborhood of Cape Hatteras I believe.[31] They are only sent from Hampton Roads once a week so we shall have to wait till the next steamer comes down, & then till one of the Gunboats come down from Beaufort. I suppose we shall have letters now by Wednesday or Thursday. We shall probably go to B[eaufort] our selves in about 10 days. We are making a longer stay this time than we ever have before as we have been underway very little & so saved our coal. We none of us expected to stay so long & only laid in mess stores for 30 or 35 days, so that now nearly all the messes are almost entirely out & have to draw ships provisions from the Paymaster.

The *Octorora* went to Beaufort friday & I sent you a short letter by her.[32] In it I believe I told you that I would enclose you a Confederate note, & after words sealed the letter with out putting it in. I will try & not forget it this time.

I have not answered Elizas letter yet. at the which I feel sertain squams [qualms] of conscience considering that I was complaining of he[r] neglect only a short time ago. However I will try & write her before the mail goes.

I wish I had some new[s] to write about, but there has not been a single thing happen worth writing about for a long time. I think it is more than a week since we have even been underway so we have not spoken any vessels or picked up any new[s]. Oh yes there has one thing happened which I am almost ashamed to write about—confound it. I do not know but I told you in my last, for it happened about a week ago.

One afternoon we saw a steamer standing in, but as soon as she saw us, (at least we inferred so by her movements) she turned & stood off again. after considerable delay & with out any orders the *Penobscot* started in chase but the *P* at best is not a fast boat, (not so fast as we are by a good deal, & as her machine[ry] was under repairs that day it is fair to suppose that he could not go as fast as usual.) & the result was as might have been expected. At about midnight she returned & reported having chased the steamer for some time & fired several guns at her but was unable to overhaul her. That the vessel was a very suspicious one as she showed no lights & paid no attention to his signals. So probably we lost a good prize by not going out our selves. Well "it is all in a life time." I have been studying pretty hard lately & have very little time to spare for either reading or writing. Study is a capital thing to make the time pass away quick it is astonishing how short the days seem now.

Well I will not write any more now. paper is paper now, mine (or rather O[diorne]'s for I have been using his lately) is all gone & I had to borrow this so I can not be so extravigent as to use two sheets. Love to all & do excuse this shocking writing of your loving son's

Henry

U.S.S. *Cambridge*
New Inlet
Sep. 16th 1862

Dear Mother

The Steamer *Maratanza* has just arrived from Hampton Roads to releave the *Octorora* who is going north, she leaves tomorrow so I shall have a chance to send letters by her.[33] I wrote one to Eliza this morning fortunatly tho' I did not know that I should have a chance to send so soon.

The *O*[*ctorara*] came down from Beaufort yesterday morning, & brought one mail. I received three letters two from you & one from Tom Peck. One of yours was dated July 27th with a little note enclosed from cousin Lu the next day announcing the birth of Ruthie. What a shame I should have had to wait so long for that letter of all others. The cause was its being directed to Fortress Monroe. My other letter was Sept 1st[.] I also received several papers & a *Monthly Journal* for which I am very much obliged.[34]

I sent a letter off for home yesterday so I have not much news to tell you. One thing tho' I am very glad of, & that is that the Capt. of the *Maratanza* is senior officer here. They say a new broom sweeps clean & so I am in hopes he will give us something to do. There are two here senior to us now so we shall not have command on either side I suppose, so much the better!

I am very glad to hear that nearly all my friends are in the service now. I think I may say all, for any one who is not patriotic enough to go now I do not care to have for a friend. Of course there are some cases when a man is justified in staying at home, but I think for young unmarried men to shrink from the contest now is a shame & a sin too.

I am real glad Joe has gone, for I never would have had any thing to do with him if he had not, & you know I like him ever so much, & perhaps I should have felt worse than he would, about it.

I want you to keep me posted as much as possable as to the news generaly for we get so few papers that we can only form a general idea of how things are going, besides two thirds of the time when papers do come on board the cabin & Ward Room menopolise them & we other officers have to be satisfied with what we can hear which is of course highly colored. For instance the *Maratanza* came here to day direct from H.[ampton] Roads, & I am as wise now as to the news as I was yesterday[.] One says "no news" another "First rate news things begin to look brighter" but if asked to specify he will change the subject as soon as possable. A third say the Rebels are giving us h--l every where & are on the borders of Pennsylvania & still another that Jackson & his whole force has been bagged, but that of course is too good to be true[.] He is a troublesome customer.

The weather is getting cooler & my health much better. I received 9 stamps in one of my letters yesterday. We shall to go Beaufort in a few days now. I will write again from there. Good by love to all & dont forget that *Photograph*. I think Joe might have sent me one of his. No more at present from your loving boy

Henry

Marginalia—Col. Wild is a brick! I made our Gunner Wild by telling him about the liquor scrape in Phila[delphia] where he belongs. in fact if it had been on board of a merchant ship I think we should have had a fight on the subject to see who was right the Tavern Keepers or the Col. Hurrah! For the "Old Bay State."[35]

U.S.S. *Cambridge*
Off New Inlet
Sep. 20th 1862

Dear Mother

Once more I take up my pen this week to write you another letter. This will be the third letter which I have written to you since sunday, so I shall expect a good big one in return. I think we shall go to Beaufort tomorrow or next day which I shall be glad enough of as our mess is very short on stores, in fact if it had not been for that sloop which I told you of in my last we should have had to have come down on our rations. This is the longest cruise that we have ever taken down the coast, being over six weeks.

I sent you a letter day before yesterday by the *Octorora* who was going north & which I suppose you will receive before the one which I sent to Beaufort the first of the week.

I have got one of my bad colds again, how I managed to pick it up I do not know, but am painfully aware of the fact that I have caught it in some way.

I am afraid my last chance of promotion is gone now, as by a recent Act of Congress Ensign's are required to be from 25 to 35 years of age & to have seen 12 years sea service & as a Master is a grade above Ensign I think I may as well "Hang my harp on a willow."

Good if true the *Mystic* has just run alongside & reported that there is a Rebel ram in by the Fort mounting three guns to a side. So we may have a chance for a fight. I wish we had a little larger force on this side tho'. The *M*[*ystic*] is the only vessel in company & her battery is no heavier than ours. Let her come tho' I say if we can't thrash her we can at least try.[36]

I want you to send me a few things that I am in need of (or shall be as soon as cold weather sets in, & I suppose it will take all of a month for them to get here) A Box sent by Express & directed. Blockading squadron off Wilmington N.C. via Beaufort NC would probably come through safe, it would be as well, when the box is expressed to take a receipt & send it to me by letter, so that if there were any trouble I could have it hunted up. I think it would be all right however as several of the officers have received packages in that way.

I want 4 French flannel shirts. (I left two at home so I shall only want two new ones) That pair of thick boots that I left at home when I was there in May. An India Rubber Cap (with flaps so to cover the shoulders), four or five hundred cigars if they can be obtained any way reasonable which I am afraid they can not as of course I do not want a poor article & I wont pay more than $5 & dont want to more than $4.50. If the cigars can not be got send me a *nice* pipe (with a good long slim Amber mouth piece etc.) (Measharm) [Meerschaum] & some Killi-cance tobacco (say 2 lbs) send me also a lot of stationary ink etc. I like this kind of paper the best.

I want some more socks also. This is all I believe, no it aint. I want two pr. draws (flannel). If I think of any thing more I will put it down before this letter goes. I do not like to trust money in letters now its so uncertain which [when] you will receive them there but keep account of the costs. If there is any thing else that you want to send in the way of Books it will be a good chance by the way that reminds me, please send my Geometry. No more at present love to all from your loving son

Henry

22nd We are going to Beaufort tomorrow. I have just been writing to Lu, as I received a letter from her today she has a bit of information for you & the rest of the family. She is a little darling & I thought I would give her the plesure of telling it. My cold about the same from your loving son

Henry

Sept. 24th 1862[37]

Dear Mother

We are not at Beaufort yet so I think I may as well add a few more lines to my letter before I send it.

It has been blowing a gale for the last few days & as if we went up to B.[eaufort] we could not get across the bar the Capt. thought it would be best to stop here. The gale has broke now so I suppose we shall go up tonight. We were in hope the *Massachusetts* would be down before this as we are all very anxious to hear the news. I hope it will be good, when we do get it. Things looked rather bad at the last accounts. We expect a draft of men by the *Massa*[*chusett*]*s*. The Capt. has applied for 25 & 5 marines. we need them very badly for the ship has not been properly manned since we left Baltimore & we have discharged several since then. Our crew now consists of about half darkies who of course in an action can not be depended upon, & it would probably require force to keep them at their guns.

The Captain told me yesterday that he expected Mr. Huntington would leave soon as his class have been ordered to Newport for examination, & that when he went I should have to take charge of all the small arms drill—quite a task for one that never had more than two weeks drill himself but I intend to do it & *well* to[o], for tho' I have drilled little myself I have had a good chance to watch others & I hope to give him satisfaction.[38] decidedly my star is in the ascendent. I think it quite a compliment as there is one officer on board who has been in the army (three months man) & one or two others who have had more chance to learn than I have.

By the way I want you to send my clothes brush & a Log Book. The one I have now I got at Lincolns.[39] it is 13½ in. by 8½ in. & about ¾ in. thick[.] I would tell you how many pages but it is too much trouble to count them. Send me two Mr. O[diorne] wants one & will settle with me for it. About those shirts, I do not want any collars on them an[d] I prefer to ware white. Do send me the prices of every thing & not make me have to ask several times as I did before for if I cant buy my own clothes etc. now I dont know when I shall become a self supporting institution.

Good by now love to all I will write again from Beaufort.

From your loving son

Henry

Send a good lot of writing paper. I will send it all back to you again. My cold is better to day.

U.S.S. *Cambridge*
Off New Inlet
Sep 22nd 1862

My dear Sister

I received your nice long letter (of the 8th) this morning by the *State of Georgia* who arrived from Beaufort. & I hasten to answer it so that you may hear from me by return of mail.

I hope you will duly apreciate the effort, for I have a very bad cold & this afternoon a racking headach so that I can hardly see.

I received your letter before I was up this morning & read it in my cot. You are a little (no big) darling & I wonder how it was that your older brother & sister had the heart to torment you so when we were *young*. Well I will try to make up my share of it now by loving you---well, as much as I *know* you do me. I would more if I could but you see you wont let me. I love to have you write me as you did this last time, though *big brother* as I am, I feel very much like crying over it. The fact is you must write oftener, dont wait for answers & I wont, for if we do I shall not get a letter from you much oftener than once in 5 or 6 weeks.

Now I am going to tell you a bit of news about my humble self. I have not told any one else, so you can have the pleasure of telling Father & Mother. but dont say any thing outside of the family. You see yesterday morning when I was on watch, the Capt. came on deck, after the usual salutation I of course walked over to the Port side of the deck (for it is always proper to let the Capt. have the starboard side & I have not been in the habit of talking so much with him lately as I used to)[.]

He took two or three turns up & down the deck, & I thought he looked astonishingly good natured at me, but was not sure, (for lately I have been rather impressed with the idea that he was a little *down* on me). Finnely he stopped in the gangway & beckoned to me to come over which I did. He then asked me how long I had been to sea, which I told him. If I had been Chief Mate, I told him no. Whereupon he held forth, that he was pleased with me & thought that an Ensigns position would become me (or I would become an Ensigns position). & tho' I was not quite old enough (25 years is the proper age) & had not been to sea long enough (12 years is the time) & had never been chief mate (which is indispensable) still he though[t] he should be able to get me the rank on account of the time I had been in the Navy (one year in the navy worth a dozen any where else?) At all events he would try, & thought he could safely promise before the year is out that I should be an Ensign.

Now to define. An Ensign is the next grade below a Master, he is a Ward Room officer (I believe), is by right (not by sufferance as a masters mate is) a Watch Officer & last but not (by any manner of means to be considered) least his pay is $1,200.00 per annum, or $100 a month & a ration.

I did not intend to let any one at home know about it at first, as I thought that if I should not get it, there was no need of making others bear my disapointment with me, but on second thoughts I changed my mind, for at all events it shows the good will of Capt. P.[arker] & if I do not get the position it will be through no fault of mine but only on account of my age.

So you must not set your minds to[o] strongly on it for it would be not at all supprising to me if Capt. P. was not to succeed.

Now aint you much obliged to me for giving you the first knowledge of all this & the fun of telling it? I think you owe me several kisses on account which I shall be very happy to receive on the first opportunity.

We picked up eight contrabands this forenoon, from Wilmington.[40] They brought papers from there as late as the 20th which state that the Rebels are beating us every where. I hope it is not so. We heard by the *S. of G.* [*State of Georgia*] (tho' they had no date as late as the 20th) that Burnside had whipped Jackson & driven him out of Maryland. I wish we could know exactly how things stand but we have no chance to keep our selves posted here.

The Contrabands say that neither of the Iron Clads up at Wilmington is launched yet so the report of the *Mystic* that they had seen one must have been a mistake. They say they are both to be like the *Merrimac*. This is the most intelligent lot that we have ever picked up.

So Joe is not going after all? Well of course if the Doctor would not pass him he could not but I am sorry he did not show more *will*. I can not conceive of any young man's being *willing* to stay quietly at home and do nothing, when the Rebels have actual[l]y invaded one of our states & the Government want[s] every man it can get, why dont he try to get into the Navy if he can not go in the Army. I should think he would be able to raise influence enough to get a position, as Capts. or Paymasters Clerk either of which are good positions. Any thing but staying at home & doing *nothing*.

I received a letter from Tom Peck the other day, he sais Josiah Bellows is trying to get a position in one of the New Hampshire Regts. (14th I believe)

Where is Charlie Soule? I thought he was in the 4th Battalion (or 44th Reg.) but do not find his name amongst the officers.

By the way has either Dan or Henry Wells of Brooklyn entered the service? Where is Geo Long now? did he get the position of *Major* for which he applied?

I think Grandpa will be pleased to hear about my probable promotion & increase of pay. Give my love to him & tell him about it.

Is he at home now? I have not heard of him much lately.

I was very much interested in your account of Walpole. I should judge by it, that it is not so pleasant a place as it used to be. I should like to go up there again tho' to see the old place for a day or so, no much longer tho' unless during the gay season when there are plenty of people there.

I wrote a letter to Mother a day or two ago which will go in the same letter mail as this.

Good by now. I want to lie down a while & see if I can not get rid of at least a part of this headach for I have got the watch from 8 to 12 to stand tonight. Love to all & write very often to your loving sailor brother

Henry

At Sea
Sept. 26th 1862
U.S.S. *Cambridge*

Dear Mother

I wrote you a few days ago about some things that I wanted & tho the letter has not gone yet, it is sealed & stamp on so I can not open it. I do not want you to send the things just yet as there is some doubt as to whether we shall coal at Beaufort any more. I do not know any thing certain about it yet but if it should be true a Box directed there would not probably be received, at least for some-time. The report is that the worms eat the bottoms of vessels not coppered so badly that owners refuse to allow their vessels to take coal there any more with-out the Government will pay for the damage done, which I do not think it will, in which case we shall have to coal either at Port Royal or Hampton Roads the latter I think & sertainly hope.

We are on our way there now (to B.) but (if what I hear is true) we shall be the last vessel that will go there.

A night or two ago the Steamer *Kate* succeeded in running the Blockade from Nassau, not on our side of the shoals however.[41] This morning two schooners attempted the same thing on our side, one got in & the other I believe was sunk. We did not have a hand in it as we were down at the edge of the shoals signaling the vessels on the other side. It was rather a singular affair & the less that is said about it the better.

We were in hopes that the *Massachusetts* would come down before we left the station, in fact we waited four or five days for her but she did not come & we were obliged to start as our coal would not hold out any longer.

I hope to find several letters waiting for me at B. also some good news from the Seat of War, we are in a dreadful state of suspense just now. Imagine how you would feel at home not to see a paper for a week or two. & then when we do get news, we know it is 10 or 15 days old & every thing may be at the time just the reverse of what we hear.

I have not time to write more now as I have got to go on watch very soon. good by ever so much love to all at home from your loving boy

Henry

I think would be as well to have the things all ready so that you can send as soon as you hear from me. H.

U.S.S. *Cambridge*
Beaufort N.C.
Oct. 1st 1862

Dear Mother

We leave here today for our station off Wilmington N.C. & as I have a few spare minutes I think I can not devote them to a better purpose than by writing you a short note.

We are going to carry down to Wilmington 75 rebels, prisoners taken at Fort Macon & else where & who have been exchanged. It is not very pleasant to have such a crowd of them as, if they should take a notion to rise they might give us a good deal of trouble. I guess we can manage them tho'. There are three Lieutenants with them. Yesterday was an important era in the cruise of the U.S.S. *Cambridge*.

I was laying down, in the steerage, (having quite a severe headach) when I heard quite a bustle on deck, & the Officer of the Deck, Quartermaster & half a dozen messenger boys singing out for "Mr. Wells—where's Mr. Wells?" so I went on deck to see what was the matter. When I got up Mr. Maies told me that "*Capt. Parker was on the Rampage*" on account of nearly all the officers & men being on shore on liberty leaving no one on board to do the work (Mr. Strong, the ex.[ecutive] Officer among the rest[.] You know the 1st Lieut is supposed never or at least very seldom to leave the ship but Mr. S makes it a practice when in Port to be on shore all the time & in that way shirks his duty on the other officers.) The boats were all away too, but one, & I was ordered to take that one and go on shore [and] hunt up the officers in general & Mr. S in particular & order them to report on board *at once*.

When they got off—well, I tell you what, I would not have taken the reprimand that Mr. S. received for $500. On the Quarter Deck too! I have been expecting it would come for some time. Capt. P. is a quiet man & will stand a good deal before he will say anything but when he *does* get going stand clear! He astonished us all I can tell you.

My application was forwarded this morning (with Capt. P. approval) for an appointment as Act. Ensign & as Old Golie is away & Rear Admiral Lee in his place I think my chances of success are better than they otherwise would be.[42] My age is the only thing which will stand in my way I think. If you have the origanals of those letters of recommendation that you had last spring when that application was made I think you had better send them to me as possably they may request them (tho' I dont think they will).

I went ashore in Beaufort this time but have not time to tell you about my experiences there now.

Good by I will write again when we get settled down again every thing is all in a mess now.

My cold is better but I have very bad headachs. Nux vomica is what I ought to take I think but mine is all out.[43] Give my love to all from your loving son

Henry

Writing awful—please excuse[.] If you can not find those Boots of mine *dont* bear another pain. This is the third letter I have sent since I arrived here.

Do you think it would do any good to write to Mr Rice. if so it might be tried.

U.S.S. *Cambridge*
Off New Inlet
Oct. 5th 1862

Dear Mother

There was a mail left here day before yesterday but I had no letter ready & only had time to scratch off a few lines just to let you know that we were all alive & well here & had not been captured by the Rebels.

The day we left Beaufort we received on board 59 Rebel prisoners who had been exchanged & who were to be sent on shore at Ft. Fisher.

It was rather a ticklish thing having so many of them on board & we so short-handed[.] Luckily the afternoon we sailed, 4 new Marines reported on board to fill up our guard. There were two or three Lieutenants & several non-commissioned officers among the Prisoners.

The senior sesesh officer wanted to mess in the Ward-Room (as his rank (?) entitled him) but Capt. P. told him he did not recognize any such officers & should not treat him any differently from the rest of the prisoners[.] The Ward-Room officers refused to have him mess with them. He was very sea-sick & when at 8 P.M. the prisoners were all ordered below he asked permission to stop on deck, but that the Captain would not allow, & so we took compassion on him & let him sleep in the Steerage. He was very greatful & said he hoped he should meet us again under different circumstances. He was a gentleman & if it was not that he is a Rebel I should say that he was a very nice sort of a man[.] he was taken at Ft. Macon & belongs at Beaufort.

We were all very anxious while they were on board. We kept 8 sentries (sailors)

on the spar Deck & 5 marines on the Gun Deck during the night, the Officer of "the Deck" carried his arms & all the rest were ready for a call at any moment, I slept with my revolver under my pillow & kept my hand on it. We kept the lamp burning after we turned in & at 10 p.m. the Seargent of Marines came down to put it out, in doing so he touched my cot, & I was up & had my pistol pointed at him before he had time to turn, it was lucky he had not got the light out or I might have shot him—probably should—. I was up two or three times during the night as were most of the other officers.

We got down off here early in the morning before daylight. We made our night signal, but either the signals were damp & did not burn well or there was some mistake in burning them (which I think most likely) so the vessels blockading (*Mystic* & *State of Georgia*) could not make them out & thought we were a vessel trying to run the Blockade, in their hurry to get after us they ran foul & the result was, the *M*[*ystic*] got her side stove in & two boats smashed, & the *S.*[*tate*] *of G.*[*eorgia*] had her stern torn nearly off, rather worse than ours was last winter. Our Carpenter has been at work on the *Mystic* ever since & her damage is nearly made good, with the exception of boats. The other will eventualy have to go north but there is no telling how long they may keep her here first.[44]

In the morning after daylight we ran in towards the Fort under a flag of truce. When with in about a mile of [or] mile & ½ we sent a boat in to communicate, with Mr. Strong, Lieut. Harris 9th N.J. (who came down in charge of prisoners) & the Sesesh Lieut.[45] A boat met them from the shore & they made arrangements to send a vessel out after the Prisoners. About three hours afterwards a little river steamboat came out to us with a Rebel flag & a white one flying. It was hard to see that flag so near us & not be able to pull it down.

They took the prisoners & we were glad enough to get rid of them, they were a miserable looking set, only two or three of them had any uniforms but I noticed they had all taken good care during their stay in our lines to provide themselves with India rubber blankets & good stout boots.

I noticed one or two of them after they got on board the steamer, take hold of the dirty little flag that was flying on the flagstaff aft & *kiss it*, done for effect I guess. As a general thing they did not seem to fancy going back over & above much & some of them I am told offered to take the oath of allegance if we would let them go back to Beaufort, but they repented too late. They all had the chance offered them before we took them on board and refused, some declaring that "all they wanted was a chance to kill about a dozen D--m Yankee[s] & then they would be willing to die."

While we were up at Beaufort the steamer *Sunbeam* was captured of[f] this place.[46] It was just our luck to be away at the time. They took her right out from under the guns of the Fort, & did not get hit once.

The Yellow Fever & Small Pox are raging ashore here, the latter disease was brought by the Steamer *Kate* which ran the Blockade a short time since. They are dying in Wilmington at the rate of a bout 12 or 15 per day.

We picked up 21 contrabands to day, one party came off in a fine large sailboat—how they managed to get clear with her I dont know. There were 15 of them the rest came off in two small boats, each party was entirely independent of the others. I do not know what the duce [duece] we are going to do with them all.

I went on shore in Beaufort this last time, I have never done so before you know, & of my own free will,·never will be guilty of doing such a thing again. It is the most miserable place I ever was in not excepting Port Elizabeth, Algoa Bay. [South Africa] (which I always thought was the last place that was made when the world was created, & all the material all expended except sand.) There are only one or two side walks in the place & even in those the sand is almost as dark as in the street. If you ware shoes you may expect to have them full before you take three steps from the boat. The ladies (?) there will not look at a *Yankee* officer but always turn their heads away when one passes[.] when our troops first went there they used to spit at them but, they have got over that pretty much now. I thought I would take a walk thro' the Grave Yard, but the Pigs soon drove me out. They pasture them there. The graves are all bricked over to keep the swine from rooting up the bodies.

I was very thirsty while I was on shore & tried to get something to drink but had to go to so many places before I could find *any thing* that I almost began to think that they lived with out drinking there. I went to one of the Hotels (?) then to a Bar Room (where they had nothing but empty bottles, & a few nut shells on the floor which I believe on my honor the man put there himself to delude strangers into the idea that he had sold something once). Then to the jail & finaly when I was quite in despair I saw an old negro woman pumping some water, so I hastened to her & asked her to let me drink out of her bucket which she did. I had quite a little talk with her. I would like to tell you all she said but I know I can not do the subject justice & so will not try. When I got tired of walking round I persuaded a barber to cut my hair for me for a compensation after which I returned to the ship quite disgusted with things in general & myself in particular for having been such a fool as to go on shore there.

They are the laziest set of people I ever met with. I do not know what they will do if their slaves are taken away from them, they certainly are not fit to take care of themselves, perhaps the Government will take the matter in hand & make some appropriation for the *poor exmasters*.

The storekeepers seem to think there that they are doing you a great favor to sell you any thing for which you ought to thank them instead of the contrary you generaly have to hunt them up if you want any thing. Well I will not write any more on that subject & that reminds me that I have written a pretty long letter so I guess it is most time to close.

Give my love to all the family. I hope in the course of the week to hear from home again. Good by now, love to all over & over again from your

Henry

I see by the papers that Col. Wild has lost his arm. Poor Mrs. Wild. how dreadfuly she must feel about it. has he come home?[47]

U.S.S. *Cambridge*
Off New Inlet
Oct. 6th 1862

Dear Lu

I have just come off watch without any particular object I sat myself down here at the desk & began to look over the things (a little of every thing) that it contained, when Durgin asked me as tho' it was a matter of course "what I was going to write?" & I answered a letter with out hardly knowing at the time what I said. Now you see it wont do for me to tell—fibs—so I am going to write to you as I promised to. You may thank Mr. D's question for it I guess, tho' as I have not much of any thing to do between now & dinner (sertainly nothing so pleasent as writing) I might have come round to it in the course of 10 or 15 minutes with out his help.

Confound him he has got a going now & I am afraid I shall not write very connectedly. his tongue is worse than bell's & when it once gets agoing it is almost impossable to stop it. He wants to know if I am "writing to my girl?" I tell him no. "Why dont I then" etc. etc. entirely oblivious to the possibility that I may not be sufficiently fortunate as to have yet found any young lady who will receive my attentions. He is planted now right opposite me with his feet higher than his head eating a pickle, he says "don't laugh at me, write your letter"! which is good advise so I will try & get ahead as fast as possable.

Yesterday we picked up 21 contrabands, 8 of them came off in the morning watch in two canoes & the rest came off at about noon in a little sloop Yacht (about 26 feet long) it was rather to bad, the boat belonged to a young lady, had been made a present to her. The Master had taught one of the darkies to sail it & "Dat's what he got by it" for he ran of[f] with the boat & took 12 others with him. I hope there will not any more come off. we have too many now & I dont know what we shall do with them unless some off the other vessels will take them off our hands. I wish they would give us prize money for them. the *Cambridge* would then have more coming to her than any other vessel in the squadron I am thinking. We have changed her name to *Contraband* among ourselves.

Here comes John with the dinner so I will knock off & finish by & by. I wish I could sketch I would like very much to give you a likeness of that coloured individual.

Well dinner is over so now I will finish my letter.

I went on shore the last time we were in Beaufort. I dont know as it is worth while to try to enter into any description of the place. I did not see much of any thing while there but a few houses which looked as tho' the[y] might have been built just after the flood, and a great deal of sand. I dont think I shall ever trouble the place again with my presence[.] I can pass the time away much more to my satisfaction on board. The ladies there are almost all sesech & will not look at the horrid Yankees (while they are looking at them). I heard a Piano playing in one of the houses (the only instrument of the sort in the place I guess) & walked down past the house to hear it, it sounded so pleasant. The blinds were all shut but I suppose some one was on the lookout for as soon as I got abreast of the building the tune suddenly changed & I heard a female voice singing *Dixie* with great emphasis. The chorus especially fervent. I keep [kept] he[r] playing it some time, out of spite, before I went away.

There are a good many soldiers stationed there[.] I think they are worse off then we on the Blockade, *any thing* would be preferable in my mind to staying there.

We had a live Major General (Foster) on board here while at B.[eaufort]. he came by invitation from Capt. P. to visit the vessel, with his staff.[48] we dressed the ship with flags to receive him.

I wrote to Mother yesterday & in my letter to her, I told all about those prisoners that we brought down here from B, so I think it is hardly worth while to tell it all over again, for of course you will see her letter.

It was pretty hard on them was it not, to land them here where the Yellow Fever is raging? Well they should not be Rebels & then they might stay north where it is healthy. I dont know but it is better that they should die of Fever than that they should have a chance to kill a lot of our men first, tho' it does seem horrid to say so.

I will not write any more now[.] Give my love to all my friends & keep lots for yourself. dont fail to write often to your loving brother

Henry

I will enclose you a North Carolina Bill. I dont know as I shall give it to you but you may take care of it for me.

U.S.S. *Cambridge*
Off New Inlet
Oct 12th 62

Dear Mother

The *Mahaska* leaves for the Roads this afternoon & I have just time to write you a few lines.[49]

Since my last, we have had a boat expedition, unsuccessful I am sorry to say.

The object was to burn the Rebel Steamer *Kate* which lies inside under the guns of Fort Fisher, the expedition was commanded by Lieut. Bunce of the *Penobscot*.[50] All our officers volunteered but Mr. Strong & myself were the only ones permitted to go except the Doctor. (No, Mr. Huntington afterwards received permission & went in Lieut. Bunces boat.)[51] There were three boats at the first attempt which was on Wednesday night, two from this ship (one in charge of the Lieut. & the other in Mr Strongs (in which I was) & one from the *Mystic* in charge of another Master.

After dark this steamer towed us in as near as it was safe for her to go, & when we shoved off the Pilot told us that we were abreast of the Inlet where we wanted to go in, instead of which we found on pulling in that we were four or five miles to the southard[.] & before we could recover the lost ground the tide had turned & was running out so that there was hardly enough water for us to go in & would sertainly not be enough for us to get out two or three hours later, (in reconnoitering we got our boat half full of water in the breakers.)

We were therefore obliged to give it up for that night and return to the ship, all on account or [of] the stupidity & ignorance of that infernal Pilot of ours. I wonder that the Captain tolerates him on board, for he is no more a coast Pilot than I am, & he is notoriously a great coward if not something worse[.] I believe there is not a man in the ship but what dispises him.

On Thursday it blew fresh from the Southd & East[ward] making so heavy a surf that we did not attempt any thing. on Friday we saw a schooner alongsid[e] of the *Kate* apparently taking out her cargo, so we determined to try again that night, & the *Mystic* not being on hand we only had two boats. it was just as well tho', for we found the surf so high that even if we succeeded in running it without staving our boats we should get every thing, ammunition[,] combustibles etc., wet which would destroy our chances of success. so we were obliged to give it up, & I suppose we shall not try it again. I am exceedingly disapointed, as I had thought that the time had arrived at last when I should have a chance of doing something. & I fully intended to have earned my straps in the affair. I think that that was Capt Parkers thought when he gave me the preferance over the others.

I have now volunteered in advance for any thing that may turn up, & hope before long I shall have a chance.

I will enter more into particulars about the expedition some other time when I have more time than now.

There was quite a serious casualty occurred yesterday on board of the *Maratanza*. I have not heard all the particulars yet but it seems she got too near in & the Fort opened on her. one shell went in aft & killed a Masters Mate & one man & wounded four others. We did not see it as she is on the other side of the shoals.[52]

We have not had any mail for some time, we expected the *Penobscot* down from Beaufort to day but she has not arrived as yet, much to my disapointment as I like to get my letters on sunday better than any other time. I always somehow feel nearer home on that day, & wish I could be with you especialy in the evening when I imagine you all, round the Piano singing the old familiar tunes.

I wrote you a letter before going in the boats the other night, in case any thing should happen, but shall not send it now, especially as our attempt turned out so poorly.

We received to day a draft of men, of which we were very much in need, also two of those that deserted in Baltimore. I am very glad they have come for before their arrival we had more niggers that [than] white men. & now I guess we have full as many of one as the other. The Black men may be well enough in their place but are not the sort of material that I should fancy going into a fight with. The probability is in case of action that we officers would have to shoot two or three of them our selves in order to make the rest do their duty. I am thankful that my Division with one exception is composed of white men, & that one I guess will do pretty well.

Good by now, love to all, from your loving boy

Henry

U.S. Steamer *Cambridge*
November 5th 1862

Dear Mother

It is some time since I have written, partly because I have not had much to write about & partly because my last letters staid here a good while after I wrote them on account of one of the vessels going off with out our mail for which piece of kindness I hope they will not get a letter for the next two months.

I have not heard from home now since the 7th of October, through some kink in the transportation of the mails, which is rather agrevating & now we are on our way to B. just as a steamer was expected back on the station who would bring the mails so I shall have to wait another week I suppose. We waited for the said steamer (the *Monticello*) as long as we possably could but were obliged to start this morning having bearly enough coal to get through.

The *M* has staid away four days over her time, for some unaccountable reason, she most alway[s] stays longer than anyone else.

Rather an important occurrence happened on our station day before yesterday which I will tell you about. The vessels on our side consisted of the *Mystic*, *Mount Vernon* & *Daylight*. The night before the *D.*[*aylight*] was sent up the coast to guard some small inlets & in the morning at about 10 A.M. we heard her firing. The *Mystic* had been sent down to the reef to communicate with the vessels on the other side, so we sent the *Mount Vernon* up to see what was going on & to lend a hand, (we could not go ourselves as we were nearly out of coal & the Senior Officer wished us to wait till the *Monticello* arrived if possible). The *Mt. V* was soon out of sight. There was not much more firing but we soon saw a dense black smoke which led us suppose that they were burning a vessel.

At about 8 o'clock P.M. the *Mt. V* returned & reported having burned the Br.[itish] Barque *Sophia* from Nassau, which the *D.* had driven ashore. After boarding her, for some unaccountable reason two of the *D.*'s boats tried to go on shore and got capsized in the surf which was running very high. The *Mt. V* sent her boats in with a line to haul them out, one anchoring just out side of the breakers & holding on to one end of the line, while the other one ran in with it. They got in all right but instead of launching one of their boats & trying to haul out by it, they all commenced hauling on the line & thus dragged the fourth boat into the surf in spite of her anchor & the men pulling with their oars[.] so finnly the officer who was in charge of her had to let go the line to save himself, which he did not do however untill his boat was full of water. The surf was getting higher all the time & it was impossable for those on the beach to get off with out assistance, which neither of the vessels could render them as their best boats were on shore already & to send in the smaller ones would only be to sacrifice there men. So the *Mt. V* came down to report to us. She brought 5 prisoners, part of the crew of the Barque the Captain of her was drowned trying to get on shore. her Log Book was a sick list you might almost say for while in Nassau she had lost almost all her crew from Yellow Fever, & every entry seemed to contain either a death or a new case[.] she shipped a new crew at N.[assau] but I believe there were only 7 on board when she ran ashore. Her mate says that her Cargo Saltpeter, salt, cannon, etc. was estimated at Nassau to be worth over $100000. & if they had succeeded in running in [it] would have sold for $500000. It is a pity we could not have taken her *alive.*

Early in the morning we sent the *Mt. V* up again, first supplying her with our Matallic [Metallic] Life Boat & plenty of rope but at about nine o'clock both she & the *Daylight* came back the Rebels having planted a battery there during the night & driven them off. So we lost from the *D.* An Ensign, a Paymaster, & 11 men with two boats. & from the *Mt. Vernon* an Ensign & 5 men with one boat.[53] In the afternoon a Flag of Truce came off from the Fort for the mens effects as they had (of course) taken them all prisoners. The boat brought off several letters from the Prisoners. It seems that at daylight a party of 25 Cavalry with some artillery came down on the beach & demanded their surrender. They had no arms to speak of as most of them had been lost when the boats capsized so of course they had no alternative but to surrender at discretion. They all say that they have been thus far treated as well as curcumstances would admit of & had no cause to complain & their captors had allowed them to send for their baggage.

I suppose you will be surpprised to hear that a Paymaster is among those taken prisoner, but I do not suppose you will be more so than we were. What business he had in a boat expedition is more than I can imagine & I think that *he* is served about right. Those who gave bonds for him when he entered the service will not fancy it much I guess.

It is very hard to get at the truth in such cases as this as to who is to be blamed for the loss but the general opinion seems to be that the fault (?) lies principaly with the Captain of the *Daylight* who (his men all say) fired shell into the Barque *after his boats were alongside of her*, which forced them to shove off again to save themselves when they got caught in the breakers & capsized.[54] I hope whether that is true or not that he will be turned out of the service for he is a disgrace to it. He makes his ship a perfect Hell to every soul on board, & goes about his deck cursing & swearing like a Pirate. He is a Volunteer I am sorry to say or rather I am glad, that the regular Navy is not disgraced by such a man. It does seem as though the Government picked out the poorest of the volunteer officers to take commands, that are in the service. Men that could not get a vessel in the Merchant Service being too well known to be trusted.

The *Daylight* captured a small schr about a week ago which was sent north.[55]

I wrote a letter to cousin Lu last Tuesday. I directed it to New York. I hope she will get it. Have you heard from Mrs. Greely yet?

I hope that I shall find the Cadet Regt. at Beaufort, it would be very pleasent[.] I should see so many of my old friends. E[liza] says I know a lot in the 44th. Who are they?[56]

I wonder if my box will be there.

Give my love to all the family & remember me to my friends. Good by from your loving son

Henry

Please excuse two sizes of paper. I did [not] notice till after I commenced that the one I was writing on was an odd sheet.

4

"The Bold and Daring Act"

Prisoner of War

Shortly after Henry's 5 November letter to his mother concerning the loss of men and boats in the surf, it is ironic that he would be involved in such an incident less than two weeks later. At 8 o'clock on the morning of 17 November 1862, lookouts on the *Cambridge* spotted a schooner near Masonboro Inlet about twelve miles northeast of Fort Fisher. Captain William A. Parker immediately ordered the ship underway toward the vessel. As the warship approached her prey, Parker ordered the thirty-pounder Parrott gun fired at the schooner. The gunfire prompted the master on board to run her ashore. Parker ordered a boat, under the command of Acting Master William H. Maies, to board the schooner and burn her. Maies had orders not to risk getting too close to the vessel if he believed the high surf would endanger the mission.

The schooner was the British *J. W. Pindar*, loaded with salt. Maies and his men managed to set fire to the vessel but in the heavy surf the boat capsized and "with difficulty" they reached the shore. From the *Cambridge* Parker observed the trouble and sent two other boats to communicate with the stranded men. Acting Master's Mate Henry Wells commanded one boat and Acting Master's Mate Odiorne the other. In the heavy surf Henry Wells swam ashore with a line, but it parted and Mr. Odiorne followed with another line. As Odiorne reached shore about thirty armed men came upon the naval party and took them all prisoner. Captured were Acting Master Maies, Acting Master's Mates Wells and Odiorne, and ten men.[1]

On 18 November, the Confederate captors took Henry and the other prisoners to Camp Heath, just north of Wilmington. The next day they sent them to Wilmington under guard. Here Brigadier General William Henry Chase Whiting, who commanded the district of Cape Fear, questioned them personally. Afterwards they marched them to the town hall, and that afternoon they started back to Camp Heath. At 8 AM on the twentieth, the Confederates placed the captives on rail cars for a trip to Richmond and they reached Weldon, North Carolina, that evening. Here they separated the officers from the men, and the officers stayed at a hotel during the night. On the twenty-first, they resumed their trip, arriving in Petersburg, Virginia, at 1 PM. They were placed in the county jail, which Maies described as the "most filthy place imaginable it being under ground with a box in one end for the common uses of nature[.]" Here, they strove to get the men to take an oath of allegiance to the United States and one of the men did so. On the morning of 22 November, the guards roused them at 8:30 and moved them once again to the rail cars for the final trip to Richmond, arriving in the city at 11:30 AM. Transported to Libby Prison, they only remained a short while. At 3 PM they paroled the three Union officers and promised that they would go North by the next flag of truce boat, which left on 31 November.[2]

U.S.S. *Cambridge*
Off New Inlet N.C.
Nov. 30th /62

Sir,

I learn from refugees from Wilmington, that the officers & men captured from this ship by the enemy, were carried immediately to Raleigh or Richmond, and consequently we have had no communication with them. I shall forward Mr Wells' effects to you by the earliest opportunity, probably by the supply ship on her return next trip.

I am, sir, very respectfully
F.W. Strong
Ex. Officer U.S.S. *Cambridge*

To
Thos. G. Wells Esq
Brookline, MS.

U.S. Transport Steamer *New York*
Hampton Roads
Dec. 1st 1862

Dear Father & Mother

I have just been released on parole from Richmond. We leave here for Annapolis tonight & I hope to be able to come home in a few days as of course I can not serve any more until exchanged.[3]

I can't say I have enjoyed my trip thro' secesia much, but I am lucky in not having been detained long.

I am decidedly "*hard up*" having no money & only an undershirt that I can call my own.

My clothes were sent ashore to me when I was taken but I never received them

& had to shift the best way I could[.] I traveled from Wilmington NC to Richmond with only shirt[,] pair of drawers, shoes, & hat, all of which I borrowed from the men. Mr. Odiorne was no better off.

I do not think you had better send me any thing tho' as I can not tell where I may be. I can get along I guess till I arrive in New York & then I will go to Uncle P.[arkhurst] for money.

I have a very bad cold but other wise pretty well, tho' used up (about) & shall be glad of a quiet spell at home.

I sent you a letter by Flag of Truce when I was first taken which I hope you received for if you did not this might take you by surpprise. Not knowing that I had been taken. Perhaps it would be better tho if it were so, & you would then be saved all the anxiety for me which you would have felt if you had known I was *locked up*.

There are about 350 or 400 of us aboa[r]d this boat including 16 officers. We left Richmond yesterday morning & City Point in the afternoon.

Good by now. love to all from you loving

Henry

U.S. Steamer *Cambridge*
Hampton Roads VA
December 17th 1862
Mr Thomas G. Wells

Sir:

Your note of the 29th ult. [ultimo] has been received, and in reply I have to inform you that your son Henry W. Wells was taken prisoner near Wilmington N.C. on the 17th November at Masonborough Inlet. He was endeavoring in the most daring and gallant manner to rescue a party of men who had been wrecked on the beach in a storm; for this purpose he volunteered to swim through the heavy breakers with a line; having effected this in company with Mr Odiorne, an armed body of about 30 men suddenly appeared, and took them prisoners.

I fear that your son and Mr Odiorne must have suffered very much, as they had left their clothes behind them in the boat, before they attempted to swim through the breakers and the wind was blowing quite hard; but I have heard that their captors treated them very kindly, and sent them to Richmond; where I hope they will soon be paroled. I shall be most happy to hear from your son when he returns home.

very respectfully
your obedient Servant
William A. Parker
Commander

U.S.S. *Cambridge*
Beaufort N. C.
Febry 17th 1863
Mr Wells

Dear Sir:

Your note of the 6th December announcing your safe arrival to your family and friends has been received; and I congratulate your on your delivery from the hands of the enemy.

I think you deserve much credit for the bold and daring act of swimming through a heavy surf with a line, for the purpose of rescuing the officers and men who had been wrecked while destroying a rebel schooner in the attempt to run the blockade.

Be assured my dear Sir that your gallant efforts were the admiration of every one on board this vessel, and had the enemy allowed you a little more time you would no doubt have succeeded in saving the whole party.

For this noble act I think you deserve promotion to the grade of Actg Ensign; especially as I consider you competent in every respect to perform the duties of an Ensign with credit to yourself and with profit to the government.

I should be happy if the Hon[ora]ble Secretary of the Navy would allow you to return to this vessel as Actg Ensign

Wishing you all success in life, and a brilliant career in your profession, I remain dear Sir,

Sincerely yr friend
Wm. A. Parker

Commander

5

"Coolness and Gallantry under Trying Circumstances"

Service in the North Carolina Sounds

Hampt[on] Roads
Feb. 20 1863
Gunboat *Ceres*

Dear Mother

I am ordered on board this vessel[.] I only had 15 minutes notice. We are going to Newburn.[1] The vessel is a mere cocle [cockle] shell[2] & you may never hear from me again. Most of the officers have refused to go & resigned. I wont. The Capt says he will go & I'll not desert him.

Good by love to all from

Henry

U.S. Gunboat *Ceres*
Pamlico Sound
Feb. 25th 1863

Dear Mother

We have run tho [through] a fearful ordeal but are safe now. I wrote you just before starting & I suppose you received my letter. I had only 15 minutes notice before leaving the *Minnesota* & as we started a half an hour afterwards I only had time to write two or three lines. This vessel is one of the old New York side wheel Tow boats [with a very heavy battery and bulwarks] are all ironplated with Boiler iron to keep off musketry which is of course an additional weight.[3] All the officers but one resigned when they found where she was going but the Admiral would not accept it & told them they had got to go & if they would not do duty they should go in irons & be tried by Court Martial when they arrived. So they concluded that as they had got to go they might as well be free & therefore they consented to do duty.

We left the roads at midnight (Friday night)[.] it was a beautiful calm night & we hoped we should be able to get round with out having any rough weather but we were mistaken. Every thing went well to Sat.[urday] afternoon when it commenced to blow from NE & the sea began to rize. we were then off Oregon Inlet, & had no hope of getting in that night. our boiler was leaking very badly so we could carry very little steam & were in mortal fear every minute that it would give out altogether. As it grew dark the wind increased & the sea began to run very high which caused the vessel to labor badly. Every sea that struck her under the guards would almost knock us off of our feet & shake every timber in her. at about midnight she commenced to leak badly the water got up over the fireroom floor & we had to put her before the wind so the pumps could free her. We threw over board about a ton & a half of shell & should have put the guns over, if the wind had increased any more, which Provedentialy for us it did not. I never looked so anxiously for daylight as I did that night every minute seemed like an hour. It came at last & thankful enough we were to see it. As soon as it was light enough we ran in for the land which we made a little to the northard of the light House on Cape Hatteras[.] we then ran between the Diamond Shoals & the Cape[,] the water breaking on both sides of us & the weather so thick that at times we could not see the land which was only about ½ a mile or a mile from us. Nothing but Gods mercy ever carried us thro'[.] The Capt. said he believed that his wifes prayers were the only thing that kept him above water, & I felt that my mothers might have some saving influence as well. it was a most horrible suspense, it makes me shudder to think of it, tho' I dont think I realy felt afraid till it was over & I looked back on that sea of breakers. it seemed impossable to believe that we could have come thro' them. We had no choice, it was a matter of life & death to us. for our little boat would never have lived to have gone round out side, & it was our only hope to make a bold dash. Our danger was not over however when we had run thro' there for we had yet to get into the Inlet where so many of Burnsides expitdition were lost. When we got off the entrance it was a fearful sight, the sea was running very high & breaking right across the entrance so we could not tell where the channel was for one place looked the same as another, all one sheet of foam. We had no choice but to run thro' however for the gale was increasing every minute & we could not depend on the engine which the engineer reported liable to break down any minute. So we did not stop to think about it but pointed her right for the center or the breakers & clapped on all steam, &—for about ten minutes I dont think I breathed for if we touched the bottom or the man at the wheel made the least mistake that would have been the last of the *Ceres* & of all on board. We were all happy at the end of that time & I hope sufficiently thankful to God for his great mercy.

I have been so near death by water twice lately that I begin to think I was not born to be drowned. however I have not such a strong faith in that theory as to want to go round Cape Hatteras again in the *Ceres* or any other such craft. If ever I am sent round again in such a craft I think it will be the last cruise I will take in a Government [vessel]. I am willing to stand any thing in reason but as to being sacrificed in that sort of way I dont fancy it.

I expect we shall have considerable fighting to do on board this vessel, which I am not at all sorry for, but I *do* wish I had a little pleasanter set of messmates. They are a good natured set enough for all I can see but there is not a particle of refinement of [or] decency in any of them. Our officers consist of an Act. Vol. Lieut. Commanding, three masters mates & two engineers. (we are to have one more of the latter). We have about 40 men. I am senior (next to the Capt) on board but as the Executive Officer has been on board for a long time in that capacity I do not want to displace him. especialy as he is a good deal older than I. The Capt. said that I could have the position if I wished but I told him I did not care for it. You may direct my letters to Newbern N.C. untill I send you different word. Good by now. My hand is so cold that I have not been able to write very well but I hope you will be able to read it. Love to all from your own son

Henry

We are now on our way to Newbern. We as well as the vessel being pretty well used up I guess we shall stop there some days. I shall have a chance to see the Bonds & Willard I hope.

U.S. Gunboat *Ceres*
Pamlico Sound
Feb. 27th 1863

Dear Mother

I started a letter home last night & now I will commence another so that if another chance offers before we get to Newbern I shall not miss it. You will probably be surpprised at seeing my letter still dated in the Sound, but I have allmost come to the conclusion that this is the only place where any letters will ever be dated from this vessel for we are hard & fast aground on what is called the Royal Shoals where we have laid ever since last Monday, and as there is a sort of Quicksand here I am beginning to think we shall not get off very readily.[4] Tomorrow will decide the question tho' I suppose. I suppose it is very wrong but realy I shall not be *very* sorry if we do not get off tho' of course I shall do my duty in assisting in ever[y] means in my power to get the vessel clear. but the fact is we have been used so shabbily in being sent out side in such a miserable concern that I think the powers that be will be served well right to lose the vessel, tho' after we got into Hatteras Inlet of course the danger to which they exposed us was over & our present difficulty might have occurred to any vessel running up & down the Sound.

When we first got fast & found that we could not clear ourselves an officer was sent to Hatteras Inlet in a boat to try to get one of the Tug boats there to come to our assistance but none of them could come, so after waiting there a day for the mail steamer, he went in her to Newbern, & yesterday the Gunboat *Lockwood* came to our assistance.[5] But we had laid here so long that I think the sand must have bedded up round us, at all events she could not start us an inch but tore all our cleats out & parted our hawser (a new one) several times. We lightened the ship of every thing except the guns (we could not get those out with out heaving them overboard as we have no spars, & of course we did not want to do that) but it was no use. After working at us all day the *L[ockwood]* went back to Newbern & I expect every minute to hear that she is in sight again bringing down a schooner to take out our battery & every thing else "getatable".

We have just been at quarters exercising. I have command of the 1st Division & a 30 pdr. Parrott very much the same as that which I had on board the *Cambridge*. We have a *very* poor crew, nearly all landsmen, however I guess I shall be able to make a pretty good fight when the time comes.

The steamer is not in sight yet & as it is after three o'clock I suppose when she does come we shall not be able to do much to night.

I expect when they get hold of us again they will either get us off or tear us all to pieces. We are strained so badly now that I am afraid that she will have to be repaired again before she can do much service.

I wish I was back on the old *Cambridge* again. I did not know when I was well off while I was on board of her. There are better vessels, but I know now that there are also some a thousand times worse.

I care more for the men I have to assosiate with than the vessel itself & I can not say that I have a very exalted opinion of my companions on board here. They are well meaning fellows enough but one can not take any great pleasure in their society. I miss Odiorne I can tell you.

Perhaps I may by chance, if this boat is lost, get down that way, but I am afraid there is not much hope of that & I expect I shall stay here in the Sounds for some time to come.

My cold still hangs on tho' it does not trouble me much. I am used to them you know. otherwise I am pretty well only somewhat used up as you may judge from the experiences I have told you of in this & my last letter.

Our accommodations are very poor on board here. We have berths to sleep in but no place what ever to put our clothes, so we have to live in our trunks which is not very convenient, as you may suppose.

My principal amusement here is to get the "captain on the string". he is a *Copperhead* of the most copperish stamp & thinks Horatio Seymore of New York & Geo[rge] B. McClellan the only true Patriots in the country.[6] & would vote for the latter for President. Would also like to see the Union restored by leaving New England out in the cold & was quite indignent when I respectfully hinted that I thought the said states were quite as able to take care of themselves as any other part of the country. He thinks that the spirit of infidelity (i.e. Unitarianism) in that part of the country had a good deal to do with bringing on the war, etc. etc. etc.

He is not a regular officer but an Act. Vol. Lieutenant. He was a master on board the *Minnesota* when I was in her the first time.

I suppose E[liza] is at home now. give my love to her & all the rest write to me often, at Newbern.

Good by, from your ever loving son

Henry

U.S. Steamer *Ceres*
Royal Shoals
March 3rd 1863

Dear Mother

As I believe there will be a chance to send this afternoon I will just write you a few lines tho' I sent off a long letter day before yesterday[.] I dont like to miss a chance but you must not expect a very long letter for since we have been ashore here we have had so much to do that it is hard work to find time to eat & sleep.

We have lightened the vessel of almost every thing getatable but still stick fast, yesterday we had two steamers fast to us. Today we have got a Wrecking Schooner trying to heave us off. she has not started us yet but she *may* be able to. Mr. Ryan, the Ex Officer has been out of the ship most of the time since we have been here up at Newbern & else where, on duty so the other masters mate & myself have had to stand watch & watch. Then when we are heaving & trying to get off I have to be up for Mr Hudson has not been to sea a great deal & does not understand how to go to work.[7] We have a miserable crew & some of the Petty Officers are as bad as the men so that we officers have to take right hold & show them how, to do every thing[.] So we do not have time to do any thing for ourselves at all.

I have hardly looked at a book since I have been here.

I have only received one letter from home since I left & that was a note from you which reached me the day Friday that I left the *Minnesota*. It is not strange however as I suppose it is hardly time for your letters to get to Newbern yet it makes me feel sort of home sick tho' for all that.

You must tell me all the news about Eliza. I suppose she is having a splendid time[.] I wont write any more now as I want to lay down. If the vessel does not leave to night I will add more to this before I send it. Tell Lu I want her to write to me. I have not time just now to write to her, to ask her myself.

Good by love to all from your *castaway*,

Henry

March 4th We are off & will probably be in Newbern tomorrow if we do not get ashore again. We are waiting now for a steamer to tow us up as we have no coal. Good by in haste from

Henry

US Gunboat *Ceres*
Newbern
March 8th 1863

Dear Mother

We have arrived here at last & I am thankful for it for I had begun to think that the Fates were against us. We have had nothing but a *ceres* of bad luck ever since she has been out.

The wrecking schooner that I spoke about in my last letter succeeded in pulling us off, after which we had to wait two days for coal as our fuel was all expended. When it did arrive we started but when we were with in about 15 miles of Newbern, it gave out so we anchored & fitted out a party to go ashore & get wood[.] I went with it. we were all armed of course & rather expected to have a brush with the Rebs before we got off. but every thing passed off quietly & we got about 3 cords of wood. We then started again but after going about 5 miles we got aground & had to lay by all night. In the morning we got off but our wood was all gone so we had to send ashore for more. Just as we were getting ready to go ahead again a schr. came to us with coal & our provisions (which we had taken out to lighten the ship when on Royal Shoals). After getting that in, we started & that time we succeeded in getting thro' (tho we grounded once on the way) & arrived here late yesterday afternoon.

We worked the best part of last night getting our guns on board, & have been coaling (nice Sunday work) all this afternoon. We start tonight on an expedition where I do not know, but I suppose we shall have some fighting before we get back. We are in a nice state to go. Our engine is about used up with our late experiences & need[s] a thorough overhauling. The Chief Engineer told the Captain this morning that if he went he must take all the responsibility as he (the Engineer) would not take any as he did not consider the Engine fit to run. Then our crew have hardly been drilled at all so we do not feel very sanguine of being able to do very good service.

I have not been able to go ashore on Liberty yet & so have not seen any of our friends[.] When I was on the wharf last night getting in the guns I spoke to the sentry & asked him about where to find them etc. When I asked him if he knew Sargeant Welman, he said "O yes we all know him, he's a bully fellow, has got first rate pluck & ain't a bit airish, every body likes him." I sent my card to him by the sentry who said he would take it as his quarters were not far from his.

I can not write any more now as dinner is ready. Give my love to all & write often to your loving son

Henry

U.S. Gunboat *Ceres*
Swan Quarter[8]
March 13th 1863

Dear Mother,

We leave here to night for Newbern so I will add a few lines to the letter which I wrote before the expedition started but did not have a chance to mail on account of our hurried departure.

We left *N.*[ewbern] Sunday night before dark[.] The Transports had a days start of us so when we arrived here we found the troops had all debarked. In company with the Gunboat *Lockwood* we then went up the Pungo River to create a diversion in their favor.

Several landings were made but I was not in any of the parties as I was very unwell for two or three days. I was not particularly sorry that it happened so, for such proceedings as were carried on there are a disgrace to the service. They were regular plundering excursions, some of the officers had the (what word shall I use?) to take Albums, Photographs & such things from houses, articles which could be of no manner of use to them & which were probably of great value to the ladies who owned [them]. One officer (not of our vessel) had the meanness to take the last pound of sugar that a woman had, who had a little baby. She begged him not to take it & said he might take any thing else in the house if he would only leave that as she could not get any more. Another took a work-box & three half Dollars.

Our Captain who was senior officer made them carry back the sugar & pictures & wrote the lady a not[e] of apoligy for their having been taken but we carried off a lot of Bacon, & Poultry. Thats all fair tho' I suppose.

We staid up the river two days & then as we had neither seen or heard any thing of the soldiers we came back here to await their return. They got back last night & are nearly all on board the transports now. as soon as they are all off we shall leave N[ewbern].[9]

I hope we shall stop there a little longer next time, so that I can have a chance to see the boys.

I long to hear from you all, & have only had one short note since I left home. of course you have written, but I have been moving about so that I have not been able to get them.

I believe I told you in my last to Direct to the "*Ceres* Newbern." Good by now it has gone 8 bells (8 P. M.) & I have got the middle watch so I want to turn in early. Love to all from your loving son

Henry

Newbern, March 15th. I received Lu's letter & a short note from you last night.

Capt. P. letter (copy) was enclosed in L's. We had some fighting here yesterday & are hourly expecting an attack on the Place by the enemy in force under General Hill or Longstreet.[10] Do what you like with Capt. P's letter. I hardly know what to advise[.] if I was at home I should try again but now you must at home judge what is best[.] The letter seems as [a] very good one dont you think[?] Good by in haste with much love from

Henry

U.S. Gunboat *Ceres*
Newbern N.C.
March 18th /63

Dear Lu,

I received your letter a few days ago & as I suppose I can count on a quiet half hour this morning I will try & answer it. The Capt. & all the other officers excepting two of the Engineers, are ashore. I am therefor[e] in command & can do as I please & as it *dont* suit me to stay on deck all the time I have come down here to write leaving one of the Quartermasters on deck to look out for the vessel & call me if I am wanted. The boys are cleaning up our cabin & the only dry places are the berths so I am setting in mine with my Portefolio on my knees, & if my writing is not very plain you must make allowances. I'm afraid I am [not] going to have such a quiet time after all for since I commenced writing I have been called on deck twice "such is life".

Monday I went ashore on liberty & had a first rate time seeing all the boys. I first went up to the quarter[s] of Co. B. 45th & saw the Bonds there they (after we had had a good long talk & smoked sundry cigars) went with me to see Willie Welman.[11] He is getting along nicely now, he looked very pale & thin to me, but you know I have not seen him before since he left home[.] Those that have been with him think he looks first rate. He says they could not have wounded him & hurt him less. It must have been dreadfully tedious for him tho' to have had to lay in the Hospital so long. They all say he bore it splendidly tho' & never complained at all. every body seems to like him & between you and I, I think he just is a tip top fellow. He seemed very glad to see me & I'm sure I was to see him.

After I left him we (Bonds & I) called on the Windsors. The Adjutant was not at home but I met him in the street just before I went on board.

I suppose you have seen in the papers by this time of the little brush that we had with the Rebels here. We arrived from the Hyde County expedition just in time to have a hand in it. It did not amount to much but it was a pretty impudent thing on the part of the Reb's to come & plant artillery right under our noses in that way. The Gunboats soon drove them off tho'.[12]

We are expecting every day to be sent to Plymouth as they have gone off in that direction.

I received a nice long letter from Eliza yesterday with a note from Mother & a Tin Type of Uncle Hamilton for which I am very much obliged. I also received a Weekly Transcript.[13]

Tell Cousin Lu that unless I am greatly mistaken & I dont think I am, she owes me a letter & I can not give her any farther extension of time but request she will forward it at once.

As to my being an "Old Fellow" or not, I think it is hardly worth while to answer that question as you called me by that name two or three times in the course of your letter.

Well I am about at the end of my paper so I guess I will not write any more now.

Give my love to all & keep lots for your self from your loving brother

Henry, who wants to hear from you very often

U.S. Gunboat *Ceres*
Newbern N.C.
March 21st /63

Dear Mother

I have a half an hour before supper & I dont think I know of a more satisfactory mode of spending it than in writing a few lines to you[.] this is not to be considered as a specimen of my penmanship tho' for I must write fast or the boys will want to set the table before I get tho' [through].

I wrote to Lu a day or two ago. Yesterday I received a letter from you, dated, (let me look) . . oh yes, March 15th & today three papers, Two Journals & one Tribune which were very exceptable. It has been wet weather ever since I wrote last so I have not been on shore except that once, which I told you about. I mean to go tomorrow if I can.

You have spoken in both of your last letters of one which you wrote me & sent to the *Minnesota*. I have not received it, but have written to a friend on board there to look it up for me.[14] But if there was any thing especial in it you had better write it again as I think the chances are that that [it] is lost.

Are you doing any thing about my promotion. I am sorry Capt. P. did not write to Washington but still that last letter is so very strong that it does seem to me as tho' they could not ignore it. do as you think best about it tho' at home. I want to get out of this & if promoted probably should as this thing dont want an Ensign on board.

I am real glad that Mr Clarke has got that position at Harvard Colledge if he wanted it, & it dont take him away from us, which I suppose of course it does not or you would have mentioned it[.][15]

It does not seem to me that Aunt Marcia has any occasion to feel very anxious about Tom, he will be home all in good time & proud to tell of his experiences with the Southern Privateer. Our family seems to be a little unlucky about getting caught. I hope Uncle Lyman will not get into the same scrape. I believe I mentioned in Lu's letter having received Eliza's letter.

The Boy wants the table now so I must close Love to all from your son

Henry

I have heard nothing of my accounts yet. Have written twice. It will be all right by & by of course only the delay is not very pleasant.

March 22nd I went on shore this morning but forgot to take this with me so I will add a line. I saw the Bonds & Wil[l]ard of course—all well. We leave I believe in a day or two for Plymouth.

By the way you know this is a great fever & ague district can't Dr Hunt put me up some medicine for that disease & I might as well doctor myself as to go with out having any thing or be poisoned by my body always providing I am so unlucky as to get the pest festered in me.

I shall write again in a day or two. Love to all

From Henry

U.S.S. *Ceres*
Plymouth N.C.
March 26th /63

Dear Mother

We are now up the Roanoke River as I told you I thought we should be in my last. We arrived here yesterday & last night we were doing Picket duty about 6 miles above here looking out for a Rebel Cotton Clad which is expected down the river, if she comes I think we shall give her a pretty warm reception for we have on this station the *Com.*[*modore*] *Perry* & *Southfield* both Ferry Boats with very heavy batteries (the *S* especially)[.][16] Last night the USS *Underwriter* arrived on this station so we feel very strong. The 27th Mass. Vol. are on shore here but I dont know any of them so I have not been out of the ship. The place does not look especialy inviting.

The *boys* have got a set of *Bones* down here & they are making such a confounded racket that I can hardly hear my self think.[17] —There goes quarters so I must leave off for the present.

—Quarters being over I shall now proceed.

Sunday I was on shore again at Newbern & had a very pleasant time part of the time with the Bonds & part with Welman. He seems to me to be looking better now than when I first saw him & seemed to be in a very good spirits.

In coming up here we passed Roanoke Island & anchored there for a few hours so I had a chance to see the place where that famous Battle was fought. The batteries looked formidable for vessels to encounter I can tell you & it must have been hot work shelling them out.

I can't say that the officers here (that's with two or three exceptions) improve much on acquaintance. Our Captain especialy is about as disagreeable a man as one often meets, sweet as honey one minute & sour as a crab apple the next. The last mood is the most frequent & then he does nothing but growl. he carries it to such an extent however that no one pays much attention to him.

He does not trouble me much for I have been in a man of war as long as he has & know the rules too well to give him a chance very often. I came near getting my self into a scrape the other day tho'. He wanted some thing done in an unreasonably short time & I told him flatly that a green crew like ours could not do it in any such time[.] Whereupon he commenced growling that I got a little out of temper & told him what I thought of his vessel & those on board of her, & you may be sure it was not a very complimentary speach, taken it all together. I never saw a man as mad as he was. I thought he was going to send me to my quarters but he thought better of it & did not. I was wrong that time but he is a very unreasonable man & wants his officers to do all sorts of things which they have no business to do. I told him that morning that I did not come on board to be a Boatswains mate & did not intend to act in that capacity. You see while we were ashore on Royal Shoals I worked like a horse because the vessel was in a bad fix & we had very few men on board that knew any thing about a vessel. I suppose he thought from that that I would be fool enough to keep it up but he has found out his mistake before this & dont trouble me much now but makes the ship a hell for some of the Poor fellows.

My direction is the same as before (Newbern NC) Love to all from your son

Henry

March 31. We are on our way back to N[ewbern] being about used up as regards Boiler etc. They will "*have*" to give us some sort of repairs before we can run any more, if there is any faith to be put in Engineers. I guess we shall stop a[t] Newbern some time. Good by love to all from

Henry

U.S.S. *Ceres*
Off Roanoke Island
March 31st /63

Dear Eliza

I received your letter some time ago & ought to have answered it sooner but the fact is I have not been in a writing mood lately for various reasons, partly because I have not been very well & partly because during the last week we have been doing Picket duty up the Roanoke River above Plymouth N.C. looking out for Rebel *Cotton Clads* which are expected down every day. That same Picket duty is no fun I can tell you in a narrow crooked river like the R[oanoke.] We have to be on the Alert the whole time night & day ready to go to quarters at a minutes notice so that when off duty one does not feel like doing much besides eat drink & sleep. (smoke too, always find time for that). If those are not reasons enough let me know at once & I will send you another lot next time if I have not forgotten them.

Oh Eliza you talk about the people in Canada being rather Sesesh in their ideas but if you could only hear some of the officers on board here talk—here—taking the pay of the Government & talking worse treason than I heard while I was a Prisoner in the South. it is enough to make one heart sick.

I get dreadfully indignant every now & then & let out on them, but it dont seem to do any good & I get called an Abolitionist for my pains.

Now I aint that altogether but I believe in supporting the administration thro' thick & thin, Emancipation Proclamation & all, for I believe that is the only way in which we can ever succeed in crushing out this Rebellion & I wish every "Copperhead" in the country was locked up or hanged—"Them's my tenix".[18]

I suppose you have heard from home of my experiences on board this vessel. We have had a great time since I joined taking it all together. To commence with we were sent round Cape Hatteras & very near lost in a heavy gale of wind off there. Then we crossed Hatteras Bar (Inlet) when the chances were ten to one against our getting thro' the sea was breaking so badly there. (We had to try it tho' for we should certainly have been lost if we had staid outside) Then, on our way to Newbern we got aground on Royal Shoals in Pamlico Sound & lay there 10 days working hard night & day before we could get off. We had to take every thing out of the vessel[,] Guns Provisions, Iron Plating, ammunition etc. etc. We thought of course that when we got to Newbern we should be allowed to have a short resting spell to get things straightened up etc. but no. we were only given 24 hours to get every thing on board again & to coal. And then had to go off on an expedition up the Pungo River to cover a lot of our troops who were on a raid in that direction. We were gone about a week & returned to N[ewbern] just in time to assist in repelling the attack which the Rebels made on that place on the 14th of March. We were shelling them for several hours. The loss on our side was very small & there were only two men hurt on the Gunboats. We staid there about a week & then news having been obtained that the Enemy had gone off in the direction of Plymouth we were sent there. We arrived on the 25th just too late to join in the fight which they had there[.]

There are several Gunboats on that station but the Rebels made their attack in such a manner that they were not able to do a great deal. It did not make much differance[.] Their moral effect was enough to keep them at a respectful distance

& the troops on shore did the rest. Since then we have been stationed above Plymouth to give the other Gunboats warning if the Ram came down[.] Our Boiler has been leaking a great deal all along finerly it got so bad that it was hard work to keep the fire burning under it, so we are now on our way to Newbern to try to patch it up. It wont be much use tho' & we shall have to come North after a new one before long. They may put us on guard duty two or three months tho' at some place where we shall not have to keep up steam, (Newbern for instance).

I wish I could get back to the *Cambridge*, there are better vessels I know, but I have found out by experience that there are plenty a hundred times worse & she was at least a very comfortable vessel to be on board of. However, it dont make much differance. I am bound to stay in the service as long as the war lasts & then I shall "shake the dust off my feet." & go back to the old Merchant Service again.

I have just been trying to draw the *Ceres* for you for you "special benifit", how do you like it? "Big thing, but can't see it." The *C*[*eres*] used to be a Tow boat in New York Harbor, she has now iron bulwarks thick enough to keep out musket balls & heavy enough to make the vessel a very slow coach. She mounts 4 guns[,] 2 30 Pdr. Parrotts Rifles, & 2 24 Pdr Dalgreen [Dahlgren] Howitzers one on each side[.] the rifles are on Pivots & can be used either way. The battery is altogether to[o] heavy for us & together with the Plating brings the vessel so low in the water that her guards drag and she can not go more than six miles an hour.

Now just look but that there was a drop of red ink on the table which I had not the bearings of, & you see the consequences[.] Now I could not think of copying a whole sheet so I'm going to let it go dont you think that is the best way?

I have just read over your letter to see if there are any questions to answer, & as I believe there are not, I will now bid you good by as we have just anchored at Roanoke Island & I want to go on deck & see what is going on[.]

I shall send this via Home as you may be there. Love to all at home any way (for if you are not they will read it there before forwarding it wont they Mother?)

Write again soon to your loving Brother

Henry

U.S.S. *Ceres*
Washington N.C.
April [n.d.] /63

Dear Mother

It is nearly three weeks now since I have written home not without a good reason tho' for you must of course have heard before this of the siege of Washington, at which our little *Ceres* has born no mean part, & has won a great name from all that have witnessed her "daring deeds". I will now try & give you an account of my doings & seeings since I wrote last.[19]

You know we left Plymouth for Newbern on the 31st of March expecting as I wrote you to remain some time at the latter place for repairs, but we no sooner arrived there than we were ordered to coal up at once & leave for Washington N.C. which place was attacked by the Rebels under Gen Hill.

We only stopped about 3 hours at N[ew Bern] & I did not get a chance to go on shore. We arrived in the Pamlico River on the 2nd of April & ran up to within a bout 8 miles of W[ashington] where we met a fleet of Transports with troops who could not get up any farther on account of the Batteries that the Rebs had planted on two Points, Hill's & Rodman's. (the former about 7 & the latter 2½ miles from Washington).[20] Gen's Prince & Spinola were in command of the forces.[21] After communicating with them we ran up a little farther & joined the Gunboats *Lockwood* (3 guns) & *Allison* (Army boat) 2 Guns & Sloop *Grant* (1 gun).[22] After firing a few shots at the Battery on Hill's Pt we came to anchor for the night. The *L*[*ockwood*] had two shot holes thro' her when we arrived. In the morning we opened fire again but as the Rebs did not reply we soon knocked off. In the afternoon we were reinforced by the Gunboats *Southfield* 6 guns (very heavy), *Seymore* 3 guns & *White Head*, 4 guns[.][23] We then shelled the Battery for about two hours, the Rebs finding it too hot to reply most of the time & when they did no one was hurt. The *Ceres* tho' our Capt. was not Senior Officer went nearer to the Battery than any one else. At dark a boat from each vessel was sent to run the Blockade with ammunition. Mr. Hudson took charge of ours.[24] (Mr. Ryan was sick. & since I swam myself into a sesech prison & never got so much as thanked for it, I have never volunteered for any thing & dont intend to, tho' I shall *always* be ready to obey orders.) We towed the boats up as far as the Battery & then left them to make their way up. We then laid Buoys in the channel opposite the Pt. (the Rebs having sunk the old ones). Capt McDiarmid then determined to try & run the Blockade. There were only three Gunboats above, *Louisiana, Com.*[*modore*] *Hull* & *Eagle* (Army boat) & we knew they were *very* short of ammunition. It was a very hazardous undertaking but I think justifiable under the circumstances. Before starting we ran alongside of one of the Transports & took on board a large amount of Powder & shell and then pointed our Bow up river & put on all steam (They fired up with pine wood & *tallow* (a whole barrel)[.]

When we got nearly up to the Point we struck on some spiles that the Rebs had driven before the place was taken originaly & which had never been removed. I thought at first that we were stopped, but our little Boat forced her way over & went a head again. The Rebs then opened on us with three guns & made the shot hum round us in a most disagreeable manner as long as we were within range but Providentialy we were not hit once. our Pilot got frightened or else was half traitor. I am not sure which & after we got by said he was unable to take the vessel farther until daylight, so there we had to anchor right between the two Batteries & expecting to be blown out of the water in the morning. At daylight we started again & succeeded in getting past the other Battery without receiving a shot[.] the only way I can account for it being that when the Rebs saw us at anchor the[y] supposed we were disabled by the other Battery & so moved their guns to get a position with them from which they could destroy us & we ran past before they could get their guns in place again. I tell you it did one good to hear them cheer from the Gunboat when we came up to the town. I guess the Reb's did not like to here it much tho'. In the afternoon (4th April) we took on board 2 companyis of the 27th Mass. Vol. & went down to take (?) Rodman's Pt. Batteries[.] We caught a tartar tho' for the Pilot (d--m him) ran us aground right square in front of the Rebel Guns & they opened a hot fire on us with 3 field piece[s] using shrapnell (shell filled with lead Balls)[.] We sent the soldiers away in boats as fast as possable & sent them back. Several of them were wounded & the only wonder on my part is that there was not regular slaughter among them. The vessel then swung round with her bows towards the Battery & stuck fast. So there we were, could only bring one gun (mine) to bear on the Rebs[.] I stuck to it like a good fellow, took the Lock string my self & dismounted two of their guns & kept the other one pretty quiet considering one of my men was mortaly wounded[.] he was right alongside of me when I was sighting the gun, a shrapnell exploded in front of us & a piece of it entered his thigh, he died on the 9th inst. After dark they sent a flat-boat to us from town & we lightened the ship of every thing that we could get off & at 12 m[idnight] floated. Ran up to the town & anchored. I got a good deal of credit for my share of that fight from Captain McD[iarmid] & also from Brig Gen. Potter who was on board.[25] On the 6th we did not do any thing. The Rebs amused themselves (as in fact they did all thro' the whole affair) by firing at us occasionally but with out doing much damage. Sometimes one of the boats or a house would get struck, but on the whole their shooting was very poor & in a little while we got so used to hearing their shot & shell flying over us that nobody paid much attention to it except indeed our Executive Officer who has during this siege displayed about as much cowidice as often falls to one mans lot to show. The men all dispise him & the Capt. says he shall try to have him turned out of the service. What makes the matter worse is that he is the hardest kind of a blower always talking about what he has done or can do. During the fight on the 4th he left his gun when the firing commenced & went below.

On the 7th a Naval Battery was established on shore near the banks of the river on the extream left wing of our lines to look out for a Cotton Clad which was expected down the river & protect that part of our lines generaly. They took one of our 30 Pdr. Parrots & a 12 Pdr. Rifle Howitzer from the *Louisiana*[.] I was placed in command with an officer & 20 men under me, wan't that a big thing? They told me it was[.]

Mail going Good by finish next time—Love to all.

Henry

Washington N.C.
April 14th 1863

Dear Mother

It is some time since I have written to you but the reason has been that I could not send them if I did. We came up here (Ran the Blockade with ammunition) about 10 days ago & have been closely besieged ever since. I am temporarly detatched from the *Ceres* now & am in *Command* of the Naval Battery which has been established here for the time being. I obtained the preferment for having (so the Powers that be say) "distinguished my self for coolness & Gallantry under trying circumstances["] in a fight we had on the 4th inst.

We have had a very trying time our force being altogether too small for the defense of the place[.] Last night a large steamer the *Escort* & two schooners ran up bring[ing] about 400 men with plenty of ammunition & provisions[.][26] We were getting *very* short of the two last[.]

The *Escort* runs down again to night & I shall send this by her. I received by the *E*[*scort*] a letter from you (of 26th) & one from Cousin Lu it was cheering I can assure you. We have had nothing but cannonading all the time here. I have got so used to it now that I hardly pay it any attention unless they are firing at me. I will write you more at length soon & tell you all about my Battery etc. Good by now love to all, write often (direct as before) to your loving son

Henry

I would write more if I was sure of you getting my letter but it has got to run the Blockade of Rebel Batteries before it can reach you & I know what that is now by experience.

Henry

U.S.S. *Ceres*
Off Rodman's Pt.
April 21st /63

Dear Mother

I closed my last letter rather abruptly as the mail left sooner than I expected but I will now try & finish my account of the Siege. I left off I believe just as I was going to tell you about the Naval Battery. When I got on the ground I found it was on the extream left of our lines facing the river. The inclosure was about 40 ft. square & I had to attend throwing up the work for which I was supplied with a crowd of contrabands, & I fixed it just as I wanted it.

When I first landed I was introduced to Maj. Genl Foster who did me the honor to say that he "was glad the Battery was to be in such good hands"[.] So much for Rodmans Pt, tho' I am sure on that day I had no idea that I had distinguished my self till the fighting was all over.

It took three or four days to get the Place fixed up properly but when I got thro' I dont think a Regiment of soldiers could have driven us out of it. The Parapet was about 5 ft. high with a ditch outside about six feet deep & 10 broad at the top, with a pallisade of Picketts all round. Gate & draw bridge all completed. We called it Fort McDiarmid at which my men were rather indignant as they said it ought to have been named Ft. Wells. I had two guns, a 30 Pdr. Parrott mounted on a circle at one of the angles so that it would sweep in any direction. & a 12 Pdr. Rifle Howitzer on a field carriage. (There were embrasures in each of the four walls so that [it] also could be used in any direction). My second in command was Mr. Harper one of our 3rd asst. Engineers, who is a first rate fellow by the way. & my garrison consisted of 20 men.[27] We quartered in the loft of an old Barn close by. So much for the Battery.

I have just been trying to draw out a little Plan to show you the position a little. I am almost ashamed to send you the result of my labor but I guess I will on the whole.

The Batteries opposite Ft. Washington were first unmasked on the 10th inst. when they sent a perfect storm of shot & shell at the Ft. & all down the line. They did very little damage tho' for the soldiers all had bomb proofs to go into. After they had kept it up for about ½ an hour the Ft. opened & soon compelled them to cease firing. On Saturday morning the same thing was repeated. In the afternoon the General came over to my Battery & asked me if I would take my field Piece over to the Fort in the morning to lend a hand to return the Rebels fire. Of course I was willing enough so I got permission from the Senior Naval Officer & in the morning moved the Field Piece over, & took a position on one of the Platforms in the Fort. At about 9 AM the Rebels opened fire with six pieces & what with the fire from our Fort & the bursting of shell it seemed like one continued explosion for the whole 45 minutes that the Bombardment lasted. I worked the Howitzer my self & got the credit of making very good shooting. I believe the Rebs thought so at all events for they seemed to pay especial attention to the part of the work on which the Piece was placed, & the Barracks behind us were riddled with shot & shell. No one was hurt, in fact it did not seem to me as tho' there was much danger behind a parapet as high as ones head & I think I rather enjoyed the fun. After the firing was over I took my Gun back & I did not take it there again as we were short of ammunition. Every thing along about that time began to look rather dark[.] we were very short of Provisions, & ammunition of all sorts[.] Plenty of long faces were seen about enquiring what sort of a place Libby Prison was etc. On the 13th we were cheered a little by two schrs running the blockade with ammunition & provisions but still the fleet below did not seem to show any inclination to force the Blockade & we heard that the land expedition that started for our relief had gone back. Capt. McDiarmid persuaded the Senior Naval Officer Comm'd'r [Commodore] Renshaw to let him run the Blockade in a schooner & try to wake them up below. He started on the night of the 13th, after he had been gone an hour or so we heard a tremendous firing from Hill's Pt & we thought that he was catching it severly but soon after the Battery on Rodmans [Point] opened & then all commenced firing & we thought there was going to be a general attack so every body went to their posts. At a little after 11 P.M. I heared tremendous cheering from the gunboats in the harbor & a vessel blowing off steam[.] Soon after I assertained that the Transport Str. *Escort* had run the Blockade with 5th R.I. [Rhode Island] Vols. on board, not a man was hurt. She brought also such a supply of provisions & ammunition as to put all ideas of starving or giving up entirely out of our heads.

The next night the *Escort* ran down again with Gen. Foster on board who left in order to take command of a relieving force. Capt. McDiarmid returned the same night.

On the morning of the 16th we woke up to find the Rebels gone[.] The cav[a]lry went out to recinoter but did not find any one with in five miles of the works. The *Ceres* went down off Rodmans Pt to see if the Rebs had left there also. Not seeing any thing of them one of the boats was sent in to have a closer look. When about half way between ship & shore a party of men who had been conce[a]led by Rifle Pits sprang up & opened fire on them with rifles. Mr. [Thomas] Mallahan 3rd Asst. Engineer was killed instantly by a Ball thro' his head. The men all jumped out of the boat & keeping her between them & the enemy managed to Paddle her out with there hands till the vessel could pick them up. Later in the day our forces took possession there & also of Hills Pt. & that ended the siege.[28]

I have got a bad cold in the head & have done nothing but sneeze ever since I commenced writing this. I know I have made lots of mistakes but dont feel well enough to look them up you'll excuse them wont you?

Bad new[s] from Charleston aint it?[29] Good by if any one should see Odiorne ask him if he found my Revolver, Log Book or any other of my things. The *Cambridge* is in Boston I think you said. Love to all from

Henry

U.S. Str. *Ceres*
Pamlico Sound
April 25th /63

Dear Lu

I received your letter of the 12th yesterday & will answer at once so as to set you a good example you know.

We left Washington N.C. last night & are now on our way to Newbern but how long we may stay there I cannot tell.

We have had a pretty rough time of it lately & I have seen fighting enough to last me for some time as a matter of choice. The little *Ceres* always had a good name in this Department, but now there is nothing like her & every body talks about her doings, in fact I am proud that I belong to her tho' if I had my choice I should prefer to be outside on Blue water for if I stay here all summer I am afraid I shall not enjoy very good health for this is a horrid climate.

What do you think of me now hey? A large thing was it not, "Commanding Officer Naval Battery." I had a great time while I was there. My second in command Mr. Harper (an Engineer) is a first rate fellow & then there were two companies of the 44th Mass. quartered close by us the officers of which were jolly good fellows & we used to have great times together. By the way there was one gentleman (a P.B.) attached to the Quartermasters Dep. of the 44th named Page that I got accquainted with.[30] One day he was at my quarters & I showed him my Photograph Book. He opened it & exclaimed the first thing. "What's the matter?" "Do you know Mr. Clark?" I told him I rather guessed I did. Why said he "my parents go to church at Indiana Pl." "So do mine (sais I.) Where do you set?" "On the right as you go in about half way up, where are you?" "On the left." He knew the Bonds by sight & recognized the Photographs. He then turned over some more & set up another shout over Charlie Lovett, & then Horace Noble (but you dont know him). That was jolly wont it?

I could not help feeling sorry all the time to think Joe was not there, if he only had been what a time we would have had. The Regt. were all there except two comp[anies] who were left at Newbern & as bad luck would have it Charlie Soule was in one of them so I have not seen him yet.

Tell Joe that I am going to write to him soon tho' I am asshamed of him for neglecting me for so long. I have written to him twice since receiving a letter from him. I am very sorry he is in such bad health but the climate about New Orleans is enough to kill a horse & I am not very much supprised that he was not able to stand it.

Tomorrow is Sunday & I hope I shall have a chance to get ashore & see the Boys. The 44th have gone back to N[ewbern] since the siege was raised so I shall see my friends in that Regt. too.

I see that the papers say that Gen. Foster had a whole Brigade at Washington to defend the place. Now we who were there are not going to be *done* out of our glory in having successfully defended the place by any such yarn. There were not more than 1400 men there & I think hardly so many. They consisted of 8 companies of the 44th Mass. Part of the 27th Mass. & small detachments of the 3 NY Artillery & 3rd N.Y. Cavelry. There was also a part of a company of N.C. Vols. However having Genl Foster there was worth a Brigade & perhaps the papers seemed in that way. There is only one opinion of *him* in this Department.

What do you think? Capt. MacDiamind said in his official report on our proceedings during the siege. about me? It ran something in this way. "I would especialy call the attention of the Dept. to the gallentry & coolness of act. Masters Mate H.W. Wells. No commanding officer could be better supported & I would respectfully recommend him for promotion to the rank of act Ensign which I think he richly deserves." That's about the gist of it. I suppose you'll think I'm getting a bit proud & egotistical. I dont know but I am, & at any rate I have a right to be so after such a [left blank] as that I think.

Well if I dont get my appointment now between Capt Parker & Capt. MacD. I shall be very much tempted to throw my Masters Mate appointment into the fire & leave the service in disgust. I have been disapointed now so often that I have not much faith in getting it tho'.

So Mary is coming out to make a visit. Just my luck to be away[.] I wish you would ask her if she does it on purpose, on the whole tho' I guess you need not, it would not sound very well I'm afraid. Oh, Dear I sometimes wish I did not go to sea & then I would not have to be away from home so much, & you would remind Mary that she owes me a letter. I should like to hear from her very much.

I have not time to write any more now. Perhaps when you show this letter you had better keep back this half sheet then if I get my Promotion it will be a supprise & if I do not every body at home will not be disapointed.

Good by now give my love to all & write often to your Brother

Henry

Those numbers on the page have nothing to do with the letter.

US Str. *Ceres*
Newbern N.C.
April 27th /63

Dear Mother

I have received two or three letters from you since I last wrote you one of them being the long looked for letter which you directed to the *Minnesota*. I only wish I could have got it when it was first written[.] I am sure it would have had a good effect, & what you predicted in it, has since proved to a certain extent true.

I am glad you saw Capt. Parker[.] I hope he applied for me to be sent back to his ship. I'll know better than to growl when I'm well off, next time. I am sorry the old ship was in such a mess when you went on board. I should like to have you have seen her when she was all trim & neat ship-shape (but not *Bristol fashion* as we used to say, *thats* English).[31]

The officer who told you about my things must have been, by your description, Mr. Taft, Captain's Clerk, he used to be Paymasters Steward & is the gentleman we had so much trouble with in our mess at first. After he got *broke in* & used to the ways on board ship tho' I found him a very pleasant shipmate.

Have you seen any thing of Odiorne? I understand his engagement is broken off. I guess its just as well for them both if it is so. He is too young & has not seen enough of the world yet to think of getting married.

By the way now I think of it, I wish you would send me a few Postage Stamps I am about out.

Did you ever get that scrap of a letter that I wrote while in Washington N.C. to run the Blockade? it was only a few lines written in pencil. I wrote it out in camp one day as I was afraid you might hear some report or rather about the *Ceres* & be anxious.[32] I find that they had a yarn flying round Newbern that we were sunk or blown out of the water, or something of that sort. I sent it by an officer of the 44th who was going to try & run past the Batteries that night.

I have had a first rate time since we arrived here. The 44th Mass have come down from Washington & relieved the 45th as Provost Guard in town[.] the 45th are in camp now just outside near Ft. Spinola. During the siege I got acquainted with nearly every officer in the 44th & those that I dont know[,] know me so its all the same & whenever I go ashore I have no lack of company & of the right sort too, thats the beauty of it. its refreshing to get into the society of Gentlemen occasionaly. Yesterday I was out to the Camp of the 45th & had a very pleasent time[.] I took dinner with Will. Henry & Willie Wellman were full of business getting things fixed up so I did not see much of them. Willie looks first rate tho' now & is jolly as can be[.] He was fixing a cellar in his tent.

While I was there Cousin George came out in a Buggy (I had met him once before so it was not a surpprise)[.] He has been very sick as I suppose you have heard, but is better now tho' still pale & rather weak. I staid out there about 9 hours, called on both of the Windsors, & was introduced to a number of officers who it would have puzzled me to have named five minutes after. I rode back to town with George. He is going home as soon as he can get a good opportunity but does not like the regular boats as they go so crowded.

I am going to take dinner with some of the 44th officers to day if I can get away from the ship, it is a little doubtful however as there is to be a Court of Inquiry as to the cause of our getting aground on Royal Shoals.

We are going back to Washington tomorrow or next day, perhaps. The Engineers say we cant get there that the Boiler will not hold out, but I have my doubts. That confounded Boiler has been "giving out" ever since I have been on board & I dont "see the point."

Evening—I have been on shore all the afternoon & have just got off. The officers of Co. D. 44th Mass invited Mr. Harper & myself to dine with them. They gave us a *splendid dinner*. Four courses & (dont look solemn Mother) plenty of Wine & Ale. We had a first rate time & none of us drank more than was good for us.

Cousin George came off on board this morning to see the Boat. I guess he did not think much of her. I was almost ashamed to take him into our quarters for they would be considered a disgrace as a merchant ship & are hardly passable for a Gunboat.

I heard while on shore that another expedition has gone off, & that the 45th are with it. I will not vouch for the truth of the report I shall know certainly tomorrow.

Good night now. I've got the middle watch & want to go to sleep Love to all from

Henry

Brookline, Mass
April 29, 1863

Dear Henry,

Your promotion of Acting Ensign, was received on board the *Cambridge*, at the Navy yard, & has been forwarded to you at Newbern, by mail to day; Odiorne received his at the same time.

You will see the appointment detaches you from the *Ceres*, & holds you waiting orders; you will of course at *once* forward your acceptance to the Department with the accompanying oath properly subscribed, & I would at the same time inform the Department that I should wait orders at Brookline, Mass. & then come home as soon as you can.

Truly your
Father

U.S.S. *Ceres*
Newbern N. C.
May 1st 1863

Dear Mother

I received your letter of the 21st a day or two ago & also by the same mail Mr. Clarks sermon & a Journal.

I saw the sermon at the 45th Camp & glanced over it there but was very glad to get it myself & I set down & read it carefully as soon as it arrived. I think it is first rate, just what I should have expected from him.

I could not help laughing right out when I came to what he said about the Boston Courier.[33]

I received a note this morning from Mrs. Harris, (where I have neglected to call thus far) She said she hears much to her supprise that I was in the *Ceres* from L. Bond, & hoped I would call. it was a very friendly note & I shall go there tomorrow if nothing happens.

I think the *Ceres* will either stay *here* for some time or else go to Baltimore[.] We certainly can not cruise any more if there is any faith to be placed in Engineers. Our Boiler leaks so badly that there is a *small river* running across the fire room floor all the time. We were ordered back to Washington N.C. but the Engineers reported that the Engine would not take us there so we are now waiting to see what they are going to do about it.

My cold is nearly over now thanks to Dr. Arnts medicine which I brought with me, I suppose.

I am very sorry to hear such bad news about Tim Peck but I should think a sea voyage would do him a great deal of good.

I wrote to J. Wellman a few days ago. I wonder if he received the letter. it was directed to Brookline in care of Father as I believe they do not have a Box at the Post Office.

Father gave me credit for what I did not do about laying those buoys. The Captain & Pilot did that assisted by the Capt. of the *Seymore* & I was left in charge of the *Ceres* to look out for them (the work was done in small boats, of course).

I hope Mother that I shall bear my honors in a proper spirit. I dont know but what I was a little crazy for a day or two but that has passed off now & I am as *calm* and *sedate* as ever.

I wish if there is any doubt about Capt. P[arker]'s letter having been received at the Department that he could be asked to write again for I should like very much to get back to the C[*ambridge*] again or at all events out of these Sounds[.] This is a kind of *going to sea* that I dont fancy.

I am very glad to here that LaLa is better. I hope to hear from her soon as she owes me a good long letter. Lu is also my debtor.

We have not heard any thing from the Expedition that left Sunday, yet, or at least not here on board.

Every thing goes on quietly except—but I guess I had better not mention is [it] at present.

Good by now love to all from your loving son

Henry

Tell Ben that I am very much obliged to him for that sample of his drawing. What I should like very much to have a picture of the *Ceres* & *Cambridge*.

H.

The Little *Ceres*

Ye friends of Neptune listen now
We'll sing to you a ditty
It's bout the little *Ceres* bold

That hails from New York City
Her guns tho few are manly armed
We'll break treason foul asunder
And when they shout they will cry out
Lookout for Yankee Thunder

Her fight at Roanoke will prove
That her crew were for the Union
And for that cause our nation's laws
Would protect our great Commander
As long as our flag our nations brag
Is from her Flag staff flying
So long we swore it shall be there
Till all 'neath it are dying

The Union by our Fathers made
To the whole world is a taken
For it we fight for our cause is right
And it never shall be broken
While others dare our Flag to tear
So it prove a traitorous knave
It shall be said when we are dead
That the *Ceres* crew were brave

Composed by one of the crew of the USS *Ceres*

[note with no date addressed to]
Hamilton Willis Esq
Brookline Mass.

U.S.S. *Ceres*
Off Newbern
May 7th 1863

Dear Mother

I have received my long waited for appointment as Act[ing] Ensign. It arrived day before yesterday. At the same time I received Fathers & Lus letters.

I hoped I should be able to get home but Com. Davenport will not let me go till he can hear from Admiral Lee as they are short of officers here in the Sounds.[34] So I suppose I shall be detained here for the preasent at least. It was rather a disapointment but perhaps it will all turn out for the best.

Capt. McDiarmid was quite put out that "Capt Parker should have got ahead of him" & sais that if he could have forseen that I was going to be made an Ensign he would have recommended me for an Act. Master. I'll get it yet if I stay with him, I guess.

I want to have a *sack* coat made (cloth), with the proper straps & lace (lace ¼ or ⅜ in.) (single breasted of course for a sack) Call & Tuttle have my measure.[35] I want too a Cap with Band & wreath & anchor on it. I lost my cap, Band, & all over board up at Washington.

I have got one pair of straps here but can not get any lace so I should like to have enough sent me for two coats. Please have the things *ready* as soon as possable, but dont send them till you hear from me again for I can not tell where I may be till I hear from the Admiral[.]

I am very glad that Odiorne has got his appointment also.

I am Executive Officer here now & have a nice *little* state room all to myself. I am writing here now. The Capt gives me full swing to do just as I please. I just heard one of the men out side of my door saying. ["]By - - she is going to be a man of war now that's sertain[.]" I've been astonishing some of them since I took charge they have been used to having too much of their own way & I shut right down on them the first go off. The old men of wars men like it but the new men who have never been in any other vessel dont know what to make of it.

I cant write any more now as I've no time for I'm full of business getting the ship to rights painting etc. Good by love to all from

Henry

$1200. a year & a ration $9. A Large thing aint it. I am going to arrange it so Father can draw half of my pay at home.

[A letter in the collection dated 7 May detached Henry and Acting Volunteer Lieutenant MacDiarmid from the *Ceres* to serve as members of a summary court-martial on the 8th.]

Newbern
May 12th 1863
U.S.S. *Ceres*

Dear Mother

You must excuse my not having written for so long. But I have had very little time for anything since I obtained my promotion, for I am now of course, Executive Officer here & have been as busy as a bee getting the ship into decent trim. The Capt. gives me full swing to do as I please & I have every thing to suit my self. I think I may say with out boasting that the *Ceres* looks like a different vessel from what she did the three weeks ago.

I have begun to relise already the differences in my position in many things from what it used to be, But I cannot say that I feel at all dissatisfied therewith.

On the 8th I received an order from Com. Davenport, "to consider myself temporarily detatched from the *Ceres* & report on board the U.S.S. *Hunchback* for duty on a Court Martial." Hm! What do you think of that? Can you immagine me setting at at [a] table, one of three, listening very gravely to evidence, examining witnesses etc.? & then passing sentence on the accused?

We were trying a charge of theft. Lt. Comd. McCann & Lt. McDiarmid (our Captain) were the other two members of the court.[36]

Its all very fine, but I can not say that I fancy that sort of work and hope I shall have no more of it.

I dined with Captain McCann that day which I liked better than sitting on a Court with him.

Sunday I was out to the camp of the 45th Mass. & saw all the Boys Henry Wheellock included who I have not met before in fact I had forgotten that he was in the Regt.[37] I had quite a long talk with him about Walpole etc. Did you know that Charlie Titus was in the Navy? He is in the *Sonoma* Paymasters Steward with Ned Bellows who is Paymaster.

A mail arrived last night. I did not receive any letters from home but as I did not expect any I was not disapointed for I suppose you thought me on the way home. It was rather hard luck to get served as I was I think.

I received a letter from Joe and was very glad to hear from him.

You must excuse this miserable writing as it is a hot miserable day[.] There is a breeze springing up now tho' I am glad to say. By the way did I mention to you that I wanted some white clothes. I left 3 vests & one Pr of Pants at home. I shall want two more Pr. of pants & a linen Coat (sack of course).

Good by now love to all & keep on writing to your ever loving son

Henry

Did I tell you in my last letter that I have a state Room now? and quite comfortable. Tho I should like very much to be out of these Sounds. I think we shall lay here in Newbern for some time.

We have just heard of Hookers defeat.[38] Wha[t] will they try next?

I have heard nothing from the Admiral yet.

U.S.S. *Ceres*
Off Newbern N.C.
May 18th 63

Dear Mother

A mail arrived yesterday but I did not receive any letters at which I was rather disapointed as I thought that you had had time to receive my letter which I wrote after receiving my promotion, but I suppose you had not however for I know you would write as soon as you heard that I was to stay here.

Mr. Ryan (act Masters Mate) has been dismissed from the service on account of his conduct at Washington[.] I am rather sorry for him[.] He wanted to leave the service, but to be turned out is rather hard lines. I was in hopes they would mearly except his resignation but they did not & Com. Davenport has ordered him to leave the Department at once.

It only leaves one Masters Mate here so that I shall have more to do than ever & shall have very little time to my self for any thing.

Capt. MacDiarmid told me today that the Commodore was talking of detatching me from this vessel & ordering me to his Flag ship (the *Hetzel*) as Ex. Officer in place of an Act. Master who is there now & would be sent here, as he (the Com.) dont like him.[39] I'm not sure that I should like the change much, off course on some accounts it would be a good thing for me as I should be in a larger vessel & so be a (*Bigger Bug*) but then I dont think my chances of Promotion would be very great (you see I'm not satisfied yet) as the *H*[*etzel*] always lays here doing nothing & then again I'm not at all sure that I should get along well with the Commodore (so called, he is only a Commander, but has charge, under Lee, of this Squadron) who is rather a curious customer.[40] So I shant worry about it, but let the matter work it self out in its own way. I think my *choice* would be to stay where I am, as by doing so I should probably get home sooner. & then I shall try all I know to get sent to a larger vessel & so get clear of the "Sounds of North Carolina."

Last Friday I was ordered to set on a Board of Investigation to enquire into certain charges made on an Act Master here. A.V. [Acting Volunteer] Lt's. Bhun & MacDiarmid were the other members.[41] I think its a pretty large thing, only two weeks an Ensign, & to have been ordered on two Courts. I dont like it tho', except that it keeps my name before the 'Powers that Be' which of course is desirable.

Saturday I called on Capt & Mrs Harris but did not find them at home[.] I after words met Capt. H. however & found that he had just been on board the *Ceres* to see me. He allowed she (the *Ceres*) reminded him *very much* of the Ship of the Line *Columbus* (which ship he was in one voyage) except of course the side wheels size & a few other things. We had quite a laugh over the *great resemblance*. I also saw Charlie Soule & Scudder (I've forgot his first name) he is in the 45th Regt but is at present act Quartermasters Seagent for Capt Harris.[42] He lives in Linden Place you know.

I can not write any more now as I ought to be on deck in fact I stole from Uncle Samuel the time necessary for writing this as I ought to have been on deck all the time & that must account for the style of writing[.] The Mail closes tonight however & I did not like to miss the chance.

Good by love to all from your loving son

Henry

U.S.S. *Ceres*
Off Newbern N.C.
May 25th /63

Dear Mother

I received your short note inclosing Mary's letter yesterday. I am sorry you should have not received my letter. I have written three time[s] since I received my Promotion.

I have not heard any thing from the Department yet but am afraid there is no chance of my being detached. Is there any one in Washington who could put in a word for me to get me ordered to the *Cambridge*, *Cannandagua* [*Canandaigua*] Capt. Parker's or any other good vessel? It would be a great favor for I dont want to spend the summer here a bit. it is getting Hotter and hotter every day & I feel proportionately out of spirits. It is a sickly climate here at best & the sooner I can get clear of it the better.[43]

Capt. McD[iarmid] went off to Plymouth yesterday so I am in command Pro Tem. He went to get us all some money from the Paymaster which will be welcome enough, for we have been hard up for some time.

I went on shore yesterday after noon to see Gen. Wild who was very cordial & very busy as he was just moving into a house so I did not stay long, but he wanted me to come again.[44]

I then call[ed] on Cates & Mr. Harris. I like the Captain very much. When I left there he came down on board with me to see the vessel.

Every thing is quiet here & one day is the same as every other.

I have plenty to do tho' on board here & have little or no time for reading or any thing else.

Why dont Eliza write to me realy I shall begin to feel quite hurt if she ignores my existance so intensely. I believe I owe Lu a letter so I must not growl at her for not writing[.] I will try & answer her last soon if I can rais[e] time.

This is an awful scrawl but I can hardly call my time my own so I write fast expecting every minute to be called on for some thing or other[.] Every minute or two some one raps at the door. "Come in," "Mr. Wells may I go on shore sir." "No, your quarantined" (i.e. Liberty stopped for some offense) "For how long, sir," "A month" "I knew I was wrong sir but aint that rather hard" "No that'll do" & the door shuts. I write a minute or two & then I hear the Quartermaster singing out, Mr. Wells, Mr. Wells, their making signals from the Flag Ship. Down goes my pen & out I bolt on deck to discover what the Q.M. might to have known, that the signals are not for us but some other vessel. Rap, rap, there it goes again lets see what he wants. It was one of the Berth Deck cooks who wanted to know if the Black List men might leave their work for a few minutes to draw small stores.[45] ("Yes" & bang goes the door again—& so it goes all day long—so much for being Executive Officer.

I guess I will not write any more now as there is some work going on which I want to look out for. so I will bid you good bye. I hope you have not forgotten about those letter stamps. I can not get any here.

If we have any friends who are in office at Washington I think what I spoke of in the first of my letter might be accomplished with out much dificulty & realy I think it would be better for me every way if I can get away from here.

I wrote you in one of my letters which I think you did not receive that I wanted a cloth sack coat made with the lace (¼ in) on the sleaves & shoulder straps, [drawing of an anchor on a shoulder strap]. Also some white clothes. I believe I left vests enough at home & 1 [P]R Pants so I shall want 2 Pr of Pants & Linnen Coat (sack same as one wears ashore). Dont send them yet tho' only have it ready[.]

Good By now love to all from your loving son

Henry

U.S.S. *Ceres*
Off Newbern N.C.
May 26th /63

Dear Lu

I hope you will excuse my having delayed answering your letter for so long but realy I have had a great deal to do lately & very little time to write.

We have just got back from an expedition down the river where we have been since last Friday. When we started our Capt. was at Plymouth on business so I had command of the vessel till Sunday, when he joined us. The Rebs burnt two (only one the other was saved) schrs that were coming up the river loaded with coal for the Government so we were sent down in company with the U.S.S. *Brinker* to keep the river clear & to destroy all the boats we could find.[46] We went up all the creeks in our small boats & expected to have some pretty hot work with the Guerilles but they did not trouble us. We destroyed a large number of canoes & flat-boats. I should have rather enjoyed the whole thing but I was unwell at the time & having so much responsibility on my shoulder[s] did not tend to make me feel any better[.] Then being so short of officers made it doubly hard as there was only one deck officer besides myself. So that take it all together I was quite ready to resign my command to Capt. MacD[iarmid] when he returned.

I received a letter Sunday from Eliza & to day one from Mother dated North Conway.[47] I am so glad she has gone on that trip. I am sure it will do her lots of good & Uncle Hamilton is just the person to make it real jolly for her the whole time.

I long to see Baby now that she has begun to talk. she must be dreadful cunning. What is Ben Bolt doing now?[48]

I received a nice long letter from Mary a few days ago which I have answered.

I find a great deal of trouble in getting money here so as soon as I can see the Paymaster I am going to make arrangements to have $50. a month made payable in Boston to Father[.]

I wish you would tell him I will let him know as soon as I can fix it.

I am going to see Capt. Harris tomorrow to see if he wont let me have my Box directed to his care as I want the things very much but dont want to run any risk of losing them[.] I shall try & find out before I mail this letter.

I want to have my straw hat & all my thin underclothes sent, & some Books too, especialy Shakespeare. I dont know exactly where my Edition is but you'll find it somewhere. I want also to have a pair of straps (I dont care about them being very nice ones) & lace ¼ in. enough for one coat. Please tell father.

Good night now dear love to all from your own brother

Henry

27th—Capt. Harris expects to come home soon to take a commission in the 2nd Mass. Artillery so send my box by Adams Express at once H.W. Wells "Act Ensign" U.S.S. *Ceres* Newbern. Get a receipt for it & send to me by mail.

U.S.S. *Ceres*
Off Newbern
May 30th 1863

Dear Mother

I received your letter dated North Conway a few days ago. I am so glad you have taken a little vacation from your cares at home I know it will do you lots of good. I can see you now in my minds eye riding off with uncle Hamilton leaving care behind, & laughing at Uncle H's fun. He must be a real jolly person to travel with, knows every body & can tell you a bout every thing of interest.

We are laying here at Newbern now like Mr. Maccawber [Micawber] waiting for something to turn up.[49] I wrote to Lu about our last expedition, down the river. I suppose you have seen the letter. It was quite a good thing for me as I had command of the vessel for the first few days our captain being up at Plymouth.

Capt. Mac Diarmid has just received a very complimentary letter from Admiral Lee on his doing up at Washington N.C. & those of his command. I expect he will have a better vessel before long[.] He says if he does he shall recommend me for an Act Master & a command so I wish him the best of luck of course. I do not think however that I shall be able to get a Masters appointment just yet as I have not been an Ensign long enough I believe.

I was on shore the other day & took a ride with Capt. Harris round the Fortifications. I had a very good time but it was fearfully dusty. He is talking of going home & taking a commission in the 2nd Mass Artillery. he has been offered a Major's appointment I believe. I saw Charlie Tule & F. Sendden for a few minutes.

I have not been over to the camp of the 45th for some time it is very much out of the way, & to[o] hot for so long a walk. I wrote Lu to have the Box sent on at once by Adams Express, be sure & get a receipt for it.

We are having very disagreeable weather now. A real good rain would be very acceptable all round I think. To day it is overcast but stiffling the air seems perfectly dead & I feel like a *wet rag*. The last news that we had was that Vicksburg was probably taken & we are waiting anxiously for the confirmation of that report. I dont believe it[.] I have been disapointed so often by the rumors in the newspapers that I make it a point not to believe any thing till it is confirmed.

I am glad that the Villandingham has got his deserts & now if they would only lock Wendell Phillips up in Ft Warren or some other safe place I think it would be just what he deserves also for he sertainly has spoken as much treason as the other.[50]

It is my watch on deck so I guess I had better be there. Please tell Uncle Hamilton that I am very much obliged to him for that valuable work which he sent me of peotry [poetry] & Engravings[.] I will send him in return some of our *Cerious* Peotry [poetry] in return.

Good by now Love to all & write often to your loving son

Henry

I will answer Elizas letter in a day or two. I suppose you will be home by the time this letter gets that [there] as so I shall direct to Brookline

U.S.S. *Ceres*
Hatteras Inlet
June 7th 1863

Dear Mother,

It is some time since I have written home & realy I have no good excuse to offer except that I have had a very lazy fit on & have not felt up to doing any thing. It is nearly two weeks since I have heard from any of you but I suppose there are letters at Newbern for me & that I shall receive them in a day or two. We have been down her[e] three days now. We are "Guard vessel" & have to board all vessels going in & out to see that their papers etc. are all right. I dont like the work very well, but the station is a good one as we get good salt air here, no muscuitos Plenty of fresh fish Eggs etc[.] it is also a healthy place. We shall not stay here long I think, we only relieved the *Lockwood* for her to go & get a supply of provisions coal etc. She ought to be back by day after tomorrow.

Have you seen any thing at home about getting me detached[?] I dont know whether it can be managed but do hope it can[.] Capt. MacD I think will leave us soon & have a better vessel so the sooner I can get away too the better I shall like it.

I suppose you have sent my Box. I hope so at all events as I need my thin clothes very much. & I dont expect it will get thro' in less than a month of the starting.

Every thing about here has been so quiet & stupid since you last heard from me that realy I am at a loss what to write.

There does not seem to be any war news at present[.] Grant seems to be at a stand still & I suppose the next that we shall hear will be that he has retreated. I try to keep up good courage, but in such an atmosphere of Copperheadism as there is on board here it is hard to do so.

I quite lost my temper this morning, with one of my messmates who was talking his *Copper* sentiments & threatened to kick him off the Quarter Deck if he did not shut up.

It is not much use to fight against them tho' for the Capt. is worse than all the rest put together. The other day I asked him after one of his long tirades against our Government & a glorification of England, what he came into our service or to our country for if he thought the other was so much better (he is a Scotchman you know). He would not see the point & did not answer my question.

Now as I have filled up my sheet I will close my letter. Good by from your loving Henry Give my love to *all hands*—

U.S.S. *Ceres*
Off Newbern
June 10th 1863

Dear Eliza

I do believe that I did not answer that letter of yours that I received some time since. If I did not pray forgive me for realy I did not intend to neglect writing for so long.

Am not I in Luck. I only heard to day by a letter from Mother (June 3rd) that my box had started & on going to the Express Office I found it there. I could hardly believe my eyes when I saw it as people generaly have to wait four or five weeks for any thing coming that way. In fact they told me at the office that such a thing did not happen more than once in about five hundred times. I found every [thing] just as I wanted it. That Coat fits to a charm. Cap Ditto etc. Tell Lu I will take fine care of her Atlantic's. I am every so much obliged to Uncle H for those books & will answer his letter soon. I wish I was at the "Jmh" now I think it would be sort of jolly dont you?

I am very sorry to hear such poor accounts of your health but I guess a trip to the mountains will bring you round all right.

We came up from Hatteras Inlet yesterday where we have been laying for a few days past in order to relieve the Guard vessel to get provisions. I think it is about the best station on the Sound. & [I] should like very well to be stationed there during the hot months. It is a dreary monotonous life there but then it is a healthy place. & that covers a multitude of evils you know besides none of the stations are noted for being especialy lively. I almost wish the Rebs would come round here & give us another warming up & I also should not mind getting a bar in my straps. I should not be surpprised if Capt. Mac Diarmid left us before long as he will probaly get a better vessel. There is some talk of transferring me to the *Delaware* but Capt. Mac D has objected so strongly that I hardly think it will be done, at least not at preasent.[51]

I dont know but Mother may be right (she is very apt to be) & that I am better off here than I should be else where but I find it very hard to think so.

Things often turn out so different from what one expects that I have almost made up my mind that we might as well let things take their own course & "trust to luck" to pull men thro'. I should feel miserable tho' if I thought I had to serve out the war in these sounds.

The 44th have left here now so I dont take much interest in going on shore as the 45th are too far off to go to very often. I think I shall try & get out there to-morrow tho' if we do not go to Washington N.C. as there is a rumor of our doing.

I cannot write any more now as it is getting late. Good by love to all & write often to your loving brother

Henry

Why dont Lu write?

USS *Ceres*
Off Newbern N.C.
June 18th 1863

Dear Mother

(There – I've commenced on the wrong side of the sheet to begin with, pretty well that.)

It is my morning watch but as it is raining hard so I cannot wash decks or go thro' any of the usual routine of morning duty I have just come in here to steel a few minutes to write to you, but I warn you to begin with that I do not intend to write a very long letter. My box arrived all right as I wrote Eliza a day or two since. Was it not lucky it came thro' so quick[?] it started (by your letter) on the 3rd & I received it on the 10th & might have had it a day sooner if I had had any ideas it was there. Every thing was very satisfactory. I believe there was not a thing in it that was not just what I wanted[.] I turned over the Jelly & sardines to our mess as I could not have enjoyed them so well to have kept them all to myself but the crackers I have been selfish enough to keep for "my own private tooth" (as Mr Maies used to say) & eat them in the mornings with my coffee when I first get up. You know I have a weakness in the way of hard crackers. I was glad enough to see that old order Book & Note Book again[.] I supposed that they were lost with my revolver etc. Did Odiorne save my Log Book too? I hope he did, for as it was my first cruise in the Navy I valued it a good deal.

The Department have made another change in the Uniform but I believe (I have not seen the General Order yet relating to it) that it does not effect my grade at all, or at any rate but little which I am very glad off. I think it is not a fair thing to make us vollunteers change our uniform so often.

We expect to go to Washington N.C. soon & from there to Plymouth to carry the Fleet Surgeon round he is going to inspect all the vessels in the squadron. Day before yesterday I was over to the Camp of the 45th & had a very pleasant time with the draw back of being caught in a Thunder Storm which as I went out with white clothes was not pleasant[.] Will Bond has been sick but is better now. I was with Will Wellman for a little while but as he was very busy I made my visit short. They are expecting to go home in about three weeks. I can not write more now so good by. Love to all from your loving son

Henry

U.S. Str. *Ceres*
Off Newbern
June 18th 1863

Dear Lu

I received both your letters yesterday[.] Where one of them has been for the last three weeks I am at a loss to know for it is dated on the 25th of last month. However better late than never.

Captain Mac Diarmid has been detatched from this vessel & ordered to the *Victoria* off Wilmington. Our new Capt. Act Master Foster will take charge to-day[.][52] I have seen him as he has been on board here once or twice but dont like to form too hasty an opinion of him but I will wait till I know him better before I tell you what sort of a man he is. All I *know* now is that he is very unpopular on board the *Delaware* of which vessel he was Executive Officer but he may ware better as a Captain.

In your letter you expressed surpprise that I should seem to change my opinions of Capt Mac D so much as my letters seemed to indicate. I will try to make the matter clear to your inquiring mind.

You see when I first came on board here Capt MacD took a sort of dislike to me with out any cause whatever & as a natural consequence I reciprocated with all my heart. When we got ashore on Royal Shoals he began to open his eyes a little for both his other Mates were in a nautical point of view a couple of *fools* (my private opinion is that they were about the same in any other) & tho' I say it myself he found it very convenient to have a seaman for an officer. So that what with that & my always talking right up to him he found it best to leave me alone & then after the Washington scrape he seemed to think no one was equal to me[.]

So it does not seem to me very strange that such being the case I should look less at his faults & more on his bright side. I still say however that he talks confounded treason but I dont think he means all he says by any means & he will fight like fun. I dont think him exactly the right man to command a man of war but where you find one better among the Vollunteers there are a dozen worse so I wish him good luck & a better vessel than the *Victoria*[.] I think the change will be any thing but a benefit to me but that of course can not be helped. I cannot write any more now. Consider this the answer to the *short* letter & I will write another soon in answer to the long one.

Good by love to all & write soon to your loving brother (who is in great haste to get this letter finished in time for the mail)

Henry

I'm all out of breath writing so fast.

USS *Ceres*
Off Newbern
June 24th 1863

Dear Mother

I have not much time but as a mail leaves today I will write you just a line so that you need not be anxious about me. Mr. Hopkins our Master's Mate has been quite sick for several days so that as I am the only deck office[r] on board I have my hands full.[53] I am on deck from five AM to 8 P.M. after which I have my Log to write, etc. so I very seldom get to bed before 10 or 11 o'clock. So you see I am pretty well driven. Capt. MacDiarmid has left us as I believe. I wrote Lu in my last, his successor Act Master Foster, has been on board now for about a week hardly time enough to form an opinion of him. I guess I shall get along well enough but I am inclined to think it will be a hard matter to please him & be popular with the men as I have been as he is inclined to be very taught on them & as Ex Officer of course I shall have to carry out his orders[.] One thing I like & that is that he seems to be a man who will support his Executive which is a great thing. He is a good Republican which is quite a relief after having to listen to so much Copperheadism as I have had to for the last four months.

I am very sorry that I could not have been at home to have seen Ruth christened[.] it would have been so pleasant to have been all together then.

I will write to the Aunties as soon as I can find time to turn round. I have just got Mr. H[arper] up on deck & I want to go & stay with him. Poor fellow he has had quite a siege. I have got a lot of work going on also which wants attention so I must close now. I hope next time I shall be able to write you a better letter aint this fine writing[?]

Love to all from your loving son

Henry

I received your letter of the 15th inst.

U.S.S. *Ceres*
Off Newbern
June 30th 1863

Dear Mother

I am afraid that you will think it strange that I have written so little of late but as I said in my last I have had so much to do that I could hardly find time on account of the sickness of the only other line officer on board.

He is getting better now I am glad to say & I suppose I shall have a little more leasure in future which will be very acceptable[.]

Yesterday I went on shore for two or three hours to try to hunt for the Paymaster who is ashore here somewhere but did not succeed in finding him. I want very much to see him to make arrangement about half Pay & also to draw what is due me which amounts to over $400. I believe. Our accounts are to be transferred to the Paymaster of the *Hetzel* which I am very glad off as it will be much more convenient for us.

I was with Scudder for a couple of hours & had a very pleasant time, he is the only one of my friends left here now & he is going home next week. I shant care much about going ashore after that for I can not see much pleasure in going ashore just for the sake of getting rid of money, Com Davenport notwithstanding who thinks a man cannot be a gentleman unless he spends every cent of his pay. His ideas of a gentleman (he held forth on board here the other day when he was taking dinner with Capt. Mac D) differs very materialy from mine. I may be wrong, but if he is right, I have no ambition to be a gentleman after his stamp.

Capt. Foster is trying to get one of the men on board the *Delaware* made a Masters Mate & ordered to this vessel. I hope he will succeed I am sure for I dont fancy being so short of officers.

I hardly think we shall get North before August for so many troops have left the Dept that it is necessary to keep a strong Naval force here[.]

We may get away sooner tho' & I hope we shall. I shall do all I can to get out of her when she does get away from here for I am homesick to get on Old Ocean again.

Two steamers have got in this week from N York & I have recd no letters but hope for better luck next time.

Good by now love to all & write as often as you can find time to your loving son

Henry

I recd. two papers Journal & Advertiser

U.S. Str. *Ceres*
Hatteras Inlet
July 8th 1863

Dear Mother

I dont know what you will think of me for not having written for so long. I have been very busy of late, but as my last two letters were full of excuses on the same subject I will not bore you with them now. We have been laying here since I last wrote. I like the station very much except that (as yet) I have received no letters. In fact I believe it is now nearly a month since I have heard from home.

It is very healthy here & I always feel stronger and better when I am on Salt water than I do on fresh. Our men have given us good deal of trouble since we have been here. Four of them deserted on the night of the fourth but on the next day by the aid of a Steam Tug we caught them. They stole a Pilot boat & started for Baltimore. One of them before starting stole nearly $170. from two of his messmates[.] We have them all in irons now waiting till we can have a Court Martial convened to try them which will not be I suppose until after we leave here[.] Three other men went ashore on liberty for a few hours & staid three days[.] they wandered off some 20 miles & I had to go after them with a party of soldiers for they had got licquer & were raising the very d--l every where they went. You see nearly all the men have enlisted in the 1st N.C. Artillery so that there were no one to look out for them but women & old men. In one or two cases they turned families out of doors in the night & took charge of the houses.

In going after them I had an all but serious accident befall me. I walked square into a bog hole stepping from hard ground to above my waist in soft mud. Fortunately it was very narrow & I got out with out much trouble but if it had been two or three feet wider it might have ended my "adventure". I almost ruined my new sack coat but I am not inclined to growl about it as I might have fared worse[.] I was in a nice mess as you may imagine so I went down [to] the water took my clothes off & washed them. I got well laughed at you may be sure but I could blame no one for that[.] I did the same my self (after I got out). I did not catch the men after all & when I got back to the ship I found they had got there before me. They were all put in irons of course so that we have about ⅓ of the crew in irons. Pleasant that.

On the 4th I went off on a sail with Mr Rafferty. I had a very good time & got well sunburnt[.] My lips especialy blistered up badly. They are a little better now but still troubling me. I begin to feel quite old now 22 years! I wish I could live them over again.

We had quite & excitement yesterday. in the forenoon the Str. *Neptune* went out bound to Port Royal.[54] At 1 o'clock P.M. while we were at dinner the Quartermaster reported firing outside[.] we all rushed on deck & with our glasses could see the *Neptune* coming back full speed with two schrs in chase firing at her[.] We slipped our anchor & started out to fight the two Privateers as brave as you please[.][55] in going out we passed the *N*[*eptune*] & spoke her & they seemed sertain that the schrs were Rebs so we cleared for action & stood down for them[.] they both hove too apparently waiting for us, & signaliying to each other[.] they were too far off for us to read their flags. Just as we were debating whether we were not near enough to put a Parrott shell into one of them they hoisted numbers which we soon made out to be *Martha* [*Matthew*] *Vassar* & *Geo*[*rge*] *Bacon*, U.S. mortar schrs. Capt. of the *M.V.* came on board[.] In his boat was one of the old *Cambridge* men who told that there were a lot more of them in the schr. They had tried to board the *Neptune* but the Capt would not heave too & I dont blame him much under the circumstances.

Good by now Love to all from

Henry.

U.S. Str. *Ceres*
Off Newbern N.C.
July [before the 15th] /63

Dear Father

I have just succeeded in making arrangements about my half-pay & I enclose you the Ticket I sent home by Mr. F. Scudder $160.00/100 which I hope came to hand.

I do not know exactly how much money I owe you[.] I believe it is some where in the neighborhood of $230.00/100 but am not at all sure but what it may be more as I do not know what my last things cost. I wish you would pay yourself however & after that as I have no particular use for the money you may as well take it for the use of the family. I shall have nearly $60. per month left which is plenty & to spare for me & I had a great deal rather have the money doing some good than laying in the Bank. Now Father I'm your son you know &

have a right to offer it, so you must not refuse to take it. I only wish there was five times as much.

We expect to go back to Hatteras soon which I am very glad of for it is much the healthiest station in the Sounds & though the best. I would like to have my letters directed to Hatteras Inlet instead of Newbern for the present. There are all sorts of rumors flying round here about Charleston being taken etc. Gen. Foster has gone—some where, no one knows where, some say to relieve Dix. others to New York to enforce Martial Law there during the Draft but it is all guess work. There is an expedition going off from here somewhere to day.

The Rebs seem to be getting pretty lively on the Coast. I wish I could get in one of the vessels after Privateers. That is the cream of the service now. What a daring thing that was at Portland. They deserved success for their boldness & I'm glad enough that we have got such a smart set under "Lock & Key."[56]

I'm glad Capt. Parker has got such a good command. The *Tuscarora* is a splendid vessel, & if he meets any of the Privateers they'll find a tough customer[.] It was pretty hard for Lt. Cm. Miller in the *Ericsson* to have to run from the *Florida* was it not?[57] I dont see what else he could do tho' under the circumstances. He is the same man who was Executive Officer of the *Cambridge* you know.

I can not write any more now as I have got to see about getting acquisitions filled out at the store ship. The Court Martial has not come off yet.

Good by. love to all from your loving son

Henry W. Wells

U.S.S. *Ceres*
Hatteras Inlet
July 15th 1863

Dear Mother

The *Lockwood* has just arrived & we are going back to Newbern so I am just going to write you a few lines before we start as the mail boat leaves there tonight so we shall miss her but as she passes here the *L[ockwood]'s* boat will board her.

I received three letters today the first that I have had for a long time. Two from you & one from Lu. One of yours enclosed a Photograph of Aunt Lucinda (which I think is capital) & a letter from Odiorne. I wrote you a day or two ago. I hope you received the letter for I have written too little lately to be able to afford that one should misscarry[.] You must excuse me Mother dear but I dont feel much *up* to writing lately somehow. I am not more than half well, tho' a long way from being sick I hope. I dread leaving this station at Hatteras tho' I'm afraid of these Sounds[.] What did Mr. Knapp say about my chances of getting detached? I want to get out on the coast again more than a little I can tell you[.]

I was talking with one of the Surgeons before we left Newbern & he advised me to get out of the Sounds if I could. If I only could look forward to our being sent North I would wait until then but they keep putting it off & putting it off until now I have got sick of thinking about it. Pshaw! now I did not mean to write a lot of stuff to make you feel uneasy about me but confound it I can't help writing as I feel. If it had not been for these deserters we might have staid here but, they must be Court Martialed so we have to go.

So Father has joined the Union League[.] Did I ever tell you that I belonged to it? I joined it in Baltimore some time a go—a year ago last May.

We have heard of the fall of Vicksburg. a great thing for us is it not? I am sorry Grant paroled the officers tho' I think we ought to have held them. We are all anxiety to hear from Meade now[.] I hope he will be able to Bag Lee & his army but if he will only give them a good thrashing again I shall be pretty well satisfied.

Tell Lu that I will write to her after I get to Newbern when I will try & send her a good fat letter.

I believe I told you about the *Privateers* in my last. one of them has been in here ever since & we have great arguments as to what would have been the result if we had had a fight[.] We tell them that we should certainly have taken them both at which they are very indignant & express them selves as having been highly amused at seeing such a small affair coming out after them.

Has Scudder got home yet[?] I sent some money by him $160. I'll send more soon by letter.

Good by now & good night from your loving son

Henry

Lots of love all round why dont Eliza write to me? Direct to Newbern as before

U.S.S. *Ceres*
Off Newbern
July 21st 1863

Dear Lu

I have just set down to write you a promise in stead of a letter for it is very late & I have got to get up very early. I will try & write you a long letter soon but this time you will have to put up with my "Phisog" [Physiognomy]

I received a letter from you a day or two ago which makes the second one since I wrote to you which is rather jarring to my *feeling*. "Cause why" – cause I ought to have answered the first & did not. We expect to leave for Hatteras Inlet day after tomorrow which I am glad enough of.

What news we are having! Good from the Seat of War but bad enough at home. We heard now however that the mob has been put down in New York & that the Draft will go on. I do not think that $300 clause is a fair thing exactly but that does not excuse mob Law nevertheless. I am glad they were put down so quick in Boston.

Realy Lu you must excuse my writing (or scrawling) any more to night. Tear this up as soon as you succeed in translating the contents.

Love to all from Your loving Brother

Henry

I'll write soon

U.S. Str. *Ceres*
Off Newbern
July 26th 1863

Dear Lu

As I suppose I may have a quiet morning I will try & write you a letter.

I suppose you are keeping house now for Grandpa & that the rest of the family are scattered. It would not be a very favorable time for me to come home would it? I suppose you would not object tho'.

I dont expect to stay here much longer now, but I hardly think that I shall be able to come to Brookline[.]

The fact is I have been quite unwell & I'm afraid my lungs are effected. I have had a medical survey held on me & they recommended to the Admiral to send me to sea. You need not feel anxious tho' I think for the Doctors tell me that they do not think it is any thing very serious yet, & that the pure salt air if I take proper care of myself will make me all right in a little while. The worst of the whole thing is that I must leave off smoking (at least for the present). They (the Doctors) did not tell me so but I can feel that it hurts me & therefore do it on my own hook. I hope my orders will come soon. Two, or three weeks at the farthermost ought now to finish, (I hope for good) my fresh water cruising. Hurrah for old Ocean! say I[.] I shall be glad enough to ride over its old waves again[.] I believe I was made for a sailor, dont you? I like the life so well.

We are still here at Newbern & I hardly think we shall get away this week. The weather is very hot & disagreeable & I am longing for a change[.] Capt. Foster dont seem to like the idea of my going, but he behaved very well about it & put a big spike in my wheel when he handed my application to the Commodore[.] He told him that he thought that I deserved consideration after all I had *suffered* for my country in Prison etc. The Capt was kind enough to say that he knew he should not gain any thing by a change. For my thinking that there were plenty more Ensigns in the sounds said yes plenty that I would not give one d—m for. but of course he said, he did not wish me to stay at the expense of my health.

Did you get the Tin Types & how do you like them. I sent three & will put another in this letter. You can give away what you dont want you know[.] I have got one full length one but it is most to[o] large to go in an envelope & as it is not very good I guess I will not send it. If you have any taken send me one.

Nearly all the Troops have left on an expedition. You will hear about it in the Newspapers as soon as I shall I guess.

I want to write you a good long letter but realy I cannot think of any thing interesting to write about so I guess the best thing I can do is to send love to all the family & bid you good by write often to your loving brother

Henry

U.S. Str. *Ceres*
Off Newbern
July 30th 1863

Dear Mother

It is some time since I have written you or received any letters. I am not in very good health just now but hope soon to get sent out on the Blockade or home, where I hope I shall get better. It has turned out just as I feared from the first. I can't stand this climate. While we stayed at Hatteras I picked up a good deal but since coming back here I have lost all I gained there & have been quite unwell. I have been spitting blood for some time past as I did not cough I thought at first that it did not amount to any thing but one day when I was at the Hospital seeing about some of our men I mentioned it to the Surgeon. He at once took me into his office & after examining me for a while, advised me to call for a "Medical Survey" in order that I might get sent away from the Sounds as he did not think I ought to remain. I accordingly called the Survey. The Board were of the same opinion as Surgeon Nelson & have recommended to the Admiral that I be sent to sea.[58] They told me however that they thought that no serious consequences need be found if I took proper care of myself & that the salt air would soon bring me up again. I am waiting anxiously now for my orders but I suppose it will be at least two weeks & probably more before I shall hear.

My old headachs have come back again & take me all together I am getting to be a rather useless member of society here[.] I have not laid up exactly tho' Mr Hopkins has a good deal of extra duty to perform which properly would come on me. Capt. Foster is very considerate & tells me not to do a bit more than I feel able to.

I have not smoked for a *whole week*. What do you think of that? I miss it more than you can think, but I have made up my mind to leave it alone until I get well. I have no intention of giving it up all together, as long as I go to sea, but I do not mean to ever allow my self to smoke so hard again as I have for the last four months. I wish I was near enough to you to get a kiss for being a good boy

& leaving it off. Oh Dear I wish Ben could act the Brother for me three weeks & let me take his place[.]

Well well I suppose I shall get home one of these days. The war begins to look like drawing to a close don't it? However I suppose there is plenty more fighting for us to do after we finish up what is on our hands now. The French must be routed out of Mexico & the English made to smell a little Gunpowder before I for one will be satisfied.

We hear that the Admiral has gone down to Wilmington with the *Minnesota* & two Iron Clads[.] I hope I may get there before an attack is made. I would like very much to help take that place[.] I have been on the Blockade there so long.

Every thing is quiet here. an expedition left a few days ago & has not yet returned[.] I believe Gen. Wild's Brigade went. Good by love to all from

Henry

US Str *Ceres*[59]
Hatteras Inlet
Aug 3rd 1863

Dear Mother

We are back again at the Inlet at last & I hope we may stay here as long as I have to remain in the Sounds for this is the only place where I can feel half like a man.

I received your letter of the 27th of last month from Hopkinton[60]

I hope you & Father are enjoying your journey. I am glad you left the Baby, for tho she is a[s] good as can be, still babies are rather a trouble when one is moving about & a child crying in the cars is one of the most terrible noises I know of. I suppose Ben has ceased to be considered in the light of a child now. I am sorry to hear that he takes such a notion to ships etc. but perhaps it will wear off. One sailer in the family is quite enough I think don't you? We must make a landsman of him, if possable.

Why dont Eliza write to me? I believe I have only received two letters from her since I left home[.] She finds time enough to write long letters to other people & I think she might spare me a few minutes occasionaly. However if she don't feel inclined to do it of her own accord I dont wish to press her.

I am sorry that Father will not take that money but if he will not take it altogether I want that whenever there is any thing that is wanted in any way but which you feel as tho you could hardly afford, you should remember that there is the money, what there is of it, perfectly at your disposal. Now do think of it for it would give me great satisfaction to feel that my earnings were doing something to make others more comfortable & happy. For instance Dont Lu want riding lessons? Eliza is out of health & she might be able to go on some journey that would do her good[.] Why bless you mother I could[n't] find a way to spend $100 a month, let alone a year. Now dont forget to spend some at least of that money for me.

I received a letter from Mary the other day. I like to hear from her very much. She writes a first-rate letter.

Where is Uncle H. now? up at Conway?

I long to see Lu & you all again but of course it is impossable for me to tell when I may get home. By the way where is Cousin Lu now I wonder if I owe her a letter. I received one from her ever so long ago & I think but am not sure that I answered it. I am afraid as she does not write that I did not so if you will tell me how to direct I will try & make my peace with her.

We have got another Masters Mate now which lets up on me a great deal. I nomenaly caught a watch but in reality do nothing of the sort as by permission of the Capt. (very considerate of him by the way) my Quartermaster stands in my place when I dont feel like being on deck. Capt F. is very careful of me. I only wish he would be a little more considerate with the crew. He is rather a Tartar & I am afraid when I leave she will be a sort of floating Hell for everybody, as it is, its just enough & it comes harder because they were rather slack when Capt Mac D was on board.

When I sat down I did not think I should be able to write more than two pages for I had nothing to write about but I seem to have arrived at the end of my paper & of a stupid letter I'm afraid.

So good by[.] Direct to Hatteras Inlet at the present Love to all from

Henry

Gaston House
Newbern
Aug. 14th 1863

Dear Mother

I received your letter of the 7th today. I am up here at Newbern on duty. (The *Ceres* is still at Hatteras) & I expect to go back tomorrow. I have been getting money from the Paymaster for the vessel & have at present about me over $1500. not a very pleasant charge I can assure you.

I rec'd a note from Capt. Foster to day telling me that we shall go North very soon. I hope it is so & I hardly think he would have written if he had not been sure. However the Admiral is here & I am going to try & have a talk with him tomorrow & if possable get him to send me away with out waiting for the action of the Department. He can do it if he has a mind to & as Capt Davenport is very friendly to me perhaps he will. I have been a little better lately the air at Hatteras agrees with me.

I received Lu's letter enclosing one from Eliza. Both of which I will answer as soon as I get back to the vessel.

I enclose $20. would send more but do not like to risk to much in one letter.

Good by. Love to all. I will write you a better letter as soon as I get where *I can do so* with any kind of satisfaction to my self or you. I am sorry [you] did not enjoy housekeeping, but I suppose it was rather hard to be left so again. Well good by again from your loving son

Henry

Marginalia, penned by a family member—"On the envelope was written with a pencil—'Detached from the *Ceres* & ordered to report to Capt Boggs off Wilmington N.C. for such duty as he may assign to me.' H.W.W. Aug. 15th"

6

"The Papers Cry Out against the Wilmington Blockade"

Back on the Wilmington Blockade

U.S.S. *Montgomery*
Off Wilmington NC
Aug 20th /63

Dear Mother

I am out of the sounds at last I am thankful to say & have just joined this vessel. Off course I can not tell you much about how I shall like her yet, & if I could I have not time for the mail is going off directly.

I am afraid it will be a long time before I get home for this vessel only left Boston a short time ago & is in good repair.

Direct U.S.S. *Montgomery* off Wilmington N.C. via Beaufort N.C.[1]

I can not write any more now for the mail leaves directly[.] I have received several letters from home lately which I will answer soon.

Good by. Love to all

From

[The bottom portion of this page is missing.]

U.S.S. *Montgomery*
Off Wilmington N.C.
Aug. 24th /63

Dear Mother

I wrote you a few lines the other day just to tell you where I was as the mail was just closing, but I will now try & write a little more at length. I believe that the last time I wrote you a letter was when I was in Newbern getting discharges for some of our men on the *Ceres* & money for the officers. (I'm not sure that that was a letter either I believe I only wrote a few lines in pencil). I saw the Admiral the next day, or rather Com.[modore] Davenport, who saw him for me & he detached me from the *Ceres* & ordered me to report for duty to Capt. Boggs of the U.S.S. *Sacramento*[.][2] So I hastened down to Hatteras got my effects & proceeded at once to Beaufort N.C. where I found the *S[acramento]*. I was in hopes that I should have remained on her as she is a fine boat, but she had her full complement of officers so I merely took passage in her down here & was ordered to report on this vessel. She was in Boston last spring & perhaps you saw her when you was over to the Navy Yard to see Capt Parker. There is not a vessel on this station that can beat us in point of speed. I think she is a little larger than the *Cambridge*. Her battery consists of four 8 in guns, one 10 in gun & one 30 Pdr Parrott, (which latter I have charge of, dont you think I ought to know how to use it by this time?) The officer[s] are a Vol. Lieutenant in command a Act[ing] Master for Ex. Officer, four Ensigns Paymaster, Surgeon, five Engineers three Masters Mates two Clerk[s] & a Pilot. Off the first two I have very little to say of & wish I had less to do with. The Capt. might do well enough in a merchant vessel but is no fit man to command a gunboat[.] how he ever managed to get such a vessel as this, is a mistery to every officer on the station. I only hope he wont keep her long. The Ex[ecutive] Officer is a—fool. I know it is wrong to use such an expression but it expresses my sentiments to a *T*. The rest of the officer[s] seem to be a very pleasant set. The Doctor especially I am inclined to like very much tho of course I am not very intimately acquainted with any of them yet. He reminds me very much of Tom Pecly he belongs to Brookline & lives on Washington St.[3]

We have a very pleasant Ward Room. The only fault is that there are not State Rooms enough. There being but six for nine officers, so that we have to put two in three of the Rooms.

I received a letter from Eliza before I left the sounds & also one from Louisa which I will answer soon, before the mail goes if I can find time.

I enclose another $20. note. if you have any use for it keep it, otherwise hand it over to Father. I sent one in my last letter also.

Good by now love to all from your loving son

Henry

U.S. Str. *Montgomery*
Off Beaufort N.C.
Sept 3rd /63

Dear Mother

We have come up here to coal & I have just received your letter of the 17th. I was doubly glad to receive it as it was altogether unexpected for I did not suppose I should get any more letters for some time. But it seems that they were very good on board the *Ceres* & forwarded them at once.

I received another letter from Odiorne. You know he is on the *Wissahickon* now & from all accounts I am afraid he has got a pretty hard vessel & is not very well contented on board of her.[4] I begin to think we were all spoiled on the *Cambridge*[.] Such men as Capt. Parker are not to be picked up every day.

By the way the *Cambridge* is here now. I was on board of her this afternoon. She looked as natural as could be. Most of her old officers & crew are gone but still I found a few familiar faces on board. The Ex[ecutive] officer Mr. Strong, Paymaster & Engineers were about all. They seemed very glad to see me & I passed a very pleasant hour there. She is going north again as she has broke down.

There are no less than six gunboats laying here now & all except ourselves disabled & going north. It is a great pity for we need them badly now as we are very short of vessels on the Wilmington station.

My health has improved very rapidly since I came down here & I hope soon to be able to report my self all right. I raise very little blood now. Since I came down on the station I have commenced smoking again moderately, only twice or at most three times a day. I dont believe that that much will hurt me a great deal, & I find it very hard not to smoke at all.

I did not know that you were looking forward to my setting up housekeeping. Who shall I have to keep house? Thats the question. I wish I could answer it. Not thro' any discussion of my love of home tho'.

I dont think Lu would ever consider to it would she?

I can hardly realize that Laura Hooper is married. Give my love to her when you see her. I am glad to hear that Eliza is getting along so nicely. I have been meaning to write to her for some time but have not done so as yet. in fact I do not have a great deal of time here as we have only three watch officers.

I must bid you good night now Mother dear for it is after 10 o'clock & I have got to go on watch at 4 A.M. Love to all & write as often as you can to your Loving son

Henry

U.S.S. *Montgomery*
Off Wilmington N.C.
Sept. 5th /63

Dear Mother

The *Sacramento* leaves here to night so I will write you a few lines. I wrote to Eliza a day or two ago & the letter will go by this mail.

Every thing is very quiet down here[.] We never know what the news is on the station till we get the New York papers & then we find out what we have been doing.

When we were coming down from Beaufort we chased a steamer for two or three hours, which had a very suspicious appearance, but tho' we were gaining on her our Captain chose to give up the chase as it was taking him out of his course, as if that was of any consequence compared with the capture of a Blockade Runner. We tried to solace our selves with the idea that perhaps after all she might be all right, but the next morning when we were on our station we saw a steamer inside of the fort so exactly like the one that we had chased the day before as to leave hardly the shaddow of a doubt but what she was the same. I am in hopes that the Senior Officer here will take the matter in hand & get us a new Captain, but am afraid there is no such good luck for us.

Capt. Boggs has gone away from here on sick leave. He was Senior Officer here and he will be quite a loss to the station.

What is the news about Uncle Lyman have you heard from him yet? I saw a list of the Officers of the *Brooklyn* & noticed his name was not there.[5] I suppose he must have been detached & ordered to some other vessel. It is very often done when a vessel is going home & those that remain are short of officers or men either. I wonder[why] he did not write tho'.

I have not written to Cousin George yet but I will soon. I do not have so much spare time here as I used to on the *Cambridge* as we have only three watch officers[.] The Masters Mates are not allowed to take charge of the deck here, but stand with the Ensigns. There are three of them. I've got the best one of the lot with me, his name is Walker & he is a smart intelligent fellow. The other two are not much account.

In regards to my health I think I am progressing slowly in the right direction. I have not raised any blood to speak of for some time & I feel generaly better & stronger. The salt air is doing more for me than any medicine could have done I think & perhaps it was better that I did not come home. I wish I could look forward to seeing you all again a little sooner than I seem likely to, but there is no help for it but to wait patiently I suppose.

I enclose $20.00 Please do not forget to let me know when you receive money so that I may not be anxious about it. Send me papers often for I can not get them ashore now as I used to in the sounds.

Good by now with Lots of love to all the family & friends from your own

Henry

U.S.S. *Montgomery*
Beaufort N.C.
Sept 8th 1863

Dear Mother

We are still here at Beaufort but expect to leave tomorrow for our station.

I understand that a mail got in last night & in that case I am in hopes that I shall hear from home tho' it is rather soon I'm afraid.

We are very anxious to get the news now for there is a report here that France has recognized the Southern Confedrecy & if that is the case of course we shall have another war on top of this one.[6] I'm sorry if it is so. I would have much rather they would have waited a while till we finished what we have on hand. However I guess we can manage them but every one will have to work with a will tho'.

I'd give a quarters pay if I was in a Man of War now instead of a nondescript craft like this. Oh! this is a great old boat. I hardly know whether to make fun of her or to be angry. Every body from the Ex[ecutive] Officer to the messenger boys want to get away from her tho' she is a fast vessel & a first rate sea boat. The Commanding Officer is what d—ms her. He does do the strangest things. He took a set against me when I first came on board because I protested against certain arangements which he saw fit to make & which were not in accordance with the rules of the service. The other day he came along while I was on watch & commenced grumbling about the Officer of the Deck not paying sufficient attention to the ships duty & I told him flatly that I did not take any interest in the ship & cared very little how the work went on. Of course he was very angry & talked a way for some time. after he got thro' I asked him if he wanted to know why I said so & then I told him why I was dissatisfied (It is too long a story to enter into—all about the internal discipline etc. of the ship) & after about two hours talk I made him acknowledge that under the circumstances he did not know but what he might be dissatisfied himself if he was in my place[.] He said he was not aware of a good many of the thing[s] which I mentioned but that now he did know of them there should be a change. & Things have been a little better since[.]

The vessel is a good deal more like a merchant man than a man of war tho' he tries to make her so I think. However it is a poor rule that wont work both ways & that same idea of his has got me out of what otherwise might have cost me a Court Martial. The fact is the men are very discontented & as the discipline of the ship is very slack it makes bad work some times. The other morning one of the men was very sulky & disobeyed my orders[.] he agravated me so (I had a bad tooth ach[e] at the time & of course was not in a very forgiving state of mind) that I struck him which is contrary to the Articles of War. he reported me to the Captain but all the satisfaction that he got was that he deserved more than he got. However it is not right to strike. I never did it before since & have been in the Navy & do not intend to do it again if I can help it. For I think it cowardly to strike a man where he has not the option whether he can return the blow or not. I dont think if I had not been in pain at the time that I should have lost my temper for I generaly pride my self on having a pretty good control of it.

I can't write any more now—Thats a wrong story, I could but have not any thing in my mind to write a bout so I will bid you good by—love to all from your own

Henry

I enclose you the *Big* tin type. It is not good & I did not mean to send it, but Lu said she wanted to see it so there it is. I had to cut it down in order to get it into the envelope.

Henry

Sept 8th. We got our anchors the other day all right. Night before last a steamer ran the blockade[.][7] we chased her for about 80 miles but she was too fast for us. The Captain wanted to give up the chase sooner but we officers all went aft & protested against it & told him that we would report him if he did not chase her as long as she was in sight as there is always a chance when steamers are running at full speed of their breaking down. That rather frightened him & he kept on as long as we could see her & then we told him we were satisfied.

When we got back on the station we found that two new vessels had come on the station[,] one of them being the *Tuscarora* commanded by Capt. Parker.[8] He is senior officer [at] Hampton Roads now & they are expecting every day to be ordered to Baltimore for repairs.

Capt. Mac Diarmid was on board here last evening. he has applied for the command of this vessel. I wish he may get her, for with all his faults he is infinitely preferable to our present Captain.

Did I tell you that we reported him for not boarding that last steamer that we chased. he got a reprimand for it.

One of the steamers, the one that we chased coming down from Beaufort is laying inside of the Fort now, at least we are very sure that it is the same one for she is a very peculiar looking vessel & one not easily mistaken.

Last night we had quite an excitement. we saw a steamer running out & slipped our chain. as usual however we did not try to catch him so he was soon out of sight. In coming to anchor again our chain snapped so we had to keep underway all night as both our anchors were gone.

They are hard at work this morning trying to get them again. The one we slipped I think we shall get tho they have parted the Slip Rope, but the other I guess we shall not see again. The Rebs have fired several shots at us for we are very close in & now they have just landed something from some boats in the Sound abreast of us which appear to be Field Pieces. if they are they will probably drive us away before we can get the anchor unless the other vessels come in & help us to silence them. I have very little faith in any thing that we can do in that way.

I dont exactly understand about the money. If I remember right the first Payment at the Navy Agents was to be on the 31st of July. So that now Father ought to have three payments instead of two—one for July 1 for August & 1 for September. If you have not sent the things which I spoke of in my last letter please add some napkins & a ring for the same.

I am getting along nicely now, in regard to my health & begin to feel like a well man again & I dont know any thing about symptoms so its no use to ask me.

I will not write any more now but if any thing especial occurs before this goes I will add a few lines. Love to all Good by from your loving son

Henry

I thought it was not very complementary to send me my own letters back, torn up—see enclosure.

U.S. Str. *Montgomery*
Off Cape Fear
Sept. 12th 1863

Dear La La [Eliza]

I received your letter some time ago & ment [meant] to have answered it sooner but I have not had much time lately so you must excuse me. Hello! I have just looked at your letter & find that it is dated Aug 2nd I realy had no ideer[idea] that it was so long since you wrote & realy I feel ashamed of my self to have delayed so long. however better late than never you know.

I suppose you will be home or soon going by the time this letter gets there. I hope the last part of your visit has been as pleasant as the first was. I wish I could have been up there with you for a couple of weeks in stead of sweltering in those horrid sounds of North Carolina. I'm thankful that I am out of there tho' my present vessel is not a very pleasant one to be on.

We were up at Beaufort a few days ago. We found the old *Cambridge* there broken down & going north. I found several of my old shipmates there & enjoyed seeing them very much[.] The old boat looked as natural as could be & I would give a good deal to be back on her again tho' Capt. Parker is not there now.

We have a very pleasant set of officers on board here in the Ward Room. Our mess consists of a Master, 4 Ensigns, Paymaster[,] Surgeon, Chief Engineer & Pilot. The Room is quite large & pleasant but we have only six State Rooms which is not so desirable as we have two in a Room & I never saw a State Room yet that was large enough for two. My chum however is a tip top fellow. (old enough to be my Father tho' & an old sea Captain) he is a Mason & we get along first rate. The Surgeon (D. F. Lincoln) is a Brookline man, but I hardly think you know him as I never heard of him before.[9] he is a very pleasant fellow, quite young, & reminds me very much of Tom Peck. I like him very much. I dont know as any of the rest need especial mention, they are all good fellows in their way. The Ex[ecutive] Officer dont know much but does as well as he can. The Doctor & I are the only unmarried men in the mess.

Two of the Engineers were married the last time they were at home & are consequently eternally writing to their wifes [wives] letters of four & five sheets of paper all crossed. I dont see what they can find to write a bout, it is all I can do to fill up one. Perhaps one of these days I may know better. Who can tell. Our Captain E.A. Faucon is about the meanest man[10] — do you remember Capt Whitting of the *Falcon*? Well he reminds me very much of him. By the way he is the same Faucon mentioned in Dana's *Two Years before the Mast* but he must have changed greatly since then if my memory serves me.[11] He is too old to command a vessel in my opinion[.] At all events, he is not fit to be in a Gunboat.

Our vessel is very fast, we can beat any thing on the station.

Write me again soon, dont delay as long as I have done please. letters are about the only comfort one gets on the Blockade. Give my love to all friends, Good by from your brother

Henry

U.S.S. *Montgomery*
Off Cape Fear
Sept 20th 1863

Dear Mother

As I have a quiet hour before going on watch I think I can not employ it better than by writing home.

I suppose you are at church now hearing Mr. Clark preach[.] How I wish I was with you there is not a sunday goes round but what I think of that dear little church of ours & wish my self in it. I do not believe that there is another in the country where the people are so united or one so near my beau ideal of what a christian church ought to be. I would rather be like Mr Clark than hold the highest commission my Country could give. I wish I was good enough to be a minister but my call does not seem to be in that way so I must ever plod along as well as I can in the profession which I've chosen & which I suppose I am better fitted for than any thing else. It is very hard to be a Christian on board of a ship & tho' I make good resolutions at the beginning of the week I find at the end very little satisfaction in looking back. there are always so many thing[s] left undone which ought to have been done, & the contrary, that one gets quite discouraged. My Hymn Book is a great comfort at such times. There seems to be something in it for every mood.

We have service on board here every Sunday prenoon but it seems to me like a perfect mockery, for the Captain humbugs & torments Officers & men the whole week & then musters them on sunday to hear prayers. Sunday before last when we were in Beaufort we had a specimen of his religion. he finished the service with the Lords Prayer something in this manner—"for ever & ever Amen, I take this opportunity to tell you men that I'm not satisfied with the way you coal ship if you dont do better tomorrow etc. etc" I can't take much interest in such religion as that & I think the less one has of it the better. If only those attended his service that went of their own free will I fancy he would have few hearers.

We have not had any mail since we let Beaufort. We are expecting a vessel tho now every day & then I suppose we shall get one. I shall not be able to hear from home quite so often here as I used to when in the Sounds.

I wrote you a few day[s] ago & enclosed a letter for Cousin Lu Greely as I do not know her address. Also a $20. I hope you received it all right. it went north by the Gunboat *Sacramento*.

The last week has been quite stormy. the weather is getting quite cool now.

I am getting a long nicely in a sanitary point of view & am picking up flesh very fast so I think you need not feel anxious about me any more even if I dont tell you exactly how I feel in every letter.

Good by now, it is almost time for me to go on watch.

Give my love to all & write very often to your loving son

Henry

U.S. Str. *Montgomery*
Off Cape Fear
Sept 25th 1863

Dear Lu

The Transport (Gunboat, Beef Boat, or what ever they call her) *Newbern* arrived here this morning & by her I received your letter of the 13th (also a Journal.)[12] So I have set down to write at *once* to answer you, to make amends for my delay the last time.

We are as stupid as you please down here & have very little excitement. What we have had too has not been of a very pleasent sort as I will tell you. In the first place a day or two ago we went in chase of a very suspicious looking steamer, she altered her course & stood away when she saw that we were after her & we crowded all the steam on that we could raise to catch her. We gained on her fast & fired several shots at her to make her stop but with no effect[.] at last after dark she burnt a signal light. it was not a regular signal & did not mean any thing but nevertheless tho' we might have been up with her in half an hour our Captain made it an excuse to give up the chase & go back.

Every officer in the ship was indignant about it & the men were almost in a state of mutiny about it. It was the most outrageous thing I have heard of since I've been in the service & I think any man who would do such a thing must be either a traitor or a coward. We officers consulted together & have made up our minds that it is our duty to report the affair as he has done the same thing before tho' never in quite so barefaced a manner.

I dont know how long I shall be able to stand the sort of humbugging which is going on board of here continually. I expect to get into some scrape before long as he has taken a special dislike to me. I think I know the reason to[o]. Did you ever read Dana's *Two Years before the Mast*[?] He is the same Capt. Faucon mentioned there[.] The character that Dana gave him nearly ruined him & has caused him to have a profound antipithy to all young *Gentlemen* going to sea.[13]

It is a long time since I have read the book & I want very much to have it sent to me as I would like to refresh my memory a little.

I had a row with him yesterday & he was going to put me under arrest, but thought better of it & after talking it over had the frankness to acknowledge that he was as much to blame as myself (for mind you, I freely own that I was not *all* in the right) & concluded to call it square. He was on deck nearly all my watch this morning & worried me most to death[.] I've not got fairly over it yet. He did nothing but growl & find fault the whole time either at me or the men till at last I wished him to a sertain place most heartily. Well well it is a long road that has no turning.

Our Surgeons name is Lincoln (D.F.) & a tip top fellow he is[.] I enjoy his society very much & we are getting to be first rate friends. I was not aware that I had said any thing in any of my letters which would lead one to suppose that I did not like my messmates for the fact is quite the contrary[.] They are all quite a pleasant set of fellows & I like them better & better every day. My chum especially who is an old Sea Captain, an Act Ensign named Paterson.[14] we get along first rate together, in fact like brothers (Masons) (which we are). The other two Ensigns are both good fellows in their way. Our Chief Engineer is rather an original sort of a character but I rather like him. He is caterer of the mess. The Paymaster is a curious man but improves very much on acquaintance[.] With the junior officers of course I do not have much to do but they seem a very pleasant set. the master's mate in my watch is a very nice sort of fellow, gentlemanly etc. & of course proportionaly disliked by our Skipper. He is the best Mate on board nevertheless & knows his business.

One of our men died last night of Typhoid Fever. Our Surgeon & that of the *Maratanza* are holding a Post Mortem examination on him now[.] if I had not been writing I think I would have witnessed it. I suppose we shall bury him this afternoon. His name was Quigley. he belonged to Boston.

What a host of engagements have come out this summer[.] I'm afraid that by the time I get home there will be no one left for me. The Home Guards seem to be doing a flourishing business, but I hope "Blue and Gold" will not be altogether ignored. I'm glad to hear of Ned Hoopers engagement please congratulate them both for me if that would be a ship shape proceeding. Also those of the others which I know.

So you make all the cake do you? I should just like to drop in to tea some night & try it[.] Of course that would be my only object in coming. Can you make

Bread? That is a very necessary accomplishment if you are going to keep house for me, but on the whole dont you think we had better let Mother keep house a little while longer. Much as we love each other I dont think we could have a happier home, do you darling? I dont want another unless I get married (which is not very likely, at least at preasent) & then I suppose it would be necessary. I'll tell you what we may do tho one of these days perhaps, we'll reverse the case & keep house for Father & Mother when they get old & so keep up the dear old home for the younger children to love as we do. I think that will be the best plan dont you.

Well here I am on the eighth page so I guess I may as well close now. I wont say because I think you must be tired of reading but because I want to add a little to Mothers let[t]er which I wrote a day or two ago.

Write me again soon. Love to all & remember me to the rest (that is, friends etc.) from your loving brother

Henry

Montgomery
Off Cape Fear
Sept 25th 1863

Mother

The *Newbern* arrived to day bringing our mail & I was disapointed in not receiving any letter from you but I suppose there must be one on the way some where.

There are a few things that I want to have sent me & I think that they had better be started as soon as possable for they may be a long time getting thro'. I ought to have a new Uniform Coat but I will try & do with out that for a while.

but I guess I had better tell you what I do want instead of what I dont.

In the first place I want a good Rubber Coat a long one which will reach below my knees. Then I want two more pairs of Draws (Flannel) ½ a Doz sheets for my berth (I never used to care for them & dont now except for the appearance of the thing. I dont know as ½ a Doz is enough either. What do you think?) Two or three more Pillow cases (white). A Pair of Congress Boots (I like those better than shoes as I'm not then bothered with strings).[15] A pr. of warm Gloves (a neat pr. you know[)] & one or two neck-tyes. I also want some good books (I am read out) I want something worth reading & which will be of some benefit to me. I am getting disgusted with my self & my Novels.

But what ever you send put in Dana's *Two Years before the Mast* as I want to refresh my memory as to my present captain. You can fill up with any thing you like. Address the Box to me with the ships name. In care of Act. Master Cass U.S. Store Ship *Wm Badger* Beaufort N.C.[16]

Good by now love to all from

Henry

Dr Lincoln wants a few books & as I was sending I told him we had better get them all in one lot. I'll enclose a list of what he wants. He will settle with me for them. NO -- send the List to Wm Lincoln Esq. 15 Central St. Boston & he will get the books & send them out to be put in my box

U.S.S. *Montgomery*
Off Cape Fear
Oct. 4th 1863

Dear Mother

Service is just over so now I am going to employ my time before dinner in writing home.

Since I wrote you last one of our men has died. We ran off a little ways & buried him at sea. It is the first time I have ever witnessed an Ocean Burial. The man's name was Quigley & he belonged some where in Boston I believe. I wonder if he is any connection of the Harness maker (or what ever he is) of that name in Brookline. I did not know him at all, he was taken sick very suddenly a day or two after I joined the ship, in my watch. I sent him below & had the Surgeons Steward called to attend him, but never supposed it was any thing serious. There was a Post Mortem examination held on him.

The Rebels ran a steamer ashore below here a few days ago & burnt her. We went down there & shelled the wreck for a while to destroy the machinery[.][17]

I never want to get into a fight in this vessel. that work satisfied me of our efficiency, tho' I have never felt much doubt on the subject.

Nobody seemed to have the least idea about their duty except the Captain (I'm willing to give the Devil his due) who handled the ship very well. The men in the Powder Division did not seem to know the difference between a 10 in[ch] shot & a Parrott shell & when they found out, they did not know where to look for them. Several times I had to wait ten minutes before I could get any thing to load with. The worst of the matter is that no steps seem to be taken to remedy the matter either because the officers that should attend to it do not know how or do not care. The Captain seems to look on our being in a condition to fight as being of a secondary consideration & grudges every minute devoted to exercise. & the First Lieutenant has not the first idea of an Executive Officers duty so that between them both we are in a very bad way.

Hurrah there is a steamer coming in so I guess we shall get a mail. it is nearly two weeks since we have had one.

I expect three letters at the very least for my last receipt from you is at least a month old.

I think I wont write any more till she gets in.

Oct 5th. The steamer proved to be the *Victoria* & she brought us a mail.[18] I only received one letter from home (Sept. 9th) at which I was very much disapointed. Especialy as the letter received was not of so late a date as the one I had by the last mail[.] There must be some letters floating round for me some where I am sure.

I received a letter from Capt H.H. Foster of the *Ceres* by this mail. The *C*[*eres*] is in here now & I am very glad of it as I dare say I may need a friend here before long. I dont think I can contain myself much longer but now if I get into any scrape I shall have both my old Captains here to testify as to my character since I've been in the service. I have not seen Capt. P[arker] yet. He seems to have kept track of me tho' for he sent his regards to me by our Capt. when he went on board to report.

Last night another steamer ran the Blockade.[19] we went to quarters & *by mistake* our chain was slipped[.] The man who had charge of it having (I rather think purposely) misunderstood the order. He was terrably rated for it & we let go another anchor tho the alarm signals were repeated & I saw a strange steamer very near us going to the southard. A few minutes after the *Victoria* (Capt. MacDiarmid) which was the vessel that gave the alarm (she is too slow to chase herself) passed within hail & asked if we saw his signals, & if so why we were not under way, when our Capt. had the face to claim credit for having slipped. However it was no use to slip unless we chased & Capt. MacD. was very angry & did not use very respectful language. I think he will report Capt. Faucon & certainly hope so.

Our men are almost in a state of mutiny & it would not surpprise me if they did revolt before long if there is not some change. I think he is a secessionist[.] At all events he is not fit to command a Blockader. It is not much use for the Officers of a ship to report the Captain or we would have preferred charges against him long ago. but now I am in hopes that Capt. MacD will do it & if he does I think we can bring evidence enough against him to get him kicked out[.]

It is no wonder that the papers cry out against the Wilmington Blockade. One or two such captains as ours would spoil any Blockading because they not only do no good themselves but prevent others from doing it.

There I wont write any more about that it makes me boil over with indignation to think about it. We picked up a canoe a day or two ago containing a dog[,] negroes 4 men 2 women & a child.

I enclose you $20 also a Confederate note. Good by now love to all from

Henry

U.S.S. *Montgomery*
Off Cape Fear
Oct. 10th 1863

Dear La La·

Another vessel arrived on the station last evening & brought a large mail. I received three letters one of which was a nice long one from you which I hasten to answer as the mail will leave this evening on one of the vessels which is going to Beaufort for coal.

Capt. Parker is here now in Command of the *Tuscarora* & is Senior officer on the station. I have just been on board there to see him. He received me very cordially, congratulated me on my promotion & expressed a great interest in my welfare generaly. I had intended to have asked him if he could not get me transferred to his ship but he forestalled me by saying that his vessel at preasent had her full complement of officers, but that if any of them should be detached or sent away in prizes he would have me transferred to her as he would like very much to have me with him again. Was not that pleasant? The *T*[*uscarora*] is a splendid vessel, a regular Man of War & mounts a very heavy battery. she is just the boat for all the world that I should like to be on board of either for Blockading or fighting especialy if we have a war with any foreign power. She seems to have a very pleasant set of officers. nearly all of them are regulars.

Perhaps I may not be so lucky as to get ordered to her but at all events it is very pleasant to me to have Capt. Parker *want* me there.

We have quite a strong force here now & I am in hopes we shall be able to make the Blockade more effectual than it has been heretofore.

We have had a good deal of excitement here for the last few day[s] from vessels running or trying to run out, but we have not caught any as yet. Last night a steamer tried to get out but was driven back.

I am very glad that you are having, or rather have had, such a pleasent time at Conway & also that it has done you so much good.

I wish I could have been with you for a few of those days[.] I do not think it would have done me any harm & it would sertainly have been very pleasent. This is weary work to make the best of it & it comes doubly hard when one is dissatisfied with their position, as I have had good reason to be with mine here. I feel happier to day than I have for some time past tho' in the prospect of getting to another vessel, & feel as tho' I could "even love Becky Case". I hardly dare think of it tho for is [it] seems as tho it would be almost too good luck.

I have noticed that since Capt. P.[arker] has been here that Capt. Faucon has been a little more civil to me than before. I expect Capt. P. has been talking to him of me, indeed he told me as much.

Capt MacDarmid who used to command the *Ceres* is here too on the *Victoria* & he is trying to get me made an Master[.] So you see I stand pretty well with those I have served under if I dont with my preasent Captain. (I feel as tho' I would like to use a strong adjective every time I mention his name, in connection with it)

Can there be much good in a man who can not find a single soul in a large ships company like this, but what most cordially detest him?

He may be a very pleasent man ashore (the Call's say he is) but preserve me from such afloat is my prayer.

But the subject is not a pleasent one to me & I'm sure it can't interest you much so I will drop it.

What a number of engagements have come out this summer. Who is the Mr. Lincoln that Clara Lothish is engaged to? any relation to the Lincolns of Brookline[?]

In one of Mothers letters yesterday I received a jolly little Tin Type of Ruthie, she looks very different from what I remember of her[.] I am afraid I shall hardly know her Lady ship when I get home[.]

I think it is hardly a square thing to have Babies growing so out of all reason. Dont you think something ought to be done about it? I wish to enter my protest in due form against her growing any more till I get home.

Please inform Ben Bolt that his letter was duly received & an answer will be forthcoming shortly. I was very much interested in his account of the Fall of the Great Elm.

There has some company just come in so I can not write any more now.

Good by. love to all & write soon again to your loving brother

Henry

U.S.S. *Montgomery*
Off Cape Fear
Oct. 12th 1863

Dear Mother

An unexpected opportunity has offered of sending letters so I will write you a few lines as I do not like to miss any chance of letting you hear from me.

I despatched a long letter day before yesterday which I hope will be duly received as I enclosed $20. & a $5. Confederate note. I also wrote to Eliza by the same mail. Why dont Lu write again it seems a long time since I have heard from her?

By the last mail I received two letters from you one dated Sept. 19th (Mother & Bennie) and the other the 29th which last by the way, came via Washington D.C. thro some carelessness of Post masters, for it was directed planly enough I'm sure.

I hope Geo. Long will succeed in getting his commission that's if he would like to serve in one of those regiments. If I was in his place I should rather stay where I was tho' I think. I have kept putting off writing till now I suppose it is too late as he will probably be on his way home. Im sorry but there it is. I dont have a great deal of time & what I have you at home have the first claim to, I've no other excuse to offer.

I'm sorry you did not like the Tin Types the large one *was* very poor but I did not think the little ones were so bad considering that I was rather "under the Toad" at the time. I guess I look a little heartier now. at all events I feel so. How

Baby must have altered since I was at home[.] That Tin Type was not any thing like the Picture in my minds eye of the little darling. I long to see her again. Can she talk much yet? You dont tell me half enough about her.

I have received several newspapers but the Tribune which you spoke about in your letter has not yet come to hand. I am much obliged to you for sending me so many[.] We can not buy papers here & our only chance of getting them is thro' the mail.

Every thing is going on here much as usual. Was it not nice in Capt. Parker to say that he wanted me back in his ship? I hope that there will be a vacancy soon for I have quite enough of the *Montgomery*. The Capt. has been very civil tho lately & has left me alone for which I'm sure I'm much obliged for if he had kept on much longer as he was doing I am afraid I should have laid my self liable to a Court Martial by telling him what I thought of him. "All I ask is to be let alone."

We have some of the greatest hands here to write letters that you ever saw[.] There are two of the Ensigns who always write 16 to 20 pages of this kind of paper double lined for every mail. & our Engineer last mail sent his wife *21 ft* of letter, it was written on Fools Cap half sheets pasted together & writing on both sides.[20] what do you think of that? He says he has *only* got *two* feet written now & so can not send any letter home this time as that would be too short. Well I guess I can not write any more now for the Boys are waiting to set the table for dinner[.] Send my love to all from

Henry

Have you sent the Box yet?

Enclosed please find $10. (Confederate)

U.S.S. *Montgomery*
Off Cape Fear
Oct 13th 1863

Dear Mother

I sent you a letter yesterday but the *Newbern* has just got in & as letters by her will probably get home first I will write you a few lines by her.

There has another vessel just arrived on the station. I do not know her name but she is very much like the *Ceres* & looks as natural as life.

We had a row on board here this morning amongst the men. One of the Petty Officers got pretty severely hurt. There is to be a Court Martial to try the offenders & I am ordered to act as one of the members—just my luck! I dont like it at all it is unpleasant duty at any time but especialy so when the Officers belong to the same ship as the man, or men, to be tried, for of course one must pass sentence according to his oath, a matter which a party of sailors are not very apt to consider,

& consequently are apt to feel a dislike to any officers who find it necessary to punish any of their number severely.

Well there it is, one can not expect to have all pleasant duty & no disagreable but it does seem as tho I had a little more of this work than my share.

The boat has gone for the mail but I hardly expect any letters as we had a large mail Saturday[.] I am rather in hopes my Box may be here tho I dont know but it is most too soon to expect it. I hope you sent it at once for I need some of the thing[s] very much especialy the shoes.

The mail has come on board. I received Cousin Lu's letter & some papers. My Box did not come but *I do not* feel disapointed for I hardly expected it so soon.

Cousin L says that Lu says I owe her a letter. There must be some mistake about that I am quite sure I have answered all her letters which I have received[.] however to make matters straight I will write to her by next mail for I always like to receive her letters.

Tell Cousin Lu that I will answer her letter very soon.

I wrote you a long letter on the 10th & enclosed $25. But the "V" was a Confederate Note so I am afraid Father will hardly want to take it for what is on its face. In my letter yesterday I enclosed an "X" of the same valuable description.

I will enclose in this $20.00 in good money to add to my *stock*.

Good by now. Love to all & write often to your loving son

Henry

U.S.S. *Montgomery*
Off Cape Fear
Oct 17th 1863

Dear Brother Bennie

I received your letter a few days ago & I will now answer it. I was very glad to hear from you as you have not written to me before for a long time.

I do not think I shall go back to the *Ceres* again, she has gone home to be repaired & to have a new boiler. Do you know what a Steamboats Boiler is? If you do not perhaps Father will explain it to you.

I hear that you have been promoted at school & am very glad of it. What do you study now?

I hope you will always be a good boy at school & do what the teacher tells you.

So you saw the fires in Hopkinton. I read about them in the Newspapers. Did you have a pleasant visit with Aunt Lucinda? Did you see Mrs. Stanwood while you was there?

I was very much interested in your account of the fall of the great Elm tree & shall like to see the piece of wood that you got from it when I come home. I think it very doubtful however whether I shall be able to make a ship of it for you, for

I am not much of a Jack Knife Carpenter & I'm afraid that that is not the right kind of wood to whittle boats out of.

It is almost dinner time so I can not write you any more now as the Boys want to set the table.

Give my love to all the family & write to me again some time when you have leasure

Good by from your
Bra Hen[21]

U.S. Str. *Montgomery*
Off Cape Fear
Oct. 18th 1863

Dear Mother

There is a vessel to leave tonight for the North so I write you a short letter to go by her.

The *Maratanza* had just arrived from Beaufort & I suppose she has a mail for us but we have not communicated with her yet. I hope that we shall however before the mail closes.

I wrote a letter to Cousin Lu yesterday. I have directed the letter to Brookline as I think she can have hardly gone out West yet, but if she has you can forward it you know.

I have commenced a letter to Ben which I will finish by & by[.] I dont think that I have much tact for writing childrens letters.

What has possest the little scamp with the desire to go to sea? It will never do in the world to allow him to foster that idea. One sailor in a family is enough in all consecunce [conscience] & we must try to make something better of him.

I have not been very well for the last few days & have consequently been rather homesick. I think that if after a month or so longer I see no prospect of a change, I shall apply for a leave of absence, for tho at times I feel quite smart, still at others I am quite miserable & I think it would do me good to be quite at home for two or three weeks with my Mother & sisters to take care of me. I have held out against my sick feelings since I have been down here but if I get home I give you fair warning that I'm going to give right up & require lots of nursing.

There has been nothing going on here since I wrote you last. Capt. Mac Diarmid has been detatched from the *Victoria* & ordered to the *Howqua*.[22] The *V*[*ictoria*] is ordered home. He does not like it much & I dont blame him for feeling as tho' he was rather hardly used, for he had expected to be ordered to a better vessel, with good reason too I think, & the *H*[*owquah*] is nothing but a Great Tow boat Mounting 4 guns. She is off New Inlet so he will not even have the privilege of going north.

Captain Parker is still here, but I have only been on board his ship once as she has kept off outside most of the time since she has been here.

Since I wrote you last I have been in another Court Martial. We had to try four of our men for fighting & trying to knock each others brains out with a Flat Iron etc. It took us two days to get thro' with the cases. Dr. Lincoln was Recorder of the Court. The more I know the Doctor the better I like him, he's a tip-top fellow & no mistake. He reminds me very much of Tom Peck in a great many things.

I had a very severe headach last night & am not altogether clear of it now so I hope you will excuse any mistakes that I may have made for I do not intend to look the letter over. I sent home $20.00 by the last letter & will send $20.00 more in this. Good by love to all from your loving son

Henry

U.S.S. *Montgomery*
Off Western Bar
Oct. 20th 1863

Dear Mother

There has a steamer just arrived here which will leave tomorrow for the North & I have just time before supper to write a few lines for I pride myself on never letting a mail go with out some sort of a letter going home with it.

I received a letter a day or two ago from Lu which I will answer soon but shall not have time to do so by this steamer.

Dont be thinking that we have changed our station by the way I have headed this letter. Off Wilmington, Cape Fear, or Western Bar all means the same thing.[23]

Every thing is very quiet here & no excitement. Last night when we took our station the Rebs fired two shots at us but did no damage[.]

As it was too dark for them to be able to tell whether their shots struck or not I suppose they thought it would not pay to fire any more. At all events they did not.

The *Tuscarora* is still here, but the *Victoria* has gone home & Capt. Mac D has joined his new vessel which is off New Inlet.

I am afraid the lost letter I wrote was rather blue. I did not feel very well at the time & I think my state of health is very apt to effect style of writing.

I hope you have sent off that box before this, but if you have not I want that coat that I left at home converted into a uniform one. Ornements the same as that sack that you sent with the addition of a 5 point gold star on each sleave above the Lace[.] I also want another vest & pants. I guess in the whole you had better have them ready & send them in a seperate package *after* I receive the other things as I dont like to risk too much in one lot.

Can'nt write any more now as the Boy wants to set the table.

Good by love to all from your loving son

Henry

Enclosed please find $20.

Oct. 21st. I keep thinking of things which I want. The fact is I have been out so long that I almost need a new fit out. My shirts are all in a very bad state of repair & my stockings – well last Sunday I over hauled the whole lot to find a pair to put on. I managed to pick out two stockings out of the stock (not mates) which appeared to be sound, but sorrowful to relate on putting them on I had the mortification to see my great toe laughing at me thro' one of them. Do relieve my distress by sending me some more, or else a Ball of Yarn.

I'd like to have a pair of slippers very much etc. etc. etc. etc. etc. etc. Only send me what you think I want. Good by

Henry

U.S.S. *Montgomery*
Off Western Bar
Oct. 22nd 1863

Dear Lu Lu

I received your letter a few days ago & as I want to have another very soon I think the best thing for me to do is to hurry up & answer.

Confound it I believe some of these fellows are crazy. The Paymaster has been tormenting me ever since I set down to write, more than half an hour ago.

I am very glad to hear that Henry Bond has reenlisted & I hope that his old comrades will follow his example. Does not Will Bond think of going back[?] I thought he would be one of the first to do so. & how is it about the Windsors? are they not going. I suppose Willie Welman will be out again before long, of course as an officer, at least he seemed to talk as tho' he should before he went home.

I am very glad Luie dear to hear that you have taken so much interest in our church of late. I fully agree with you in thinking that there is not another one equal to it in the whole United States, & that our Hymn Book is as near perfection as can be. It is a real comfort. I read mine every sunday & have a little church in my head all to my self & so generaly pass a happy hour or so[.] but from the time I take it up until I lay it down I cannot help wishing myself in the dear little chapel in Indiana Place.

What a good man Mr Clark must be to be able to draw all his congregation so closely to him so that tho' they may be thousands of miles away still in spirit at least they join him on the sabbath.

I remember (I shall never forget it) the sunday when I first felt as you do now & my experience was much the same as yours. Mr Clark if he had known how I felt could not have preached more directly at me than he seemed to that day. & what is more he has not left off since. When ever I hear him (*so* seldom!) I always feel as tho what he was saying was meant especialy for me. I wonder if Mother remembers that Sunday[?] but of course she does, she loves us all too well not to remember what effects us so nearly. & I think that perhaps it is more owing to her influence that we feel so than to any thing else. Oh Lu its not every one that has such a home as we have had. We owe our Parents a debt that all the love & obediance that we can give will never half repay. I think I never half apreciated what home was till I left it. I hope Ben will do better & be a comfort to Father & Mother as they grow old. Of course Ruth will. I believe she is a little angel. Do you suppose there ever was such another Baby?

I wish I could give you any encouragement to expect me home within any reasonable time but I can not see much prospect of it at present[.] I can see nothing ahead but a dismal vista of Blockade with the possability of a trip to Norfolk in a few weeks to repair our windlass which is broken, & a still more remote one of being able to get transfered to the *Tuscarora*. However when I have been out a year I intend to apply for a leave of absence for a short time, tho' I doubt if they will pay any attention to it.

Have you had any Photographs taken lately? if you have any be sure & send me one. I have not got you in my book yet you know & I dont like it at all, at all.

I am sorry to hear that you have all got colds at home. I have done all I could in the matter & taken one my self out of sympathy. You talk about its being hot weather at home but I have had to wear white clothes & straw hat here on watch & been half roasted at that. How'll that do for October.

The Rebs continue to run the Blockade here about as they please but I guess we shall stop them after a while as the Powers that be are beginning to wake up & are increasing the squadron very fast.

I'd like to catch some of them, for a little prize money would not be unexceptable & I think its about time I had a little luck in that way.

I cann't write any more now for I'm tired & have a headach (I'm very sorry to say that is a very common thing with me of late) so I want to get a nap before I go on watch.

Love to all the family & friends etc. Good by. Write me a good long letter soon.

From your loving Brother

Henry

U.S.S. *Montgomery*
Off Western Bar
Oct. 25th 1863

Dear Mother

Sunday has come round again & so I'm going to write to you especialy as I feel decidedly homesick today. I am on the sick-list now with one of *my* colds a regular *sneezer*. I dont suppose you will require to know any of the symptoms by letter as you have seen me have so many. I do not remember ever having one of this sort at sea before & I think it is hardly a fair thing. It is not so bad you know when I have my mother to take care of me but here its most too bad. I did not like to lay up but it was very damp & drizzly last night & my chum, Mr. Putnam (who does not stand watch regularly being sailing Master) would not hear of my taking the deck, but took my place, so I had a quiet night. My head this morning feels like a lump of lead so I have put my self as I said before on the List for I am sertainly too stuped [stupid] altogether to do duty.

I have not taken any medicine as yet & dont know as I shall. I think perhaps it will be as well to let the thing work it self out.

I am thankful that I am an Ensign instead of a Mate tho' for I have now got comparatively comfortable quarters & can take pretty good care of myself which would be a difficult thing to accomplish, to say the least of it, in a Steerage.

The *Clypso* [*Calypso*] arrived yesterday & brought us a mail[.] I was disapointed in receiving no letters from home, but I had a very pleasant one from Eliza (at Conway) Also one from Capt. Foster of the *Ceres* & a lot of newspapers.

I have not received a letter from you for some time, but I suppose that there is some good reason for it so I wont complain, but I can not help feeling a bit disapointed when a mail arrives with out bringing me a letter from you.

The Bell has just finished tolling so all hands are at church now. I generaly go for the sake of setting a good example tho' I do not feel as tho' I derive any advantage therefrom, but today I think it more prudent to stay where I am as it is very cold on the Berth Deck & I might make myself worse.

If I was at home I think I should run that risk tho for the sake of going with you to hear Mr. Clark. That would be something worth while.

I am real glad to hear that Lu has begun to love our church[.] I thought she would after a while[.] Your children Mother have to come to it sooner or later. home influance does not go for naught.

Do you remember when I was a small boy how I used to complain about having to go to church & say that when I grew up I never would go near one? You used to say then that I should be glad one of these days & thank you for insisting on my going, & I'm sure I do now. But it seems as tho my boyish determination was to be carried out per force for it is so seldum that I can go to church.

I am longing more & more every day to get home if it is only for a week but I do not think I had better ask for a leave of a[b]sence just yet. The longer I wait the better chance I shall have of getting it I think. Time does drag dreadfully tho', it seems more like eighteen than eight months since I left home. I suppose it is because I have been sick so much of the time.

I am living in hopes that something will turn up before long that will bring me home.

I think we shall go to Norfolk before long as we have broken our windlass, possably we may go still farther north, who knows. or perhaps we may catch a prize & I may be sent home in her. I am afraid that last chance is rather a poor one to calculate on as even if we do take one my chance of being put in charge is rather bad as there are other officers here that have been in the ship longer than I & have therefor a better right. We shall leave here tonight or tomorrow for Beaufort to get coal. We are all run out & have hardly enough on board to take us there. We are waiting for the *Tuscarora* who will probably be here to day.

Night before last we ran in very close to the fort & anchored on account of seeing a large steamer in side apparently intending to run out (she was Bark rigged & I should not wonder if it was the *Sumpter*.[24] The Rebs saw us & fired about 20 rounds of rifle shell at us[.] They flew all round but we never budged an inch & finnly [finally] they got tired of it & knocked off. None of their projectiles struck us tho' some came pretty near.

I will not write any more now as I want to lay down but if I have time after the *T*[*uscarora*] arrives perhaps I will add a few lines.

I am afraid I have not written a very pleasant letter but you must make allowances for my cold etc.

Good by. love to all from your homesick Boy

Henry

U.S. Str. *Montgomery*
Off Beaufort
Oct. 30th 1863

Dear LaLa [Eliza]

I received your letter of the 18th to day & haste[n] to answer it.

I have not written home for several days & I feel rather ashamed of myself, as in my last I wrote that I was sick & of course you will all feel anxious to hear from me.

I am still on the sick-list & feel rather blue. I'm beginning to feel afraid my cold is going to settle on my lungs but perhaps the *Medico* will be able to prevent it. I dont cough much yet.[25]

I tried to go on duty the day we arrived here partly on account of some slurring remarks that the Captain passed (& which one of the officers was officious enough to tell me of) about officers laying up. I stood two watches & then broke down[.] The doctor protested at first & then put his veto on my trying it any more. He is taking excelant care of me, but I dont know, I am beginning to feel rather discouraged & want to get home, it does seem as tho I had hardly seen a well day since I got home from Richmond[.]

I hoped when I got down here on salt water that I should get well but it seems that is not to be. So now as I said before I am about discouraged, & want to come home. Dr Hunt might be able to cure me.

I think if I dont get better soon I shall ask for a leave of absence or a medical survey for I'm neither use nor orniment here.

There—I think Ive written enough about myself & too much too[.] I'm afraid but I cann't help writing as I feel.

I've not received my box yet but perhaps shall tomorrow as some of our officers have gone up to Newbern & I think very likely they may find it there.

You must excuse my not writing a longer letter but it makes me feel dizzy to write & I want to lay down. I get tired very quickly & have to lie down during the greater part of the day.

Good by now, love to all the family from your own

Bra Hen

P.S. Private

I dont like it a bit that mother has been sick & I not told any thing about it. I was wondering why she did not write. When I read about it my first thought was that I would not say a word in my next letter about my own health, but I concluded that would be unkind to say the least of it so changed my mind. but please dont let them do so again, you dont know how badly it made me feel when I heard about it.

Promise me in your next letter that you wont. Otherwise I shall be immagining all the time that some one is unwell.

Henry

U.S. Str. *Montgomery*
Beaufort Harbor
Nov. 1st 1863

Dear Mother

I have just set down to write you my usual sunday letter.

I feel better to day than I have before since I was taken sick & hope I am going to get well again, or at least so that I can go on duty for I dont like being confined below at all. It makes me feel altogether too homesick for comfort or peace of mind. I had to back down on my first determination of not taking any medicine & have been setting up a small "shotacary Pop" inside of me.[26] The "Medico" has taken me in hand & realy I think he has done me a great deal of good, tho' I do make faces at his medicines.

My principal trouble now seems to be that I have lost all my strength. I can not set up more than two or three hours with out being so tired that I have to go & lie down for two or three more to get rested. I suppose it is partly owing to my not having eaten much lately, but I have no apetite & if I eat much it rises up in my throat causing a very oppressive feeling something like Dyspepsia, I immagine.[27]

I have more or less headach all the time & can not read much. I cough a little but do not think that that amounts to any thing. & I raise a good deal of thick Phlem (is that spell[ed] right? I mean *flem*)

Add to all that that I am terribly homesick & I believe you have Diagnosis of my preasent state as near as I can give it [to] you.

We had a mail yesterday but I did not receive any letters from home. I have received several papers lately, & a day or two ago a letter from Eliza which I have answered. Why dont Lu write? I have not heard from her for some time.

Our men are just on the verge of mutiny & if they do break bounds the Capt. will have no one but himself to thank for it for he has fairly driven them to it. Since we have been in here he made them work coaling ship from early in the afternoon one day until eight A.M. the next with out a drop of water to drink tho' there was plenty on board the ship. His reason being that he did not want to use water out of the Tanks but would get it from shore. Some was got in the morning which was hardly fit to drink & as there was no one to watch it the men I dare say wasted it so that it was all gone as I said before, & he would not send for any more. He kept them coaling all last night, & they are at work now (Sunday forenoon)[.] I dont know whether he will knock them off for Prayers or whether he will give us double allowance next Sunday, probably the latter.

The men would not work during the night, that is they worked so slow as to accomplish nothing, hoisting in 53! buckets in one watch.[28] They threw lumps of coal at the lanthorns & were finaly so mutinous that four or five Marine sentries had to be posted to watch them, armed.[29] I cant write any more now for I am tired & want to lie down. Good by. Love to all the family from your loving son

Henry

I have not received the box yet but shall soon, I dare say. Enclosed please find $10.00.

U.S.S. *Montgomery*
Off Beaufort N.C.
Nov. 5th 1863

Dear Mother

Yesterday there was a Medical Survey held on me & I am ordered to Norfolk Hospital for an indefinite length of time[.] The surgeons found my Lungs to be affected & reported me as unfit for duty. I can not find out just how bad they are. Dr. Lincoln says two months is the least time that I can hope to be fit for sea duty but the others say much longer.

When I get to Norfolk I shall apply for leave of absence. if they refuse it I think I shall resign for I do not fancy staying in a Hospital for two months & no sertainty of getting out [of] there. I will wait tho' till I hear what you think at home[.]

Write to me as soon as you receive this direct to Naval Hospital Portsmouth Va.

I shall probably be there in about six days from date.

I should be very sorry to have to throw up my appointment which I worked so hard to get, & hope that there will be no necessaty of it. I guess they will give me a leave of absence.

I shall go on board the Transport *Newbern* to day but she has got to go down off Wilmington before she goes North.

Good by now Give my love to all the family. In great haste from your loving son

Henry

Marginalia—Henry struck out a repeated line and wrote, "I'm crazy and blind."

7

"It Makes Our Life Here Seem Doubly Monotonous"

Duty in Florida

USS *Admiral*[1]
Narrows[2]
Feb 7th 1864

Dear Mother

We are going down the bay & I have just time to write you a few line[s] to send ashore by the Pilot, just to let you hear the last of me you know[.]

I received your note yesterday & was very glad to hear from home again before sailing.

I hope Father received the note I sent him enclosing $100. on Friday. I have not time now to tell you all about my doing in New York but I will do so after I join my vessel.

This ship is a very fine one & bran[d] new! I was afraid when I left home that it would be other wise as I heard that the *A*[*dmiral*] was the same steamer which used to run "down East" from Boston & not a very sea worthy vessel. I did not say any thing about it when I was at home for fear that you would feel too anxious about me. & of course if she had been ever so bad there would have been no help for my going in her.

Please excuse this horrible writing the vessel is a propeller & sails badly.

I am nicely & hope to continue so.

Good by – lots of love to all the family from your loving son

H. W. Wells

U.S.S. *Admiral*
At Sea
Feb. 10th 1864

Dear Mother

As we are to stop at Port Royal for a few hours I thought I would just scribble off a few lines to you, & mail it there.

We are having fair weather & are getting on nicely. it was a little rough on Monday and there was a good deal of sea sickness but every body is all right now. There are quite a number of Ward Room Passengers so we have to berth two in a room. My chum is a.a. [Acting Assistant] Paymaster Franklin who is going out to join the *S*[*c*]*iota*. it is his first trip.[3] He's a very pleasant fellow a little green tho' as I found to my cost this forenoon for he left the Bulls Eye light open in our room & a sea came in & completely drowned every thing. Our beds & mattrass were all soked. It required a good deal of Philosophy to keep in good temper but with the help of my pipe I managed not to swear much tho' I'm afraid to night I shall miss my comfortable bed at home with Bennie for a warming pan, much. We passed on Tuesday a Gunboat towing a Monitor bound south.

To day we chased a Blockade runner but she proved too fast for us. In doing so we had a very narrow escape. The vessel is new this being her first trip & of course nobody on board has had time to find out much about her. While we were chasing & had got up a heavy head of steam some of the officers smelt fire & on investigation we found that the wood work round the funnel was on fire there having been no sheathing on it. If it had not been discovered, in 15 m[inutes] later it would have been all in a blaze & heaven only knows what the consequences might have been for not only have we a green crew but there is a draft of nearly two hundred men on board & it would have been next to impossable to have keep [kept] them in any sort of order. However as it was it was soon got under—[control.]

I can not write any more now. Love to all the family. Tell Uncle H[amilton] that I've not forgotten his Photograph & I will send him my address as soon as I know it myself.

Good by for this time dont forget to send me lots of papers. When you know how to direct them, send the Army & Navy Journal occasionaly.

No more at present from your loving son

H.W. Wells

U.S.S. *Admiral*
Key West Fla.
Feb 14th 1863 [1864]

Dear Mother

We arrived here in Key West this morning & as it was Sunday I have not reported yet but have been cruising round (Thermometer 100° with winter clothes on – whew – think of that –) eating Bananas & smoking. I thought I would not write again until I joinee [joined] my ship (I wrote from Port Royal & by the Pilot at New York) but I changed my mind as I find there is a steamer going out in the morning & I know it will be a satisfaction to hear from me if it is only a few lines in pencil. It will have to be a very few too for it is just on the verge of 10 P.M. when the lights must out.

I have not seen Capt Welch yet but shall tomorrow probably[.][4]

My vessel is at Indian River on the east coast of Fla. I believe. how I'm to get to her I dont know but shall find out I suppose tomorrow.

I expect I shall have to stay here in Key West for some time. if I do I will write no more at present.

Love to all. In great haste from your loving son

H. W. Wells

Marginalia—[at top of page a drawing of a hand pointing] Take notice how the pages are numbered. I made a mistake.

Key West
Feb. 17th 1864

Dear Mother

I am still here at Key West & do not think I shall get away this week. My vessel is blockading at Charlotts Harbor, about 120 miles from here on the West Coast of Fla.[5] I am going up to join her in the U.S.S. *Honduras* which vessel is repairing here & will hardly be ready before some time next week[.][6] I could not stay on board of her as they are painting so I am stopping at the Russel House the only Hotel here & which is about equal to a 19th rate boarding House in a northern city in point of accommodations, & of a first class New York Hotel in charges.[7] They set a very poor table, but there is plenty of fish & Turtle so I manage to get along[.] One would think that the Beef tho' came from Noah's Ark it is so hard & tough, & the butter – well the less that's said of it the better. The rooms are miserable I've had better in a sailor boarding house.

The town is quite small & quiet & there is little or no business done here except what is brought by the Army & Navy. I'm told its the largest *City* in Florada Tho I hardly think there are as many inhabitants as in Walpole & is certainly not so fine a village. it is rather pretty tho' the houses are all surrounder [surrounded] with coconut trees & there are plenty of flowers in the gardens.

There is not much fruit raised here but vessels from Havannah bring over plenty of Bananah's & oranges & I've seen some Guavas. I've half lived on the first since I've been here.

Capt. Welch boards here & I gave him your note of introduction. He was very polite but some how I dont *take* to him much tho he spoke very pleasantly of you & Father & wished to be remembered when I wrote, hoped if he could at any time be of service to me I would consider him & etc. etc. in fact I have no reason for not feeling perfectly satisfied with my reception.

While I was on the *Admiral* I wrote you two or three short notes in pencil just to let you keep track of me. I hope you have received them. I believe I have not told you any thing of my visit in New York yet so I will try now & post you[.]

I met a very pleasant fellow in the cars & talked & smoked with him all the way to New London. On the boat I shared my state Room with Mr. Field. I told him at the Depot in B that he could have half of it if he wanted it supposing he would (if he excepted) share the expense. but that never seemed to enter his head he thanked me for the use of it & went off in the morning before I turned out.

As soon as I got my breakfast I went over to the Navy Yard & reported & found that there was very little prospect of getting off for several days tho at the Admiral's office, I was told that she would sail the next day. I then went over to Uncle P's & found Aunt Katy at home (the young ladies came in a little while after). I was very much supprised to hear of Uncles sudden start, as you must have been at home, but the worst of it is they dont know where he is, he did not tell them exactly where he was going & has not written yet.

Auntie asked me to stay at their house but I thought I should rather put up at a Hotel so after staying for about an hour I went back to the City[.] before going however I was introduced to Mrs. D.J. Wells. She is quite small dresses in black does not talk much but is very pleasant[.] I should not think she had a great deal of character, her forehead is very low. & I should not call her very pretty.

I put up at the Astor House as you know & after dinner I called on Dick Lovett & had a very pleasant chat with him.[8] In the evening I went over to Brooklyn again & found the whole family at home during the first part of the evening[.] The Boys kept me down stairs smoking. Henry was at home. he is First Lt. in the Marine Artillery now. When we went up into the Parlor I found beside the family a young lady cousin of theirs who was making them a visit[.] I can not remember her name but she was very pleasant & also very pretty, handsome, or beautiful. I dont know which term to use, hardly, but I guess the second will express my meaning best. Henry was *very* attentive but as she is older than he I dont suppose it means any thing. We had some music & then Played Whist & I was beguiled into staying until 1 AM. for after I got up to go nothing would do but I must go down and have a smoke befor[e] I went.[9] So we did not keep the Ladies up much after twelve. I was assured that the Ferry Boats ran all night but when I got down to the South Ferry I found that they did not run after 12 m[idnight]. Did the Wall St. run? No, only the Fulton: There was a pr[e]tty mess I had been on my feet all day & was not in very good trim for a long walk so I went back to Chilton St but the house was all dark so I thought I would not trouble them but started off for the Fulton Ferry. It was nearly three when I got over to the Hotel & as I was rather faint I thought I'd get some oysters before I turned in so I traveled along till I found an oyster celler open & then sailed in. I found the place filled with Soldiers & civilians all gloriously drunk & directly they commenced a row & down came the Police & for five or ten minutes Babel could not have held a candle to the uproar all of them shouting & cursing together. They quieted down after a while & the Police took out some of the drunkest & then I got some oysters. It was pretty late when I turned in, & I took my breakfast at about 10.30 AM. next. so that morning, after breakfast I went over to the Navy Yard & reported my self & then went back to the Hotel & kept quite until evening reading the Atlantic Monthly. In the evening Dick Lovett came to see me & we coursed up Broadway & round to Delmonico's.[10] We smoked *10* cigars apice between 6:30 & 11:30[.] What do you think of that. On Friday I drew my advance & mileage ($22.) (I sent home $100. Was it rec'd) I have not got any more paper so I will tell you the rest next time I write.

Good by give my love to all the family[.] I would send you some Bananas but I am afraid they would not keep.

I will try to find how my letters should be addressed before I close this letter. Good by again.

from your loving son
H.W. Wells

Marginalia [written sideways on another page]—
Direct to
Act Ensign
H. W. Wells
U.S.S. Gem of the Seas[11]
Eastern Gulf Squadron
Key West Fla.

Key West Fla.
Feb. 18th 1864

Dear Mother

The mail did not leave yesterday as I expected so I will write you a few lines in addition to what I mailed yesterday. When I closed I was telling you about my stay in New York so I will finish that subject first. The Str. *Admiral* went into commission on Friday so I thought it was but to get my baggage on board which I did in the afternoon & then went over to Aunt Katies to spend the night. in the eve Dan & I went to the German Opera ("Tannahausa") [Tannhäuser][12] I did not like it much. I dont think it begins to compare with the Italian.

I was provoked with my self for going for I know I should have had a pleasanter time if we had stayed at home & besides I caught cold there & did not get over it for nearly a week.

The next morning after breakfast—(I took mine at about 8 am with Auntie—the establishment is much like a hotel. no one gets up until they get ready & every one does as he or she pleases so I did not see any of the family in the morning) I went over to the Navy Yard to see how matters looked telling Aunt Katy that I should be back to dinner, but when I arrived I found the vessel hauled out in the stream & on boarding her was positively informed she would sail at noon. I did not believe it tho' & as I heard the Paymaster say he was going over to the city on some business I thought I'd go too as I hoped to get a letter from home. So I did & was paid for my trouble by finding a note from you. I got back before 12 but did not go on board cruised round the Yard etc. & got some dinner at a Eating house first. Later in the afternoon I repaired on board but we did not sail to [till] Sunday noon.

While in New York I saw the Italian Iron Clad *Re de Italia* she is a very fine ship.[13] I wish we had a few of her class in our Navy.

I believe I have told you all the incidents worth mentioning that occurred on our voyage out.

My chum was a very pleasant fellow but it used to amuse me to see him dress[.] it used to take him from an hour & a half to two hours to perform his toilet. He required four different basins of water to perform his ablutions—etc.—

He had never been to sea before & I found his ignorance to my cost for one day he left the air port open in our State Room & we shipped a sea in there which drenched both our beds & spoiled one of my books etc. I find it dull work staying here. I've been reading the III vol of Phillip 2nd (Prescotts).[14] I attended a Masonic Lodge last evening, & shall go again to night as there is a special meeting.

I cant write any more now. love to all. Please tell Uncle Hamie my address. Act Ensign H W Wells U.S.S. *Gem of the Seas* East Gulf Squadron Key West, Fla. I depend on hearing from him. Write to me often & send me lots of papers. Good by from your loving son

H.W. Wells

Key West
Feb 23rd 1864

Dear Mother

I have just heard by the mearest chance that there is a steamer to leave this afternoon for the North. The mail closes at 4 P.M. and as it is now about 3 I have not much time to write but still I dont like to have a mail go with out your having some new[s] of me.

I am still stopping here at the Russel House & I'm afraid I shall not get away from here this week from the apperinces [appearances] of things. I find it very dull here there is nothing in the world in the way of amusement going on here &

I find it hard work to kill time. It was stormy all the latter part of last week so I could not walk out much

I have thus far had no means of getting introduced into what little respecteble society there is here, & of course I have no inclination to go in any other. I've made one first rate friend here tho' & that is Judge Boynton of the Prize court.[15] He is & [an] old retired Naval Officer & boards here at the Hotel. he seems to have taken a fancy to me & talkes with me when ever he gets a chance. The other day a steamer came in from Havanah bringing mails & late papers. There is no news depot here so one can not buy papers but after breakfast while I was setting on the piazza smoking the Judge came along & beckoned to me & asked me to go up stairs to his room, so I went up & he opened a package containing a whole file of New York papers which he had just rec'd[.] "There!, said he, now we'll read them together" So he & I set there all the forenoon smoking & reading, occasionaly he'd comment on an article & we'd discuss it together (he's *sound* on the *goose* belongs to the Union League & believes in Lincoln) also a bit of an Abolishinist too tho' a Virginian.) In the course of our conversation we got upon Naval subjects & I happened to let drop how provoked I was at being sent to a sailing vessel. He took it up at once & said if he got a chance he would speak to the Admiral (with whom he is very intimate) & get him to transfer me if he could, after I have been here a little while. Was it not kind of him? Last night he told me that he had mentioned me to Capt. Temple (Fleet Captain) & that he (Capt T.) had promised to bear me in mind & transfer me to some regular man of war as soon as an opportunity offered.[16] Of course it dont do to build too much on it as he may forget but it was never the less kind of the Judge.

I can not write any more now tho I've plenty to say, but must bid you good by[.] Love to all the family from your son

H.W. Wells

I dont know whether you will be able to read this letter I've written it in such a hurry. I know I've made lots of mistaks. please excuse them

U.S. Barque *Gem of the Seas*[17]
Charlotts Harbor Fla.
Feb. 29th 1864

Dear Mother,

I have at last arrived at my destination. I joined this ship on the 27th & am just beginning to get settled & acquainted a little.

I can hardly tell you much about the ship or my messmates yet but I will try & let you know as much about them as I do.

The ship ought to come first I suppose. Well, she is a small affair (371 tons)

& mounts 4 32 Pdrs. & one 20 Pdr. Parrott Rifle. As far as I have been able to see the crew seem to be a very good set of men especialy the Petty Officers which is a great thing. She has been laying here ever since the 20th of August 1863 & has not been under weigh during the whole of that time so you can judge what chance there is of my gaining experience in handling a vessel. However they are talking of going out on a short cruise in the course of two or three weeks.

I guess I shall like the Captain very much[.] every body else does at all events & that is a good sign, but he has not been in the ship long and may change tho' I dont think he will[.] at all events he is a Mason so he & I are not likely to quarrel. His name is Rockwell (Act. Vol. Lieutenant).[18] Our Ex. Officer is a German named Leinas[.][19] He's all right I think. He plays a first rate game of cribbage at all events. His rank is Act. Master. there is another Master on board named Winslow but I was sent here to relieve him & he will leave us as soon as the *Honduras* gets back, as also will Act[.] Ensign Jenks who has also been detatched. There is one other Ensign on board named Bliss, who seem[s] to be a very pleasant fellow[.][20] he is about 40 years old I should think, perhaps not so much tho', & plays cribbage at which I just beat him six games out of eight. Last night I served him worse still for I only let him beat one. The "Medico" is quite an old man but seems very pleasant. His name is Walton.[21]

The Paymaster is a young man a gentleman & a good fellow I should judge. So much for our mess. We are all "down Easters" except the Ex. Officer. There are two Master's Mates, but I have not got acquainted with them much yet, in fact one of them went off in a sail-boat on an expedition the day I joined & has not got back yet[.] We dont expect him before the last of the week.

Our quarters are very poor indeed. The Ward Room is small & we have to berth two in a room. However I am inclined to make the best of it. & I hardly think I shall stay here long. in the mean time we are laying back taking life very easily living on venison, Green Turtle oysters Game, etc. We are laying in a harbor full of islands & the Islands full of game[.] somebody goes on shore most every day. There are no Rebs with in 40 miles & when we want a brush the boats have to be fitted out for three or four days service.

I want you to send me my gun & fixings belonging thereto. You will find a lot of Patent Wads Cartridges caps etc. in the middle small draw[er] of the secretary in the "Junk". send my game bag also, & the spare cleaning Rod if you can find it. its in the junk, or my little room. put in also some cotten rags for cleaning. I think you had better take the Gun-Case & all & *box* it up as it will probably get hard usage coming down. If you can find the old gun *cover* put it & the rags in the Gun case as they will keep things from rattling about. Direct it in good large letters (can't you get some one to *paint* or *letter* it.) Act Ensign Henry W. Wells, U.S. Bark *Gem of the Seas* East Gulf Blockading Squadron Key West, Fla. (Direct my letters same way.) & send it by Adam's Express.

Be sure & send me plenty of caps ("Eleys patent water proof".) I dont know how many I left on hand. Do start it as soon as you can for I'm in a great hurry for it. I expect to have great sport.

By the way I made a great mistake in my last letter my friend the old naval officer is not Judge B but Capt. Carpenter, Prize Commissioner.[22] They addressed him as judge quite often, hence my mistake. Capt Welch has just been appointed Prize Commissioner also so they are working together. Capt W. came to me the day before I left & told me that he was quite intimate with the Admiral & that he would try to get him to transfer me to some other ship soon. Between him & Capt. C I think I stand a good chance in the course of two or three months of getting into something a little more serviceable. in the mean time this place is one of the most healthy on the whole coast which is certainly a blessing. Capt. W wished to be remembered to you Father. I guess I shall save money here for one cant spend it & our mess bills thanks to the woods & waters are very small.

I can not write any more now as the Boy wants to set the table. Love to all

from your loving son
H.W. Wells

U.S. Barque *Gem of the Seas*
Charlotts Harbor
March 3rd 1864

Dear Lu

As I have a half an hour before dinner I think I will employ it in writing to you.

I am just beginning to get settled now & I guess I shall like my new ship very well[.] I shall get a good rest on board of her at all events. & as I [have] been pretty well knocked about for the last two years I suppose that I ought to be satisfied.

Just now we do not have so much leasure as we shall by & by, as one of the watch officers is sick & another away. So there are only three of us left but it wont be for long. Mr. Bliss will turn too in a day or two & the other will come back & then we shall be in clover. all I want is my gun & then I shall try & make my self as contented & happy as may be until such time as the Admiral may see fit to send me to another ship.

By the way one of my messmates (& my room mate that is to be) lives on Heath St. Roxbury, almost in Brookline. You know where Mr. Wellington lives? Well he lives opposite. His name is S.T. Bliss, Act. Ensign.

We had a court martial yesterday on board here to try a man for refusing to obey an order as usual I was dragged in as a member of the Court. I thought as I had only just joined I was going to get clear. & so I should have for by the first order I was not detailed. but on the Court assembling, the prisoner objected to

Mr. Bliss on account of his having made the remark, after, he was arrested that if he had his way he'd hang him. So I had to take his place. just my luck.

Well I dont think I will write any more now. I have been here so short a time that I have not a great deal to write about & I have kept you all pretty well posted as to my doings before I got here.

I guess I shall have to find a new shoe maker next time I come home[.] Rooney cheated me horribly last time I was there.[23] My Congress Boots burst out before I had worn them a week & my other boots, (one of them) the counter in side has torn down so I can not put it on.[24] Ask Father to send me a pair of *low* light shoes when he sends the gun.

Give my love to all the family. & remember me to my friends. Have you got the Photograph of Miss Williams yet? By the way how were those new ones of mine? If there are any to spare send me one. I can return it you know unless I can exchange with some of my messmates. I take lots of comfort out of my Photograph book.

Good by.
From your loving brother
H.W. Wells

U.S. Bark *Gem of the Seas*
Charlotts Harbor Fla.
March 13 1864

Dear Uncle

I received your letter a day or two ago & hasten to answer it. I hardly expected to hear from you so soon, but I hope you will not consider your promise redeemed, but will let me hear from you occasionaly when you feel in a writing mood. I am waiting impatiently for that Photograph. I want it to fill up the space opposite to Miss Phillips in my book.

I wish I could be home on or about the last of April but I suppose there is not the ghost of a shaddow of a chance that I shall be. In Naval Circles an officer is considered as moraly dead when he is ordered to the East Gulf Squadron for there is no such thing on the books as getting out of it when fairly caught. If you apply for a leave of absence any time within the first year the Admiral looks up in astonishment & tells you, you have only just joined[.] then if you dont look sharp keep quiet & above all out of sight the first thing you'll know your ordered on board his *Prison* ship, the US Str. *Stars & Stripes*, the punishment of which lies in having to associate with the worst set of officers in the whole Squadron. "& besides" the Admiral always manages to keep about a Dozen watch officers on board of her so that being so many there is nothing for them to do. "Taking it By & large & all round" its about the tallest note I've heard of.

If after an officer has been here *over* a year he wants to go home[,] he is informed that he can not possably be spared, as he is just getting acquainted with the coast etc. etc. So as near as I can find out I may as well make up my mind to spend the rest of the war in this part of the world. I dont want to go to the prison ship so I shall not ask for a leave but I do not dispare of getting transferred to some steamer nevertheless.

In the mean time I am having a very good time here & if the principal object of life was to lay back & take comfort I could not well be in a better position. This vessel has not been underway since last August. & we are of about as much use here as a spare pump with no handle. There are several inlets within 30 miles of us & small sloops & schooners can run in & out as much as they please for all we can do. We have two tenders however which do all they can to keep the trade down, one is a sloop of about 20 or 30 tons with a Howitzer on board & the other is a little *mite* of a schooner with a crew of 7 men in charge of a Masters Mate. There is first rate hunting & fishing round here also plenty of oysters so we live first rate.

I hope mother will go out West I think it would do her lots of good.

I can not write any more now as I must go on watch. Please remember me to Miss "P".

I will therefore bid you good by *In statu*[*s*] *quo, ne plus ultra.*[25]

H.W. Wells

P.S. How will my quotation compare with your Hingham one at [the] town meeting? *Hic Jacet, Habeas Corpus!*[26]

U.S. Bark *Gem of the Seas*
Charlotts Harbor
March 13th 1864

Dear Mother

The supply steamer *Union* arrived day before yesterday & by her I received three letters (from Tom, Uncle H. & Si Bellows) much to my suppise as I did not think it was yet time for me to hear.[27]

I am getting along very pleasently here, much more so than I expected[.] I dont understand why it should be so but at present I must say that I think I have never felt so contented since I've been in the U.S. Service.

Perhaps if I was in more robust health it might not be so pleasent to be so inactive but as it is the quiet life which we are leading here is very agreeable to me. I dont want you to think from that that I am sick or even ailing for with the exception of a sprained foot (not bad, only a little troublesome at times) I am well enough, only I dont feel very strong.

Our Captain is a splendid fellow & no mistake. He is one of those few men who can, while in command be on friendly & familiar terms with those under them with out losing his own authority & their respect.

He comes in here quite often & sets & talks by the hour as jolly as you please. (He's chock full of fun) with out any assumption of superiority, but when he is on the Quarter Deck he's Captain, & no one forgets it.

Our Ex. Officer understands his business very well, much better than most Volunteer Officers. & we get along pretty well, tho' I dont like him so well as the Captain. He plays a dreadfully strong game of Cribbage[.] I have my hands full to hold my own with him I can tell you. We have played a great many games but keep along about together the whole time. The other officers are quite pleasent. I like my chum Mr Bliss very well. I think I told you in my last that he is almost a Brookline man. He also plays a fine game of C[ribbage] tho not so strong a one as Mr. Leinas.

The Captain has just come in so I shall not be able to write any more for some time I expect, for laughing, or at least not very connectedly. He's going to take Dinner with us to day. I expect we shall have a great time but it seems to be a subject of lament that we have no wine in the mess to add to our feast but I guess we shall get along well enough with out it.

The Tender *Georgia* got back three or four days ago[.][28] she has a Masters Mate in command & 7 men for a crew, belonging to this vessel. The Mate brought back one of his men under arrest for mutinous conduct & on Friday we tried him by Court Martial, but as the charges were not proved we acquitted him much to the disgust of Mr. Edgecomb the Masters Mate.[29] Of course I was a member of the Court, in fact as there are only three line officers who are competent to sit there seemed to be no choice for the Captain to make as it requires Three line & one Staff Officer to comprise a Summary Court. He wanted me to act as Recorder but I told him (*not* in so many words) that I could not *see* it. so finely he let me off & Mr. Bliss had to do it.

There has been very little going ashore of late on account of our boats being all out of order & undergoing repairs. We are getting them into pretty good shape now. Yesterday the Captain invited me to go on shore hunting with him so I borrowed Mr. B[liss]'s gun & we started off[.] we did not have very good luck. The Captain shot one Curlew & one Blue Bittern or Marsh Hen. & I got two of the latter. They are about the size of a chicken (with very long legs & necks.) They are a strange looking bird. Their feathers look more like hair than any thing else & are a dirty blue. They are very good eating however. I hope my gun is under way before this. I want it very much. I wonder if you thought to send my long Boots. I wish I had them but for got to mention them when I wrote before.

In shooting wild fowl one can not be very particular about his steps & the ground is apt to be very muddy.

I notice my fingers have stained this paper. I hope you will excuse it. I thought they were clean.

March 16. I had to leave off writing the other day so that the boys could set the table & have not had much opportunity of writing since or perhaps it would be more correct to say that I have not improved what time I have had. However I will finish my letter now as I expect the *Union* will be back before long.

Our Dinner Sunday was quite a success. We live first rate here I can tell you. Yesterday the Captain & Paymaster went off on a foraging expedition to a Plantation (if it deserves so high sounding a name) of a Union man (so called) named Brown & returned in the evening with a Deer[,] a lot of string beans, eggs (50¢ a dz), Lemons[,] bananas etc. etc. quite a boat load. We have a garden on one of the islands where we raise potatoes & squashes[.] & now we have just got an old sloop alongside fitting her up to go for oysters of which there are any quantity a few miles from here. A week or two ago we received a seine from Key West & as soon as we get the boats in order we are going fishing. There are lots of mullet here, besides various other kinds.

Day before yesterday Mr. Leinas started off on an expedition with the Launch[.] we expect him back tomorrow morning. I wanted to go but there was only one boat & if I could not have a boat to myself I would rather stay on board.

Be sure & send me one of my Photographs. Mr. Bliss has some of his own & I want to exchange with him.

I am glad Eliza has gone to Norfolk. I am sure she will enjoy her self. I hope she will write to me[.]

I hope Luies lameness is not going to prove serious. Have you concluded not to have Dr. Hunt any more.? Uncle H. sais you have consulted Dr. Wheaslehoft in her case.[30] One might as well have the best advice that there is to be had as long as they have to pay the price any how.

He also sais that Grandfather is not well[.] I hope he is all right by this time.

Why don't you go out to Chicago? I think it would be splendid for you. Do go, it would do you lots of good & you owe it to us children (I dont know where the philosphy comes in for that tho' I am afraid the debt is all on the other side.) to take good care of your self & not loose your health. I wish you would take my money & go, I know it would never give me half so much satisfaction in any other way & I do want you should have a little rest from your cares. How is your lameness now I hope you have got entirely over that trouble.

How is little Ruth getting along now. Who takes care of her nights now Eliza is gone?

I am glad Father received that money from New York all right. I was a little anxious about it. I still owe him $10. besides the expense of sending the Gun etc., which I will forward soon. My advance is not worked up yet so I can not draw anything at present, you know. & I always like to keep a little money by me in case of immergancy, so I wont send what I have on hand.

My health is quite good & I think I am growing stronger every day.

Give my love to all the family Good by (I need not ask you to write often for I know you will as often as you can. I hope I shall hear from Uncle H again too (I have answered his letter) & from Lu. I wrote to her by the last mail.)

From your loving son
H.W. Wells

How do you like my signature?

U.S. B.[ark] *Gem of the Seas*
Charlotts Harbor, Fla.
March 27th /64

Dear Mother

The U.S.S. *Honduras* arrived yesterday & by her I received your letters of the 29th & 6th the latter enclosing one from Lu. I see by them that you have not then heard of my arrival here & of the sort of station I'm on. What do you think of it now?

Every thing goes on here like clockwork. A day or two ago Mr. Leinas & I dined with the Captain. It was a very pleasant complement for him to ask us, & all that sort of thing but pshaw! his steward can n't come to time with ours & so far as the eating goes I should have had a better *feed* at home (i.e. the Ward Room) [.] We had a jolly time tho & I dont care how soon he invites me again. Perhaps you would like to know our Bill of Fare. Well we started with a smashing Clam chowder (the Capts favorite dish & which he helps to with a bounty that does more credit to his hospitality than to his judgment of the capacity of his guests—*inards*,) Then Pork Stake & Oyster Pies, then Apple Pie & cheese, & last but not least coffee & pipes.

A very good dinner but we have better every day if the powers of our steward be taken into consideration. For we have one [o]f the best men in that department that I've ever seen on board ship. He makes the best coffee I ever drank.

Our boy tho' is the greatest case[.] he is a contraband named Enoch (Black as the Ace of spades) we have a great deal of fun with him, he's a comical darkie. Last night I set him to open a bottle of ale & I thought I should have died laughing at him. He is dreadfully afraid of it & it is amusing to see the air of releaf which he puts on when, not caring to lose more than half of it, one of us take[s] the bottle from him & open it our selves. Last night however I was playing Cribbage so I let him go ahead. I wish I could give you the faintest idea of his proceedings. it was very comical to see but now I've got started I hardly know how to tell it. I watched him as he twisted the wires off. he was trembling all over & kept his thumb prest down on the cork as hard as he could. Well, said I, is there much "Pop" there Ennie? "I reckon so, sar he, he's startin now, sar, he's give, giving to go." & go he did sure enough & the ale commenced flying all over every thing. he stood there perfect picture of helplessness with his eyes big as saucers till I grabbed the bottle from him just in time to save about a glass. I heard [him] then let off such a sigh & "gracious" (it ought to have been "Golly") that it completely capped the climax & I laughed till I could hardly keep my seat.

He is a good boy tho & honest. He picked up two cents on the floor the other day & brought them to me to see if they were mine. There are not many boys in the Navy white or black that would not have put them in their pocket & said no more about it.

You mentioned aunt Abel's death in your letter but I believe I told you that news first.

By the way while I think of it allow me to defend Dick Lovett in that smoking score, in the first place it was *not* Lent, for he said that evening that he did not care how much he smoked for that in a day or two Lent commenced & that as he did not know of any thing that would cause him greater self denial than to stop smoking, he had made up his mind to keep it by not using Tobacco. So I helped him lay in a stock of smoke before hand. So for me I dont smoke so much as I used, & I use mild Tobacco at that. but I enjoyed those 10 cigars & I aint a bit sorry that I smoked them, *there*! I would not do it very often tho', in fact I've given up my cigars on ship board it is too expensive a habit altogether.

I have received three or four papers since I've been here the one I got this last mail was the latest date on board. At least I've not seen any that were latter, & it has been the rounds.

How is Grandfather now! I am sorry to hear that he is in such poor health. I hope he will soon get well & strong again.

I am glad Eliza is having such good times at Norfolk[.] I must try & find time to write to her, but the fact is we have so little to do here that it is hard to accomplish any thing strange as it may seem.

I shall probably answer Lu's letter before the mail goes.

How is Ben Bolt flourishing[?] tell him I want *he* should write me a letter.

O—Ruth—I wish I could tote her round for about half an hour this fine afternoon[.] Does she improve in her talking much yet?

The other day the Capt. & I took a sail over to the Plantation & dug some potatoes. Capt R.[ockwell] said he wished *Gideon* could see us, as in that case he might start us off some where & send us home.[31] He has been down in this Squadron over two years now & think[s] it is most time they gave him a furlough but the Admiral can n't see it in that light. We had a very good time but stove our boat in beaching her. however with the help of a few nails knocked out of some barrel hoops & a piece of old Deer skin which we found on the beach we made her tight enough to get back to the ship. I hope I shall get my gun next time the *Honduras* comes up[.] I am waiting very impatiently for it.

When I have been ashore I have borrowed Mr. Bliss's but I don't like to. I much prefer using my own shooting gun & letting others use theirs.

Well I seem to have written a pretty long letter, when I sat down I only intended a page or two at the most & [to] finish some other time but I have kept writing one thing after another as they occured to my mind with out taking notice how much paper I was covering.

I wrote to Cousin Lu a few days ago but have not sent the letter yet.

Good by now love to all the family, from your own loving son

H.W. Wells
or
Henry

I like the last, best writing to you [Refers to signing the letter "Henry" and he drew a hand pointing to his name.]

U.S. Bark *Gem of the Seas*
Charlotts Harbor Fla.
March 29th 1864

Dear Lu

How are you?
I'm going to wrote
You a note.
Golly.

I received your hiferlutin letter a day or two ago & as I have got an hours leasure this morning I think I may as well devote it to you.

The Captain has just got back from a two days expedition down to Fort Myers where the Refugees are. he had a great time & nearly drove us all mad with laughing, telling us his experience & with an account of an expedition that they went on, down there, a while ago. He can make a good story out of most any thing.

He says they (the Refugee soldiers) landed at a place where the Rebs had a station & found it deserted. after they had been overhauling things for about ½ an hour, not keeping much look out it seems one of them suddenly discovered a man with a musket standing at the edge of the woods close by watching them with a great deal of interest. He turned out to be a Rebel Picket & had been there ever since their landing feeling very much slighted at not having been taken any notice of. When he found that they had at last concluded to notice him the following conversation insued. "I say strangers, who be yeon?" "We be Yanks!" "Yeon don't say so! Sure?" "Sure" "Wall I want to know." "But who be yeon" "Wall I reckon I'm a Reb picket, I seay?" "Wall what is it" "Would yeon take a feller on?" "O yes" "Wall my turn is up with the Southern Confederacy to day. & as I don't want to lose any time I reckon I'll go along with yeon." & he did sure enough & is now in the 2nd Fla. Regt. I wish you could hear the Captain tell the story[.] it is too rich for any thing, tho' it may seem rather flat on paper.

He is trying to get a leave of absence & I think he deserves it, he has been out her[e] more than two years & was only married a few weeks before he left home. Thats what I call a pretty hard case. I wish him every success in his endeavor, provided I can get away also, but tho it may be very selfish, I dont want to see him leave while I'm attached to the ship. "We ne'er should see his like again" I'm very sure. He is just the opposite of Capt. Faucon in every respect. & he is liked by every one that has any thing to do with him.

Mr. Leinas & I are playing a match at Cribbage, noting the games in a little book. We have been at it about a week now & have played 99 games of which I have won 52 & he 47 so you see we play pretty evenly. Last night we played 35 games. It made a strong impression on my mind for I had the middle watch & as I got no sleep in the first worth counting I was horribly drowsey & had to drink a Bowl of Ale eat a piece of pie & smoke a pipe before I could get my self into any kind of trim for a 4 hours walk. & this morning I never turned out till they were half thro breakfast.

Well I seem to be getting along towards the end of my paper so I guess I will not write any more now. How about Geo. Duncan? Good by. Love to all the family from your Poor brother wearing his life out on this terribly harassing Blockade in the service of his country

H.W. Wells

April 5. – Mr. Leinas has 92 games & I 111.

Hail Columbia!

I say Lu, I want a scarf, neck handkerchief you know [k]nit or embrordered do you think you could make me one? They are first rate to cover up ones shirt bosom when you cant get them starched. if you can I want one "neat but not gaudy genteel but not extravagant" & you can send it in a letter.

Charlotts Harbor
April 5th 1864

Dear Mother

The *Honduras* is coming in on her way to Key West, she is very much behind her time & as I sealed up my letters several day[s] ago I thought I would add a line or two so that you might have the latest news of me.

I have had a very bad cold since I wrote last but am much better now in fact I have got about over it. I was not obliged to go off duty tho' I think I should have if there had been more watch officers.

I had a bit of a row with the Ex Officer the other day. I guess the wrong was pretty equaly divided. he provoked me by the way in which he corrected an order which I gave. (which was right in every other ship that I've been in but was not the way *he* wanted it done) He has a right to have things done as he pleases but he had not right to address me as he did so I got angry & told him in pretty strong language what I thought of it, manners & all. The Capt took it up on the part of the Executive but I had a talk with him & soon satisfied him that the wrong was not all on my side & the matter has all blown over now. I dont want to quarrel with Capt. R for I never was with a Capt. (unless it was Capt Parker tho' they are as different as can be) who I though[t] took more pains to make his officer[s] comfortable & I think there would be a poor return.

This *is* a lazy life & no mistake we have four watches. The men are mostly old hands & do not want much drilling so that we have little to do but eat drink & sleep. I am reading 'Eyes & Ears' & like it very much. Have also read about two thirds of Lords history, which I also find interesting.[32]

I hope to get my gun when the "H" comes back. I shall write to Eliza next mail. I am hungry for Photographs can't you feed me? Take lots of comfort out of my Book. I feel a placid satisfaction with my self every time I look at Father & Grandpa. I want Ruth, awfully, & Lu in *walking* costume. Good by the Boatswains mate is just shouting forward. (whistle) whirr, whirr, whirr. "Do you hear there? all you that have got any letters bring them aft, & put them in the mail bag at once."

So good by with lots of love to all from

Henry

U.S. Bark *Gem of the Seas*
Charlotts Harbor
Apr. 8th 1864

Dear LaLa [Eliza]

Marginalia—Ben's baby name for Eliza. L.W.

I received your letter yesterday & will answer at once trusting to luck for a chance to send.

We are in rather an out of the way place here & can neither receive nor send off mails so often as we used to off Wilmington.

This is a great old station tho' its a notch beyond any thing I've seen before on the Blockade[.]

We are laying in a land locked harbor with plenty of game on the Islands all round us, lots of fish oysters, Clams, etc., every thing in fact that heart could wish or stomach crave for, but no Rebs. Nothing ever runs the Blockade here. the ship never gets underway. (I beg her pardon, she was underway once & moved three times her length since she has been here a period of over nine months.) So we have nothing to do but eat drink & sleep, Hunt or fish when we feel like it or lay back & smoke & read. Just now I am very well satisfied for I suppose as I am not very strong yet this sort of life, in this climate which medical men say is the best in the world for people who ar[e] troubled with their lungs, is probably the best thing which could have happened for me.

The *Gem* must be of the Glass Diamond class I think for she is a poor concern. Was good enough once I suppose but a miserable old trap now. I expect she will have to go home before long. her decks leak so badly that the Medico think[s] it will make it very unhealthy for the crew[.] I dont feed my self up with any idea of going north in her tho'. Admiral Bailey has a knack or his Fleet Capt. has it for him which is the same thing, of never for getting one, so as I've only just come down I shall in event of her going home, get transferred to another vessel.[33]

I have sent home for my gun & mean to have a good time while it lasts at all events. I want to serve my country but if they wont give me a chance why there it is. I dont see what I can do about it.

We have a splendid Captain. His name is Rockwell Act. Vol[unteer] Lieutenant. He is as jolly as can be & dont put on any airs with us officers when off duty but comes right in to the Ward Room & sets & talks with us by the ½ hour together. When on duty tho' he's Captain & no mistake. It is not every man that could do that.

He is not *too* refined, but what would you have. One can't expect to find perfection in this world of *sorrow* specialy on the Blockade. & now that that I have disposed of the Captain wont you walk into the Ward Room & I'll introduce you to the officers[.]

The appartment is quite small & cramped. it is about 14 ft by 12. We only have three State Rooms for five officers. I am sitting at the table which fills up about the whole Room, writing to my older sister. On my right sets the Doctor studying German. Dr. Walton allow me to introduce you to my sister. "In your ear" dont get to talking with him, he[']s horribly long winded & prosey. He is quite an old man looks rather seedy, wears specticles, full black beard & whiskers, mustach, medium height, thin & spare. On my left was Mr Colby, but he[']s just gone out, so I can not introduce him[.] he is a young man not much older than I am, if any, a native of Vermont & Paymaster of the *Gem of the Seas*[.]

My Room Mate, Mr. Bliss Act Ensign is in his berth & from sundry groans which I hear coming from that direction I judge he is finding it hard to get to sleep. He is quite a large man some would call him fat, with big black whiskers, etc., about 40 or 45 year[s] old I should judge. I like him well enough tho' he is not very popular[.] The men hate him.

The last but [not] the least of our mess is Mr. Leinas who as Executive Officer ought to have been mentioned first. He is a German with a big mustach & aman who tho' I keep on moderately friendly terms with, I have no respect for what ever as regards his character. he is a good enough officer as they go now adays, but I have yet to find a single gentlemanly trait about him.

That is all of our mess & I am not going to describe the rest of the officer[s]. For that matter I think I have about killed that subject any way.

I saw Capt. Welch in Key West. I boarded at the same Hotel while I staid there that he did (not very strange by the way as there is only one in the place & a very poor one at that.) I am sure I dont know whether I like him or not. Do you know him? & if you do, do tell me what your opinion is & I will endever to regulate mine accordingly[.] I always like to act on sensible advice where I've not made up my mind beforehand.

I am glad you are having such fine times at Norfolk. after all there is a good deal [of] facination about a military life. I sometimes feel as tho' it will be most unbearably dull when I go back into the merchant service.

I have never been in Norfolk so of course I can not place you. It must be very plesent for you having an old friend like Waldo there to go about with you. O but wont B[rookline] be dull when you go home after so much excitement.

I expect you will get so grand with your Generals Admirals & Commodores that you will before long quite turn up your nose at a poor Ensign. We are all useful in our way, (tho' it would be hard to define the usefulness of this crowd here.)

I guess in [the] future the Adj. Hinckley will find something else for you to shoot at in stead of his cap when there is any Pistol practice on the carpit.

I never have seen the *Wyandot*[*te*], but have seen her sister ship. she is not much like the Old *Cambridge* & only half as large.[34]

I guess I wont write any more now but if the mail does not go off very soon I may add a few lines. if I dont good by remember me to the Gen'l & Mrs. Wild also to Waldo Hinckley & any of my friends if there are any more of them there.

From your loving brother
H.W. Wells

U.S. Bark *Gem of the Seas*
Charlotts Harbor
Apr. 9th 1864

Dear Mother

We received a mail a day or two ago & by it I received your letters of the 13th & 17th of March, & a whole lot of newspapers including an Army & Navy Journal for all of which I am much obliged. We get very few papers here except those which come by mail & by both of the last I have rec'd the latest papers which have come on board.

The Schr *Ariel* came in this morning with a prize & is going to Key West so I have not much time to write but I cant let her go with out your having at least a few lines from me.[35]

I dont feel very bright this morning so you must put up with a stupid sort of a letter. I went to bed quite late last night & hardly got to sleep when crack crack went the rattle—

My time is getting waisted at a scandalous rate. The Capt. & the officer in command of the Schr have been in here for the last hour shinning cuffers.[36] So that it has been impossable to write & now I must close up in a hurry for I can hardly keep my eyes open for as I was telling you when they came in—We all had to turn out to supprise quarters & exercises for nearly an hour then the Capt asked us down Mr. Leinas Bliss & myself into the cabin & we set there smoking, yarning & drinking—what shall I call it?—Wine?—for nearly two hours, & as I had the morning watch & had to turn out at 4 a.m. you may suppose I did not get much sleep. Well well this is a great old ship!

I wrote to Eliza yesterday but did not think then that there would be a chance to send letters so soon or I should have written you also. I received a nice long letter from her by the last mail. I have directed to Care of Brig Gen. E. A. Wild, is that right.

I have not seen that Life of Butler but should like to if you think it worth while to mail it.[37] I have enjoyed Eyes & Ears very much & like Beecher better now than I used to. I respect any man who can write such a book as that.

I hope Lincoln will be reelected. I see there are several candidates in the field however.

I am going to write & give those fellows on the *Montgomery* a piece of my mind.

My health is improving very fast. I had a bad cold a week ago but it is pretty much gone now.

Cant write anymore, I wrote Uncle H a rather foolish letter. hope he wont stop writing tho'. I write a good deal as I feel generaly & sometime regret having sent letters after it is too late.

How is Grandfather? I hope he [h]as got quite over his sickness. give my love to him & all the rest of the family. I shall expect to hear from Lu next mail. Tell Father that I shall send home an allotment as soon as I can arrange it. My advance pay has prevented it before. Good by from your ever loving son

Henry

I don't like "H.W. Wells" to *you*.

I love to see "Mother" at the end of my letters & perhaps you *may* feel the same to have "Henry" in yours. I like to write it so at all events.

US Bark *Gem of the Seas*
Charlotts Harbor
Apr. 12th 1864

Dear Mother

Yesterday was one of my White letter days. The *Honduras* arrived & by her I received your letters of the 27th (enclosing Lu's & the Photographs) & 31st of March, also my gun. every thing was satisfactory about it except the screw driver belonging thereto which is missing[.] I think I lent it to Uncle H.[amilton] but am not sure. it had a black ebony handle. it is of no great consequence & I can get along very well without it. but should later to know where it is. The cleaning rod is not hurt at all & I am glad Aunt Martia took the responsibility of sawing it off rather than leaving it out.

I did not expect that you would send any powder & was very much supprised at finding the flask full, agreeable so however. I can get that here, from Gunner Ferguson (my old shipmate) of Key West.[38] I am very glad you sent such a good supply of caps. did I have all those on hand or did Father buy them? The fishing tackle is not of the right sort to be of much use here but it was very thoughtful of you to send·it. I dont care much about fishing any way. In this part of the world hooks & lines are voted too *slow* & we use nets.

All the officers admire my gun very much & say it is the finest piece they have seen on the coast.

I dont like that Photograph of Uncle H. at all. it dont do him justice at all & besides it is a poor picture. Chute would have done better.[39]

I exchanged mine for one of Mr. Bliss. When I gave it to him I asked him how he liked it. He said, "First rate, but it looks a d—n sight better than you do. I think it flatters you very much" complimentary wont it. If one wants a candid opinion about himself or his belongings there is no place like shipboard for getting it. I will send you his Photograph. you may keep it till I come home. it is a very good likeness.

I think we shall have another boat expedition before long as we hear of Rebs in the vacinity. I probably shall go.

I am very glad to hear that you have decided to go to Chicago[.] I think it will do you good & am sure it will be a comfort to poor Cousin Sam. Dont let the want of money stop you a minute. What a seige you have had from that fall[.] I hope by this time you are entirely over it.

I am sorry you can not get letters from me oftener but I write as often as there is a chance. You have been real good about writing to me. it is a real jolly to get so many letters. Will E[liza] come home if you go to C? I had a letter from her the other day as I believe I told you & have answered it. Is Aunt M. still staying with you. Give lots of love to her if she is. I remember my visit at Sanbornton [NH] with a great deal of plesure. What started Aunt Jessie off to New Orleans did Uncle Lyman send for her or was it one of her own ideas.

I am much obliged to you for the complement on my letter "on company paper"[.] I do not consider said paper waisted when sent home. I am afraid this one wont receive any such praise. I have got to go on watch in a few minutes so cant write any more now. Will if I have time add some more before the mail goes. Love to all from your

Henry

Apr 14th. Great excitement. Rebs threaten an attack on Ft Myers. (Refugee Camp) They have called on us for reinforcements. Nothing decided yet but I guess a party of 25 men will go in charge of Messers Leinas & Wells. There are reported to be about 300 Rebs. There are about 30 refugees at the Ft (so called) & about 50 or 60 more off on a scout. may or may not get back in time. Will write more at length soon.

from your loving son
Henry

Our Capts name is C. H. Rockwell.

U.S. Bark *Gem of the Seas*
Charlotts Harbor Fla.
May 1st /64

Dear Mother

It seems a long time since I have written home, in fact it is three weeks but there has been no opportunity of sending [mail] since I returned from the expedition which I mentioned in my last letter & as I have not felt very bright since I got back I have kept putting off writing until I should feel more in the humor.

That was a great affair, that Expedition. Mr. Leinas & I went with 20 men in the Launch[,] 1st cutter and Tender *Georgia*. I manned the *G*[*eorgie*] with my men & took my boat in tow. We were gone from the ship six days but did not have any fighting after all at which we were all very much disgusted. We started on Friday 15th of April in a gale of wind & raining like *smoke*. The Launch is a very fast boat & I nearly carried away the spars of the *Georgia* trying to keep up with her. We arrived at Punta Rassa, about 12 miles from Ft Myers at 7 P.M.[40] I camped there & the Launch went on up to the Fort. There was a steamer laying off P[unta] R[assa] with some Refugees which we were to carry up as the steamer drew to[o] much water.

The Launch did not get back until about noon the next day so I amused my self drilling my men & hunting[.] When she did come she brought down the *Rosalie* (our Tender) & together we loaded up with the Refugees & their families & started for the Fort![41] Such a getting up stairs! The river is full of oyster beds & the channel very crooked, we got ashore about once in five minutes on an average. When she struck all hands had to jump overboard & *lift her off.* It was great old navigation & a notch beyond any thing I've seen before. My Boys worked splendidly tho' & I was quite proud of them. We only got about half way up that night for after it got dark it was all most impossable to find the channel so after working until midnight I thought the boys would be better for a little rest so we anchored & waited till daylight. In the morning we started again but the wind died away soon after & for the last four miles we *poled* along. When we arrived at the Fort we found that there was no hope of a brush with the Rebs. For a party which had been sent out from the Fort had ambushed the enemy & thrashed them three times & driven them off. They captured 36 horses but no prisoners, neither Gurreliers [Guerillas] or Refugees being inclined to give much quarter when they fight.

Ft Myer hardly deserves such a name. It was orignaly a trading station & during the Indian war a Block house was built there. Since the place has been ocupied by the Refugees they have built three more blockhouses & thrown up a light brestwork connecting them, & enclosing the settlement which consists of a dozzen or more *houses*? & stables for horses (sheds, rather). We found about 300 men women & children there of which 170 are soldiers. That number tho' includes those which we brought up with us. After dinner Mr Leinas[,] two other officers & my self started off on a ride. I had rather a different mount from that which I enjoyed while at home I can assure you[.] I had to use a *club* to get any thing like a gallop out of him. but then, I had the satisfaction of knowing that he was a śesesh horse & that I was setting on a śesesh saddle, oh such a one! you ought to have seen it. I wont attempt to describe it for I could not do the subject justice. We started off into the woods but had not gone far before we saw unmistakable signs of there having been some one round very recently for there were tracks of two horses not half an hour old going towards the Fort & from it full speed in the last direction. as we had not brought our arms (a piece of folly which I protested against when we started) we turned back & followed the tracks to a thicket close by the Fort where the Horses had probably been tied while the riders were making their observations. We then went & got our revolvers & started off again to see if we could not scare up a little excitement. I borrowed a spur tho before we started out the second time for my wrist was most broke with beating the brute which I rode. When we had got about six miles from the Fort, Mr Leinas who was a few rods ahead suddenly stopped & came back full gallop & reported that there were a party of horsemen ahead. we immediately formed in line (4 of us) & rode towards them. as soon as they caught sight of us they spread them selves across the road & out into the bushes on both sides. & we counted 8 of them, which we thought if they were rebs, were about a fair match for us. just as we were getting our pistols ready however the Lieutenant who was with us recognised them as a party of cow hunters who had been sent out from the Fort a few days before. after talking with them a few minutes we rode on again for about three miles but finding nothing we turned back. The next morning we started back for the ship but on arriving at Punta Rassa we found a steamer & two Tenders there with a reinforcement for Ft Myers from Key West, consisting of three companies of the 2nd U.S. Vol. (colored) & two pieces of artillery. so as our orders were that if reinforcements arrived to assist in transporting them up the river, we had to stop & load up again. it was too late to do any thing that day tho'so the troops were all landed on the Point[.] They were quite a fine looking set of darkies, take them as a whole & seemed well up in their drill. The Reg't was raised in the District of Columbia & not more than half of them are contrabands.

In the morning I loaded up the *G[eorgie]* with ammunition & provisions, & started for the Fort in company with the *Ariel* (Tender) we had quite an exciting race up. The *A[riel]* was the fastest boat & had a Pilot on board, which we had not. but then she was larger & got ashore harder than we did & was not so easily got off. First one would get ashore & the other would pass her amid the triumphant shouts of those on board, but pretty soon that one would come to grief & the other get ahead. One time we both stuck fast close to each other & then it was fun to see the Boys work to get off first. In the end we got up about five minutes ahead.

It was blowing so fresh we did not go down again that day but a party of us went off to ride instead. We had a first rate time[.] I had a very good horse that time. In the evening we had a military wedding & a Ball which were both rich affairs in their way. I could hardly keep sober while the marriage was going on. The man who acted as chaplain made a horrible mess of the service not being a *very* good reader. He repeated some sentences over three or four times before he could get them strait enough to suit him. After he got thro' the Commanding Officer of the post pronounced them man & wife.

I thought I should have died laughing when the dancing commenced. They tried to dance Cotillions but made a most ad libertim affair of it every one dancing the figure that suited them best.[42]

The next day we went back to Ponta Rassa & from there returned to the ship where we arrived the day after, all of us pretty well used up. Mr. Leinas caught a horrible cold, but strange to say I did not, tho' I have not been well since I got back. I have been in a curious state, not exactly sick but feeling very unlike making any exertion.

I think we shall go off on another *raid* before long, it is talked of. I shall go if I can but may not be able to as Mr. Bliss will want a chance.

The *Queen* arrived a few days ago & I was disapointed in only receiving one letter from home.[43] I expected two or three at least as it was nearly three weeks since I had heard. It was dated Apr. 10th, & contained the particulars of the burning of the Winthrop House. I had a letter from Joe also. He tells me he is to leave Capt McKim's office.[44]

I will try & see what I can do for Bennie in the way of eggs. I have never tried to blow any but will do the best I can. There are a great variety of birds here, if one could only find their nests. Has he got any turtle eggs? As for stamps, I can do nothing in that way here. I think I shall add to my collection of shell[s] quite largely before I leave here, as the beaches are covered with them in great variety.

I suppose you must be in Chicago now from what was said in one of my last letters but I shall direct this home to father & then if you are gone they can forward it to you. I am real glad that you decided to go both on your own account & Cousin Sam's. Has cousin Lu received my letter?

Well I think I have written a pretty long letter this time, but will close now as I want to write to Lu. Good by love to all the family. if you are out west give my love to cousins Sam & Lu & the children. From your loving son.

Henry

U.S. Bark *Gem of the Seas*
Charlotts Harbor Fla.
May 3rd 1864

Dear Lu

Do I, or do I not owe you a letter? I am strongly under the impression that I answered your last but if I did I forgot to "make a note o' it," so as I value your correspondance very highly & do not wish to give you offence by not answering your letters in due season I'll just indite you a few lines just to make a sure thing of it.

Is Uncle Hamilton married yet? if he is I shall rely on you to give me a full & graphic description of the wedding in all its particulars. Are they going or gone up to Conway? That was the origanal plan I believe.

Have you received, at home, that Photograph of Mr Bliss which I sent. & if so how do you like the looks of my chum? He is a curious sort of a man, at times I hardly know what to make of him. we get along very well together but I dont think he is one of those who would be apt to make many fast friends being a little to much in clined to look for the "mote in his neighbors eye."[45] he is an old shipmaster & I manage to pick up a good deal of valuable information from him at times when he get[s] started.

Oh dear I've got to go on watch so I shall have to put off this letter until I'm off duty again.

May 4th. Well now I guess I will finish this letter. Let me see, I had lots of things ready in my mind to tell you yesterday but I am afraid I've slept them all away. In my letter to mother I have told her all about the expedition that I went on so as you will probably read that I will spare you a long account here. By the way has mother gone out West yet, & how long does she intend to stay when she gets there? I have heard very little of the plans as yet. Has Eliza got home yet? I wonder if she received my letter, & if so why she has not written. I suppose she is having such a jolly time that she does not find much leasure to write.

I am sorry you dont hear from me oftener but I write as often as there is an opportunity of sending letters. I have only received one letter from home for a month, how about that? I have written to Joe & directed as he wished to the care of the Neptune Insurance Co. Tho' from what he said in his letter I should judge he was not quite sure of the place, thats his look out tho'[.] Was there any hitch about his leaving Capt. McKims? It seems to me a little strange that that office should so suddenly be obliged to curtail to the extent of one clerk. I am afraid the trouble was that Joe paid a little too much attention to Miss Howes at the expense of his business. I suppose they are engaged fast enough?

I am waiting impatiently for that Photograph of Jennie Williams. Mind & follow her up & make her "fork over". Give my compliments to her & tell her that I have a blank in my Photograph book (made for the occasion, between you and I) which I am very anxious to fill. When are you going to have some. I want one of you very much. Tell you what I'll do, you have some taken without saying "nothing to nobody" I'll pay the dammage & take half, which you shall exchange with any one you like, that I know, & send me the proceeds what do you say? is it a bargain? The other half dozzen & all the extra ones you can get being of course your sole & undivided property. If you dont like that—make up your mind before you read any farther "Honor bright". why you may keep them all except the best one which you must send to me or the two best if you set in two different positions. Strange as it may seem however I greatly prefer the first arrangement. I would make a proviso that Mother should have the second best (you see I'm very selfish) but I know that you would give her the first choice with out my saying any thing about it so I leave that out of the arrangement. I will enclose the money $3.00. if the price has risen let me know & I will make up the differance. On the whole I'll send a "v" & you can take the balance & buy a birth day present for your self & consider your self kissed when you get it.

There, I am not going so write any more now so good by. love to all the family[.] Tell me a bout Grandfather when you write[.] I hope he is getting better[.] Mother said in her last that he was quite unwell, but that was some time ago. Write lots to your loving brother

H.W. Wells

U.S. Bark *Gem of the Seas*
Off Charlotts Harbor
May 8th 1864

Dear Mother

We received a mail yesterday & I found in it your letter of the 18th enclosing Lu's. also a whole lot of newspapers, Army & Navy Journals Registers Monthly Journal etc. etc. which I was very glad to get. I was much interested in that article on T. Starr King & also in your account of his funeral.[46] You know I attended his church once or twice last time I was in San F[rancisco]. Mr. Bliss has also heard him preach several times & has been very much interested in reading the accounts of him.

The musquitos were so thick in Charlotts Harbor that they almost drove us all crazy. Bars did ent seem to have any effect at all & they would make nothing of biting thro' a thick blanket & sheet. They were bad enough in the day time but at night O it was horrible, at last the Captain concluded that he could not stand it any longer so we got underway & ran out of the harbor & we are now laying off the outer buoy, about 4 miles from the land.

It is much pleasanter here in some respects than in-side being cooler & there being no musquitos but I am [certain] unless we move back by & by that Bennies Eggs & my shells will be at a discount, for we shall not be able to go on shore much from here. By the way I hope Ben & Ruth are nicely over the meazles by this time, for of course the last will have them.

Why is it that in none of your last letters you speak of going to Chicago? you surely have not given up the idea.

I am much obliged for all you[r] good advice in my last letter from home don't ever think that I dont like to have it or am "glad when your done" for tho' I may not profit by it as much as I ought, I like to be talked to never-the-less & then you know you always sweeten it with a little pat on the back at the end which is very gratifying to my self-love, & if there was ever so much which was bitter to read (which there seldom is, perhaps never) the little sentance at the end, only a line perhaps, "so many manly traits," or some thing of that sort smooths it all over. (The same as I used to do with the cat when I was—major—while patting her suddenly draw my hand in the wrong direction to make her mad & then smooth her off again until she would purr. The difference being that in my case the roughing up was wonten & in yours—motherly. for who should tell one his faults (i.e. rough up his fur) if not his parents.) so as I read you can imagine me with my face a little flushed scowling a little perhaps till I get to the soothing part then the scowl passes away a smile takes it[s] place & the flush assumes a decidedly differant character. Then I light my pipe & think it over the result generaly being that I feel sure that the first part is just & the last very generous but perhaps not quite so just. Then I make lots of good resolutions &, (alas that I should have to make such a confesion), forget them again. For instance last night I held a conferance with myself while I was on watch & the result was that I made a resolution to smoke only half the amn't of Tobacco per diem that I have heretofore. A very good resolution you will say, but shall I keep it? is the question I ask my self with a good deal of doubt. Well I have not smoked this morning (which will account for such a stupid letter) & I shall not be able to this afternoon as I shall be on watch so I begin well at all events.

You need not send any more messages to Enoch for I shall not deliver them[.] I cannot allow him to be spoiled in any such way. at present he is all together too well trained to think [of] disobeying any order he may receive & we intend to keep him in that happy state of discipline.

How did you find out that there were beautiful flowers on the islands hereabouts? I never have seen any of them & I dont think I'm a "Groper" tho you did call me one.[47]

I am afraid you will be anxious about me it is so long since you have heard. it is not my fault tho', there has not been a mail left the ship since I got back from that expedition, I wrote you a long letter a few days ago, but it is still in my portfolio waiting for transportation.

I can not write any more now. I wrote to Lu a few days ago, it will go at the same time with this. Love to all the family. Good by, write often to your own loving son

Henry

U.S. Bark *Gem of the Seas*
Charlotts Harbor
May 17th 1864

Dear Lu

You're a trump. [hand-drawn playing card with heart] I have received *lots* of letters from you & I love you lots for it. So now, old 18 year old, see what you get for writing to your brother. I am sorry you can not get my letters oftener but what "can't be cured must be endured". We get mails however I'm happy to say a great deal oftener that [than] we have a chance to send them. So dont measure your letters by the number you receive but send at least two for one or I shall not consider the account square, unless indeed a Photograph is enclosed in which case I will be magnanemous & count the letter & picture combined as equal to one of my essays, or popular (at home) writings.

You have done very well so far, mind you keep on or I shall call you a two short of what aint trumps [a hand-drawn two of clubs playing card] & you will have to see me in your minds eye coming at you with two "clubs".

I like the Photograph of Uncle H very much or rather the Photograph of the Hat with Uncle H. in it. I think I should have liked it better if the said hat could have played a subordinate part & Ham-let himself been the principle attraction.—Please excuse me I wont do it again.

You say in your last letter that you saw an account in one of the papers of our expedition do please forward it at once[.] I should much like to see what could have been said about it. In future if you see any thing conserning us in this vacinity do send on the paper at once for our edification it is so refreshing to see what tall yarns the newspapers correspondences can spin. Especialy send me the paper that has the account of the Tampa expidition. I expect they will make a great story out of it, but in truth as near as I can find out it was a most disgraceful affair.

You must miss Uncle Hamilton ever so much. by the way did he remember the ring etc.? That *was* a novel idea of yours. I wish I could have been to the wedding. I never saw any of my near relations married, I suppose now I shall have to wait until you or Eliza make up your minds to abandon your state of single blessedness.

I suppose Mother must have left for Chicago by this time unless the children have been sicker than you thought when you last wrote. but I dont like to think that for a moment.

By the way I asked *you* to make that Cravat. I want a neat & proper one & am willing to trust your judgement in the matter. When are you going to have it done?

Why dont Eliza write to me? I am realy ashamed of her. She has got such a lot to write about too. Does she think I dont take any interest in all her doing down in Dixie?—If so she is very much mistaken.

I am sorry your allowance came to grief. I wish I could help you in any way. Dont be afraid to call on me if you are very *hard up*.

If I dont get some more Photographs soon there will be wailing & *smashing* of teeth round here[.] I'm *wild* for them. Has Eliza had any new ones taken? if she does & does not send me one I shall—I dont know what I shan't do. So see that she is warned in time of the fearful responsibility resting on her shoulders.

I hope you got my last letter (May 3rd I believe) I expect great results from that: that is if you take up with my first offer. but perhaps you will not like to enter into a Copartnership in which your face is to be the whole capital.

If I was not too much exausted from that mighty (mite-y) effort in the first part of this letter I'd put a Pun in here, but I feel that I am not equal to the attempt.

May 20th. Well I guess I will finish my letter to day as the *Honduras* will probably be along soon. Yesterday the U.S.S. *Clyde* was here & left for Key West.[48] I intended to have sent this letter by her but she went off very suddenly so I had not time to finish it as I was on watch when she left. I ran below for a minute &

closed up Mothers letter (which I hope she has received by the time you get this) very abruptly but thought it would be better to let yours wait as I know that we shall have another chance in a day or two. I am pretty well now only I have got a fit of the blues & feel as tho' I could eat any body up that says a word to me. I am going off on a Pilgrimage before long. I have applied for the Command of the Little *Georgia* for a cruise all by myself (I mean of course no other officer) & I dare say if I am alone for a while I shall feel better. besides I shall have a good chance to get birds Eggs shells etc. The Captain has promised to let me go but has not set any time yet.

This leaving off smoking has taken all the vim out of me I believe. No I dont either. I know I shall be all the better for it in a little while only I'm a sailer & I like to have my growl. Oh dear I wish I was where there is a little more excitement, it is horrible dull here. We have nothing to do but to eat drink sleep & grow fat. I expect I shall weigh 300 at least if I stay here a year, now that I dont smoke to keep the flesh down.

Dear Lu I wont tire you by writing any more to day[.] I feel rather down in the mouth as I said before tho I dont know exactly what is the cause. So I close at once.

Love to all the family & remember me to my friends. Write often to your loving brother

H.W. Wells

U.S. Bark *Gem of the Seas*
Charlotts Harbor
May 18th 1864

Dear Mother,

Yesterday the Str *Clyde* came in bringing us a mail, in which I found amongst other things your letter of the 24th. Please dont apologise any more for giving me good advice or for blowing me up when you think I require it. I dont need to be told that it is kindly ment. I assure you, & I think it does me good to get such letters occasionaly. The fact is the life that we are leading here is enough to make any one lazy, let alone one who as you very justly say is predisposed that way. But I'm going to try to reform at all events & I have *made a beginning*. I have not had a pipe between my teeth for a week & have only smoked two cigars. I dont mean to say that I shall not smoke *any* more because I think very likely I shall, but I am going to break my self of the *habit* of smoking, & make like wine, a luxury not to be induly at except on occasions. I reserve to myself however the right to smoke in my night watches when I happen to be very sleepy & find it difficult to keep awake except by artificial means. Now I know you will be glad to hear that. Perhaps I should not of thought of doing that if it had not been for your letter.

In your last letter you spoke about my opinion on the Slavery question &

mentioned that a warm friend of mine expressed regret that I had not defined my position on that subject more clearly. I should like very much to know who that friend is. (I *think* I know who you mean)

I dont know as I can expres[s] my self very clearly on paper but I will try to tell you just what I think on the subject, in as few words as possable. I think Slavery is a *sin* & I would never countenance it in any way shape or manner. it has always been a curse to this country & *now that we* are *at war* I never want to see any peace made without its being distinctly understood [that] slavery shall cease to exist [throughout] the United States. Not only because it is a wrong in itself but because I do not believe that we can ever have a firm union again until it is done away with.[49] I can not help feeling too that God never allowed this horrible war to come to pass with out some greater object than that we should cut each others throats until we are both exausted & then settle back to the same old place where we started from.

Therefore I believe that *I* am fighting for the Union *&* the *extinction* of *slavery*. What is to become of all the Darkies after the war is over is more than I can tell & I leave it to wiser heads than mine to decide. So far as my personal feelings are concerned I dont like negroes, but I dont see what differance that makes if I'm "Sound on the Goose" (that is if I am) & I dont know what business even my warm friends have with my private feelings [as] long as my actions correspond with what I know to be right & just.

If I dont think a negro is equal in interlect to a white man what then? Neither do I think the Chinese or the Turks or the Arabs are. I consider that the Negro however is about the lowest grade of humanity that we have & I think the state in which they live where they are left to themselves as in Africa sufficiently proves it[.] I suppose all started fair in the beginning & look where Europe is & then where Africa. if the negro was ever in a worse condition than they are now they must have belonged to the brute creation & if better, why did they not keep so? Of course the negro of this country have borrowed some of our civilisation & while they stay with us they may retain it (precious little most of them have) & improve on it, but I dont think that proves any thing, for it is only borrowed after all & I firmly believe that if sent back to Africa & Colonised away from the Whites, that in a few generations they would relapse into Barberisom again.

But as I said before if they are ever so low I do not think that gives us any right to buy & sell them[.] Now that is what I think about it. I'm not ashamed of what I think, & I can not see where you have any cause to be, or any of my friends dissatisfied with my views even if they dont agree in all points with their own. We certainly do agree in the main point which is the abolishion of slavery & if any of my friends (true) think that I am very far astray in the rest they had better write & argue the point so as to get me into the fold. I am open to conviction if any one can prove to my satisfaction that they are right & I wrong. That's a fair offer I'm sure.

I wonder if this part of my letter will please you as much as the first. I'm afraid not but if you attack me & talk of being ashamed when what I may have expressed on any subject, is spoken of why you must expect me to exhunerate myself as far as I can. I've not said half what I want to but I will bank up the fire for another time.

I am very anxious to hear from home again for I hear that the Small Pox is raging about Boston & vacinity & the children being sick too makes me feel rather nervous. I received Lu's letter with Uncle H's photograph & card. I was just a little disapointed that you did not send me a piece of the cake not that. Pshaw. I dont know what I am thinking of.

It is too bad they could not have had a finer day for the wedding. I am glad however that you was able to go. You seemed to think it very doubtful whether you would be able to or not when you wrote. Eliza must have been very much disapointed to have missed being there.

By the way did they find that negative at Black & Batchelder of yours? & have you had any new Photographs struck off?[50]

We have moved back into Charlotts Harbor again, but I am not sure that we shall not go out side again soon. in the mean time I will see what can be done in the way of Eggs etc.

I have kept very quiet lately & have not been out of the ship at all. I have not felt very smart but I dare say that is partly owing to my leaving off smoking for I should think that any such change as that in ones habits would naturaly have some such effect at first.

It was very hard to keep from lighting my pipe after meals for the first two or three days, but on the whole I have not found it so difficult as I had supposed it would be. however I must not crow until I am out of the woods for the desire may come over me again too strong to be resisted. Tho I think not.

I've seen so many try & so few succeed in throwing off the habit that I dont dare to feel too confident & I should *not* advise you to send me out a box of first rate Cigars just to try the strength of my resolution.

19th I had to leave off, & wanted to finish the letter to day but [Str][51] *Clyde* came in last night & is going to sail at once for Key West so I must say good by love to all in great haste from

Henry

U.S. Bark *Gem of the Seas*
Charlotts Harbor Fla.
May 22 1864

Dear Mother

I sent you off a letter two or three days ago but as the *Honduras* will probably be here in two or three days on her way to Key West I will write you a short letter.

Every thing goes on as usual here & we have no excitement at all. The weather is most too hot for one to go on shore much & even if it were not I doubt if I should care to go. I'm a stay at home bird, & very seldom leave a ship to which I am attached of my own free will & accord unless it is on some expedition against the Rebs. I was in hopes we were to have another expedition soon it was talked of but for the last few days I have heard nothing of it, so I suppose it is given up. The fact of the matter is that the Rebs are reported as mustering very strong up Pease Creek & have a piece of Artillery with them so I suppose Capt. Rockwell considers in this case that discretion is the better part of valor.[52] & realy it always has seemed to me rather an unwise thing to do for we *know* that there are no blockade runners up there (at least the scouts from Ft Myers say so & they are to be relied on) therefor[e] all we could hope for if we went would be a fight in which we should probably be outnumbered ten to one & ambushed at that[.] However the responsibility would not rest with me if we did get cut up a little & I'm bound to have a hand in all the sport that's going. I call it sport for those Gurillers [guerillas] are no better that [than] thieves & murderers & I should consider it a good work to rid the world of a few of them.

May 25th The Captain interrupted me yesterday to go sailing with him. we did not get back until late & then I had to go on watch so I was obliged to put off finishing this until to day.

I have been on a Court Martial nearly all day & am rather tired. We have tried two men or rather a man & a boy. The first pled guilty of disobedience of orders & we punished him for it, but the other we had the satisfaction of acquitting. I dislike such duty exceedingly & am always glad when the evidence is such that we can conscientiously acquit the Prisoner.

Have you received my last letter? If it was not gone I should not send it now, but write one instead that perhaps would please you better. Convictions come over a man very forceably with out his knowing or intending it & such an one has taken its abode in me within the last few days with out my knowing exactly how or why.

Partly from a book that I have been reading I guess. but I can not write any more now. I am going to start to night on a cruise in the *Georgia* to be gone a few days. Good by, love to all from your loving son

Henry

U.S. Bark *Gem of the Seas*
Charlotts Harbor Fla
May 28th 1864

Dear Lu

I received your letter of the 15th yesterday telling me the sad news of Henry Bonds death. If he had fallen in battle I should not have felt so badly for then we should have at least had the consolation of knowing that he fell in a cause worth dieing for, like a man, with his sword in his hand, facing the enemy, a glorious death, but to be murdered in an ambulance after having been wounded & carried off the field.[53] Oh it is to[o] horrible to think of. I know that it is wrong to feel revenge but one thing is certain if ever I get foul of a party of those infernal gurrillers I shall not try to take any prisoners for I suppose if I did I should not be allowed to hang them. but no one could blame me for shooting them first & taking [hanging] them afterwards. I hope that a just God will make me the instrument to avenge them for the horrible deeds they have perpetrated during this war.

Poor Henry! what a satisfaction it must have been to him to have his father and Ria with him during the last few hours[.] Oh it must be *very* bitter to die among strangers. I hope if I ever face that I may be killed at once since I can never hope to be where my friends could reach me. It would save a world of mental suffering & longing for the loved ones of home. I hope if that time ever should come that I may be a[s] ready to go as he was.

The last time I saw him was at Newbern when he was in the 45th. You know he was gone before I got home. I wish you could get me one of his Photographs (in uniform if you can)[.] I should like to have one very much. Do you think you could? If you go over to the Plains give my love to them all.

I received a short note from Mother dated Syracuse[.] I am glad that she has at last got fairly started & hope she will have a grand time. I suppose of course the Baby is well or she would not have left. I am very sorry to hear such poor accounts of Grandfathers health[.] I hope he will soon be better. I am very glad he has given you a watch. it is time you had one & I know of course if he gave it to you that you would have to go a long ways to find a better Grandpa dont half do any thing. Give my love to him. I consider any thing given to you as a special complement to my self. You and I'se chums as the sailors say.

I dont think Eliza is a very good corispondant to me. You are the best one I have after Mother. I am real glad you have taken such a start at writing for I do love to hear from you. You who are at home can not appreciate the egerness with which a mail is seized on board ship & how anxious every one is to get letters from home & friends[.] if you could you never would grudge the short time that it takes to scribble off a few lines now & then to cheer our hearts & break in on the monotony of our swell life here on the Blockade. But I have no business to say a word to you for I see your familiar hand writing on the back of a letter almost every mail latterly.

Both you & Mother speak in your last letters about being anxious at not hearing from me. I was afraid you would be but it was no fault of mine for I sent off a letter as soon as there was a chance after the Expedition which was not howeve[r] for some time. I never keep you in suspence in regard to my movements any longer than I can possably help. & our mails are so irregular here that it is never worth while to be anxious on account of letters delayed.

I think in my last letter I mentioned that I was going off on a cruise in the *Georgia* (Tender). I did go but was recalled after an absence of 24 hours on account of one of the masters mates having got into trouble which made them short of officers on board. I was sick when I started & that night the musquitoes were so thick that I never slept a wink until after daylight but walked the deck the whole time which did not make me feel any better (strange to say) so I was not very sorry to come back. The Diagnosis of my ill health may be thus set down 1st slight indisposition, caused by not smoking? 2nd Bad toothache. 3rd (Night before I went away) Tooth very bad, could not sleep, so took a dose of Laudanum to make me (a tea spoon full almost) but it did not have the desired affect & I found my self in the morning with a bad headach, sick at my stomach & my tooth aching like *time*.[54] 4th No sleep next night on the schooner on account of the musquitoes 5th About used up. I did not go onto the list [sick list] tho', I have to be *quite* done up before I do that.

Tuesday we got a mail & papers up to the 16th. The Glorius News pretty nearly cured me & I think I shall do very well now.[55] If Grant will only take Richmond I dont think I shall ever *want* to be sick any more. We are very impatient to here later news. we have all great faith in Grant but still are very anxious.

The Rebs seem to be having things pretty much their own way in the Sounds. & the news seems bad from Louis[i]ana but never mind if Grant & Sherman succeed it does not make much diffirance.

What does father think of the prospects of a war with France? it [seems] to me as tho' it was not at all unlikely.

How I wish I was in a good smart Steam Sloop of War. The ideer of being shut up here in an old box of a craft like this that can not get out of her own way in such stirring times as these is enough to drive me crazy.

I do think it is too bad there are a lot of fine steamers in Boston & New York all fitted out only waiting for men to man them[.] I dont see why they dont take such vessels as these which are of no manner of use to any one, put them out of Commission & place the officers & men in those steamers where they could do something—"Them's my tenix"[.]

Uncle Parkhurst has got back from New O[rleans] has he? it always seemed to me a sort of Wild Goose chase that he went on & I am not at all supprised that he has returned—with out catching the geese?

Do you realy think that there is any chance of their comming to Boston & if they do, do you think Dan & his wife will come with them? I dont know what else he could do tho, for I do not believe him capable of supporting him self.

You speak of my crevat as tho' you had already sent it. have you? I have no doubt I shall like it when it comes[.] I did not say any thing a bout the color for I thought it would rather trust your taste than mine. Now dont be naive old lady.

I have got that Photograph of Ned Wilder, you did lend or give it to me. I am not sure which but if you want it back you shall have it—when you send me some to take its place.

If baby has any taken and I dont get one there will be a row right straight[.] I am not going to be forgotten I assure you.

Have you seen Dr Lincoln? I have had a letter from him in which he tells me he has resigned & is at home[.] I dont blame him for leaving the service if he could not get out of the *Montgomery* except in that way[.] He sent me his Photograph so now I have two of him & if you want one you may have it.

You must miss Mother lots how funny & lonesome home must seem with out her. I would love to see you all but on the whole I guess I will not come home until after she gets back.

I hope Bennie will be a powerful good boy & not give her any trouble[.] he has commenced well mother tells me. I wish I was a little boy & could be with my mother. No, no I dont, I am glad I am a man & able to fight for my country & for *right* in this terrible struggle. I remember I used to wish once that I could have lived during the Revolution. My wish has come home to me with interest for what was that compared to this one[.] If all ones wishes & whims were to come to pass what a world this would be.

Well I guess I will not write any more now. Give lots of love from me to all the family & write to me when ever you dont know what else to do. Good by from your loving Brother

H.W. Wells

U.S. Bark *Gem of the Seas*
Charlotts Harbor
May 29th 1864

Dear Mother

I received your pencil note dated at Syracuse, day before yesterday & was very glad to hear that you were at last fairly started on your journey. I hope that you will have a first rate time & that Bennie will not give you any trouble. If he could only appreciate the merits of the case I am sure he would not. How I should like to change places with him for the next two or three weeks! I dont think I have ever been on a journey with you since I have was a little boy. I remember some 14 or 15 years ago going on to New York with you to meet Father when he came home from California the first time. & also one or two·trips from old Walpole to Boston, especialy that time when I was laid up with chilblains at Auntie Bonds the whole time I was there.[56] You used to take care of me then. *How* I should like to travel with you again & change places.

I am glad that you have taken Ben with you[.] are you surpprised that I should say so? I am afraid you have good reason to be, but when I remember how much I used to think of a journey when I was of his age it would be very selfish of me to grudge him the same delight & as I can not be a little boy any more I will dream that I am in his place & enjoy it with him. I should think he would be a much better traveling companion than I used to be[.] he is so wise & asks so many apt questions that I should think that it would take away a good deal of the tediousness of riding in the cars to listen to him & answer. If I remember right I did not used to be a very good boy in the cars. I have an indestinct recolection of a trip to Windsor Vt with you & Uncle H.[amilton] during which I was very naughty & cried all the way much to Uncle H's visible disgust & probably of every body in the cars.

I am afraid Aunt Lucretia will not recognize much in my Photograph that will remind her of the little Henry that she used to know. I think I shall have to go out to S[yracuse] to see her some time—When this war is over.

How sad it is about poor Henry Bond it must be a terrible blow to them all at the Plains. To be murdered too while wounded & helpless it is too dreadful to think of. Such things bring the war home to us all with terrible force.

I have been feeling very revengeful ever since I heard the news & I am afraid that it would go hard with a gueriller if he got with in range of my revolver just now. I know that is [it] is wicked to feel so but it is hard not to on such provocation, but I try to suppress it[.] I should like tho' to have a fight with them.

We have heard news up to the 16th & are very anxious for later dates[.] They have sent me a lot of papers from home & Lu wrote me a nice long letter. I wont write any more now. I shall direct this to Father as you may be home before it arrives. You have not told me how long you was going to stay. Love to all at home or in Chicago from your

Henry

U.S. Bark *Gem of the Seas*
Charlotts Harbor Fla
May 31st 1864

Dear Father

I have just been looking over my account book & I find that I still owe you that $10.00 which I borrowed while I was at home[.] I was under the impression that I had paid it back to you & am sorry that I should have neglected it so long.

I also owe you something more tho I do not know exactly how much for Photographs shoes etc. So I will enclose you $20.00 which I hope will cover it all, if it does not however I wish you would let me know what the balance may be.

I shall send you my allotment ticket soon, should have sent it before now but the Paymaster is lazy & keeps putting off making it out.

I have written to Mother & Lu both of which letters will go with this. In

Mothers I have enclosed one of my sleeve buttons which is broken, if she is not at home I wish you would have it mended for me & send it back. & also send me a watch key[.] I have lost the only one I had.

We are very anxious to get latter news from Virginia. Out last dates are the 16th. We hope next time to hear that Grant or Butler are in Richmond tho' I'm afraid we shall be disapointed. The campaign has commenced grandly has it not? except in Louis[i]ana, there, Banks seems to have got pretty well used up.[57]

What do you think of the aspect of our Foreign affairs? Shall we have a war with France? it seems to me not unlikely.

I wish you would write & tell me your opinion on matters & things generaly.

Mr Leinas & I are playing a match at Cribbage, who will get the most games in 1000. We stand now at L. 408 W. 462 so I feel pretty secure as to the result. It would be hard to be beat on my own game, he is a strong hand tho'.

Good by now, love to all & write soon to your loving son

H.W. Wells

U.S. Bark *Gem of the Seas*
Charlotts Harbor Fla.
June 7th 1864

Dear Lu,

Day before yesterday the *Honduras* arrived bringing us a mail & I received your letter of the 22nd ult: enclosing that *horrid* Photograph of Eliza, & the Neck Handkerchief which I like very much. Please consider your self kissed for the same. I hope Eliza has not had any of those Photo's struck off. (the one you sent me I judge from there being no artists name on it to be a Proof.) The face it self is not so bad but according to my ideas she show[s] very bad taste in the position, it looks *so affected* – dont you think so? I suppose not tho' as you say you like it. I wish I could agree with you, but I'll be shot if I *do*. I hope if E has any others taken that I shall be favored with one[.] I hope she has got over her sickness by this time.

Have the family given up Dr Hunt altogether? I am very sorry to hear such poor accounts of Grandpa's health[.] I hope it will not prove any thing serious. Give my love to him.

I am glad that Mother is having such a nice time[.] I heard from her once at Syracuse & I hope to hear again soon from Chicago. How long does she intend to be gone?

To return to the all absorbing topic of Photographs – so you have taken up with my last plan? Well I am satisfied perfectly. I thought most likely that you would prefer the 2nd & in fact I dont think on the whole that my first proposition was hardly a fair one any way, towards those who you exchange with. So you may consider the whole set as your birth day present – only be sure & choose mine first before you let other people overhaul them. & remember that if you have two or more different positions I shall expect one of *each*. Dont you think that that is fair?

I hope I shall get one of them in the next mail but perhaps that is most too soon.

I will enclose you the one of Ned Wilder (if I dont forget it as you did the tie.) You are welcome to have it back for I think it is a dreadful poor one, dont you? honest. I am afraid if you dont get that Photo of Miss Williams pretty soon they will be all gone. You ought to make hay while the sun shines you know.

I think it is about time Ruthie had hers taken[.] How I should like to have a good picture of the little darling. Does she talk much yet? & how does she get along with out Mother? I should think she was old enough now to miss her a good deal.

I received a letter from Joe in the last mail if it deserves that name. it covered three pages of large blue paper & I could & do generaly write as much on one of these, half pages. Between you & I & the main mast. I guess you were right about there being some sort of a riff between him & Mis A. he did not tell me so, (if he had I should not have told you any thing of it) but I judged as much from the way he denied his engagement on which (tho' I did not believe it) I congratulated him in my last letter. What is he doing now? anything? I have lost the address which he gave me, as I shall probably write to him before the mail goes please tell him that I have directed to Brookline when you see him.

So you dont want me to go on any more expiditions? Well perhaps I shan't, but it will not be for not having the Good will to go, only for want of a chance. It is horribly dull here, it is breeding season so there is no hunting & if there was it is too hot & the muscuitoes are too thick for one to think of going on shore for pleasure. If it was not for our mails & an occasional expedition the life would be unbearable. it is all most so now. I require excitement & when I dont have it I get as blue as indigo.

Oh Dont I wish I was in the Army of the Potomac now! or even on James River or in the old Sounds of North Carolina, where they seemed to have enough to do just now to keep them from getting rusty. any thing would be better than laying here doing nothing while there are such stirring times all around us.

There are some new steamers that have just joined this squadron & there are more coming so we are beginning to have faint hopes that these old sailing vessels will be relieved & put out of commission. I dont expect to get home even if the vessel does go north however as I should probably be detached, but I dont care for that[.] I am not *very anxious* to come home again just yet & had just as lives stay on the Blockade a few months longer if I could only get where there was something doing, & in a decent vessel. Not that I should not like to be at home you understand only I have been off duty so much since I have been in the service that I think I ought to be willing to take a good spell this time Dont you? I can not write more now as Enoch wants to set the table for Dinner. So I will bid you good by. Love to all the family & friends[.] Write as often as you can to your loving brother

Henry

U.S. Bark *Gem of the Seas*
Off Charlotts Harbor Fla
June 12th 1864

Dear Mother

I have got just five minutes to write you a half a dozen lines. Yesterday our Tender the *Rosalie* captured a steamer (pretty well that for a sloop) & she will leave directly for Key West in charge of Mr. Leinas. I dont belive tho' that she will prove a Prize for I dont think she was trying to run the blockade, & even if she was she is not worth much as she is & old affair & has no cargo. Her name is the *Emma* late *May Flower* a blockade runner captured by the *Union* & sold in Key West.[58]

Oh dear here is Enoch wanting to set the table. So I can not write any more tho' I hope you will think even these few lines are worth three cents, as they tell you that I am pretty well & *dont smoke* yet.

I have not heard from you for some time. I enclose you a very pretty Photograph, I think, of the Episcopal Church & Parsonage of Key West.

Good by love to all from your loving son

Henry

Marginalia—Received Aug 3rd

U.S. Bark *Gem of the Seas*
Off Charlotts Harbor Fla
June 13th /64

Dear Mother,

It seems an age since I have heard from you & in fact it is over two weeks & then I only had that little short note from Syracuse. I am not complaining tho' far from it. I know when you are traveling you do not have much time that you can call your own & you do not visit the West often enough for them to let you spend much of your time writing when you are there but I can not help missing my letters from Mother nevertheless & I know you would rather I would than not, when I can not get them.

Lu is a darling & writes me nice long letters very often, but tho they are real good loving sisterly letters they can not fill the place of mothers[.] You see Lu would as soon jump out of the window as say that I am not perfect in every thing whereas you are not afraid to tell me that I'm a naughty boy some times. it is pretty strong seasoning, but Cayenne when one gets used to it is not unpalatable rather the contrary. & so it is with your reproofs, they may sting a little at first, but they are always so just that one can't feel angry. & they are so lovingly administered that I am not sure but what I take a placid satisfaction in doing something occasionaly to merit them.

Perhaps I should not take it so well from Lu tho' so she had better not try it on. I prefer her letters as they are & yours as they are too.

Just think I have only smoked a pipe now, once, for over a month. & then I had the tooth ach so bad that I would have tried any thing to stop it, & that always relieved the pain. Dont you think I have done pretty well! It has been a terrible long month tho' & I have almost given up two or three times, but I am determined to give the matter a fair trial.

June 17th I had to leave off here the other day. & one thing or another has prevented my commencing again until now.

Day before yesterday the Supply Str. *Union* arrived from New York.[59] She did not bring us much of a mail, but I received your letter of the 29th ult. at Chicago, & was glad enough to hear from you again. I am afraid from what you say that you will not have much rest from housekeeping while you are away from home, but I know you are never so happy as when you are doing good & helping those who need assistance[.] So I am real glad that you are there, I know it must be a great comfort to Cousins Sam & Louisa to have you with them[.] I hope Bennie will not add to the troubles. "But if I know myself" when I was of his age & had two Companions, people went wild generaly. Do you remember the old Attic in the house at Walpole?

By the way, talking of Bennie, what made you tell him that I was going to bring him those Eggs etc.? I never said that I should I only said that I would try & I am afraid I shall have to take it out in trying. I have not been able to go on shore (except once with the captain & then of course I had to regulate my movements by his) for over two months. Part of the time we have been so short of officers that I had not time & latterly we have been laying way off out side where of course no liberty is given. The breeding season is about over so I am afraid I shall not be able to get a single Egg. I have offered to pay some of the men that live on shore near here, handsomely to get them for me. They promised well but I have not seen any result as yet.

I am very sorry but I dont think if you had wanted them yourself that I should have succeeded any better. Our ex Officer is very loath to let any one have a boat to go any where so we do not any of us get a way from the ship much except when the Captain invites us to go with him.

I never was with but very few men who were so generaly detested as this same Dutchman of an Executive Officer which we have here. Officers & men alike hate him for he is Tyrannical, selfish, disobliging, & very disagreeable. It is hard to get along with such a man, but I have managed pretty well so far & have only had two or three *spats* with him. I have beaten him that match at cribbage, that is one comfort. Mr Bliss & I are playing one new. Mr. Leinas went to Key West in that Prize Steamer which I told you of in my last. it is quite a relief to have him away even for a few days.

I think I may be able to get the shells both for Bennie & for "Wm Dall" tho' I dont know who he is unless it may be the son of the missionary.

We have got a new officer on board here now an Acting Ensign named Powell, he is from Maine and bran new in the service.[60] I dont know yet how we shall like him he is very green & will not be of any use to us in the matter of Drill for some time to come which is rather too bad, as it all comes on Mr Bliss & I. Two of our Masters Mates have left so that we are not any better, or so well off for watch officer as before.

We continue to have glorious news from the Army & I am in hopes Grant will favor us with another grand Fourth of July by marching into Richmond.

It makes our life here seem doubly monotonous & irksome to read of the stiring times elsewhere. I have got all the good will in the world to serve my country but confound it I have never had a fair chance yet except at Little Washington & that did not amount to much. Perhaps I might ought not to complain tho' for some have faired worse than I have. There is not an officer on board that has seen as much service as I have. in fact Mr. Leinas is the only one that has ever been under fire at all & he only in a skirmish or two. but that is very poor consolation.

I will return you Aunties letter. It seems hard to realize that Henry is gone. Murdered too when he was wounded & helpless. I know that God claims vengeance as his own but I hope & trust he will make me a humble instrument to carry it out[.] We have some Guerellas round here & if ever I meet any of them—well.

I can not write any more now. Love to all. I am sorry to keep hearing such poor accounts of Grandpa's health. What seems to be the matter?

Good by, if this finds you in 'C' Give my love to the Cousins & remember me to Mr & Mrs. Harris.

From your loving son
Henry

U.S. Bark *Gem of the Seas*
Charlotts Harbor
June 17th 1864

Dear Lu

The *Union* arrived day before yesterday & did *not* bring any letter from you. Now then what have you got to say for yourself old Lady. if you think I am to be neglected in that sort of way you are greatly mistaken so now take care & never do it again if you dont want me to hold an indignation meeting & send you the proceedings.

I was expecting to see one of your Photographs by this mail but I suppose next time it will come "sure pop" & that one of Jennie Williams too.

I will enclose you in this letter a very pretty picture of the Navy Club House in Key West (*if* I *dont forget it.*) I sent mother one of the Episcopal Church & Parsonage at the same place, a few days ago. if you like them I will send you more. They will do to put with the Conway pictures etc. & their you will have the Northern Pine & Southern Palm together. I have seen some very pretty ones of various scenes round the Key.

Oh dear the musquitos are perfectly horrible here. you have no idea what a real cause of suffering they can make themselves. Why for three nights I have not been able to sleep in my berth & all the sleep I have had has been on a wet deck (for we have been favored with a nice smart rain squall at about 9 P.M. every night.) rolled up in a blanket head & all. Comfortable that! I was almost afraid it would make me sick, but one must sleep somehow & an hour or so that way is better than none at all. It has not effected my health tho' as yet so I guess it wont. (D—m the musquitos!) I'm so sorry. We came in here a few days ago to get wood & water so I am in hopes now that it is on board we shall go outside again soon.

Capt. R[ockwell] & Mr Bliss have gone on shore leaving me in charge. I feel quite grand & just knocked the Pay's hat off for not being sufficiently respectfull.

We've got a new officer an Act Ensign named Fowler (I told mother that it was Powell I dont know how I made the mistake but I called him so for two or three days.) it dont much matter tho' for I dont think much of him.[61] he is *very* green. he may be a seaman but I can't see it in that light at present. & at all event[s] he is an unmannerly fellow. He has just entered the service.

I had the morning watch this morning & amused my self by giving the Chief Boatswains Mate (a man almost old enough to be *my* father) such a fatherly talking to that he almost cried, *not quite* & acknowledged the errors of his ways & promised to do better. After all his sins were more of omission than commission. & it was for the faults of others which he might have corrected & did not that I gave him his lecture for. He is a good man & capt. of my Gun, & has a little of the same failing as your self, my dear, & believes in your humble servant, in fact tho' I say it my self "as hadn't ought to" nearly all the ships company are troubled the same way.

If I want any thing done for my self, sewing & any thing of that sort there are plenty ready to do it. so there are for most of the other officers too for that matter only with this differance, that while they have to pay roundly, I can never get them to take any thing. They wont have my money. it puts me to some in convenience for I go with out thing[s] which I would otherwise have but do not like to be considered by the men as being under any obligation to them.

The other night in the middle watch I was walking the deck hot & tired fighting musquitos when I saw a man poke his head up the Poop ladder[.] I supposed he had some report to make so I walked along to see what he wanted & found him holding his Tin Pot full of iced Lemmon ade which he wanted me to drink. I could have hugged him for I was very thirsty & was just on the point of sending a boy for some water. It must seem very egotistical to you for me to write such things but after all I can not help feeling rather proud that the men should like me so well tho' I have never done any thing especialy to merit it as I know of. I never was a Tyranical officer I believe & I gennaly [generally] find that I can do more good by a quiet talking to a man when he does wrong than by threatening or reporting him. & I always try to do about what is just & right by them. & it is pleasant to see that they appreciate it.

Well I guess I wont write any more now, for you owe me a letter You know. Love to all. How is Grandpa now? better I hope.

Write often to your loving Brother

Henry

June 23rd I have rec'd your penitential letter. I'll forgive you for not writing that Sunday if you will tell me who called me a Copperhead. H.

U.S. Bark *Gem of the Seas*
Off Charlotts Harbor Fla.
June 26th /64

Dear Lu

I received your letter of the 5th a few days ago & sent you off a letter on the same day. I think I write on an average about three letters to your two which is hardly fair, but you do so well for a small girl that I wont complain. In fact I suppose a lady has a right to regulate a correspondance to suit herself so if I write oftener than you I must be at fault my self. I only wait for a *rebuke from you* to cease doing so.

I was a little bit disapointed in not receiving your Photograph in the last letter but the prospect seems brilliant for next time. I long to see little Ruthie's. Of course I dont care any thing about yours, oh no! I only want them sent as a matter of form, & you shall have them all back *when I get through with them.* I will send you another dollar to pay for them with & if that with the other is not enough let me know for remember Two dozzen Photo's was your birth-day preasent & I dont want you to pay for half of them.

By the way I sent Father $20. a while ago, has he received it? I am afraid it was on board the Str. *Pocahontas* when she was lost.[62] & I also sent home one of my sleeve buttons to be mended which I have heard nothing from. Some of my letters must have been lost in that steamer I think. I sent you Ned Wilders Photo some time ago & last time I wrote I sent one of the Navy Club House in Key West. This time I will send you the Light House on Tortugas Island.

The Yellow Fever is raging in Key West very badly but we do not apprehend much danger here[.] it has seldom been know[n] to spread to this part of the Coast so I do not think you need feel very anxious about it. I dont feel afraid of it at all & dont think I should even if it appeared on board. I have been altogether to[o] *Blue* of late to be troubled by anything *Yellow*. I wish I could get where there is some excitement I am sure it would do me lots of good. My body is well enough now but my head is all *topsy turvy*[.] That's a sweet state of things ain't it[?] I think I must have written letters that have appeared strange to you at home since I have been out here. There have been some which I have written & sent right off which an hour after I would have torn up if I could have got hold of them. I have often set down & tried to write a real jolly letter (they must have been miserable failures) when I have felt more like jumping overboard than any thing else.

Well well if I have got the blues I dont know as that is any reason that I should inflict them on you, but I wont write anymore now. I *want* to know who called me a "Copperhead" I will not tell you who I suspect, unless I find my idea correct. how I want to know & think I have the right to, & shall feel very much provoked if you evade the question. But I am sure you wont when you understand that I am in ernest in the wish. Good by now, love to all the family. & write often to your loving brother

Henry

U.S. Bark *Gem of the Seas*
Off Charlotts Harbor Fla.
July 3rd 1864

Dear Mother

I received your letter of the 19th a few days ago & was real glad to hear from you again for I have missed your regular letters very much of late. Lu has been a real good girl & has written very regularly, but two are better than one & no one can take your place to my satisfaction as I believe I explained to you in my last. Funny aint it? that it should be so.

I am afraid you dont hear from me very often but I can not help it. I never let a chance go with out sending at least a few lines, but lately there has been very little opportunity for sending any thing.

I should have answered your letter before but there did not seem any prospect of sending & I have not felt up to much of late. I wrote to Lu a week ago & the letter is in my Portfolio yet waiting a chance to send.

I was very much interested in reading the Copy of Aunt Ruths letter which you sent me, have you heard any thing further? I should think they might soon be able to come North now, that is if they want to. & I suppose that there is no doubt a bout that. I should think they ought to have had enough of the Confederacy by this time. They must have suffered a great deal. it is hard to imagine Uncle E[dwin] & auntie keeping house for the officer & taking their pay in Rations as their only means of support.

It is a pity that they did not come away in the first of it before it was too late.

I hope that the war is most over now. if Grant is only able to take Richmond & destroy Lee's army it seems to me that Peace can not be very far distant. We are all very anxious for the news, our latest dates are the 19th of June & Grant had then just crossed the James River & was attacking Petersburg. When he takes it I hope they will destroy that Jail there. it makes my bones ach[e] every time I think of it. What would not I give to be with that army now! or even on James River. Oh it *is* hard to lay here doing nothing while such stirring times are passing in other places. I'm weary of doing nothing. I used once to think it would be fine to have little or nothing to do but I dont immagine I shall ever be troubled with such "thinks" again. I have had altogether too much of that sort of thing of late.

I am in hopes we shall have something to do soon, at least some of us. I had a hint to day from Mr. Leinas that we should have another boat expedition before long on account of some information which was received a few days ago[.] If it comes off I shall try my best to get counted in. Mr. L.[einas] will of course go in charge & I know he would rather have me than any one else. & he told me that if he could fix it that way he would. He & I have got along very well of late & in fact I have [gotten] along better with him than any of the others.

We have finished our match of a 1000 games at Cribbage. I came out 42 ahead. I am playing one now with Mr Bliss for the "Championship" but it wont amount to much I guess. he has a good deal of conceit but I dont think he plays as well as Mr. L. & do not imagine I shall have much trouble it [in] beating him. We have played about 300 games & I am 30 ahead now.

I want you to send me three of my Photographs[.] if you have not got them I wish you would have some more struck off. I will send the money. I like to get those to the officers that I sail with when I can & of course they expect a return. I have one of Mr Leinas which I shall send you soon for you to look at so you can see what sort of looking men I am with & *place* me better in your mind. I cant send it this time tho' for the "Company" envelopes wont hold it.

Enoch wants to set the table for supper so good by till tomorrow.

July 4th 1864. Twenty three years old today! (I wonder what Grant is doing to celebrate my birth-day). My 23rd year has not been a very satisfactory one taken it all together. Im glad its over[.]

I hope this one will be a happier one but the prospect dont look over & above bright. I suppose the chances are that the next Fourth will still find me buried in the East Gulf Squadron, if the war lasts that long & I suppose it will. it will take a good while to get things straightened out after the Rebs are fairly whipped.

They seem to have forgotten me in Key West. I am not at all supprised at it however. When one is out of sight he is very apt to be out of mind too. I never placed much confidence in their doing any thing for me, tho' I still think they could if they were a mind to try. I have been thinking some of writing to Capt Welch but do not know as it would be best. I dont much like to ask favors of any one so that they can consider me as under any obligation. Perhaps I may write tho' I can't say. Would you?

We are going to have a dinner party on board to day. The U.S. Sch *J.S. Chambers* & 2 Tenders are laying here & the officers are all coming on board here to dine.[63]

I have got the afternoon watch & I'm glad of it for I've got a head-ach & dont feel like being jolly. I'm not sure of escaping tho' in fact I know I shall not altogether[,] for one of the Masters Mates will have to relieve me. I'll get clear of it if I can tho that's certain.

We had another Court Martial the other day, & I had to act as Recorder & had all the writing to do, only about fifteen pages of fools cap. Nice work that won't it.

I can't write any more now. some of them have just come in & it is a perfect Babel here.

Good by love to all the family. How is Grandpa now? better I hope. Write to me often.

From your loving son
Henry

U.S. Bark *Gem of the Seas*
Off Charlotts Harbor Fla
July 6th 1864

Dear Mother

I sent you off a letter yesterday but as there is a chance of the *Honduras* passing today, you shall have at least a few lines by her too.

The Fourth passed on the whole very pleasantly. The "Boys" seemed to enjoy themselves very much of course it was a holliday. the ship was dressed in Flags & at the morning quarters the Captain told them that they might sing dance eat sleep or what ever they pleased for the day, provided they did not overstep the bounds of discipline. Part of them went on shore for a ramble but were all off before dinner as the "Fatted Calf" had been killed & a feast was on the Tapis.[64]

We got two calves from Ft Myers more than a week ago & kept them for the occasion. They danced during the day (You ought to see a lot or sailors dance a cotillion, it would make you dizzy). but the evening was devoted to singing & had a good time generally.

The day was rather a dull one to me[.] I did not feel very well & every thing was topsy turvy because we were giving a dinner party to the officers of the U.S. Sch *Chambers (Jas. S)*. It went off very well tho'. the dinner was a decided success (we were not surpprised at that however as our Steward understands himself throughly & is "worth his weight in "Green Backs"["] He leaves us in a month or two his term of service being nearly out. We all intend to ware crape when he goes for we shall ne're see his likes again.)

It is not usual amongst sea faring men to pass the Fourth with out some thing stronger than water to wash it down with, but we did. There was not a drop of wine or spirits expended on board here that day unless (as I strongly suspect), the Captain of the *C[hambers]* brought on board a private bottle for himself & Capt "R" but if he did there was not enough to go round so they wisely kept it to themselves.

As I dont wish however to give you a wrong impression as to our absteniousness I may as well add that we sent to Key West for a basket of Champagne by Mr. Leinas but I suppose the Yellow Fever made him loose his memory. at all events he forgot it so we had to content our selves with lemonade & Coffee. O such coffee it would bring a man to life if he had been drowned a week. I never drank better any where, not even in Bordeaux. We are noted for our Coffee all along the coast.

Well, we were sorry to have to go with out our wine tho', but it is all the same *now* & we have the money in our pockits.

I will send you Mr. Leinas Photograph this time. Dont forget to send out mine. I wish you would send me my white coat[.] I left it in the little room I believe. You might send it the same as you did the Gun, & some "Goodies" (*that will keep*) along with it. If you send any cake be sure & make a Rich one[.] These *Sea Gentlemen* are very fastidious[.] the Captain had a very nice cake sent him & they all turned up their noses at it because it was plain. I *want* the coat & it will cost less to send it out than to buy a new one. I dont know how I came to forget it. I want a Bag of no. 6 shot. send me the price, as I shall dispose of part of it.

Good by now, love to all the family from your loving son

Henry

US Bark *Gem of the Seas*
Charlotts Harbor Fla
July 9th 1864

Dear Father

I have just five minutes to write you a letter on business. Did you recive that $20. I sent some time since. How do I stand with you now?

I enclose you this time $40. on account, & will send the allotment next month.

The Steamer is close to us so I can not stop to write any more, as I have got to get ready to board her.

Good by from your loving son

H.W. Wells

U.S. Bark *Gem of the Seas*
Charlotts Harbor Fla.
July 23rd 1864

Dear Lu

We had a big mail a few days ago & in it I found two letters from you, which I should have probably answered before, but I knew that there would not be any chance of sending till the *Honduras* got back & so have put off writing until the last minute for the musquitoes have nearly driven us all crazy for the last few days[.] We are laying inside & have been getting on board the wood & water[.] We finished yesterday so I suppose we shall go out side again as soon as we get a fair wind. I shall be thankful enough when we do for I have not had *any* sleep for two nights and feel correspondingly streaked.

The men are having a great time on deck over an auction the Master at Arms is carrying on selling the contents of the "lucky bag[.]" he makes a capital Auctioneer being very glib with his tongue & keeping the whole crowd in a roar the whole time.

The lucky bag is a large bag keept by the Master at Arms in which he puts all clothes found knocking about the decks where they had not ought to be. When it gets full (about once a month or so) it is brought up to the mast & opened. Any man can claim his clothes then if he chooses but it involves punishment on the Black List (that is being kept at work for a sertain number of days.) so generaly a large part of the things are unclaimed & are then sold at auction & the money is applied as the Capt. may direct. I believe this is going to the National Sailors Fair at Boston next November. By the way have you heard much about that affair? Circulars have been sent through the Fleet about it asking the Officers & men of the Navy to contribute towards it. The officers of this ship have all given a days-pay & I believe the men are going to do the same. It seems to me to be a very good thing.

I received the Photographs all right (three)[.] I fully agree with you in thinking the one of poor Henry Bond as good as it could be & am real glad you got it for me[.] you are a pretty good girl on the whole, tho' you did not tell me what I asked about who called me a Copperhead. you can do as you like about it[.] I want to know but if you wont pay any attention to my want why I can not help it. I shall not forget it tho' the next time you want some special bit of information[.]

I dont feel at all forgiving I assure you. You had no business to tell me of it at all unless you intended to tell the whole. I think I know who said it but may be doing a *friend* great injustice. if I am it is all your fault. I did not suspect Uncle Fred after I had thought it over a little while tho' he was the first one that came into my head. he is too strong a Copperhead himself not to know better than to think me one.

Before your last letter came I thought very likely you would evade the question & tried to make up my mind if you did to play the indignant and not answer the letter[.] I had not fully made up my mind however when the mail arrived & finding two long letters & three Photo's in it quite disarmed my resentment as you see. so I shall adopt the Passive mode of retaliation instead of the active one. in fact I am not at all sure but the latter would be spiting myself more than you, for you at home dont need letters half as much as I do. But to return to the subject of the Photo's.

What a horrid Proof that was of yours. What *shall* I do with it? its too ugly to keep & still I dont want to throw it away. I have got it in the book (Temporarily), opposite Georgie Tilden & actualy he looks *frightened.*

What possessed you to have that wash-basin hat perpetuated[?] I think it is the ugliest style of head piece I ever saw, & besides you look as prim & strong-minded as an old maid of—well any age you like between 40 and 100.

I hope you will excuse my few *wild* criticisms & send me the result of the *next* trial.

I think Jennie William's Photograph quite good. I wish you would give my complements to her next time you see her & tell her that I am very much obliged to her for it.

I shall have to stop writing now as I must go on watch. "so long".

Sunday Morning.

I got desperate last night & rigged a Musquito Bar on my berth, & slept a sleep.[65] When I woke up this morning I was nearly smothered & could hardly breath, but congratulated my self on the fact that I had not had a single bite. Judge of my indignation then on finding by undoubtable testimony that there had not (for some reason or rather probably the weather) been a single musquito on board all night. My *felinx* [feelings] can be easier immagined than described. If it had not been sunday I am afraid I should have been strongly tempted to have swore a *few.*

Have you received those two pictures I sent you & also that $1.00? I am sorry mother did not get hers it was the prettyest one of the lot I think. I sent it so you need not crow old lady. I guess I will send you another this time I have several more of them.

I am glad to hear that Cousin Isa has got home again. it must seem good to see her. Is she going out again? Give my love to her next time you see her. if I knew how to direct I would write & dont know but I shall any way, via home.

I dont think I shall follow your advice about being doubly kind to the Boy who brought me the lemonade as I do not think it good. I believe I owe my popularity among the men to the fact that I have no favorites but try to treat all justly & considerately according to their deserts. in fact I know that it is so because the Chief Boatswains mate told me so the other day when I wanted to pay him for making a pair of Pants for me. He said "You have always treated the whole ships company well & I dont want any pay for any thing I can do for you[.] Whenever you want any thing done that I can manage I shall be glad to do it for you etc." There are one or two officers on board that can not get sewing done for them on any terms. the men wont do it. & the rest have to pay fully as much as one would ashore for the same work, if not more. I would rather pay my self, for I dont like them to think that I am under any obligation to them[.] in fact I told the B.[oatswains] M.[ate] as much, that I would not consider myself so.

I feel proud that they should apreciate my intentions & be so ready to acknowledge them[.] They all seem to try to please me & do well in my watch & I have not had to have a man put in irons since I have been on board, which is saying a good deal for six months in a man of war.

We are having a sweet day of it[.] it has been blowing & raining all the morning like smoke ([in] fact, you can't see three yards from the ship)[.] I should not wonder if we had a heavy gale if not worse. They say this is the way the Hurricanes generaly commence. I dont care if it comes & blows us chock up into the bush[.] I dont think the Government would lose much by it & I am sure it would be a relief to all on board. The ship is in a very bad state now[.] the decks are horrible & leak all over. a fresh leak broke out this morning right·over Mr Bliss's berth & wet his bedding & then run down onto mine which is underneath. Pleasant that.

Well I cant write any more now love to all the family & remember me to all my friends (except those who say I'm a Copperhead).

From your loving brother
Henry

U.S. Bark *Gem of the Seas*
[August 1864[66]]

Dear Father

I enclose you my allotment ticket at last I meant to have sent it long ago but the Pay[master] kept putting it off as I was not in any particular hurry.

Did you receive the $20. which I sent you on May 31st & also $40. sent July.

I have received my prize-money for the Schr *Julia* amounting to $52.31, not much but better than nothing.[67]

I see by the Army & Navy Journal that there is a bill before Congress for admitting a sertain number of Volunteers into the Regular Navy[.] I wish you would watch its progress & if it passes or any simular bill see if you can not raise influence enough to get me nominated by some of the Powers that be. I want very much to get into the Service if I can & hope you will be willing to assist me when the time comes. I think we are booked for war for some years to come & the sooner one gets established the better.

The allotment ticket is a little soiled. I did not do it & when the Paymaster handed it to me I wanted him to copy it but he would not. I believe he is short of blanks or something of that sort.

I wish you would ask Mother to send me in a letter or otherwise some yarn, for my stockings [are] in a shocking state. I dont think that there is a pair amongst them but what has one or more holes in them.

I hope you will excuse this writing, it was done in a hurry.

Every thing is dull as ever here & I have no news.

I have written long letters to Mother & Lu.

I wish you would write me & tell your opinion on the war generaly.

I can not write any more now.

Love to all the family,

From your loving son
H.W. Wells

Next time any thing is sent out to me I wish you would send another pair of shoes. Those that came with the Gun were too small[.] I could get them on but could not wear them so I let the Paymaster take possession at cost when I found out what that may be. Please tell me or send word. My size is No 8. I belive I wear about the same size as your-self.

U.S. Bark *Gem of the Seas*
Charlotts Harbor Fla
Aug 4th 1864

Dear La La

I received your letter some time ago but have not had the courage to answer it before. You have no idea what a perilous undertaking both for body & soul it is to attempt to do any thing here, below, except eat & sleep (if you can). The musquitoes are a terrible plague. If one sets down to write he hardly gets his pen in his hand when he feels it the wish of his being first to slap one side of his face, then the other, then his writing hand (thereby in all human probability blotting his paper or driving his pen thro' it) then his foot. Clothes are no protection to such birds as these we have here. They will bite thro' a piece of sole leather as easy as sing a serinade.

The heat is intense & at last the poor Blockader after losing his temper—(there's one of the rascals round my nose now. oh dear I laid in wait for him but did not succeed in killing him)—

Interruptions are the bane of my life[.] I was called off from my writing two hours ago by the Coxswain of my boat "just for a minute" to attend to some thing about the rigging of it, & have been hard at work (looking on would be nearer the truth perhaps seeing others, but busy attending to it nevertheless) ever since. It is now most dinner time so I dont see as there is any prospect of finishing my letter this forenoon especialy as it is only just begun.

I left off telling you of the poetry of the Blockade[.] As I was saying—after losing his temper & beating himself till he is almost black & blue, swearing after each slap (for we sailors are but mortal & after a man has been bitten two or three hundred times forebearance ceases to be a virtue, especialy when he has done penance before hand by striking him self as many times & only killed two or three.) rushes on deck runinging [running] over with perspiration & oh in a sweet frame of mind believe me.

We have not been able to set in the Ward Room for three weeks before yesterday, when we had a good breeze which has kept up to day. During the first part of the time I suffered a good deal for want of sleep but now I have got a musquito bar rigged & so keep clear of one evil tho' I am nearly smothered with the heat every night. Sometimes I lay awake & listen to the *varmint* out side. They do make a wonderful noise for such little creatures. it sounds like a heavy surf beating on the shore as they make charges on the bar & then go back and make another rush.

Well I cant write any more now for it is time for the boy to set the table.

Aug 7th. I wonder if we are ever going to have a chance to send any more letters or receive any? it is nearly a month now since we have had any communication what ever with the outer world & we have begun to think that we have been forgotten altogether by the powers that be—in Key West[—]or else that the Yellow Fever has made a clean sweep of them. It is too bad just at this stage of the game, both ways. I expect you at home will be worrying about me & fearing something has happened that I dont write, visions of fever etc. rising very vividly in your minds while we here miss our only consolation for our exile by not getting our mails & being cut off from hearing the news which from the positions of the different Armies cannot fail to be intensely interesting just now.

Friday we thought we were going to have a chance to send letters for we saw a steamer out side bound for the southward.

The *Rosalie* went out to intercept her but the fellow would not stop for her so we were disapointed.

Capt Coffin of the *R*[*osalie*] is very sick so he has been brought on board here & Mr Bliss my roommate has taken his place.[68] Mr Leinas is also sick so I am for the present acting as Ex Officer Sailing Master & Watch officer, about enough for one man, that. The Capt takes part of the Ex Officer duties off my hands however which lets up on me a little. (Oh dear, dear, the musquitoes are tormenting the life out of me.)

We have had no signs of the fever up here as yet & I begin to hope that we shall weather out the summer with out "Yellow Jack's" paying us a visit. if we get thro' this month all right I think the danger will be past. Perhaps it is better for us on the whole that we are debarred communication with Key West as our news might chance to cost us dear. I suppose every thing is wisely ordered, tho' we do not always appreciate it.

Allow me to correct a mistake of yours in regard to that Noble Frigate the *New Ironsides*. You say she is always repairing. I believe she went into commission some time in the Summer of '62 certainly not later than the fall, for I saw her at Newport News when I was coming down from Richmond[.] Since then she has seen harder service than any other ship, I believe, ever did & rougher fighting & has not had any repairs to my knowledge except what little she could get done at Port Royal for the simple reason that they could not spare her off Charleston & every one of the Monitors repaired two or three times to her once.

I should think it was high time she came north to be overhauled after what she has gone thro'.

I meant to have written you a long letter but I am afraid you will have to take the will for the deed for I *can not* stand this any longer, & must go on deck. it is bad enough there but is a Paradise compared to the Ward Room.

Remember me to all friends & love to all the family. I hope Grandpa is better by this time I am sorry to hear that he has been so unwell.

I have written to Father & enclosed my allotment.

Good by, write to me again when you have time.

From your loving brother
H.W. Wells[69]

U.S. Bark *Gem of the Seas*
Charlotts Harbor Fla
Aug 17th 1864

Dear Mother

We received a mail a few days ago, after waiting about five weeks for it, & I was glad enough to hear from home again. I am afraid you must have been anxious about me, receiving no letters for so long a time, in this sickly season too, but there was no help for it.

No vessels go to Key West now that can avoid it & the regular supply steamer *Union* is quarintened at Portsmouth N.H. having got the Yellow Fever on her the last time she was down here. Our squadron dispatch boat the *Honduras* is or was in the same fix & was laid up for some time but has just got to running again so I am in hopes things will not be so bad in future.

Perhaps we were fortunate in being cut off from the rest of the squadron as we have been for the fever has spread thro' almost the whole of it & if we had had more intercourse with them we might have had it too.

We have had some sickness on board but nothing contag[i]ous. Mr. Leinas (Ex Officer) & Mr Coffin Commd'g the *Rosalie* have been sick for some time. Mr Bliss took charge of the *R* temporarily & so I was acting as Ex Officer Sailing Master & Watch Officer for about two weeks & as there was only three of us to stand watch I had my hands full. At first for two or three days while it was a novelty the Capt. took most of the duties of the Ex. on himself which I was very glad of, but he soon got tired of it & turned them over to me. Mr. L is on duty again now tho' he is hardly fit for it.

I have been pretty well this summer, better than I usualy am in such hot weather[.] It has been pretty rough here tho' what with heat & musquitoes some of the oldest settlers here say that they have never known the latter to be so bad.

I received four letters from home by the last mail (three from you & one from Lu with the Photos) some papers & Mr. Clarks book which I was very glad to get I can assure you. I am sorry to say that it was dammaged some what however tho' not so as to effect the contents.

It seems to me that either you dont get more than half of my letters or else how shall I account for the neglect which some of them receive for instance I have sent home $60.00 part in June & part in July & I believe I have mentioned the fact in about every letter I have written since. Yet I can't hear any thing of it whether it has been received or not. I suppose it must be lost but I *should* like to be sure about it one way or the other.

Another thing I have at differant times sent home Photographs of places in Key West & of one or two of my messmates not one of which (no, I did hear that Mr Bliss's had arrived) has been acknowledged[.] They were not of much account to be sure but I *do* think that they were worth acknowledging.

Now Mother this aint all meant for you but for the family generaly & Lu specialy as I have sent several to her[.] Perhaps tho' you have not received them. I sent one of Mr. Leinas & I want one of mine to give him in exchange. Please send it to me. I hope you will excuse me for presuming to growl at you. If you will only take me as an example & bear it with resignation as I do when you do me the same kind office it will be all right.

Now dont you think I have a right to feel a little put out? Supposing I had not said a word in my letters about "Butler" & "Clark's Sermons" would not you have felt so? I had not ought to have put the last in that catagory tho' as it was a Birthday present, I wish I could kiss you for it. Try & immagine that I have. I wish you had marked it a little it would have made it seem more homelike[.]

I dont exactly know how to express what I mean, but it is good to have a book like that, with passages marked in it by one we love. *I* think it doubles its value[.] That was what made me think so much of my old Hymn Book.

I am glad Mr Clark had a chance to preach to the Representatives, & gave them a piece of his mind. I hope they will benefit by it[.] It *is* a shame that those Reg'ts are allowed to go with out pay, their full pay I mean, & I am glad that Mr "C" show it up to them in the right light.[70]

Have any of my friends gone out with the new call for troops? Where is Will Wellman? is he not going? & Will Bond; if I was in his place I should sertainly go *he* has something besides his country to fight for, tho one would think that *that* was enough to call any young man into the field. I for one can not understand the apathy with which so many look on this struggle with out seeming to have the least desire to lend a helping hand, as if the welfare of the country was entirely a secondary consideration. I wish I could have as good a chance to go where the hard fighting is now being done as some of them have instead of being buried alive down here. I would not be long in "Girding on my armor" as the song goes.[71] It seems a pity in times like these that those that want to fight should not have a chance, dont it?

I think I have staid here about long enough & as soon as the Fever season is over I am going to try to get out of this if possable tho it is rather a hopeless task.

I suppose there is no hope of Joe's going to the war is there? I have not heard from him for some time. What has become of him?

I should like very much to see Sarah & Mary Brown, are they going back West again? Do remember me to them & to Mr & Mrs Brown too thro' them.

I have succeeded in getting some Pelican & Curlew Eggs for Bennie tho' I dont know whether I shall be able to get them home whole or not.

I hope soon to hear that Uncle Edwin & Aunt Ruth are with you. What an experience they must have had. I should like to hear them tell it. I wonder how they feel on the subject of the Rebelion now & if Auntie has been carried away by Southern influences. Be sure & tell me all about what they say & give my love to them when you see them.

I can not write any more now as I have got to go on watch. Good by, love to all the family from your loving son

Henry

U.S. Bark *Gem of the Seas*
Charlotts Harbor Fla.
Aug 27th 1864

Dear Lu,

I received your letters of July 18th & Aug 8th, the last, yesterday. Str. *Honduras* who has got to running again tho not altogether clear of the Fever. Your

Photographs came all right. & I like them quite well tho' I should have prefered a little more of your face. I have got several pictures of you now in groups & otherwise & there is not a front view amongst the whole of them. if you have any proofs of that Description do send me one so that I can see your sweet face looking at me (Hmm, how will that do.) You need not think I'm not satisfied tho'. I think the others are worth a good deal more than they cost. consider it a good speculation tho they do look a little sleepy. (would not you like to pull my ears now?) Best you had the impudence to tell me. I was *so* particular & hard to please & of course I must verify your assertion. I dont wish to cast any of your reflections back on you[.] Oh, No, I'll keep all I've got, & all I can get too. I've got the last in my book opposite Ben. Almost in the fore-front on "U" as Grandpa said in the story of the man who was going to war.

Father, Mother, Grandpa, & Eliza are the only ones ahead of you. "E" is the oldest you know & therefore has the precedence that is Military Etiquette you know, senior first. Ned Wilders Photo is capital, is it not? I have got him opposite Sarah Lovett the two pictures go together first rate. Give him one of mine of course. I thought Eliza was going to have some more taken, is she not? or has she had those "over the life" ones perpetuated.

I admire your circumspection in not sending the Photos all at once for fear yours should not receive sufficient attention. There would have been a good deal of danger of that unhappy result, *perhaps*.

I hope you are satisfied with the result of your War service.

Oh, Ah! I find on re-reading your epistle that instead of Fearing that your Photos would be cast in the shade, as an unassuming young woman natural[l]y would you had the egotistical assurance to suppose that I should be so absorbed in looking at your Profile that I should entirely ignore the other. Well, well, that's pretty good too, for a young lady of your size.

Ameses as you say it is well sometimes to have the agony prolonged as you pathetically expressed it so I wont upbrade you anymore on that score.[72]

I am glad you have at last come to the conclusion of telling me who it was that called me a Copperhead. I did want to know very much & after what I had said should have felt very much hurt with you if you had not told me. (consider your self kissed).

You see it is quite a releaf to my mind for I had come to the conclusion that it was not his but some one whose good opinion [edited word] (only one P.) I valued more a great deal than I do hers. I dont know whether it is best to tell you who it was or not. on the whole tho' I guess I wil[l] return your confidence only dont say any thing a bout it. I thought at first it was Miss Jenkins but I finaly set it down in my mind that it was Mrs Bowditch & I felt very badly to think she should have so mistaken me, for I value her good opinion very much.

I am sorry that any one who I looked upon as friends should think I was so depraved as to have any sympathies with that contemptible party. But I would rather it was her then Mrs B that said so. Tho I can not recall any thing that I ever said to her that would give her any foundation for saying such a thing of me.

So far as Mr & Mrs Prescott are concerned, the next time you see Miss J. please tell her with my compliments that I do not allow any one to declare to me as to who I shall associate with, & the best thing she can do is to mind her own business. I shall choose my friends & she may hers & it makes very little to me after what has been said whether she includes me in her number or not, in fact I would rather prefer she would not.

I should have respected her a good deal more if she had told me what she thought while I was at home & could defend myself than to wait until I was off again in the Service of my country to slander my character behind my back after professing to be my friend. But enough of this subject. it makes me mad to think of it.

By the way I made a mistake about Mr Bliss's residence. [In Boston] He lives in one of those houses up on the hill back of Heath St. & you get to it by going up Highland St. a Place which leads off Tremont St just beyond Heath. I am sorry my mistake should have given you & mother a tramp for nothing.

I am sorry you dont hear from me oftener but I can not help it[.] I write as often as there is a chance to send. I expect the mails will be more regular in a month or so, when the Fever season is over.

I *should* like to know if the money I sent to Father in June & July was received[.] I have not heard a word a bout it. I have begged entreated & importuned for information on the subject but no one pays any attention to the subject. Do you know any thing about it? There was $60.00 altogether. I suppose it is lost but should like to know. I sent an allotment also some time ago. if it has not been received it is important I should know it.

How I should like to have seen Uncle Edwin & Aunt Ruth. What did you mean by not telling me more about them? you ought to be ashamed of yourself. Miss—next time you write to make up for your short comings. Give my love to them when you see or write to them. What did Auntie think of her namesake Little Ruthie? Why why why, you agrivating Tweedle-pipes did not you tell me.

I read the part of your letter relating to the Cake with breathless interest & gave a sigh of releaf when I found it was decided that it should be made.

Dont you run away with the idea that we live better here than you do at home that's all humbug. To be sure we have a good many luxuries such as venison & Turtle but there are a great many thing[s] which are usualy terrible necessaries which we are deprived of. For instance we have not seen a Potatoe for over two months or any other vegetable except one or two squashes. In place of what for courtesy sake we call butter we should be nearer the point if we said oil for it is emphatically "spoon wittlers".[73] Our standard dish (for mind you we do not get venison etc. every day not by no means) is baked beans (my favorite dish) tho we only have them 21 times a week on an average their forerunner being *bean soup* by way of a change, at dinner[.] I could go on with a long list by as I am near the end of my paper I guess I wont. I am sorry to hear that Grandpa is so poorly but hope soon to hear that he is better. Give lots of love to him & also to the rest of the family[.] I suppose you will take your own share of it whether you are told to, or not. Good by, from

Henry

U.S. Bark *Gem of the Seas*
Off Charlotts Harbor Fla
Sept 4th /64

Dear Mother

I sent off some letters home a day or two ago which had been laying in my Portfollio for some time so now I think I had better write some more, so as not to miss any chance of sending which may turn up of letting you hear from me.

We are still existing here, the same as ever no excitement, no news, no anything. & worst of all no supply steamer & few mails.

I am mer[r]y about news tho' for we had quite an interesting piece of it a few days since. Farraguts new exploit, the Capture of the Mobile forts. Was it not a brillent affair? & then that fight with the *Tennessee* was it not [a] glorious fight? I think that Admiral Buchanan deserves the credit of having fought his vessel splendidly against such fearful odds after he was deserted by his consorts. I did not think any *one* vessel could have held out against three Monitors so long to say nothing of the wooden vessels. I believe in giving the "D–L his due" & I can not help thinking that he did all a brave man could do. I am glad the vessel was taken *alive* as we say as I suppose she will prove quite an acquisition to our Navy & will in part take the place of the *Tecumseh* which was blown up there.[74]

I expect that Admiral "F" will not be kept down here much longer now. I hope they will let him try Wilmington next. I wish I could be with him in some good vessel. There is some sense in the way he goes in to a fight. He is to the Navy what Grant is to the Army, & does not know any such word as fail in what he undertakes.

Oh Dear the musquitoes are bothering me so that I can not write any more now, but will wait for a more favorable time.

Sept. 9th. I have [been] putting off writing from day to day hoping something would turn up, but I dont think I had better put off finishing this letter any longer as the *Honduras* ought to be back now in a day or two.

We sent the *Rosalie* to Key West some time ago & she ought to be back tomorrow or next day when I hope we shall get a mail & some news. We are all very anxious to hear of the progress of the Presadential election our last accounts did not look so bright as we could wish.

It does seem to me that it would be almost ruin, if not quite, to have any other than Lincoln for President just now. As he said himself "Its a bad plan to swap horses while crossing a stream."

Do send me lots of papers. A great many wont come thro' I suppose but some will. The New York Herald is the only paper we see much here, & for any thing except the war news, I'd as soon have none at all. Occasionally we see the N.Y. Times & the contrast is quite refreshing.

I am real sorry that you are not very well this summer or rather have not been. I wish I was at home to *take care of you*. You ought to have gone down to the beach. Some where it seems to me, tho' I suppose you would not have liked to have left Grandpa now that he is so unwell. In fact Lu told me that that was the reason.

I am afraid that journey out to Chicago was too much for you but I wont say any thing about that, for I know you did lots of good by going, only I wish you had been well & strong. Poor Mother it seems as tho' every one took lots of good from you & make very little returns. Every time I go away from home I think of all the good you have done for me & how little I have done to make you happy in return & yet you know I love you dearly. Oh Dear I wish I was a little boy again, I dont think one improves much by growing old & going away from home.

I wish I could write my thoughts to you just as I feel, but I cant. Sometimes I think I can, but my pen wont run to day. If I could I know you would sympathize with me & comfort me[.] I know I'm a big boy to say that, but I feel it nevertheless & need it too. I'm not in a very placid & enviable state of mind & have not been for some time past.

Did you read that sermon of Mr Clarks on Life Measures? I think I heard him preach it, at all events I have read it several times since I got it. It is a good sermon & it has done me good I believe[.] He hit my case in part there tho' not altogether.

That Book is a perfect treasure. You could not have sent me any thing more exceptable, & I am not the only one that benefits by it either.

I have been very well this summer unusualy so for me. The Captain was remarking last night that I did not look like the same man I did when I came on board last winter. They all say the same thing & what every body says must be true you know.

I have *not* kept my resolutions in regards to smoking. I left it off for some time but the musquitoes were so bad that I took it up again in self defence[.] Deliberately without any qualms of conscience whatever. I thought at first I would not say any thing about it in my letters but on the whole have made up my mind that it is hardly fair to conceal my change of purpose when I blew the trumpet so loud on giving it up. I intend to leave off again by & by when the cool weather sets in however.

I am going to enclose you a Photograph of Acting Master Coffin who commands the *Rosalie* our tender. It is a horrid looking thing. Taken in Key West for all the name on the back. It looks a little like him tho'. Did you get that one of Mr Leinas?

How is Grandfather now. It must be very hard for him to have such a long spell of sickness he is so seldom laid up. Give my love to him & tell him that I hope I am to hear that he is all right again.

I will not write any more now but perhaps I may add a few lines if any thing occurs before the *H*[*onduras*] arrives.

Good by love to all the family

From your loving son

Henry

8

"I Like My New Position Quite Well"

In Command

(No 1)
U.S. Sloop *Rosalie*
Off Charlotts Harbor Fla
Sept. 15th /'64

Dear Mother

I take back all I said in my last letter about your neglect in acknowledging the receipt of Photo's, money, etc. for I have just received a letter from you which ought to have arrived a month ago for I got letters a week ago nearly that much later. I am sorry I did not wait a while longer before I commenced to growl but I guess you wont feel very badly about it. Will you? I wont do so again *never no more*.

I suppose you would like to know the meaning of the heading of this letter. So I beg leave very respectfully to introduce you to the Comd'g officer of the U.S. Sloop *Rosalie* (Tender to the U.S. Bark *Gem of the Seas*) HW Wells Acting Ensign U.S.N.[1]

Mr Coffin has been unfit for duty for some time past & as he said he was tired of the sloop I applied for her & have *got* her. Mr. C. is on board the Bark in my place. I do not know whether it will be a permanant thing or not but rather think it will[.] at least I shall probably stay where I am for three or four months & that is all I want. It will I think be a pleasent change for me as they are talking of sending me off cruising (Dont you wish I may catch some prizes?) I dont know whether I have ever described my *spouse* (the *Tender Rosalie)* to you or not, but I will now at all events[.] She is a Sloop of about 50 tons, (she used to be a yacht & is a very pretty vessel) & carries 1 gun, a 12 Pdr. Howitzer, & a crew consisting of the Commander, a Master's Mate, a Pilot and Eight men (including two Petty officers a Quarter Master & a Quarter Gunner).[2] My Masters Mate is not on board. They being short of officers on the Bark, he is detained there for the present. I am not very sorry for it as my cabin is small & not big enough for more than two to be comfortable in.

The Pilot's name is West. he seems a nice quiet sort of a man but is entirely uneducated & can hardly write his own name.

The crew seem to be a good willing set of men. The discipline has been rather slack on board here-to-fore but I am getting things straitened out a little now. When I took command I made the men a bit of a speach & told them what I expected of them & what they had got to expect from me. & I have had no trouble with any of them thus far & do not expect to.

There—I think that that subject is about written out, dont you? By the way address my letters to the Bark, the same as before, as she is my head quarters & is stationary while the *R*[*osalie*] is a wandering bird & the mails would not know where to find her.

I dont know whether I have received all your letters or not. I have received the sleeve button, two books, & the Postage Stamps. also all the Phot[o]s that have been sent I believe. Dont you think it would be a good plan to number your letters & then I should always know if one was missing. I will do so commencing with this one (No. 1) first letter from the *Rosalie*.

I am sorry that you hear from me so seldom but it cant be helped at present. As long as the Yellow Fever lasts in Key West so long will the mails be irregular & uncertain & perhaps longer. but that is the Principal cause of the trouble[.] You seem to be having a regular clearing out at home—

Sept. 19th. I was called off suddenly for some thing or rather [other] & was not able to finish my letter[.] Since then I have had my hands full I have sunk my Sloop. dont start. I did it with malice & a forethought to kill the Roaches which were so thick that no one could live with them & of course I have been all in a heap ever since. I raised her to day. I am almost used up as I have been on the beach for three days with my crew, victims to musquitoes, but shall be all right in a day or two. I meant to have written you a good long letter but the mail will go tomorrow so I cant. Good night love to all from

Henry

No 2
U.S. Sloop *Rosalie*
October 1st 1864

Dear Mother

I have got a whole heap of unanswered letters before me & the mail leaves tomorrow (probably) so I must at least write you a few lines.

I would have had a good long letter ready but since I raised the *R*[*osalie*] I have not had a minutes peace, having been to Ft Myers twice & been filled with passengers all the time, (Refugees or Officers). I am now on my way back to the Bark from my second trip to have a little rest & then go cruising. I have been rather unwell for the last day or two occasioned I suppose from laying out on deck nights in wet clothes & various other exposure. I did not mean to do it but it was your fault. I was *brunged up* wrong.

I had to carry a load of Twenty Refugees to Ft. Myers, mostly women & children. My vessel is very small & they & their baggage filled her up pretty well. It is not usual to allow them in the cabin. They have to go down forward or shift the best way they can on deck.

When I took them on board I gave orders that not one of them should go into the cabin (as is usual) & I set my face very stern (& imposing!) so none of them would presume to trouble me, very successfully too, for I saw some of them looking askent [askance] but none of them said any thing. But one thing knocked my calculations & I find I'm not hard hearted enough for such business. We started from the place where they were. (Arnolds Bay where I sunk my *Rosa.*[3] Where by the way they were landed the night before & staid all night in a pelting rain with out any protection whatever.) at about 3 P.M. & it was raining hard, with a howling wind.

I stood it for a while (in fact for the first hour or so I had my hands full looking out for my vessel, for I was carrying sail very heavily.) but finerly those poor little children looking so Pale with wet & cold to say nothing of the women, were too much for me, & I came to the conclusion that any sleep I could get in my berth would not do me much good with those little things suffering on deck. So I let them have the cabin, the women & children, that is, my softness of heart did not extend to the men & I thought they ought to be able to stand as much as I could. So they went below thankfull enough, & when an hour after I looked down & saw a row of little children, not one of them larger than Little Ruth, seven of them, laying athwart-ships on a matrass [mattress] on one side of the cabin, all asleep, dry & comfortable I felt well repaid for the use of my cabin, for it was one of the prettiest sights I ever saw. & I rolled my self up in my rubber coat & laid down on the wet deck. Well, pretty well satisfied with myself. I had them on board two days & when I landed them, one of them, an old man, came to me almost with tears in his eyes to tell me how much obliged they were etc. he said they had never been treated so well by any one since they crossed the lines. I ran away from him before he got thro' however for I did not feel as tho' I needed any thanks.

The result of it all was that I got used up over it & was quite unwell for a day or so, but am getting better now.

Matters are not going on very pleasently on board the Bark just now and I am very well pleased to be out of the way. Capt L[einas] is not a man which I want to serve under. why actual[l]y I do not believe he has been sober two days since he took command, & part of the time, the officers tell me, he does not know at all what he is doing. Nice that aint it?

I have received several letters lately from you, Lu & Eliza, also the Box, all right. Cake & all, every thing was satisfactory. The cake was very nice. I gave part of it to the Officers & the rest I took up to Ft Myers & gave it to Capt. Cranes family who are there with him.[4] One of his daughters married Act. Ensign Jenks late of the *Gem of the Seas* & she is there too. She plays the Guitar finely & sings also so I find it quite a treat to go to their house when I am up there. The Captain is I believe a Northerner by birth but has been here in Florida a good many years. (he served in the army all thro' the Indian war in this State.) The rest of the family are all Southern, but they are Union, all over. The Capt belongs to the 2nd Fla. Cavalry (Federal). They used to live in Tampa before the war, but were driven away on account of their Union sentiments.

It seems to be quite the fashion for officers to get married down here[.] I know of quite a number both army and Navy, who have done so, as a general thing tho' I think they have made fools of themselves tho'. Mr. Jenks however is an exception & has got a wife that he has no cause to be ashamed of. Perhaps *she* might have done better but I dont think he could for she is his superior in almost every point of view.

The last letter I received from you was dated at Fryeburg [Maine]. I am real glad you went on that trip with Uncle Hamilton[.] I am sure it has done you lots of good[.] he must be such a jolly person to travel with too. I [passage struck out][5] tho' I know you was glad to go there but I dont believe it did you any good.

You say you wish the Navy could vote, but I dont! if they all should go as our ship would. We had an election about a month (no it was on 4th of July) ago. The Candidates were Lincoln MacClellan, Fremont, & Handcock.[6] There were about fifty votes cast of which twenty seven were for MacC. & eighteen for Lincoln, four for Handcock & one for Fremont. The officers tho' are all Lincoln men, but one.

About that vest that Uncle Edwin has got of mine. Of course he is perfectly welcome to it & I am very glad the mistake occurred. There is no need of his ever knowing it. I do not know but I mentioned it before.

I am very sorry to keep hearing such accounts of Grandpa's health[.] I hope soon to hear that he is better. Give him lots of love from me.

Those Atlantic's in the Box were very exceptable.

Good by now. Love to all from your ever loving son

Henry

U.S. Sloop *Rosalie*
Charlotts Harbor Fla.
Oct 3rd 1864

Dear Lu

It seems a long time since I have written to you, but realy I dont know how I could have helped it. I have had very little time for any thing of late having had a horrid run of passengers which have fil[l]ed up my cabin & left me no room to do any thing.

Just now I am having a little rest waiting for the Supply Str *Union* to come down the coast. When she has gone I shall probably unless something new turns up, go off on a cruise down the coast to look after Blockade Runners[.] I hope I may catch some, dont you?

Mr West my Pilot has just moved his family down here onto one of the Keys near the Bark & is very busy getting them housed in. I hope he will get them all comfortable before we have to go away. I have been on shore all the afternoon with some of my men lending him a hand. They make houses here out of Palmetto leaves[.] They are very picturesque, & quite comfortable too, in this climate & when made properly as *we* are making this one, dont leak at all. I think it would shock a Northern house carpenter tho' to see such a house go up.

The musquitoes are still very bad here tho' not quite so troublesome as they were a month ago, but they a[re] buzzing round my head pretty thick now I notice.

I am beginning to get used to my new position now, & am very well satisfied with it, for I find more variety& excitement here than on the Bark. Still I would rather be some where in more active service than I can find on the coast of Florida.

I will enclose you one of my Photographs for Ria Bond[.] Please give my love to her, (I suppose thats proper as she's my cousin) & tell her I want one of hers in return. (There is no sort of need of telling her that I've got *one* already you know.) I want a vignette if I can get one but will take any that I can get. I wish I had a better one of Cousin Sophy too.

I believe I have received all you have sent. Your own included. I want one of those full face Proofs. if you have got one *Send it on*. I like that over the left, Photo of Eliza better now than I did at first it grows on one[.] but still I think she's good looking (no, I mean handsome) enough to have a better picture than that floating round, dont you?

What a rampage the family have been on this summer. I can hardly keep track of you all. I suppose you are settled down quietly for the winter by this time. How did you enjoy your visit to Portland?

I cant write any more to night. I'se sleepy. Love to all. How's Bennie now[?] I hope Grandpa is better by this time.

Good night. I will try & write a longer letter next time.

From your loving Brother
Henry

U.S. Sloop *Rosalie*
Estero Inlet
Oct 12th 1864

Dear La La [Eliza]

I have been owing you a letter for some time but realy since I have been in command of this vessel I have had very little time for writing.

Daytimes I am nearly always busy & evenings, well, any one that has endurance enough to sit down to write with 10 million musquitoes flying round his head goes a notch beyond me, that [is] all I can say.

The musquito season is pretty nearly over now however I am thankful to say. We had our first *norther* a few days ago, & after they set in the rascals soon leave.

I am off on a cruise now (away) & I am glad enough to get away from the old Bark. I shan't go back as long as we have a mouthful to eat on board thats certain.

I left Charlotts Harbor four days ago & took a load of Refugees to Ft. Myers with permission after landing them to go on a cruise down the coast. I was detained two days at the Fort by an accident but I am now fairly started and on my ground. To day I am laying in Estero [Bay] and my boat is off in charge of Mr. West overhauling all the Lagoons & Bays with which the place abounds. If we find nothing (& I hardly expect we shall here) I shall try the next Inlet & so on down to Cape Romano where I think my best chance lies. Now if you look at the map you can see just where I am or rather where I was for by the time you get this letter I shall probably be some where else.

I am much better satisfied here than I was on board the "*Jim* of the *Say*" as there is more variety & excitement (tho precious little of the latter.) The only unsatisfactory feature is the precarious tenure of my appointment. Capt Coffin is still on board the Bark. he has been well for some time & on duty there.

My orders here were only of a temporary nature, tho' I was given to understand that I should be kept on the Sloop, but at that time Mr. C[offin] expected to go home. whether he can, if he wants to, resume the command here, is a fact of which at present I am in a delightful state of uncertainty. Tho' I dont believe he can as I know that my being sent here was approved of from Head Quarters.

If he can get back I think he will want to however, as the Bark is not a very comfortable residence since Capt Rockwell left, the officers tell me. Capt L[einas] is a little too much inclined towards the "Flowing Bowl" to command respect from those under his orders & at the same time a little inclined to tyrannical occasionally. Well, well, if I do have to go back I shall have had a pleasant vacation at all events.

I received the Box all right. The cake was very nice. I did not eat much of it tho'[.] I was just leaving for Ft Myers when it came (not this last trip) so I left half of it in the old mess & took the rest along. When we got up there I took what was left, a nice handsome piece, up to Capt Crain's & gave it to his daughters. They were delighted with it & had never seen any thing like it before. I enjoy calling on that family very much, they are far superior to the general run of the people here & are very well educated—for Florida. Captain C. is a Northern man but his children have never been out of this State I believe. His oldest daughter married Act Ensign Jenks, who formerly belonged to the Bark but left shortly after I joined. She is staying at her fathers & is a very pleasant young lady. Plays the Guitar & sings when she is asked (with out being coaxed), & very well too.

I like to go to the Ft. just to hear her sing. She was sick this last time, so I missed the music but I sent her some Peaches & Jelly & when I came away she told me that the next time I came she would sing to me as much as I wanted[.] I think she would get tired first tho'. It is getting to be the fashion for officers to get married down here. Dont you tremble for me? Immagine me coming home with a wife that can't read or write & smokes a pipe, can swear a dead shot at 180 yards & dont care for man or D—l. There are several officer[s] here that are so mated, one of them (I blush to say it) is a Mass. man too, Lt. Ames 2nd Col[ored]. Regt. U.S.V[olunteers]. a Capt also in the same Regt. (Bartholt) is worse off than he.[7] Their Surgeon too, but he is a lucky man for his wife has another husband living. Nearly all the women that I've seen round these parts smoke. None of the Crains tho, they are a different stamp.

I had a nice old Lady among my passengers last trip named Duke, from Tampa[.] She was between 60 & 70 years old but came thro' the lines all by her self. She is on her way to Key West to join some of her children who are there. I took good care of her & kept her in the cabin. she is a friend of the Crains so when we got to the Ft I carried her to their house. She was very grateful for what she call[ed] my kindness (tho' a man must be a brute who would do less for a poor lone woman like her) & said she should remember & pray for me as long as she lived. Item—she is a Baptist, but thinks my Hymn Book the nicest one she ever saw. I like her very much & if I go to Key West shall certainly hunt her up.

I have been engaged in house building lately. Mr. West removed his family to Charlotts Harbor, & we built him a house for them in Arnolds Bay. It was (like Solomons Temple) built with out the sound of a hammer, with poles & palmetto leaves, roof & all & is as tight as a drum. How should you like to live in a house like that?

Mrs West is a nice sort of woman, but entirely with out education & tho' I have never seen her do it, I strongly suspect that she smokes. She is better than they average tho for all that & can out ride & out-shoot a great many men who think themselves smart at those things.

Well I wont write any more now. perhaps tho' I may add a line before I send this off to let you know the results of my cruise if there are any.

Love to all the family[.] How is Grandfather now? better I hope.

Write me when ever you have time[.] I dont think any body else's letters make up for yours (or yours for any one else).

From your loving Brother
H.W. Wells

No. 3.
U.S. Sloop *Rosalie*
Malco Inlet Fla[8]
Oct. 17th 1864

Dear Mother

I am afraid you will think that I neglect you at home by writing so seldom, but it seems useless to write when there is no chance of a chance to send letters. Two or three weeks ago the Admiral sent word round to the Squadron [that] all vessels must make out requisitions for every thing that they required to last them until the 1st of Jan. 1865 as there would be no more direct communication with Key West until that time on account of the Supply Str *Honduras* having broke down. That looks encouraging for us dont it? However we shall not be quite so bad off as that I think as the Tenders go there occasionaly & when they do they bring mails.

I am in hopes that I may be sent there myself soon if I stay in the Sloop, as she needs repairs very badly which she can not get any where else & I think Capt. Leinas will send her.

I have been away from the Bark about 10 days now on a cruise. I shall have to go back soon now as my provisions are nearly out. I was in hopes to take something back with me in the way of a Prize but have found nothing as yet. it is most too early in fact for the small Blockade Runners. During the summer there are to[o] many calms & heavy squalls for them to do much & so it is only during the winter when they are sure of good winds that they do much business.

I like my new position quite well tho' I get a little lonesome at times. I hope soon to get another officer when (if he is any account,[)] I think it will be pleasanter. I have got a pretty good crew & they seem to try to give me satisfaction in return for which I make them as comfortable as possable. Yesterday (Sunday), I carried out for the first time what I have always said I would do when I got command of a vessel, that is, I had service. In the morning I called them all aft & told them that it would please me very much to read a chapter in the Bible etc. to them every Sunday if they would like to listen to it. I told them that of course I should not force them to attend that they could suit themselves, but that I thought I should not be doing my duty if I let the day pass with out doing something to remind them what it was.

Several of them are Catholic's & seem afraid at first that I wanted to convert them. but I told them that that was not my object & that I did not think the Bible would hurt them. so they all concluded it would be a good thing I believe. At all events when the proper time came & I passed the word for all who wished to hear, to lay aft, every one of them came. I read to them the Morning Exercise out of the Hymn Book[,] the Lord's Prayer, then two chapters from

Matthew (VII and VIII) & closed by reading the first Prayer in the Hymn Book. I thought I would not make it too long at first & besides I had a cold & could not read very well.

You can't tell what a deal of comfort I take out of my Hymn Book, & that Book of Sermons. I take it up & open it any where. I find I can't go amis[s]. There is something good in every page. I dont know hardly which of the Sermons I like the best they are all so good.

Every one who sees the Hymn Book seems to take a fancy to it. Last eve Mr West, my Pilot, said he liked it best of all the Books I had, & wanted to know if I could not get him one. He said his wife could not read & he wanted it to read to her. The Bible is too hard for him to read out loud. he says he breaks down too often on hard words but the Hymn Book he thinks he can manage better. I wish you would mail me one[.] I think it would be put to a good use. Send one that is neatly bound & I will make him a present of it.

Oct. 19th. Something or rather, called me off & so I put this letter by intending to finish it yesterday, but I had my hands full of work all day & not a little anxiety too for it was blowing like smoke & the *Rosalie* dragged her anchors & got ashore. I succeeded in getting off however with out any serious damage & its all right now. I intend to leave her[e] for the Bark as soon as the tide turns, as if I dont the Boys wont have any thing to eat, which I suppose they would hardly like. I have been laying here in this Inlet (which is a sort of Rendevous for Blockade Runners) for three or four days hoping to get hold of some of the fellows going up or down, but with no success but Better luck next time Perhaps.

It is a great place for game here & a day or two ago I shot an Alligator with a Rifle. he was about 12 ft. long (as a rough guess. I did not go near him but once & then I left double quick for he smelt so strong of musk that it made me sick.)

The hot weather is very nearly over now & the musquitoes are beginning to leave which is a blessing[.] if it was not for them & the sand flies this country would realy be quite attractive. The soil is good & one can raise all sorts of fruit & vegetables. the woods are full of game the waters with fish & there is any amount of wild fowl along the coast in the Bays & Lagoons but Tho every Prospect pleases and only *musquitoes is* vile. I should not like to live here, for if I had quoted that line properly I should not have come far from the truth for these "Crackers" as they call the people who live here out side of the towns are the most lazy ignorant miserable good for nothing etc. etc. etc. etc. etc. etc. etc. specimens of humanity that I ever came across. The women are bad enough & (most of them) smoke & sware as well as their husbands, but they do all the work both in the house (that dont amount to much a good New England farmer would not let his cattle live in as dirty a stall as they do.) & out. The Question as to who is the best woman here is the one that can hunt Cattle best (on horse back thro' the woods) & till the most land. The men are too lazy to do any thing but hunt & drink whiskey.

They are all Gentlemen & Ladies however oh, yes, I have insulted several by calling them men & women when they have been passenger[s] on board. "Capt. this Lady wants so & so" I look round & see a woman all ragged dirty as a pig & perhaps smoking a pipe. "This woman, do you mean." "That lady sir."

One of the women will ask up the hatch for her husband. "Which is he" "That Gentleman over there?" That man—oh language is not full enough to describe them. I wont attempt it.

The tide is turning so I must go on deck. Good by, love to all. How is Grandpa now [missing text] improving. He has had quite a siege of it has he not. Give my best love to him. I hope Ruthie will brave her Photograph taken soon I want it badly. How did Aunt Ruth like her of course she did who could help it. but what did she say when she found it was named for her. & where is she & Uncle E now. Give my love to them when you write.

No more at present from your loving son

Henry

(No 4)
U.S. Sloop *Rosalie*
Key West Fla.
Oct 30th 1864

Dear Mother

Since I wrote you last I have been very sick, but am better now I'm happy to say. I was taken very suddenly while I was on that cruise (by the way I did capture a prize after all) & thought at first that I had got the Yellow Fever as my symptoms seemed to indicate it. When I got to the Bark the Surgeon took me in charge. He called my sickness Remittent Billious Fever, that was on Saturday.[9] On Tuesday the *R*[*osalie*] had to leave to tow the Prize (of which more by and by) to Key West & as I was bound to go I was carried on board.[10] I was quite sick all the time & had to keep my berth most of the way. I had a Masters Mate with me however to do my work for me.

I have been trying here to get them to send me home but they can't see it in that light.

I am certainly not fit for this sort of work & for that matter I am not sure that I am fit for the service at all now.

I get quite blue thinking about it sometimes, the least thing upsets me now, & I dont like to look forward at all, for unless I can get a great deal stronger I dont know what I am going to be fit for, certainly not for sea life.

I have not seen much fighting this war but it has used me up worse than some who have.

Perhaps a good long quiet time at home may build me up again but I can't hope for that until we have peace again if ever that happy time comes.

About that prize, it did not amount to much being only a Sloop Boat with two men on board. The *name* of the thing tho' it [is] something. The men were both known in Key West as Blockade Runners.

I have received lots of letters & papers lately & I will answer them all in due season[.] I dont feel able tho' to do much writing now.

Tell Lu not to think that I have forgotten her because I dont write for "Taint so."

By the way what was it about Willie Lovetts escape & John Thaxter's death? you said Lu would tell about it in her letter but I do not find it.

About the Army & Navy Journal I like to have it very much you can see I am alone now & have to depend on my own services for reading etc. but dont sent it if it inconviences you in any way to do so.

Bennie shall sertainly have my cabinet & I will try & help him to fill it up but dont you think I had better wait & give it to him for a birthday present? I suppose he will be very impatient to take possession otherwise I should propose his waiting until I got home as I am afraid the process of seperation of my things from Joes will give you a great deal of trouble. Does he care about the coins? Give it all to him in a "Pleasant Way" from Brother Henry.

I'll tell you about sinking & raising vessels another time. Good by now. excuse my making this letter so short but I dont feel up to writing a very long one. Mr. Coffin is going home.

Give my love to all the family from your ever loving One

Henry

(No. 5)
U. S. Sloop *Rosalie*
Charlotte Harbor Fla.
Nov. 11th 1864

Dear Mother

I am very sorry you should be disapointed in not getting a good long letter from me by this mail, but I have been so soured about & filled with passengers ever since I left Key West that I realy have not been able to find time. I have just arrived here from Tampa Bay & leave at once for Ft Myers. before I can get back the *Union* will be gone so I shall miss the mail but you shall at least have a line to let you know that I am well again.

We are all in a nice mess[.] The U.S. Supply Str *Union* went by here with out our seeing her tho she laid off the buoy & made signals for *four* hours (a nice mess for Capt Leinas for he has been drunk ever since he took command pretty much so I do not feel very sorry for *him*) I was at once despatched to Tampa to try & *catch* her (a sloop after a Steamer!) Of course I didn't, but I found Capt Rockwell there & was glad enough to see him[.] he has got command of the *Hendrick*

Hudson one of the finest steamers in this squadron, a vessel very much like the *Cambridge* only a better vessel.[11] I will send you a picture of her, one day. When Capt. R found he was ordered to her the first thing he did was to apply for me to be sent there too. Perhaps I did not feel a little proud that he should have thought enough of me to do so! and then again perhaps I did.

I should like to go to that vessel very much as I think her one of the most desirable in the squadron[.] as for *R*, I am hardly strong enough for this service tho' I may manage to get along well enough. I have got lots to write about but no time to do it in. I ought to be on deck now as there is work going on which wants an officer to look out for it. & I am alone on board at present. My M.[aster's] Mate being (by the way I have got one now) being sick on the Bark & Mr West ashore with his family for I always let him go when I first get in & let him stay until the last minute.

My church servic[e] goes on nicely. I have lots to tell you about it.

Capt. Leinas is to be relieved from command of the Bark by A.V. Lt. Geo Taylor. We are all very glad.

I enclose you a Photo of Capt. Rockwell, a good likeness but poor picture. Good by love to all, in great haste from your loving son

Henry

I hope you will be able to read this scrawl. H.

Send me out two or three of my Photos. have some new struck off if necessary.

(No. 6)
U.S. Sloop *Rosalie*
Nov. 20th 1864

Dear Mother

It is some time since I have written you a good long letter & my last one especialy was hardly worthy of the name, but I mean to try this time to redeem my credit unless something turns up to prevent.

I have had a very busy time of it for some time past, always on the move. I dont dislike it on the whole tho I would like a *little* rest. it is much pleasenter than rusting on board the Old Bark at all events.

Let me see, (i.e. look at my journal) when I wrote my last letter (No. 4. for I dont count No 5 as worthy of the name. (excuse the repetition.) I was in Key West with my Prize. I left there the day after & returned to Charlotts Harbor[.] I had a jolly time on the return trip having got pretty well over my sickness, which by the way was pretty severe while it lasted, & having two passengers on board an Ensign & Masters Mate named Trask & Andrews, who were ordered to the *Gem of the Seas*.[12] They were both good company but I liked "A" the best.

I arrived at the Bark on the 3rd of Nov. in the morning & in the afternoon started off on an expedition with two of the Barks boats in tow, the whole commanded by Capt "L"[.] I will not give you the details of that affair, the less said about it the better. The captain was drunk all the time. we had very bad weather & came very near losing the Sloop, but of course accomplished nothing, except badly damaging my vessel, for which I was not much obliged to the Captain. I hope I may never have to have him on board again. We got back from that affair on the 5th & I had plenty to do repairing damages.

On the 7th the Supply Str. *Union* came & laid off the buoy for 4 hours without any boats being sent out, when the Capt. of the *U*[*nion*] got angry & went off with out leaving us any fresh provisions or mail. There were various excuses for it but *I* think *whiskey* was the main cause of the *Union* not being recognized.

As soon as she was gone I was ordered to take the Paymaster on board & proceed at once to Tampa Bay with despatch to try & catch her there. (which I did not succeed in doing). On our arrival there we found Capt Rockwell had come down in the *Union* & been ordered to the Command of the *Hendrick Hudson* one of the finest Gunboats in this Squadron. He seemed very glad to see Pay[master] & I, & we had a jolly time as long as we were there.

I like Paymaster Colby very much. he is my 'special friend on the *Gem*. I hope some day that I shall have the pleasure of introducing him to you.[13]

We got back to Charlotts Harbor on the 11th & I had hardly anchored before I received orders to go to Ft Myers & bring down Mrs. Jenks[,] her husband having sent for her to come north to him on the *Union*. So off I went. I hurried all I could & got back just in the nick of time for when I arrived I found the *Union* off the buoy & I went right out without communicating with the Bark at all except by signal. Mrs Jenks just saved her passage & that was all.

As soon as I got back to the ship I was ordered to take the Paymaster on board again & go to Key West with dispatches, & I left that night. We had a pretty rough time going down & I lost my boat.

Before I went however I had a row with Mr Bliss & would have had a fight if I had not worn a uniform, probably. He & the Capt. both came on board tight just before we left & Mr. B seemed determined to have trouble with some one. He commenced on Mr West my Pilot but I thought if he must have a quarrel it had better be with an equal (in rank: I dont look upon him in that light, on any other terms) where it would not be altogether an onesided game, than with one who could not take his own part on account of his position. So I *took it up*.

After a while Capt "L" joined in and told Mr "B" to shut up as he was to blame. Whereupon Mr. B commenced abusing him & they kept it up until they left both too drunk to know what fools they were making of themselves.

My lines have indeed fallen in pleasent places dont you think so? I am thankful that I am in the Tender any how.

We only stopped in Key West one day. I have received several letters & papers[.] I got one by the last mail dated Aug 9th (Papers I mean) but most of them came thro' pretty well. I also received Mr Everets speach.[14]

We are on our way back now & almost to Charlotts Harbor. I wonder where I shall be off for next? I dont care so I'm away from there.

I hope you received my letter (No. 5.) as it contained a Photo of Capt. Rockwell. No 4 had one of the Key West ruins.

Well, now dont you think I have some excuse for not having written a great deal of late? Driven round the way I have been I could not seem to get a quiet moment in which to write especialy when I have passengers on board. I am afraid poor Lu will feel neglected for I have two of her letters now unanswered[.] She has been a real good girl to write to me so often.

Our accounts of the Election all seem to be so favorable that we are beginning to feel very easy as to Mr Lincolns reelection. Thank God for it for the fate of the Country seems to hang on that issue. You of course *know* now what the result has been. I wish we did the suspense is not pleasant at all.

Please tell Bennie that all the Eggs I have been able to get are, three Pellican's & three Curlew's, but that I guess I shall be able to bring him home some pretty shells.

By the way have you any use for Buck Skin. I have got four of them & can get more. Nice for silver & *such*.

I will enclose you another Photo of Key West.

I cant write any more now as it is most supper time. So good by Give my love to all the family & friends.

From your loving son
Henry

I wish Father would let me know how I stand with him in regard to money. I can't keep my account book strait with out knowing.

(No 7)
U.S. Sloop *Rosalie*
Key West Fla
Dec. 7th 1864

Dear Mother

You must excuse me for letting such long intervals come between my letters but realy I dont have much time that I *can* write & then it is *so* hot.

I am here in Key West again, for repairs this time & I rather guess this will be the last letter you will receive from the *Rosalie* as I think she will go out of commission or rather be converted into a Guard Vessel. However it will be a good thing for me I think for I am expecting in that event to get a better command, the

Schr *Annie*, tho I may not succeed.[15] They intend to transfer me with my entire crew to her, but may change their minds. I hope they will do it. it would suit me first rate. The *A*[*nnie*] is larger than the *Rosa* & will, or should, carry more men.

The cause of my coming here, was that in a gale I lost my Center Board (no blame to be attached to the Commander.) which of course disabled the vessel & rendered repairs absolutely necessary. On my way here I met General Newton & happened to be able to do him a favor.[16] he was on the Str *Nightingale* & in return he gave me a tow down so I killed two birds with one stone, made a friend of the General, & a quick passage down.

I would have written on my way down but I had ten passengers & so no come [time] to do any thing. Such is life. I want to write you a good long letter, all between you & I cofindential you know but I cant get settled down to it some how. it will come tho' one of these days but I dont know as you will be very glad to get it.

I received your letters of the 27th ult. this morning (No 4) & also No 3 when I first arrived. The book has not come thro' yet.

I am glad you got the Photo of Capt. "R[ockwell]". How do you like it? I am going to send you one this time that my crew made me a present of a day or two since. You will then see what sort of a looking set of men I'm with. Bishop is the Quartermaster. He is a Live Yankee & Jack at all Trades. I dont know any thing that he can't do. He is my right hand man. Maddocks is the Q[uarte]r Gunner, & a good steady man[.] Seely is a good man tho when on the bark he used to be thought a very sour dispositioned fellow[.] *I* never have any trouble with him tho'. Nelson Brown and Jammo are all good men enough with out any very positive character either way[.] Plume the cook is a very nice man & I like him very much. & lastly McGady, a pretty good sort of a boy on the whole, *tho* he *did* break my "monkey" (a kind of water pitcher) this morning.[17] He dont seem to take it much to heart tho' by the way. These boys are horrid careless. did I tell you that one of them in emptying a bucket of dirty water threw my silver fork & three plated ones overboard? well he did, but came aft to tell me, so frightened that I had not the heart to growl at him. I expect he thought I'd heave him overboard after them.

My service goes nicely, with the help of Bishop (who among his other accomplishments can sing very well & *has* led a church choir.) we have added singing to our worship which makes it much pleasanter. I intend when I get them a little more interested (if I succeed in doing so) to read them short services[.] At present I am trying to put a stop to swearing on board[.] The Articles of War prohibit it but I dont think I shall require their help. The men, I know respect me enough to try & please me & I dont hear an oath very often now.

I will write again in a few days to let you know what success I have in regard to change of vessel[.] The *Gem of the Seas* is going to be relieved from Charlotts Harbor in a short time & the Bark *Restless* will take her place.[18] My address will have to be changed but I will let you know in time about it. I cant write any more now it is too hot[.] Good by love to all, from your own

Henry

Tell Lu darling that I am ashamed of my self for not having written her but will try to make it up with her soon. We did not do any thing on Thanksgiving day because we did not know any thing about when it was until it was over, but I've been Thanksgiving ever since I have heard of Lincoln's reelection.[19] God bless him & help him to carry the country thro' this struggle. I dont think it will last much longer. I am very sorry to hear such poor accounts of Grandfathers health. Give my best Love to him.

U.S. Sloop *Rosalie*
On Key West Fla
Dec 8th 1864

Dear Luie [Louisa]

I must write you a few lines to day tho I dont intend to send the letter off at once, but I realy am ashamed to let the date between your letter & mine go on increasing any more. Now you see I'm safe, for there's [drawing of finger pointing] the date & I can keep the letter back as long as I please & lay it all on Poor "Uncle Sam". Aint that a good idea & a very moral one?

It is too bad to have let your letters go so long unanswered for you have been a dear good girl & have written me such nice long ones, but I have had honestly, very little chance to write of late & when I could have done so, why I had not *spunk* enough—there!

I've been rather blue of late tho' I dont know as I have had any 'special reason for it. My health has been very fair since I got over my last fit of sickness (in October) except that about three weeks ago I strained my chest badly & could not lay down for several nights, & breath[e], with any kind of comfort. in fact for over two nights I had to resort to artificial means to get to sleep at all.

For the last few days I have been writing like a race horse, a whole three months log! I only got the book a short time ago & as the vessel will probably be taken away from me I had to have it ready to turn over.

I am in hopes that I shall be able to get charge of a schr that is laying here called the *Annie*. She is larger than the *Rosalie* & tho' she can not be called a "Sloop of War" she will also escape being called a "Serving Mallet" which is a very mortifying appel[l]ation for one's vessel.

I intend to keep this letter back until the matter is decided so that you may know & I think I shall have to change my address at the same time as the *Gem of the Seas* will probably be relieved from Charlotts Harbor.

The *R*[*osalie*] is now on the Marine Rail Way (hence the heading of this letter), getting repaired sufficiently to relieve the *Annie* who is doing guard duty here. We shall probably be launched Monday, when I shall find out sertainly what is to be done with your humble Servant.

I think I wont come home this winter as you are not going to be there. Aint that good of me? 'specialy as I could not come any way. It is dangerous to apply for leave unless one has been out two years & it will be a long time before I'm thus qualified, but then perhaps the war will be over by that time & then that will be Glorious & I'll come home for a good long visit. You must be sure & write to me when you are out West. I shall depend on hearing very often, all about it.

Annie Dec 16th 1864
Well I've got the *Annie* at last, and am fitting her out. but I dont feel quite sure yet that I shall keep her for our Fleet Captain is as cross as a Bear & seems to have taken a 'special dislike to poor me. He says I want more for my vessel than all the rest of the Tenders put to gether, with out taking into consideration that I am fitting a vessel out new & *of course* want a complete out-fit. I am getting out of patience & dont care much now whether I keep her or not tho' she is a nice little vessel, larger & better than the *Rosalie*. I can't tell tho how she will behave in a sea way yet.

I am getting tired enough of Key West and shall be glad enough to get away from it. It's an awful expensive place to be in & one gets no satisfaction for money spent either. By the way talking of money draw as much as you want from my funds at home to get both Mother & Father a handsome Christmas present—dont be afraid of it—I would send money but I'm hard up at present & the Paymaster way up at Charlotts Harbor!

I received your letter Dec 4th this morning & was glad enough to see your hand writing again tho' I know I did not deserve it for neglecting you so much of late. I hope you will get this letter before you leave for the West, so as not to carry away any hard feelings against your absent Brother. I know you are *so* apt to bear malice!

The next time you write you must tell me all about the wedding[.] I shall want to hear all the particulars.

Good! one of my friends has just come on board & tells me that news has arrived from Rebel sources that Sherman is in Savannah. If its true! How are you Secesh?[20]

I hope Mother received my last letter. I enclosed a Photograph of my crew in it. I will send you one of my Cabin Boy Hugh McGady a pretty good boy in the main, & tries to do the best he knows how.

Every thing is all in a mess on board here now[.] I got the masts in last night & now we are painting fitting rigging etc. I can't settle my Self down to writing with any kind of satisfaction.

There I'm not going to write any more. *SO.*

My address will be same as before—*almost.* Act. Ensign H W Wells U.S. Schr *Annie* Key West Fla.

Good by Love to all the family. Poor Grandpa I am sorry to hear such sad news of him. Give him my best love. I wish I was at home to help you take care of him.

Be sure & write to me from the West.

From your loving Brother
Henry

Marginalia—Excuse the dirty spot

(No 8.)
U.S. Schr. *Annie*
Key West Fla
Dec 20th 1864

Dear Mother

I received three letters from home Sunday & tho' they were all rather old still they were none the less welcome. One of them, was from you (Nov 14th) one from Eliza & the other from Lu.

I also received the Hymn Book all right, & a whole arm full of newspapers, etc.

I wrote Lu a long letter a few days ago which I hope she has seed by this time.

I am still here in Key West getting the *Annie* fitted out. its tedious work & I am tired enough of it. shain't be at all sorry to go back on the Blockade. We have all been detached from the *Gem of the Seas* & the *Annie* is now Tender to the U.S. Bark *Restless* Act. Master Carter Comdg.[21] Captain "C" used to command the Tender & I hope he will remember his old feelings & give me a chance to do something. My station will still be the same as the "*R*" will relieve the *Gem*, as soon as she completes her repairs. She is here in Key West.

I like my new vessel very much & expect to be much more comfortable in her than I was on board the *Rosalie*[,] Tho I have a kind of affection for her too.

The accommodations are much better for both the men & my-self here. My cabin is quite a nice one.

The vessel has quite a reputation for speed but I shall know more about that when I have tried her. I dont like to take other peoples word for every thing. She ought to sail tho, with such a model as she has got & if she dont I shall be greatly disapointed.

There! I guess I wont write any more about her now or you will think I am infatuated. I think her name is pretty tho', dont you?

In future my letters must be directed either to this vessel or the *Restless*, it dont make any difference which.

I am very glad to hear the Sailors Fair was such a success. did I ever tell you that we raised quite a sum on board the *G of the S* towards it?

I am glad Grandpa voted at the Election. I was afraid he would not be able to. I wish I could have been home to have put in my vote. It would *not* have been a Copperhead one, some peoples opinion to the contrary notwithstanding[.]

Some of the States allowed their soldiers & sailors in the field to vote but I did not see any notice that Mass. did so. I think it was hardly fair not to give us all a chance, even tho' our glorious old State did not want any help to go in on the right side & win. I tell you what I am proud of my State & always like to have any one ask me what part of the country I belong to. I am getting sufficiently reformed too to hail as an abolishinest, tho' I am not by a long way up to Phillips and Garrisons mark yet & dont ever expect to be.[22] S[t]ill I think slavery a great moral wrong & one too, that must cease to exist before the Rebels can have any peace or be allowed to come back into the *family*.

I will try & write again before I leave here until then good by. Love to all the family

From your loving son
Henry

Capt Welch is going home. I send you a Photo of his office—upstairs—below is a Book Store as you might suppose by the style of Painting

U.S. Schr *Annie*
Key West Fla
Dec 25th 1864

Dear Mother

Christmas Day is about over but I can't let it go by with out writing you afew lines for I've felt real homesick all day, thinking of my last Christmas, at home & this one. The contrast is enough to make any one feel so I'm sure.

I've got "no one to love me" here & none to wish me the hearty old "Merry Christmas" tho' after all it would be like mockery to do it for there is not much chance for a stranger to have one here any way.

It has been a long & dreary day & I shall be glad to go to sleep & forget it.

It does seem as tho I have spent very few Christmas's at home since I can remember, but I suppose it is ungreateful for me to complain now as the two last ones found me there.

I am getting rather blue of late. I dont know what has come over me. Every thing has been going very well with me & there does not seem to be any reason for it, but I can't help it some-how[.] I have been meaning to write you a regular blue-book of a letter but on the whole I guess I wont at least not at present[.]

I'll see if I can't get to feeling better with out troubling you with my troubles first.

I expect to leave here in about three days. I shall be glad enough to go for I am sick & tired of this place & don't care if I never see it again.

I expect Capt. L[einas] wont like it much that I have got away from him, but I am very well satisfied my self with the change. I never thought much of him as a commander.

We hear vague rumors that Sherman is in Savannah[.] I hope its so! Hurrah *for him*!

Seems to me every thing looks very bright as regards war matters just now. I am surpprised tho' that Gold should keep up so tho'. I thought the Election would send it down.

I wrote you a letter three or four days ago so I have not much to tell you about. By I have received two of my Photographs.

I hope Eliza has got over that accident[.] It is a wonder neither of them was seriously hurt. I'm glad Lu showed so much presence of mind[.] It always provokes me to see folks get frightened & not know what they are about. Give her a kiss for me for *holding on*. Wont Ruthie have some Photos before long? I hope when she does she will have one in the *Post Office* for me.

I hope you will excuse my short letters of late you know I've not had much time for writing. Hope Bennie will enjoy his Cabinet.

Give my love to Grandpa & all the family. I hope Father will send me a statement of my money affairs soon so I can commence in fair, with the new year[.]

Good by from your loving son

Henry

U.S.Schr *Annie*
Key West Fla
Dec 28th 1864

Dear La La

I have received two letters from you within the last few days so I think I had better hurry up & write you before another one comes along.

I warn you before hand tho' that you wont get a long one from me to night. Cause why—cause I dont feel in a *writable* humor. I'm mad. I am, having lost mislaid or otherwise, something that I would not have had disapear for a good deal. I've been jumping round & I'm afraid swarring a little for the last half hour. So you may think my mind is not in a very placid state. I would not touch a pen on any terms if it were not for the fact that I shall probably leave here tomorrow or next day & so not have another chance.

I have been under orders since Monday night to go to Havana as soon as I could get ready for the mail, but I dont believe I shall go as a Steamer has got in that will probably be sent instead.

I would like to have gone very well but its horrid '*spensive* buying gold at present rates & spending it. So I am satisfied either way.

I have given up all idea of going to the *Hendrick Hudson* in fact I dont want to now for I like my new vessel very much tho' I dont like to say too much until I have tried her at sea. She has got very heavy masts & may prove crank[.] She *must* sail tho'. The Pilot is afraid of her, but I laugh at him, he thinks there is nothing in the world equal to the *Rosalie*.

I shall be glad enough to turn my back on this Key its a mean place & I'm sick of it.

How do you like the Photos that I send home? I think some of them are very pretty. I'll send you one or two this time.

It will be nice to have them to go in the Books along with the White Mountain views etc. I've got some of Havana too. Mind I dont give up *all* claim to them they must be kind of family property you know. I received a letter from Mother to day (Dec 18) enclosing another of my Photos (3 Recd). I hope you have taken enough of my money at home to make up my full share of the Presents to Mother & Father[.]

I wish also that you would take $10. & get some thing for your self & Lu (thats $5. apiece) as a New Year's present from me[.] I ought to have thought of it before but have been so drove of late that I have not had a chance to think of any thing. "Better late than never" tho.

Lots of love to Grandpa & all the family. Do write a little oftener than you have since I have been away. I like to hear from you ever so much.

Good by From your loving brother

"Roberto Lincoln"

Dont let 'em tear the old House down. I suppose Lu has gone by this time. My prize money will amount to about $0.001

How are you – Read?

Henry

9

"It Is with Feelings of Sadness"

The Death of Henry Wells

On Board of U.S. Bark *Gem of the Seas*
Key West Florida
January 29th 1865

Dear Sir

It is with feelings of sadness that I write to you informing you of the probable loss of the Schr *Anne*, tender to this vessel, with all on board. I do not know that I am doing aright in writing to you at present, but I will give to you the particulars of the case as far as known, in order that you may be prepared to hear the worst. The *Anne*, commanded by your son, was whilst at Key West attached to the *Restless* but the *R[estless]* not being ready to go to C[harlottes] Harbor the *A[nne]* was transferred to this vessel and sent up. The *Anne* sailed from Key West on the 29th day of December and on the 16th of January the *Restless* arrived at Charlotte[s] Harbor. Upon the arrival of the *R[estless]* Capt Carter inquired for the *Anne*.[1] We told him that we had not seen her. From that time our doubts arose as to her whereabouts. On the 20th of January while at C[harlottes] Harbor we received news from a military post, near to us, that the U.S. Schr *Matchless* had passed the day previous, a sunken schooner off Cape Romain with mainmast broken resembling the *Anne*. The only hope that we have that any one was saved is in that the Capt of the *M[atchless]* says that he saw a fire on shore and that it might have been made by the survivors. The day that the news was received at C[harlottes] H[arbor], Capt Carter sent a boat to discover the wreck and ascertain if possible the fate of the officers and crew. We were unable to hear anything further as we sailed on the 21st for this port arriving here on the 25th. Upon our arrival from C[harlottes] H[arbor] at this place we ascertained that nothing was known about the *A[nne.]*

There are now two schooners in this port bound up to find and raise the wreck if possible. They have not as yet gone on account of a heavy gale from the Northward. It is my intention to start for the North in three or four days but should I hear anything further I shall inform you, in the meantime, immediately.

We all hope and trust that your son is not lost but we have serious doubts. He was endeared to us all by his kind, gentlemanly and generous manners and as a messmate, I can testify there was no superior. The country has probably lost a brave and patriotic officer and you a worthy son.

Resp. Yours
Samuel T. Bliss
Act Ensign US Bark *G of the Seas*

To
Thomas G. Wells Esq.
Brookline
Mass.

Office of the Prize Commissioners,
Key West, Fla.
March 5th 1865.
Thomas G. Wells Esq
Brookline Mass.

Dear Sir,

I have to acknowledge the receipt last evening, on my return from Pensacola, of a letter from Mrs E.S. Wells of 10th ultimo, in relation to the loss of the U.S. Schr *Annie*, commanded by your son, Henry W. Wells, and have to inform you, that the U.S. Steamer *Henrick Hudson*, Actg. Vol. Lieut C.H. Rockwell Commandg, arrived here about the 19th ult, from off St. Marks, and Captain Rockwell informed me, that on his way, he fell in with the wreck of the *Annie*, her masts heads, just above water, that he got a rope or hawser fast, and hove her to the surface, and after a careful examination of the hull, he came to the conclusion, that she was blown up, as the port side fore and aft was blown out, he thinks by her magazine exploding, but of course, he dont know the fate of the unfortunate crew, but if they took to the Boats, they must have landed in the Enemys Country.

I have recently visited all the Blockading vessels, from Charlottes harbor, to Pensacola, and each way, inquired of all, if any thing had been heard from the crew, as knowing he was your son, and feeling an interest in him, believing him a good officer, and worthy young man, so much so, I had intended to use my influence with Admiral C.K. Stribling, when he came here again, to get him another stripe, as he undouted himself becoming an officer.[2]

While the *Annie*, was being fitted, Henry often came to see me, and the day before he sailed hence, I gave him such advice, if followed, he certainly would have been promoted.

Capt Leinas, would not have known much about the fate of the vessel, when he sailed for home.

You have, my friends, my heart felt sympathy, should any thing further be heard of his fate, I will write you.

and am most truly
your obdt friend
R.W. Welch[3]

P.S. I sent this intelligence to my wife, before I left for Pensacola.

Washington, D.C.
March 12 - 65

My Dear Friends

I have *nothing new* whatever to give you in regard to Henry, except our tender thoughts and sympathies in your sad anxiety which are new every day as we turn to you our former near friends.

I was at the Navy Dep't again yesterday, and had access to all papers which might give light upon the subject, but there is nothing whatever. I presume that you had an account of the Report made Feb 17th to the Navy Dep't by Act'g R.[ear] Ad.[miral] C. K. Stribling based upon the Report of Feb 6th of Lieut C. H. Rockwell on board U.S. St[eamer] *H.[endrick] Hudson*, Key West Fla. Squ[adron].

I thought however I would make some extracts from the Report so that if you had not rec'd it in detail you might know what had been done.

On Feb 4th Lieut Rockwell searching for the *Annie*, discovered a wreck in six fathom of water (near Malco Inlet) 10 miles off Cape Romaine (Cape Romain bearing SW lat. 26° (or thereabouts)[.][4] Lieut. Rockwell says: "I found the mast and running along side succeeded in raising the wreck sufficiently to bring her bow out of water, and identify her as the *Annie*, and discovered her condition . . . From foremast aft, her deck was entirely gone, except the port side of the trunk cabin aft. From just abaft the fore rigging on the starboard side she is entirely gone. - deck between timbers, and every thing from the keel out being cut off, with the exception of two or three of her floor timbers. - No vestige of her main mast or the sail could be discovered . . . . Anchor chains, with the jib, and a few other articles were saved. . . . . The next day with grapples and other appliances the whole hull was felt over to ascertain if any bodies of the crew could be discovered, but nothing was found except some clothing and bedding. . . . . Nothing could be found to throw any light on the manner of her loss. As I discovered her no vessel could have run her down and injured her to the extent seen, by a single blow. . . .

The catastrophe by which she is wrecked is still a mystery which unless some of her crew have been saved must I fear remain so . . . From all I can see I think she must have been blown up, and I can account for it in no other way." Then the A.[cting] R.[ear] Ad.[miral] in his Report Enclosing this of Lieut Rockwell says . . . "From the account of Lieut Rockwell I think there is reason to believe that the *Annie* was accidentally blown up."

I shall go in to the Navy Dept every now & then and if any information of any kind is received which might throw light on the fate of the crew of the *Annie* I will write you. Or if there are any questions of *any sort* which you would like asked let me know and I will at once see to having them answered. Lucia joins me my dear friends in tenderest sympathy & love. Believe me ever sincerely yours,

Fred N. Knapp[5]

Office of the Prize Commissioners
Key West, Fla.
March 15th 1865
Mrs E. S. Welles
Brookline Mass

Dear Madam,

I have to acknowledge the receipt this morning, of your letter of 7th inst. and am sorry to say I can give you no further intelligence respecting the fate of your poor son Henry. I have seen Lt Rockwell, commdg. The U.S. Steamer *Hendrick Hudson* this morning, and he thinks beyond doubt the *Annie* was blown up and his crew must have perished.

Should I come in possession of any news relating to this unfortunate disaster, I will most soundly advise you, and I will make inquiries if Henry left any thing here.

While in command of the U.S. sloop *Rosalie*, he captured, and brought to this port, as prize of war, a small sloops Boat, without name, but she was if but little value, and I doubt if there will be any residue to be divided, however the final statement of all prize cases goes to Washington to the 4th Auditor to day and undoubtably on long a list will be published.

Let me once more assure you that I will do all in my power to get information, and should any thing be found belonging to Henry, I will see that it is sent to you.

With kind regards to Mr Wells
I remain most true
your obedient friend
R.W. Welch

US Bark *Restless*
St Joseph Bay
April 7th 65

Mrs Wells

Dear Madam I have just received your letter of 19th of March And I hasten to answer it as the mails leaves in two hours[.] I will endeavor to give you all the information that I can[.] I know that you must feel the loss very heavily for there is not one in the East Gulf Squadron that knew him but loved him[.] I can[n]ot describe the feelings of the officers of this ship when we received the news of the loss of the *Annie*[.] I will give you the details of her loss for I think that I was the last one that saw the vessel before she was lost[.] I was bound to Key West in the Schr *Two Sisters* in the forenoon of Saturday, December 31st 64[.] I saw the *Annie* she was bound to Charlotte Harbor we had fine weather all day until Night at about eleven oclock[.] We were close to Key West and therefore shortened sail[.] The weather looked good but five minutes after I took in the fore sail I was struck by a heavy squal[l.] I had to reduce sail at once it blew very heavy[.] I being some seventy miles to the Southward of the *Annie* and the wind coming from the Northward she must have been struck about eight that evening and by the looks of the wreck I think that he was knocked on his beam ends and Immediately cut his Gun adrift and let it go over board and then cut away his main mast[.] I think that she must have righted up and filled and sunk[.] I arrived at Key West the Next day and then was ordered to the *Restless* the vessel that the *Annie* was attached to[.] we sailed on 12th of January and arrived in Charlotte Harbour on the seventeenth we supposed that the *Annie* was there but she had not been heard from so we dispatched a boat to Punta Rassa twenty miles below to see if we could hear anything of them[.] while there the Schooner *Matchbox* arrived and brought the news that she had seen the wreck of the *Annie*[.] she saw her twelve miles from Cape Roman land distant twelve miles and also that she saw a fire on the Beach to the Northward of Cape Roman[.] Mr Hinckley the officer in charge of the boat returned that Night and got ten days provision for his men and some extra provision for the crew of the *Annie* for we were sure that they had got ashore as the coast at that place is uninhabited and we knew that there would he know fire without some one was ship wrecked there. The boat returned after twelve days search the Fire was made by three men that had been driven ashore in a little sloop[.] They were down there hunting so we gave up all hopes of finding any one that belong to the *Annie*[.] The weather was so boisterous for a fortnight after that they could not go near the wreck[.] as soon as the weather smoothed down the Steamer *Hendrick Hudson* went to the wreck and raised her she had beat about so long that her sides were busted out and every thing washed out of her[.] They took her fore mast out and let her sink again[.] There is not the least chance for one of them to have been saved as their boat was small [and] would only car[r]y two and if any one had got into her they would have been heard off [of] before this[.] there is nothing saved but the Fore mast that is all they got out of her[.] but if ever I get a chance I will go along the coast and see if I can find anything that ever belong to him[.] I was not at Key West while he was there but all the rest of the Gentleman of this ship were there[.] he was on board of this vessel the night before he sailed he had the same crew that he had in the *Rosie Lee* [*Rosalie*.] Mr West was on board also[.] I will endeavor to get a Photograph of him and send you[.] Mrs West is living on a Key at Charlotte Harbor[.] I have taken care of her ever since he was lost[.] she has one child[.] I am trying to get his wages for her for I think that she needs them[.] Mr West had about one hundred and seventy dollars due him[.] The whole Crew and officers accounts were sent to Washington[.] There was due Henry at the time that his accounts were sent $132.18[.] That was the 31st of January[.] The only way to get the money is to write Steven J. W. Tabor fourth auditor Washington[.][6] Now you must not think that you are taking to[o] great a liberty for I numbered Henry as one of my best friends and anything that I can do for his parents I will do cheerfully so dont stop to consider about asking me to do anything that lyes in my powers[.] I don't think that you could have sent to any one that could give you more information than I can[.] Acting Ensign Bliss has gone home and I suppose that he will call and see you as he was a shipmate of Henrys and lived in Roxbury[.] if any letters come to this ship they have to pass throu my hands so if there is any comes directed to Henry I will forward them to you without delay[.] I am in hopes that my Government can spare me for a month to visit my family and when I do come home I will surely call and see you[.] Mr Hinckley one of our officers has just given me a Book that Henry gave him the night before he was last[.] I will send it and will also try to get some other things[.] if there is any thing that you can think of that you would like to know write to me at once and I will inform you if it lies in my Power[.] I procured while at Key West a Photograph of the crew to send to you but as you say you have one I will send it to one of their mothers[.] Please excuse this hasty written letter and I will remain your True Friend

J A Montague[7]
Acting Ensign and Executive Officer
US Bark *Restless*
EGB Squadron
1st Division

Notes

Introduction

1. Thomas Goodwin Wells, "Letters of an Argonaut from August, 1849 to October, 1851," *Out West: A Magazine of the Old Pacific and the New*, vol. 22, no. 1 (January 1905), pp. 48–54; no. 2 (February 1905), pp. 136–42; no. 3–4 (March–April 1905), pp. 221–28.

2. Robert M. Browning Jr., *From Cape Charles to Cape Fear: The North Atlantic Blockading Squadron during the Civil War* (Tuscaloosa: University of Alabama Press, 1993), p. 204.

Chapter 1

1. The *Cambridge* was one of hundreds of vessels purchased and converted to serve in the navy. Built in 1860, the navy purchased this screw-propelled vessel in July 1861. At 858 tons, the service initially armed her with two 8-inch guns and two smaller cannons.

2. Commander William A. Parker entered the service in July 1832, reaching the rank of captain in early 1865. He would, at the apex of his career, command the ironclad monitor *Onondaga* and the Fifth Division of the North Atlantic Blockading Squadron. While commanding this division he reacted too slowly in countering a move by Confederate ironclads in the James River. His slow reaction to the enemy's movement threatened not only his naval forces but also the safety of City Point and the Army of the Potomac. Parker was court-martialed for this and, while he was not found guilty, the department moved him to the retired list.

3. Fort Monroe was a stone and brick fort erected on Old Point Comfort to protect Hampton Roads. It served during the war as a bastion of the Union defenses in the area and a logistical facility for both the army and navy.

4. Cousin Lu was the famed novelist, short story writer, and poet Louisa May Alcott.

5. Robert D. Eldridge.

6. The Parrott gun was a muzzle-loading cannon named after its inventor Robert Parrott. It had both army and navy versions, manufactured in different sizes from a 2.9-inch to a 10-inch version. The naval guns fired a 3.67-inch to an 8-inch projectile, the last weighing 150 pounds. A wrought iron reinforcing band laid over the breech during manufacturing gave the guns more strength to keep them from bursting.

7. The sailing master was in charge of the ship's navigation as well as many other duties. He would be the individual most responsible to see that Henry learned the skills necessary for promotion.

8. The *Roanoke* was a screw frigate commissioned in 1857. The navy converted her into an ironclad and she was recommissioned in June 1863 sporting three turrets and mounting six heavy guns. She was a failure due to the weight of her armor. Her draft was too great for inshore work and her low freeboard barred ocean cruising.

9. Beaufort, North Carolina, developed on a peninsula, a mile and a half from Beaufort Inlet that runs between Bouge and Shackleford banks. Morehead City is just across the Newport

River from Beaufort and had, only in mid-1858, obtained rail connections to the interior. In 1860 it was an active seaport due to its large and sheltered harbor. It was Beaufort's relative isolation, though, and the fact that the port could only accommodate vessels of moderate draft, that had limited its utility. The town mainly exported naval stores, cotton, and various other agricultural products.

10. The 84-ton schooner *Revere*, captured by the *Cambridge* on 10 September, had a cargo of 825 bags of salt and 250 barrels of herring. She was bound from Halifax, Nova Scotia, to Key West, Florida, but tried to sneak into the blockaded port of Beaufort. Her home port was Yarmouth, England. Henry would represent and testify for the Government's interest in the prize case and deliver the documents captured on board to the federal court to condemn the vessel. There are further documents of Henry's testimony and participation in this proceeding in U.S. v. *Revere*, Schooner and Cargo, U.S. District Court of Massachusetts, Records of District Courts of the United States, 1685–2009, Record Group 21, National Archives, Boston, Massachusetts.

11. After Henry sailed the *Revere* to Boston for the prize court proceedings and remained for the adjudication, he returned to his ship, but for a short while spent time on board the *Minnesota*.

12. Captain William L. Hudson commanded the Boston Navy Yard from 1858 to 1862. He was one of the most senior officers in the navy.

13. Henry delivered the two men to testify in the court proceedings.

14. The *Minnesota* was one of the newest screw frigates in the navy. Heavily armed with forty-five heavy guns, she would serve most of the war as the flagship for the North Atlantic Blockading Squadron.

15. 17th Regiment Massachusetts Volunteers.

16. Zouave units outfitted with uniforms similar to the French Zouaves. They had jackets with open fronts and wore baggy trousers with sashes and a fez-like cap. The 11th New York, led by Colonel Elmer E. Ellsworth, were known as the "Fire Zouaves," the men drawn from volunteer fire companies in New York City.

17. Henry is referring to the Pratt Street Massacre where a prosecessionist mob attacked troops of the 6th Massachusetts Infantry. During the melee at least four soldiers and nine civilians died.

18. The Confederates used the hull and engines of the frigate *Merrimack* to construct the ironclad CSS *Virginia*. During the war and afterwards many mistakenly referred to the ironclad by her earlier name. The Confederates armed the *Virginia* with two 7-inch guns, six 9-inch guns, two 6-inch guns, and a four-foot underwater ram at the bow. Her armor consisted of 4 inches of armor backed by 24 inches of wood.

19. The Battle of Bull Run was the first major engagement of the Civil War. On 21 July 1861, the two undisciplined armies met about 25 miles west of Washington, DC. The Confederate forces under the command of Brigadier General Pierre Gustave Toutant Beauregard met the Union forces of Brigadier General Irvin McDowell. The Confederates fought a defensive action and the battle ended in a Union rout, all watched by spectators from Washington, DC.

20. The bark *Gemsbok*, built in 1857, served in the merchant service until the navy purchased her in September 1861. At 622 tons, she mounted four 8-inch guns and two 32-pounders.

21. Captain Gershom J. Van Brunt, appointed a midshipman in 1818 and captain in 1855, he was one of the most senior officers in the navy. He commanded the frigate *Minnesota*, and due to illness, the navy placed him on the retired list in April 1863. He died that December.

22. The town of Newport News is on the James River on the southeastern end of the peninsula between the James and York rivers. It is now part of the Hampton Roads metropolitan area.

23. "Shell" probably refers to a shellback, the slang term for an experienced sailor.

24. This poem comes from an anonymous letter to the editor in *The Knickerbocker* magazine, vol. 58, no. 6 (Dec. 1861), pp. 551–52. Written from the *Cambridge*, the letter recounts the funeral ceremony and service on the blockade.

25. The *Albatross* was a 378-ton screw steamer built in 1858 and acquired by the navy in May 1861. She carried four 32-pounders and one rifled 12-pound gun. She had a relatively fast speed of eleven knots.

26. Lieutenant William Gwin went on to command the gunboat *Tyler* attached to the West Gulf Blockading Squadron. On 14 July 1862, the *Tyler* was involved in a running fight with the ironclad CSS *Arkansas*. The ironclad passed down the Yazoo River and engaged dozens of the squadron's warships on her way south to Vicksburg.

27. The ship's officers and crew divided into messes and ate together. The wardroom mess included the staff officers above the grade of ensign and line officers from the rank of master and above, not including the captain. The steerage mess comprised ensigns, acting masters, midshipmen, and clerks. The warrant officers' mess included the boatswain, gunner, sailmaker, and carpenter. The officers usually selected a caterer from their group whose responsibility was to provide provisions and manage the food choices and the affairs of the mess. Each officer in the mess would contribute an agreed-upon sum of money to assist the caterer in providing better food than that issued by the navy. The caterer kept accounts and receipts of the expenditures.

28. The blockade runner *Alliance* flew South Carolina's Palmetto flag while in the port of St. John's, New Brunswick, creating a furor since it was the first vessel then to fly a rebellion flag rather than the United States flag while in port.

29. The schooner was the *Chief* out of New York.

30. Louis Malesherbes Goldsborough was born in Washington, DC, in 1805. He entered the navy as a midshipman at the early age of seven but did not begin service until 1816. He served as the Superintendent of the U.S. Naval Academy and the commanding officer of the Brazil Squadron before the war. As one of the most senior officers, in September 1861, he received command of the Atlantic Blockading Squadron and then a month later the newly formed North Atlantic Blockading Squadron. The navy promoted him to the newly created rank of Flag Officer in January 1862. After receiving criticism of his actions during the Peninsula Campaign, he resigned his position, but remained in the navy until 1873, becoming the first commanding officer of the European Squadron in 1865.

31. Adams Express was a freight and cargo transportation business.

32. Established in 1833, the Naval Lyceum at the Brooklyn Navy Yard served as a place where officers could further their knowledge of worldly subjects and ideas and fostered unity and community within the service. By the time of the Civil War, this lyceum had thousands of books, magazines, and charts as well as many specimens and artifacts from around the world. It had earlier published its own magazine.

33. The 111-ton screw-propelled *Rescue* was a tugboat built in 1861. Purchased before completion, the navy brought her into service that September. She had an iron hull and mounted one 20-pound rifled gun and one 12-pound rifled gun.

34. The *Valley City* was a small 190-ton screw-propelled steamer built in 1859 and acquired by the navy in July 1861. She had an armament of four 32-pound guns.

35. During the Civil War the word *contraband* denoted African Americans who escaped their bondage. This term originated in August 1861, when the federal government decided that they would no longer return escaped slaves and considered them "contraband of war," essentially captured enemy property.

36. William B. Cushing attended the US Naval Academy and resigned before he

graduated. The outbreak of the Civil War gave him the opportunity to rejoin the service. He would lead several daring raids, one accomplishing the destruction of the ironclad CSS *Albemarle*. He did have difficulties in his personal relationships, which Henry will bear out.

37. The Corrotoman River has two branches that join just before it empties into the Rappahannock River on its northern bank. This is about eight miles above where the Rappahannock empties into the Chesapeake Bay.

38. William Parker's report of this action is in Richard Rush, et al., eds., *Official Records of the Union and Confederate Navies in the War of the Rebellion* (Washington, DC: Government Printing Office, 1894–1914), ser. 1, vol. 6, pp. 407–8. (Hereinafter cited as *ORN*.) Henry's account follows the report closely.

39. Urbanna, historically often spelled Urbana, is on the south side of the Rappahannock River about fifteen miles from where the river empties into the Chesapeake Bay. It means "the city of Anne," named after Queen Anne.

40. Canoes in this area could be fifty feet or longer and some had sail propulsion.

41. James F. Clarke, a graduate of Harvard College and Harvard Divinity School, established the Church of Disciples, a Unitarian Church in Boston. He served as the church's minister from 1841 to 1850 and from 1854 until his death in 1888. He was a prolific author, writing some 150 books and pamphlets during his lifetime.

42. Joseph N. Miller.

43. One of the earliest Union amphibious operations, the expedition included over 12,000 troops and over 75 vessels. It sailed to attack Port Royal, South Carolina, in order to seize a lodgement on the Southern coast. After the bombardment of two coastal forts, the army landed and seized much of the area around Beaufort. This expedition facilitated future captures of strategic points, and the Beaufort area served as a logistical base for the navy.

44. The 1,867-ton *Congress* was a sail-propelled frigate commissioned in 1842. She was heavily armed with fifty heavy guns. The 1,726-ton *Cumberland* was a sailing frigate commissioned in 1843 and armed with twenty-four heavy guns.

45. This is an archaic contraction of "on it."

46. The USS *San Jacinto* stopped the British mail steamer *Trent* and removed diplomats John Slidell and James Murry Mason. This was a violation of neutral rights and created an international furor, causing great friction between the United States and Great Britain. The Lincoln administration later released the men and disavowed the actions. Henry will discuss this issue in later letters and misspell Slidell's name.

47. The executive officer on board warships is the officer next in rank to the commanding officer and is in charge in the absence of the commanding officer. The executive officer has the most difficult job on board the ship. He shoulders most of the administrative burdens, making sure that the crew performs and adheres to all the policies and rules on shipboard. He oversees the daily activities on board, including the disciplinary functions, freeing up the commanding officer to focus more on tactical and strategic issues.

48. There is no known warship stationed there whose name begins with the letter I with two guns.

49. The master-at-arms is the most senior petty officer who attends to the police duties of the ship. He makes all arrests and is in charge of those in confinement, quells disturbances, prevents smuggling on board, and oversees the lights and fires on the ship.

50. "The Bold Privateer" was a popular song during the war.

51. Warrant officers were officers holding their rank by virtue of a warrant issued by the navy board, Secretary of the Navy, etc. Promoted from the enlisted men, they comprised the boatswain, carpenter, gunner, and sailmaker. They ranked just below mates and quartered and messed together.

Chapter 2

1. The Order Book of the *Cambridge* required the master's mates to keep a journal, for the captain's inspection on the 1st and 15th of every month. In it they used the ship's log to keep notes on the wind and courses as well as making important remarks.

2. Henry probably had chronic bronchitis.

3. The *Daylight* was a 692-ton screw-propelled steamer. Built in 1860, the navy acquired her in May 1861. She mounted four 32-pounders. She was extremely slow, capable of a speed of only five knots, but managed to capture a number of prizes during the war.

4. The *Brooklyn* was one of the US Navy's most powerful warships. A 2,532-ton screw sloop, she mounted one 10-inch smoothbore gun and twenty 9-inch smoothbores. She became the flagship of David Glasgow Farragut, who commanded the West Gulf Blockading Squadron. This warship participated in some of the most heated engagements of the war.

5. Lynnhaven Bay is about eight miles west of Cape Henry, accessed through an inlet. Henry probably means Lynnhaven Roads, which is the coast adjacent to the inlet within the Chesapeake Bay.

6. The *Cambridge* towed the *A. M. Lawrence* out of danger. She was in ballast from Amsterdam to Baltimore.

7. Contemporaries used aconite for many different maladies including anxiety, exposure to hot and cold weather, numbness, colds, headaches, and more.

8. When Henry first discussed this issue he spelled Slidell's name correctly but will continue to get it wrong in his later letters.

9. Brigadier General Ambrose Burnside led the Burnside Expedition. He organized a division to operate along the east coast, first attacking Roanoke Island, NC, and then New Bern and other towns accessible to the North Carolina Sounds.

10. Collisions between vessels on the blockade were commonplace. Most of the damages suffered were superficial, but there were instances when the collisions caused enough damage to require work at a naval facility. At least one vessel (the *Peterhoff*) sank off Wilmington due to a collision with another blockading vessel.

11. The British commissioned the 3,984-ton screw frigate *Immortalité* in November 1860. She had an armament of 51 guns.

12. The *Jamestown* was a 985-ton sloop commissioned in 1845. Her 18-foot draft, and having only sail propulsion, made her less valuable as a blockading vessel. She spent most of the war on the west coast.

13. Two William Lincolns lived at 13 India Street, Brookline, MA.

14. A jibboom is a spar that extends the bowsprit.

15. An archaic expression meaning not letting an opportunity slip by.

16. He may have meant "beget," meaning to produce, to be fruitful, or to generate.

17. It is unknown what Henry is speaking about.

18. Burnside, at this point, had not arrived at his first objective of Roanoke Island, NC. He passed into the sounds on 7 February and captured the island the next day. His forces then headed to New Bern, capturing that town on 14 March.

19. The Navy Department sent Porter's Fleet of mortar vessels to cooperate in operations up the Mississippi River with David Glasgow Farragut.

20. Brown Windsor soap was popular throughout Europe. Castile soap is a cleansing product made from vegetable oils rather than lard or tallow and is still available today.

21. In 1855 William J. Hardee wrote a book entitled *Rifle and Light Infantry Tactics*, which became the standard manual for the United States Army.

22. In the February 1862 issue of *The Atlantic Monthly* magazine.

23. Lieutenant William Gwin commanded the gunboat *Tyler*, assigned to the Western

Flotilla on the Mississippi River. In July 1862, the ironclad CSS *Arkansas* attacked the *Tyler* and two other warships in the Yazoo River. A running gun battle ensued, and Gwin was able to get his ship back to the safety of the fleet. Considered one of the best junior officers in the navy, he was given command of the converted armored river steamer *Benton*. In December 1862, Confederate shore batteries attacked the *Benton* and Gwin was mortally wounded.

24. The book is *History of the Consulate and the Empire of France under Napoleon*, by Louis Adolphe Thiers. There were 20 volumes in the 1845 set.

25. Edmund N. Blunt began publishing the *American Coast Pilot* in 1796. The book contained directions and descriptions of principal harbors and coastal features as well as prevailing winds and currents to aid in the navigation of the coasts of North and South America. It was a popular publication for ship owners and masters. There were twenty-one editions published with updates.

26. This is in the January 1862 magazine.

27. It is unclear what Henry meant here.

28. Henry uses the word "tenix" three times in his letters. It is probably some sort of inside joke with his sisters since in one case he uses the word "felinx" for feelings. It seems he has made it a variation of "tenets," from the Latin *tenere* meaning to hold, as an opinion. In June 1861, federal legislation created the United States Sanitary Commission as a private relief organization. Its mission was to support the sick and wounded soldiers of the Union army and to help the dependent families. It raised millions of dollars and had the support of thousands of volunteers.

29. Edward Hooper, a teacher and administrator, served on the staff of Brigadier General Rufus Saxton. He helped to administer a project that allowed former slaves to work on abandoned plantations—called the Port Royal Experiment.

30. The navy acquired the 407-ton screw-propelled *Stars and Stripes* in July 1861. Her armament consisted of four 8-inch guns, one 20-pound rifled canon, and a 12-pounder.

31. Henry wrote her on stationery with a likeness of General George B. McClellan surrounded by flags and the words "Hope of the Nation."

32. Fort Donelson defended the Cumberland River in Tennessee. On 6 February 1862, forces under Ulysses S. Grant, with naval assistance, captured Fort Henry on the Tennessee River, about ten miles to the west. The two defenses were situated where the states of Tennessee, Kentucky, and Missouri meet. Grant began the investment of Fort Donelson before the fall of Fort Henry and forced the surrender of most of the garrison on the 16th. Grant insisted on unconditional surrender, thus providing him a nickname of "Unconditional Surrender Grant." This defeat forced the Confederate withdrawal from western Kentucky and Tennessee and the loss of Nashville on the 23rd.

33. Hailed at the beginning of the war as the "Young Napoleon," George Brinton McClellan's greatest talents were his ability to organize, train, and administer an army. Yet he was totally lacking in qualities as a battlefield commander. Lincoln gave him command of the armies around Washington and he soon became commander-in-chief of the entire Union army. His failures during the Peninsula Campaign forced his replacement, yet after the Union defeat at the 2nd Battle of Bull Run, he resumed overall command once again. Lincoln dismissed him again after the Battle of Antietam. McClellan did become a presidential candidate in 1864.

34. Satinet is a cotton fabric with a finish similar to satin.

35. The news that Savannah, Georgia, fell was incorrect. It did not fall to Union forces until December 1864.

36. The navy purchased the 329-ton, iron-hulled *R. B. Forbes* in August 1861. She wrecked near Currituck Island, North Carolina.

37. The *Hoboken* was a 535-ton steamer chartered by the Army Quartermaster's Department.

38. The *S. R. Spaulding* was a 1090-ton side-wheel steamer also chartered by the Army Quartermaster Department.

39. On 7 November a large naval force attacked fortifications at Port Royal, SC. Accompanying army forces later took over the abandoned forts and this began a huge effort to capture much of the South Carolina, Georgia, and Florida coast.

40. John Albion Andrews, elected Governor of Massachusetts in 1860, served until 1866. Senator Charles Sumner, elected to the Senate in 1851, was one of the most powerful men in the chamber.

41. "Viz" is an abbreviation of *videlicet*, meaning "namely."

42. After the Confederate defeat at Fort Donelson, Brigadier General John Pope did threaten Columbus, Tennessee, but no battle occurred.

43. The *Vanderbilt* was a fast steamer built by Cornelius Vanderbilt for transatlantic service, which he gave to the government. The navy used her as a fast cruiser, but she never used the "*C*" before the name *Vanderbilt*.

44. The Ericsson Battery was another name for the USS *Monitor*.

45. The frigate *St. Lawrence*, commissioned in 1848, was one of the most powerful ships in the navy. She carried ten 8-inch guns, thirty-eight 32-pounders, and two 12-pound guns. Her deep draft would limit her effectiveness as a blockading vessel. She would remain in the navy until the last day of 1875. Due to low tide and no wind the *Cambridge* attempted to tow the *St. Lawrence* into position to participate in the battle. The shell damage came from Confederate guns on Sewell's Point.

46. The *Monitor* was a revolutionary warship designed by John Ericcson, incorporating many new inventions and spawning dozens of similar but improved versions. Built in New York, this ironclad had a low freeboard and a revolving turret. Eight inches of iron plate protected the turret, which contained two 11-inch guns.

47. The *Nashville*, a former US Mail Service vessel, ran between New York City and Charleston. After her capture in Charleston, the Confederates converted her into a commerce raider. She ran the blockade in October 1861 and burned the American merchant ship *Harvey Birch*. She returned to Beaufort, North Carolina, on 28 February 1862 after capturing two prizes.

48. The Confederates had renamed the *Yorktown* as the *Patrick Henry*, but many still referred to her original name. The CSS *Raleigh* and *Beaufort* accompanied the CSS *Virginia* out of the Elizabeth River, where the *Patrick Henry*, *Jamestown* (also known as the *Thomas Jefferson*), and *Teaser* joined them. Both the *Patrick Henry* and *Jamestown* had some protective armor. The *Minnesota* probably had 44 guns, the *Roanoke* 44 guns, and the *Mystic* 5 guns.

49. There were no reported warship losses by the Confederates.

50. In 1852, the Philadelphia and Savannah Steamship Company built the *State of Georgia*. The navy purchased her in September 1861. A 1,204-ton side-wheel steamer, she mounted six 8-inch guns, two 32-pounders, and a 30-pound rifled gun.

51. A letter from Henry's Uncle Hamilton to Thomas Wells dated 17 March 1862 related his trip to Washington, DC. Hamilton Willis met with Charles B. Sedgwick, Chairman of the Committee of Naval Affairs, and Secretary of the Navy Gideon Welles and other politicians. He learned the Navy Department was against promoting Henry to Master at this time.

52. While in Beaufort, Fraser, Trenholm and Company purchased the *Nashville* to use her as a blockade runner, renaming her the *Thomas L. Wragg*. She escaped the port on 17 March and made several successful runs as a blockade runner. On one trip, Union warships chased her into Warsaw Sound, Georgia. Here authorities converted her back into a commerce raider and renamed her the *Rattlesnake*. The ironclad *Montauk* destroyed her in February 1863.

53. The *Chippewa* was an Unadilla Class gunboat commissioned in December 1861. At 691 tons, this class of screw-propelled warships had an 11-inch smoothbore gun, two 24-pounders

and a 20-pound rifled gun. This class was known as the 90-day gunboats because construction in some instances took only three months. They served as the mainstay of blockade duty and river work for two years from the beginning of 1862.

54. There were no Confederate commerce raiders that carried sixteen guns. Henry may have been discussing the Confederate commerce raider *Sumter*, which had actively preyed on Union shipping in November and December 1861, but in January 1862 went to Gibraltar for repairs and coal. She was trapped there by Union warships, and the Confederacy sold her in December 1862. She was not heavily armed, having only five guns.

55. This was apparently the 287-ton bark *Glen* carrying 391 tons of coal to Fort Jefferson on the Tortugas. On 23 July 1861, the privateer *Dixie*, out of Charleston, captured her, then took her to Morehead City. An admiralty court condemned the ship and her cargo. Due to the paucity of coal in the South, an auction that September that sold the cargo and the ship's gear netted her captors a tidy sum.

56. If transcribed properly this is an archaic form meaning the act of intending.

57. Union forces did seize Beaufort on March 25th.

58. Wendell Phillips was a Boston-born abolitionist. He, like some other abolitionists, welcomed the formation of the Confederacy, believing that the Southern states had a right to secede and that it would end the power of the slaveowners over the United States government.

59. Built in 1859, the *Mount Vernon* was a 625-ton screw steamer purchased by the navy in April 1861. She mounted three 32-pound guns. The *Fernandina*, also purchased by the navy, was a 297-ton bark built in 1850. The navy commissioned her in November 1861.

60. A historic homeopathic treatment for bruises, aches, and pains.

61. The *Victoria* was a small 254-ton screw-propelled vessel purchased by the navy in December 1861. She mounted one 30-pounder and two 8-inch guns.

62. The ironclad *Galena* was a more traditional-looking warship, not having a turret as did the *Monitor*. She had more guns and a lighter armor. In mid-May, she went to Virginia to strike up the James River with the *Monitor* and the *Naugatuck* in an attempt to reach Richmond. The Confederates repulsed this naval expedition at the Battle of Drewry's Bluff.

63. Referring to the *Naugatuck*.

64. Barnum's Hotel was about four blocks from the waterfront on the corner of Fayette and Calvert streets.

65. Acting Master Samuel Very Jr.

66. On 25 and 26 May, Baltimore Unionists clashed with secession-minded citizens. Dix to Stanton, 26 May 1862, in R. N. Scott, et. al., eds., *The War of the Rebellion: A Compilation of the Official Records of the Union and Confederate Armies* (Washington, DC: Government Printing Office, 1880–1901), ser. 1, vol. 12, pt. 3, p. 253. (Hereinafter cited as *ORA*.)

67. Major General Nathaniel P. Banks was a former Governor of Massachusetts. In May 1861, Abraham Lincoln appointed him a major general of volunteers. General Thomas "Stonewall" Jackson defeated his forces at the Battle of Front Royal on 23 May 1862 and again two days later at the First Battle of Winchester.

68. New York State Militia, known as the "Blue Bloods" due to the large number in the regiment that belonged to New York City's social elite.

69. The parentheses do not match correctly but this is how Henry wrote them.

70. First Assistant Engineer J. Buchanan Houston.

71. Faneuil Hall is a marketplace and meeting hall near the waterfront in Boston. Opened in 1743, it is the site of some of the most important speeches made leading up to the American Revolution. It is today part of the Boston National Historic park.

72. Perhaps relating to Burlington, Vermont, nicknamed the Green Mountain City.

73. Union Leagues were clubs of men who supported loyalty to the Union and the policies of Abraham Lincoln. They stood in opposition to the "Copperhead" Democrats.

74. Both forts are in Baltimore.

Chapter 3

1. This blockade runner was the *Modern Greece.*

2. The *Massachusetts* was a 1,155-ton screw-propelled supply ship. Built in 1860, and purchased by the navy in May 1861, she supplied the warships of the Gulf Blockading Squadron.

3. Charles Sumner was a senator from Massachusetts and leader of the anti-slavery faction as well as that of the Radical Republican faction.

4. The iron-hulled Revenue Cutter *Bibb*, built in 1845, sported experimental underwater horizontal paddle wheels. This mode of propulsion was a complete failure and the government had her converted to side-wheel propulsion almost immediately after launching. In 1847 she transferred to the US Coast Survey and provided useful service for many years. In May 1861, she transferred back to the Revenue Cutter Service, only to return in short time to the services of the Coast Survey, where she served until 1879.

5. This is the list of sick sent to the commanding officer by the medical officer. A duplicate list of names, called the binnacle list, went for posting on the upper deck.

6. This is likely the Seven Days Campaign in which General Robert E. Lee took command of the Army of Northern Virginia and launched an offensive to drive back the Union army then threatening Richmond.

7. The *Monticello*, built in 1859, was a 655-ton side-wheel steamer. The navy initially chartered her and then purchased her. She mounted one 10-inch gun and two 32-pounders. In September 1861, the navy added two additional 32-pounders. She could steam at eleven and a half knots.

8. Lieutenant Commander Daniel L. Braine, a midshipman in May 1846, remained in the Navy after the war, advancing to the rank of Rear Admiral.

9. The *Penobscot* was one of the twenty-three Unadilla Class warships and was commissioned in January 1862. One of the "90-day Gunboats," this 1,900-ton vessel mounted, in February 1862, one 11-inch Dahlgren, one 20-pounder Parrott rifle, and two 24-pound howitzers.

10. The 452-ton *Mystic* was built in 1853. The navy chartered her for the Paraguay Expedition in 1858 and purchased her in 1859. She carried four 32-pounders and one 24-pounder.

11. Acting Master's Mate William F. Durgin. He received an appointment as mate on 30 June 1862, and the navy revoked it on 17 April 1863.

12. *Leef* is an obsolete adjective meaning "willing."

13. The navy purchased the diminutive 254-ton screw steamer *Victoria*, which entered service with the navy in March 1862. She mounted a single 30-pounder and two 8-inch guns.

14. Masonboro Inlet is on the north end of Masonboro Island about twenty miles north of New Inlet.

15. The 41-ton sloop *Lizzie*, from Nassau and ostensibly bound to Baltimore, had an assorted cargo of salt, blankets, sheet tin, arrowroot, soda ash, and caustic soda.

16. The idiom "give all my old shoes" probably means give up all his efforts.

17. Charles L. Huntington.

18. C.S.I.C.S. (Confederate States Iron Clad Steamer) *Arkansas* attacked the federal fleet, fighting her way from the Yazoo River to Vicksburg. She later continued down river and broke down above Baton Rouge and was destroyed by her Rebel crew.

19. In the nineteenth century, referring to someone as a "brick" meant "a good, honest fellow."

20. Henry's new sister, Ruth Lyman Wells, was born on 28 July.

21. Tin types were photographic images placed on a thin piece of metal.

22. Belladonna and aconite are traditional medicines made from plants.

23. The *Suwanee* was a 684-ton side-wheel steamer chartered to the Quartermaster's Department.

24. The Confederates did complete two ironclads at Wilmington during the war, the *Raleigh* and the *North Carolina*. Both were Richmond Class ironclads and mounted four heavy guns.

25. The 981-ton side-wheel steamer *Octorara* carried an armament of one 80-pound rifled gun, a 9-inch gun, and four 24-pounders. She served most of the war in the West Gulf Blockading Squadron.

26. Commander James F. Armstrong. Henry calls Armstrong "captain," which was a courtesy title for the commanding officer of any vessel regardless of the officer's true rank.

27. The Confederates continually made improvements to Fort Fisher, until it was the largest earthwork fort in the Confederacy, mounting forty-seven heavy guns.

28. The *Boston Journal*.

29. The poem mentioned was one written by Louisa Alcott to Henry's brother. She describes Bennie as swinging on Hawthorne's gate. The manuscript is in the New York Public Library.

30. *Mercredi* is Wednesday in French.

31. The *Arrow* worked for the Army Quartermaster, and Confederate partisans captured her on 16 May 1862 at Coinjock, Virginia. News of this event probably reached Henry late. Henry's recent letters from home could not have travelled on this ship given the difference in dates. There is no other qualifying American ship known that sank off the East Coast during the three to four months before this letter.

32. Henry continually misspells *Octorara*.

33. The 786-ton side-wheel steamer *Maratanza* began her career in the navy in April 1862. She carried a 100-pounder, a single 9-inch gun, and four 24-pound howitzers.

34. Henry is referring to the *Monthly Journal* of the American Unitarian Society.

35. This episode mentioned by Henry occurred in August 1862 when, as a believer in total abstinence from liquor, Wild had his troops shut down a hotel and a saloon that had supplied liquor to his men. Philadelphia authorities issued arrest writs which he refused to obey. Edward A. Wild also was from Brookline, Massachusetts, and attended the same church as Henry. He earned a medical degree from Harvard and enlisted in the army at the outbreak of the Civil War as a front-line officer and not as a doctor. An abolitionist, Wild later commanded "Wild's African Brigade," made up of three regiments of African American troops. See the book *Edward A. Wild and the African Brigade in the Civil War* by Francis H. Casstevens (Jefferson, NC: McFarland and Company, 2003), pp. 5–18, 45.

36. There would be two ironclads finished at Wilmington, but neither was in the water at the time.

37. Henry treated this letter as a continuation of the preceding letter to his mother and sent it in the same envelope, so it is placed here before the letter to his sister dated Sept. 22.

38. Charles L. Huntington was a midshipman. In 1861, the Navy Department detached the First, Second, and Third classes of the US Naval Academy and ordered them into active service.

39. There was a Frederick W. Lincoln & Company in Boston that sold nautical instruments and charts.

40. One of these men was William B. Gould, who joined the crew and kept a diary of his service.

41. The *Kate*, owned by an English firm, in July 1863 ran aground on one of her trips out of Wilmington. Captured and condemned in the prize court, private interests purchased her and returned her to the blockade-running trade as the *G. T. Watson*.

42. Rear Admiral Samuel Phillips Lee replaced Rear Admiral Louis M. Goldsborough.

43. Nux Vomica is a drug made from the seeds of the strychnine tree and used for headaches and other maladies.

44. The *State of Georgia* did have to leave her station for repair work. The issue that caused the collision was the blockaders covering their lights to keep lookouts on the blockade runners from spotting them. Rear Admiral Samuel P. Lee instructed the commanding officers to cover the lights with tarpaulin hoods and to post a man at each light to uncover them if needed. *ORN*, ser. 1, vol. 8, p. 122.

45. There was a First Lieutenant Edwin S. Harris in Company C of the 9th New Jersey Volunteers.

46. On 28 September, the *State of Georgia* and *Mystic* captured the *Sunbeam* near New Inlet.

47. Wild lost his arm at the 14 September Battle of South Mountain, Maryland.

48. Major General John G. Foster commanded the Union army's Department of North Carolina.

49. The 1,079-ton side-wheel steamer *Mahaska* carried an armament of one 9-inch gun, one 100-pounder, and four 24-pounder howitzers. She was a fairly fast vessel, able to make eleven knots.

50. The *Kate*, owned by John Fraser and Company, had the dubious distinction of bringing Yellow Fever to Wilmington in the summer of 1862. She hit a snag in the Cape Fear River on 18 November 1862. They managed to save the cargo, but the ship was a total loss.

51. The men are Francis M. Bunce and Ensign Charles L. Huntington.

52. The shells killed two and wounded five. Report of Casualties, J. Corbin, *ORN*, ser. 1, vol. 8, p. 127.

53. The official report claims the loss of three officers and eighteen men.

54. Acting Master Joshua O. Warren was the commanding officer of the *Daylight*.

55. The schooner was the *Racer* from Nassau with a cargo of salt. The crew abandoned the schooner after they spotted the *Daylight*. As the vessel drifted towards the beach, boat crews sent from the Union warship managed to save her before she ran ashore.

56. The 44th Massachusetts Infantry organized at Readville, about eight miles from Henry's home. At the time of the letter, the regiment was in New Bern, NC. Most of the men were part of the 4th Battalion Massachusetts Volunteer Militia organized in May 1862. These men volunteered to join the 44th when it formed.

Chapter 4

1. William Parker to Scott, 17 November 1862, *ORN*, ser. 1, vol. 8, pp. 214–15.

2. William H. Maies, Journal, entries for 17–22 November, 1862, William H. Maies Papers, Minnesota Historical Society.

3. A parole is an agreement that the soldier or sailor will not serve in the military until formally exchanged for other prisoners of war. His captors took Henry to Richmond's Libby Prison, where he was paroled after a few hours, although he probably remained in the prison a little over a week awaiting the flag of truce boat. This was a three-story former tobacco warehouse, built of brick, on the waterfront of the James River. Belle Isle, an island in the James River, had earlier served as the prison for captured enlisted men and noncommissioned officers. By this date, however, the Confederates had closed that facility, only to reopen it a few months later.

Chapter 5

1. The town of New Bern is on the Neuse River. The spelling of the town's name has changed several times.

2. A nickname for a small light boat. The *Ceres* was a 150-ton (144-ton in some sources) side-wheel steamer built in 1856 and purchased by the navy in September 1861. She mounted two 30-pounders and two 24-pounders.

3. The bracketed words are missing from the letter and were restored by using the earlier partial transcription. Someone removed a segment of the letter post-delivery. It appears there are about six lines of text missing, and these were not in the text of the earlier transcription.

4. Royal Shoal is about six miles northeast of Ocracoke Inlet and about twelve miles west of Hatteras Inlet.

5. The *John L. Lockwood*, built in 1854 and acquired by the navy in September 1861, was a 180-ton side-wheel steamer that mounted one 32-pounder and two 12-pounders.

6. The commanding officer of the *Ceres* was Acting Volunteer Lieutenant John McDiarmid. Copperheads were a faction of the Democratic Party that opposed the Civil War and wanted peace. The Republicans gave the "Peace Democrats" the nickname of Copperheads indicating they were like venomous snakes. Horatio Seymore, one of the leaders of the movement, was the Governor of New York.

7. The two officers were Acting Master's Mates M. Tallmadge Ryan and Henry A. Hudson.

8. Swan Quarter, also known as Swanquarter, is a small town on the banks of Swanquarter Bay. It rests on the south side of the peninsula between the Albemarle and Pamlico Sounds, and about ten miles east of where the Pamlico River empties into the Pamlico Sound.

9. The Union leadership organized this expedition, the second in less than a week, to deal with some irregular troops (guerrillas) in Hyde County. The Union forces, consisting of two Pennsylvania regiments and a company of New York cavalry, landed near Swan Quarter and marched toward Lake Mattamuskeet. Here, for a couple of days, they foraged and captured citizens, bringing back to Swan Quarter sixty prisoners, including a few on a "guerrilla muster roll." Those on the roll they carried back to New Bern, and the rest they released after they took the oath of allegiance. Besides the thefts that Henry mentioned in his letter, they also took horses, oxen, carts, buggies, cotton, corn, and bacon. This expedition caused a great deal of consternation, causing the military governor of North Carolina, Edward Stanly, to write General Foster to complain about the outrages perpetrated. See *ORA*, ser. 1, vol. 18, pp. 180–82.

10. Major General Daniel Harvey Hill commanded the Department of North Carolina and Lieutenant General James Longstreet commanded the Department of Virginia and North Carolina.

11. The state of Massachusetts mustered the Forty-Fifth Infantry Regiment into service in the summer of 1862. A large number of the officers and men were from the Corps of Cadets of the Massachusetts Militia; thus, many called the Forty-Fifth the "Cadet Regiment." Henry M. Bond was an ordnance sergeant in company B and William S. Bond a lieutenant in the same company. See Albert W. Mann, *History of the Forty-Fifth Regiment Massachusetts Volunteer Militia* (Jamaica Plain, MA: Brookside Print, 1908).

12. On 13 March the Confederates attacked both Washington (North Carolina) and New Bern. The naval forces protected Fort Anderson, on the north bank of the Neuse River, rebuffing a Confederate bid to capture it.

13. *Boston Weekly Transcript.*

14. There is a short letter in the collection from W. B. Moody, a paymaster's clerk, on board the *Minnesota*. He wrote Henry on 25 March saying that they had received the letter and forwarded it to the *Ceres*.

15. James Freeman Clarke became a professor of natural religion and Christian doctrine at Harvard.

16. A cottonclad is a wooden gunboat protected from enemy gunfire by bales of cotton placed on the decks to protect the gun crews.

17. The term "bones" refers to some game of dice.

18. See the 11 February 1862 and 28 May 1864 letters for the same word.

19. At the beginning of 1863 General Robert E Lee wanted to probe the areas of Union occupation in North Carolina. Lieutenant General James Longstreet oversaw this Confederate effort and tasked Major General Daniel Harvey Hill to attack the Union garrisons at New Bern and Washington, North Carolina. Hill began his attack against New Bern on 13 March. Union gunboats and fortifications were able to successfully stop this attack. Two weeks later, on 30 March, an investment of Washington, North Carolina, led by Brigadier General Richard Garnet, began and had some success. Major General John G. Foster, who commanded the Department of North Carolina, arrived in Washington to personally lead the Union garrison. The Confederates established batteries and obstructions along the Tar River to slow down or stop Union reinforcements and posted brigades south of Washington to deal with any relief efforts. A Federal force, commanded by Brigadier General Henry Prince, sailed up the Tar River. After observing the Confederate batteries, the transports stopped and returned. A second relief effort under Brigadier General Francis B. Spinola marched from New Bern. Defeated at a battle at Blount's Creek he likewise returned with his forces to New Bern. On 4 April the *Ceres* ran the blockade to bring ammunition and extra firepower for the two gunboats off Washington. The siege continued, but on 13 April, the side-wheel army transport *Escort* managed to pass the Confederate batteries and reach Washington with supplies and a Rhode Island Regiment. General Foster escaped on this vessel and returned with additional reinforcements to relieve the town. While holding the Union forces at bay, the Confederates were able to forage for supplies throughout the area. General Hill ended the siege on 15 April and withdrew from Washington. The navy played an essential part in this effort. The gunboats protected the bridge that crossed the Tar River and exchanged fire with Confederate positions.

20. Hill's Point is on the south side of the Pamlico River, about seven miles below Washington, NC. Rodman Point is about 1½ miles below Washington, also on the south side of the Pamlico River.

21. Brigadier General Henry Prince commanded the Fifth Division, 18th Army Corps. Brigadier General Francis B. Spinola commanded a brigade of the Fifth Division known as the Spinola Brigade.

22. The *Allison* was an army tug under the command of a naval warrant officer and crewed with naval enlisted men and soldiers from the 99th New York Infantry Regiment, also known as the "Union Coast Guard." The sloop *Grant* does not appear in army sources. It is possible that Henry erred in the name.

23. These were the *Isaac N. Seymour* and *Whitehead*.

24. Acting Master's Mate Harry A. Hudson.

25. Brigadier General Edward E. Potter commanded the garrison of Washington, NC.

26. The *Escort* was a 458-ton side-wheel steamer chartered by the Army Quartermaster Corps.

27. John S. Harper.

28. Lieutenant McDiarmid gave Henry quite a compliment writing in his report to Commander Renshaw on 18 April. "I beg call your particular attention to the gallant conduct and cool bravery displayed by Acting Master's Mate Henry W. Wells. No commanding officer could have been better supported than I was by him."

29. This concerns the navy's 7 April 1863 attack with seven ironclads on the defenses of Charleston Harbor. The Confederate forts repulsed the Union attack and severely damaged many of the ironclads.

30. P.B. probably stands for Primitive Baptist.

31. "Bristol fashion" means in good order and usually appeared as "shipshape and Bristol fashion."

32. Henry is discussing the 14 April 1863 letter.

33. On 1 April Reverend Clarke criticized the Boston *Courier* for allowing men like Senator Charles Sumner and Massachusetts Governor George S. Boutwell and their followers to "croak" their dissatisfaction of the war and its antecedents. James Freeman Clarke, *Discourse on the Aspects of the War* (Boston: Walker, Wise and Company, 1863), p. 23.

34. Henry K. Davenport received an appointment as a midshipman in February 1838. Promoted to passed midshipman in 1844, lieutenant in December 1853, and commander in July 1862, he had an extremely varied career both afloat and ashore. He commanded the gunboat *Hetzel* from 1862–1864. The navy commissioned him a captain in 1868.

35. John M. Call and Thomas W. Tuttle were tailors located on Washington Street in Boston, MA.

36. Lieutenant Commander William P. McCann.

37. Henry Gassett Wheelock was a sergeant major in the regiment.

38. Robert E. Lee defeated Brigadier General Joseph Hooker at the Battle of Chancellorsville.

39. The *Hetzel*, a 301-ton side-wheel steamer, mounted one 9-inch gun and one 32-pounder.

40. Commodore Henry K. Davenport was the senior officer in the sounds of North Carolina. The term *commodore* was a courtesy title denoting that he commanded a separate group (flotilla) of vessels semi-independent from the squadron.

41. C. F. W. Behm received a commission as an acting volunteer lieutenant in August 1861.

42. There was a Henry B. Scudder in the regiment.

43. The *Canandaigua* was one of the navy's new screw sloops. They were fast and heavily armed.

44. On 24 April 1863, having recuperated from losing his arm at the Battle of South Mountain, Wild received a commission of brigadier general of volunteers. As an ardent abolitionist he recruited African Americans from the New Bern area and formed "Wild's African Brigade."

45. The black list men are those restricted for punishment.

46. The schooner the Rebels burned was the *Sea Bird*. The diminutive 108-ton screw steamer *Henry Brinker*, acquired by the navy in October 1861, mounted only a single gun, a 30-pounder.

47. North Conway, New Hampshire, in the White Mountains, attracted artists, which in turn attracted tourists.

48. "Ben Bolt" was the title of a popular poem written by Thomas Dunn English. The poem's popularity grew so that within a few years a musical arrangement was composed.

49. Mr. Micawber is a character in the Charles Dickens novel *David Copperfield*.

50. Clement Vallandingham was an Ohio politician and led the anti-war Copperhead faction of the Democratic party.

51. The *Delaware*, acquired by the navy in October 1861, was a 357-ton side-wheel steamer that mounted one 9-inch gun, one 32-pounder, and one 12-pounder.

52. Amos P. Foster.

53. Franklin Hopkins.

54. There were several non-military steamers with the name *Neptune*, but it is not clear which steamer this may be.

55. The anchor chain had a buoy attached so that the crew could retrieve the anchor later.

56. On 25 June, the Confederate commerce raider *Tacony* captured the *Archer*, a fishing schooner off Portland, Maine. After transferring supplies, the rebels burned the *Tacony* hoping the pursuing warships of the Union Navy would give up, thinking their warship had sunk. They headed into Portland Harbor and captured the US Revenue Cutter *Caleb Cushing*. Soldiers and citizens chased the rebels in two steamers. As they closed, the Confederates destroyed the *Caleb Cushing*, and the local pursuers captured the officers and men of the Confederate raider.

57. On 8 July, the Confederate commerce raider *Florida* chased the side-wheel Government-chartered steamer *Ericsson*, but the *Ericsson*, under the command of Joseph N. Miller, managed to escape in fog.

58. Assistant Surgeon Henry C. Nelson.

59. The ink on this letter has badly faded and some of the words, mainly toward the end, are best guesses.

60. Hopkinton, Massachusetts, is about twenty miles west of Brookline.

Chapter 6

1. The screw-propelled *Montgomery* was a large and fast ex-merchant packet ship. At 787 tons she was 201 feet in length and carried a crew of 143. Armed with six heavy guns, she could make eleven knots, and was capable of catching most of the blockade runners.

2. Charles S. Boggs received an appointment as midshipman in November 1826. A career naval officer, he made captain in July 1862 and retired a rear admiral. The *Sacramento* was a 1,367-ton screw steamer armed with one 150-pounder, two 11-inch guns, one 30-pounder, two 24-pounders, and four 12-pound guns. With a speed of twelve and a half knots, she could catch all but the fastest of the blockade runners.

3. Henry probably meant Tom Peck.

4. The *Wissahickon* was one of the Unadilla Class gunboats. Commissioned in November 1861, this class formed the backbone of early river and blockade operations. This particular warship carried one 150-pounder, two 24-pounders, and a single 20-pound gun.

5. Lyman Wells was an acting master on the *Brooklyn*.

6. France never recognized the Confederate states diplomatically.

7. The *Banshee* ran the blockade on 6 September.

8. The *Tuscarora* was a large and heavily armed 1,457-ton screw sloop. Both warships in the class were fast and early in the war searched for Confederate commerce raiders.

9. Acting Assistant Surgeon David F. Lincoln.

10. Acting Volunteer Lieutenant Edward H. Faucon.

11. Faucon is the educated captain who Dana writes was a "sailor, every inch of him" (pp. 148, 172).

12. The *New Berne* served as a supply ship to the North Atlantic Blockading Squadron. The navy acquired this screw steamer and commissioned her in August 1863. At 978 tons, she could make thirteen knots and initially carried one 30-pounder, four 24-pounders, and one 12-pounder.

13. In contrast to Dana's claim that Captain Faucon was a "sailor, every inch of him," his chief mate considered him "slack."

14. Probably George A. Patterson.

15. Congress boots were popular at the time. Also called Congress gaiters, they were ankle-high shoes that had elastic panels in the sides so they could slide on the foot with ease.

16. The 334-ton former whaling ship *William Badger* served as a supply hulk in Beaufort, NC, and maintained a supply of food, carpenter's and boatswain's stores, clothing, and other items.

17. This was the blockade runner *Elizabeth* (formerly the *Atlantic*). She accidentally ran ashore on 24 September and the crew destroyed her.

18. The *Victoria* was a 252-ton screw-propelled gunboat. Built for the merchant service, the navy acquired her in December 1861.

19. The *Antonica* ran the blockade at this time.

20. Foolscap paper is 8½ × 13½ inches.

21. In his 18 January 1862 letter, Henry addresses Bennie as Bra Ben.

22. The *Howquah* was a small 397-ton screw steamer with two 30-pound rifled guns and

two 12-pound rifled guns. The navy acquired her in June 1863 and commissioned her just over a month before Henry wrote this letter.

23. The Cape Fear River had two entrances. At Southport, several forts protected Old Inlet or Western Bar. Fort Fisher protected New Inlet, the northern entrance. These waterways were only about seven miles apart but Smith Island and Frying Pan Shoals separated them, requiring the warships to steam an extra 40 miles to pass around the shoals to get to the other inlet.

24. The *Sumter* was a Confederate cruiser that was active early in the war. She never travelled to Wilmington and by this date she had sailed to Gibraltar and was sold by the Confederacy that December.

25. The term "medico" is another word for a physician.

26. Henry was trying to be humorous for his mother.

27. *Indigestion* is the more common word for dyspepsia.

28. Each bucket could hold 375 pounds of coal, or about six buckets to the ton.

29. *Lanthorn* is an archaic form of *lantern*.

Chapter 7

1. The *Admiral* was a 1,248-ton screw-propelled auxiliary storeship that supplied the Gulf blockading squadrons.

2. The "narrows" is the channel that separates Staten Island and Brooklyn, New York.

3. The acting assistant paymaster was Benjamin H. Franklin.

4. Robert Williams Welch was the prize commissioner in Key West. He oversaw the adjudication of the prizes brought in by the blockading vessels.

5. Throughout the remaining letters Henry continues to misspell Charlotte Harbor, replacing the letter "e" with an "s." Charlotte Harbor is a large estuary that stretches north of Sanibel Island. The largest settlement in the area was Fort Myers, on the banks of the Caloosahatchee River. This river empties into the southern end of the estuary.

6. The *Honduras*, commissioned in September 1863, was a 376-ton former merchant vessel used as a supply and dispatch vessel for the East Gulf Blockading Squadron. She mounted a single 20-pounder, two 24-pounders, and two 12-pounders.

7. The Russell House was a three-story hotel and considered the best hostelry in the town.

8. The Astor House was the first luxury hotel built in New York City. It was considered the most prestigious hotel in the city for many years, and many famous people stayed there.

9. Whist is an old English trick-taking game extensively played throughout the eighteenth and nineteenth centuries.

10. Delmonico's is still a famous restaurant.

11. Throughout his letters Henry refers to this ship as *Gem of the Seas*. The official name was *Gem of the Sea*, without the plural "s." The *Gem of the Sea* was a bark-rigged 371-ton ship built in 1853. The US Navy acquired her in August 1861 and armed her with four 32-pounders and a 20-pound rifled gun.

12. *Tannhäuser* is a three-act opera with music and text by Richard Wagner.

13. The *Re D'Italia* was a heavily armed broadside ironclad with armor as thick as 4¾ inches. She looked very much like the US Navy ironclad *New Ironsides*.

14. *History of the Reign of Phillip the Second King of Spain* by William H. Prescott in 3 vols.

15. Thomas J. Boynton.

16. Lieutenant Commander William G. Temple was the fleet captain of the East Gulf Blockading Squadron. As the senior aid to the admiral of the squadron, he was the equivalent of a modern-day chief of staff.

17. *Barque* is a variant spelling of *bark* and is a vessel with at least three masts. The forward masts are square rigged and the sternmost fore-and-aft rigged.

18. Charles H. Rockwell.

19. Acting Master George H. Leinas.

20. Acting Master William H. Winslow, Acting Ensign John H. Jenks, and Acting Ensign Samuel T. Bliss.

21. Acting Assistant Surgeon Benjamin G. Walton.

22. Edward William Carpenter was appointed a midshipman in the navy in 1813, graduated from Norwich University, received a lieutenant's commission in 1825, and retired as a commander. The navy placed him on the reserved list before the Civil War began. The naval registers mistakenly list him as Carpender.

23. The 1861 *Boston Directory* lists bootmaker Peter Rooney and shoemaker John Rooney.

24. The counter is a perpendicular stiff material at the heel to help maintain the shoe's shape.

25. Latin loosely translated to mean "The state in which they do not have more."

26. I believe Henry meant to reflect "here lies the body."

27. The *Union* was a 1,114-ton screw steamer used as a supply and dispatch vessel in the Gulf of Mexico. She mounted only a single 20-pound Parrott rifle.

28. The official naval records record the tender's name as *Georgie*. Henry would continually call her the *Georgia*. She was a small five-ton schooner captured on 29 July 1863. The navy retained her as a tender to the *Gem of the Sea*.

29. Charles A. Edgecomb.

30. William P. Wesselhoeft was a physician in Boston.

31. "Gideon" probably refers to Secretary of the Navy Gideon Welles.

32. *Eyes and Ears* by Henry Ward Beecher; the other work mentioned perhaps relates to historian and lecturer John Lord.

33. Rear Admiral Theodorus Bailey had a long and distinguished naval career. Appointed a midshipman in 1818, he served on a dozen ships, reaching the rank of commander in 1849, captain in 1855, and acting rear admiral in November 1862 upon taking command of the East Gulf Blockading Squadron.

34. The *Wyandotte* was a 453-ton screw-propelled gunboat. The navy acquired her in 1859 and her armament consisted of four 32-pounders, one 24-pound howitzer, and a 20-pound rifled gun.

35. The *Ariel* was a 19-ton schooner captured in November 1862 and acquired by the navy in July 1863. She served as a tender in the squadron.

36. A cuffer is an exaggerated story.

37. Perhaps Samuel Johnson's *Life of Butler*.

38. William J. Ferguson.

39. The 1861 *Boston Directory* lists a Robert J. Chute as a photographist.

40. Punta Rassa, Florida, is a point just northwest of Fort Myers Beach and across San Carlos Bay north of Sanibel Island.

41. The *Rosalie* was a 28-ton sloop captured off Charleston, SC, in March 1863. The navy acquired her in May 1863 and used her as a tender in the East Gulf Blockading Squadron. She carried only a single 12-pound gun.

42. In music, *ad libitum* means music performed with free expression and rhythm.

43. The *Queen* was a transport and supply ship, a 618-ton screw steamer.

44. William McKim was the general agent for the Inland Insurance Company.

45. This comes from the Bible, Matthew 7:3–5, and relates to ignoring a glaring fault of one's own while criticizing the faults of another.

46. Thomas Starr King was a noted Unitarian minister first preaching in the Boston area and then in San Francisco.

47. One meaning of *groper* is "one who searches blindly."

48. The *Clyde* was the former blockade runner *Neptune*. Captured in June 1863, this lightly armed, 294-ton side-wheel steamer served in the East Gulf Blockading Squadron her entire naval career.

49. The frayed edges of this letter required some guesswork, represented in the brackets.

50. Black and Batchelder had a shop on Washington Street in Boston.

51. The "Str" was in the original letter according to an earlier transcription but is now missing.

52. The Peace River empties into Charlotte Harbor.

53. On 6 May 1864, First Lieutenant Henry May Bond (20th Massachusetts Volunteers) suffered a non-fatal wound in the cheek at the Battle of the Wilderness. He accompanied the wounded to the rear, sitting in the front seat of the ambulance. A band of John Singleton Mosby's partisan rangers, the 43rd Battalion Virginia Cavalry, attacked the ambulance at White Oak Church to take the Union ambulance horses. An exchange of gunfire mortally wounded Henry Bond. See Thomas Wentworth Higginson, *Harvard Memorial Biographies*, 2 vols. (Cambridge: Sever and Francis, 1866), vol. 2, pp. 12–20.

54. Laudanum is an opium-based pain killer. Many patent medicines of the day used laudanum for sleep, colds, etc. for adults and children.

55. This was probably the Battle of the Wilderness, 5–7 May 1864. The battle was tactically inconclusive, but it was the first battle in the two-month Overland Campaign, designed to destroy Robert E. Lee's army.

56. Chilblains is the inflammation of small blood vessels in response to exposure to cold. Symptoms include bumps, itching, or red-violet patches on the skin that usually clear up in one to three weeks.

57. Major General Nathaniel P. Banks had embarked on the Red River Campaign in March. There were several goals, including the capture of Shreveport, Louisiana; the confiscation of cotton; and the organization of pro-Union governments in that region. The campaign was a Union failure and prolonged the war. The Union military forces did gather thousands of bales of cotton, giving the expedition the appearance of being only a cotton raid for the benefit of speculators.

58. There is very little or nothing known about the dimensions and final disposition of the *Emma/Mayflower*.

59. The navy commissioned the *Union* in January 1863.

60. Henry misunderstood the Ensign's name. It was Albert C. Fowler.

61. Acting Ensign Albert C. Fowler entered service on 13 May 1864.

62. On 1 June 1864, off Cape May, NJ, the *Pocahontas*, an Army Quartermaster steamer, collided with the *City of Bath*, also of the Army Quartermaster's Department. The collision caused the *Pocahontas* to sink, while the *City of Bath* survived.

63. The 401-ton *James S. Chambers* was a schooner commissioned in the navy in December 1861. Her armament consisted of four 32-pounders, one 30-pound rifled gun, and a 12-pound rifled gun.

64. *Tapis* is an archaic word meaning a tapestry used as a tablecloth.

65. A mosquito bar is usually netting or cheesecloth draped over a wooden frame to cover a bed or berth.

66. In Henry's 4 August letter to Eliza, he mentions this letter, and therefore he wrote this letter before 4 August.

67. The *Cambridge* captured the British schooner *Julia* on 23 September 1861. Henry, at the time, was taking the schooner *Revere* to the prize court in Boston. Thus he never wrote home about the capture, but he was still eligible for prize money as part of the crew.

68. Henry refers to Acting Master Peter F. Coffin as Captain, denoting that he was the commanding officer of the vessel.

69. The edges of one page, front and back, of this letter suffered damage, leaving it incomplete. Fortunately, the earlier transcription captured the words. I have used the transcription when the text was missing.

70. This may be related to the 15 June 1864 act by Congress that gave equal pay to African-American soldiers.

71. William B. Bradbury wrote a song popular in the Union Army entitled "Marching Alone," which had the phrase "Gird on our armor."

72. *Amese* is an obsolete usage meaning to appease or pacify.

73. Henry misspelled the word *wittles*, the contemporary slang for *vittles*, more commonly written as *victuals*. Charles Dickens uses the word *wittles* in *Great Expectations* to mean a stock or a supply of food. Henry mentions reading this book in his 9 November 1861 letter to his mother. "Spoon wittles" also appears in contemporary books, indicating feeding an infant with soft food by spoon.

74. Henry is writing about the 5 August Battle of Mobile Bay. Rear Admiral David Glasgow Farragut passed into the bay with a large and heavily armed column of 18 warships, including 4 monitors. The monitor *Tecumseh* struck a torpedo and sank at the outset of the battle. The other warships passed into the harbor and engaged the four Confederate warships, including the ironclad *Tennessee*. The smaller and more lightly armed Confederate warships tried to escape, leaving the *Tennessee*, with Confederate Admiral Franklin Buchanan on board, to deal with the entire Union attacking force. Eventually, the Union warships overwhelmed the *Tennessee* and she surrendered.

Chapter 8

1. The *Rosalie* was a small 28-ton sloop captured running the blockade. She was 45 feet in length and had a beam of 17 feet and a draft of 3 feet, 6 inches. The navy acquired her in May 1864. There is discrepancy in the tonnage figures among the different sources.

2. A Quarter Gunner is a petty officer attached to each gun division (in this case only a single gun) whose job is to take care of the gun and all the gear. At quarters he supplies the gun crew with the primers, belts, and other paraphernalia and articles the crew needs to serve the gun.

3. According to a Florida gazetteer and the US Board of Geographic Names, there is no Arnold's Bay in Florida.

4. Captain Henry A. Crane.

5. There are just over two lines struck out. It appears that someone other than Henry did this, perhaps due to its sensitive nature.

6. George B. McClellan did run against Lincoln in 1864 as the Democratic candidate. John C. Fremont ran as the nominee of the Radical Democracy Party. Winfield Scott Hancock was not a candidate in the 1864 presidential election.

7. Probably the 2nd Regiment, US Colored Troops. There was a Captain John F. Bartholf in this regiment.

8. Malco Inlet is a variant name of Big Marco Pass. This waterway connects to Marco Bay on the north side of Marco Island and north of Cape Romano, Florida.

9. In the nineteenth century, "remittent bilious fever" most often referred to a relapsing fever with bilious vomiting and could be symptomatic of a number of medical issues.

10. The prize was a small sloop boat that had no name. She cleared from Key West to go

sponging and fishing. The navy captured her 100 miles north of her course, with a cargo of salt, stores, and other merchandise.

11. The *Hendrick Hudson* was a 460-ton screw steamer. She was the ex-blockade runner *Florida*, captured in April 1862. The navy purchased her in September 1862 and commissioned her that December. She carried two 20-pound rifled guns and four 8-inch guns.

12. Brainerd P. Trask; Andrews's first name is unknown.

13. Acting Assistant Paymaster Henry G. Colby.

14. Probably Edward Everett, a Unionist vice-presidential candidate and noted orator.

15. The *Annie* was a twenty-seven–ton schooner. Built in the North and named *Nora,* the navy captured her south of Charleston while trying to run the blockade under the name of *La Criolla.* The navy acquired her in the prize court. She was 46 feet, 2 inches long; had a beam of 14 feet, 9 inches, and a draft of 5 feet; and carried a single 12-pound smoothbore gun. The navy changed the name to *Anna* in some sources, but she was always known as the *Annie* in the squadron.

16. Major General John Newton, a native Virginian and West Point graduate, remained in the US Army and served with distinction in the Atlanta Campaign. In the fall of 1864, he received command of the District of Key West and Tortugas.

17. The men are Hiram Bishop, William P. Maddocks, George W. Sealey, George Brown, Herman Jammo, Joseph Plume, and Hugh McGady. The only exhisting muster roll does not list Nelson nor does it list him as one of the missing men within the notes made after the loss of the *Annie*. Muster Roll of the *Annie*, Muster Rolls of Naval Ships, Record Group 24, Records of the Bureau of Naval Personnel, 1798–2007, National Archives, Washington, DC.

18. The *Restless* was a 265-ton bark acquired by the navy in August 1861 and commissioned that December. She carried two 32-pounders, one 30-pound rifled gun, and a 12-pound rifled gun.

19. On 3 October 1863, President Lincoln proclaimed the last Thursday in November as a day of "thanksgiving and praise." It seems that Henry did not understand it would be a recurring national observance.

20. General Sherman's army was on the outskirts of Savannah, Georgia, but did not capture the port town until the 21st.

21. Acting Master Henry B. Carter.

22. Wendell Phillips and William Lloyd Garrison were both nationally known abolitionists, both from Massachusetts.

Chapter 9

1. Acting Master Henry B. Carter, referred to here as "captain" as a courtesy title.

2. In September 1864, Rear Admiral Cornelius K. Stribling received command of the East Gulf Blockading Squadron.

3. R. W. Welch was the Prize Commissioner in Key West.

4. The Cape is more likely Cape Romano, and there is a shoal off the cape.

5. Fred N. Knapp was the Superintendent of Special Relief of the U.S. Sanitary Commission in Washington, DC. He mentions the report of Lt. Charles H. Rockwell. This 7 February report is in *ORN*, ser. 1, vol. 17, pp. 807–8. There was no need to duplicate the report because Knapp recounted the important information contained within it.

6. The Treasury Department's fourth auditor settled the accounts and kept the financial records of the Navy Department.

7. James A. Montague.

Bibliography

Adams, Sampson, & Co., *The Boston Directory Embracing the City Record, A General Directory of the Citizens and a Business Directory*. Boston: Adams, Sampson, & Co., 1861.

Boatner, Mark M., III. *The Civil War Dictionary*. New York: David McKay, 1959.

Browning, Robert M., Jr. *From Cape Charles to Cape Fear: The North Atlantic Blockading Squadron during the Civil War*. Tuscaloosa: University of Alabama Press, 1993.

Buker, George E. *Blockaders, Refugees, & Contrabands: Civil War on Florida's Gulf Coast, 1861–1865*. Tuscaloosa: University of Alabama Press, 1993.

Callahan, Edward W. *List of Officers of the Navy of the United States and of the Marine Corps From 1775 to 1900*. New York: Haskell House Publishers, 1969.

Canney, Donald L. *The Confederate Steam Navy, 1861–1865*. Atglen, PA: Schiffer Publishing, 2015.

———. *U.S. Coast Guard and Revenue Cutters, 1790–1935*. Annapolis: Naval Institute Press, 1995.

Chambers, William, and Robert Chambers. *Chambers's Encyclopaedia: A Dictionary of Universal Knowledge for the People, Illustrated*. 10 vols. Philadelphia: J. B. Lippincott, 1868.

Clarke, James Freeman. *Discourse on the Aspects of the War*. Boston: Walker, Wise and Company, 1863.

Cogar, William B. *Dictionary of Admirals of the U.S. Navy*. 2 vols. Annapolis: Naval Institute Press, 1989–1991.

Current, Richard N., ed. *Encyclopedia of the Confederacy*. 4 vols. New York: Simon and Schuster, 1993.

Cutler, Carl C. *Greyhounds of the Sea: The Story of the American Clipper Ship*. Annapolis: Naval Institute Press, 1984.

De Kerchove, René. *International Maritime Dictionary*. New York: D. Van Nostrand, 1948.

Faust, Patricia L., ed. *Historical Times Illustrated Encyclopedia of the Civil War*. New York: Harper and Row, 1986.

Gardiner, Robert, ed. *Conway's All the World's Fighting Ships: 1860–1905*. London: Conway Maritime Press, 1979.

Garrison, Webb. *The Encyclopedia of Civil War Usage*. Nashville: Cumberland House Publishing, 2001.

Gibson, Charles Dana, and E. Kay Gibson. *Dictionary of Transports and Combat Vessels Steam and Sail Employed by the Union Army, 1861–1868*. Camden, ME: Ensign Press, 1995.

Gould, William B., IV. *Diary of a Contraband: The Civil War Passage of a Black Soldier*. Stanford, CA: Stanford University Press, 2002.

Hamersley, Louis R. *A Naval Encyclopedia: Comprising A Dictionary of Nautical Words and Phrases; Biographical Notices, and Records of Naval Officers*. Philadelphia: L. R. Hamersley, 1881.

———. *The Records of Living Officers of the U.S. Navy and Marine Corps*. Philadelphia: J. B. Lippincott, 1870.

Hamersley, Thomas H. S. *Complete Army and Navy Register of the United States of America, From 1776 to 1887*. New York: T. H. S. Hamersley, 1888.

———. *Complete General Navy Register of the United States of America, From 1776 to 1887*. New York: T. H. S. Hamersley, 1888.

Headley, J. T. *Farragut and Our Naval Commanders* E. B. Treat, 1867.

Heyl, Erik. *Early American Steamers*. 6 vols. Buffalo, NY: by the author, 1953–1969.

Higginson, Thomas Wentworth, ed. *Harvard Memorial Biographies*. 2 vols. Cambridge, MA: Sever and Francis, 1866.

Hubbell, John T., and James W. Geary. *Biographical Dictionary of the Union: Northern Leaders of the Civil War*. Westport, CT: Greenwood Press, 1995.

Long, E. B., and Barbara Long. *The Civil War Day by Day: An Almanac 1861–1865*. Garden City, NY: Doubleday, 1971.

Lytle, William M., and Forrest R. Holdcamper. *Merchant Steam Vessels of the United States, 1790–1868*. New York: Steamship Historical Society, 1975.

Maies, William H. Papers. Minnesota Historical Society.

Muster Rolls of Naval Ships. Record Group 24. Records of the Bureau of Naval Personnel, 1798–2007. National Archives, Washington, DC.

Patterson, Howard. *Patterson's Illustrated Nautical Dictionary, Unabridged*. New York: Howard Patterson, 1891.

Robinson, William Morrison Jr. *The Confederate Privateers*. Columbia: University of South Carolina Press, 1990.

Rush, Richard, et al., eds. *Official Records of the Union and Confederate Navies in the War of the Rebellion*. 31 vols. Washington, DC: Government Printing Office, 1894–1914. [Cited in the text as *ORN*.]

Scharf, J. Thomas. *History of the Confederate States Navy from Its Organization to the Surrender of Its Last Vessel*. New York: Rogers & Sherwood, 1887.

Scott, R. N., et. al., eds. *The War of the Rebellion: A Compilation of the Official Records of the Union and Confederate Armies*. 130 vols. Washington, DC: Government Printing Office, 1880–1901. [Cited in the text as *ORA*.]

Sifakis, Stewart. *Who Was Who in the Civil War*. New York: Facts on File, 1988.

Silverstone, Paul H. *Warships of the Civil War Navies*. Annapolis: Naval Institute Press, 1989.

Tweney, C. F., & L. E. C. Hughes, eds. *Chambers's Technical Dictionary*. New York: Macmillan, 1940.

U.S. Navy Department. *Navy Register of the United States for the Year 1862*. Washington, DC: Government Printing Office, 1862.

———. *Register of the Commissioned and Warrant Officers of the Navy of the United States Including Officers of the Marine Corps and Others for the Year 1860*. Washington, DC: Government Printing Office, 1860.

———. *Register of the Commissioned and Warrant Officers of the Navy of the United States Including Officers of the Marine Corps and Others to September, 1862*. Washington, DC: Government Printing Office, 1861.

———. *Register of the Commissioned, Warrant and Volunteer Officers of the Navy of the United States Including Officers of the Marine Corps and Others for the Year 1861*. Washington, DC: Government Printing Office, 1862.

———. *Register of the Commissioned, Warrant, and Volunteer Officers of the Navy of the United States, Including Officers of the Marine Corps and Others, to January 1, 1863*. Washington, DC: Government Printing Office, 1863.

———. *Register of the Commissioned, Warrant, and Volunteer Officers of the Navy of the United States, Including Officers of the Marine Corps and Others, to January 1, 1864.* Washington, DC: Government Printing Office, 1864.

———. *Register of the Commissioned, Warrant, and Volunteer Officers of the Navy of the United States, Including Officers of the Marine Corps and Others, to January 1, 1865.* Washington, DC: Government Printing Office, 1865.

———. *Register of the Commissioned, Warrant, and Volunteer Officers of the Navy of the United States, Including Officers of the Marine Corps and Others, to January 1, 1868.* Washington, DC: Government Printing Office, 1868.

U.S. Navy Department, Naval History Division. *Civil War Naval Chronology 1861–1865.* 6 vols. Washington, DC: Government Printing Office, 1971.

———. *Dictionary of American Naval Fighting Ships.* 8 vols. Washington, DC: Government Printing Office, 1959–1981.

Warner, Ezra J. *Generals in Blue: Lives of the Union Commanders.* Baton Rouge: Louisiana State University Press, 1984.

———. *Generals in Gray: Lives of the Confederate Commanders.* Baton Rouge: Louisiana State University Press, 1983.

Webster, Noah. *Webster's Biographical Dictionary.* 1st ed. Springfield, MA: G. & C. Merriam, 1957.

———. *Webster's New Geographical Dictionary.* Springfield, MA: G. & C. Merriam, 1980.

———. *Webster's New Universal Unabridged Dictionary.* New York: Simon and Schuster, 1979.

Wells, Thomas Goodwin. "Letters of an Argonaut From August, 1849 to October, 1851." *Out West: A Magazine of the Old Pacific and the New,* vol. 22, no. 1 (January 1905): 48–54; no. 2 (February 1905): 136–42; no. 3–4 (March–April 1905): 221–28.

Wells, Walter, and David Wells. "Where the Latest Wells Came From." Unpublished manuscript in the author's possession. December 2000 and April 2012.

Wells Family Papers. Library of Congress, Washington, DC.

Wise, Stephen R. *Lifeline of the Confederacy: Blockade Running during the Civil War.* Columbia: University of South Carolina Press, 1988.

Websites

https://archive.org/
https://charts.noaa.gov/PDFs/11429.pdf
www.civilwardata.com
https://ehistory.osu.edu/exhibitions/cwsurgeon/cwsurgeon/medicalterms
https://www.findagrave.com/
http://freepages.rootsweb.com/~grundyconnections/computers/medterminolgy.html
https://www.hathitrust.org
https://www.history.navy.mil/our-collections/photography.html
https://www.loc.gov
https://www.nps.gov/civilwar/soldiers-and-sailors-database.htm
https://www.onelook.com
https://quod.lib.umich.edu/m/moa/
http://research/mysticseaport.org
https://sites.rootsweb.com
https://translate.google.com
http://translate.yandex.com
https://www.usgs.gov/core-science-systems/ngp/board-on-geographic-names

NEWSPAPERS AND JOURNALS
Army and Navy Journal
Atlantic Monthly
Monthly Journal
New York Times
Raleigh Standard

Index